THE AUTOBIOGRAPHY
OF AN UNKNOWN
SOUTH AFRICAN

Perspectives on Southern Africa, 1

THE
AUTOBIOGRAPHY
OF AN UNKNOWN
SOUTH AFRICAN

by

NABOTH MOKGATLE

UNIVERSITY OF CALIFORNIA PRESS

BERKELEY AND LOS ANGELES

UNIVERSITY OF CALIFORNIA PRESS
Berkeley and Los Angeles
© 1971, by Naboth Mokgatle
ISBN: 0-520-01845-1
LC: 79-138285
First printing, 1971

Printed in Great Britain

CONTENTS

DEDICATION

This book is dedicated to the memory of my paternal grandmother, Mahlodi Paulina Kekana Mokgatle. She was a slave. She grew up alone, far away from her people and birthplace. She never owned property of her own except her children. As her story in the book will show, she was married off by someone who was not her father but who kept her as a slave. She never knew her parents; only late, by mere chance, her people discovered her, already a mother of children.

Perhaps for me, her capture during the conflict between her people and the early Dutch settlers in South Africa was a blessing in disguise. Had she not been a slave, had she not been married to a Mosotho Chief by her slave master, I would not have come into the world in the form I did. I might not have come at all. It was because of the two episodes, her enslavement and marriage, that preparation for my coming life in the world started. I am a part of her and she is a part of me. I believe firmly that as long as I live, she lives.

N. M.

London 1970

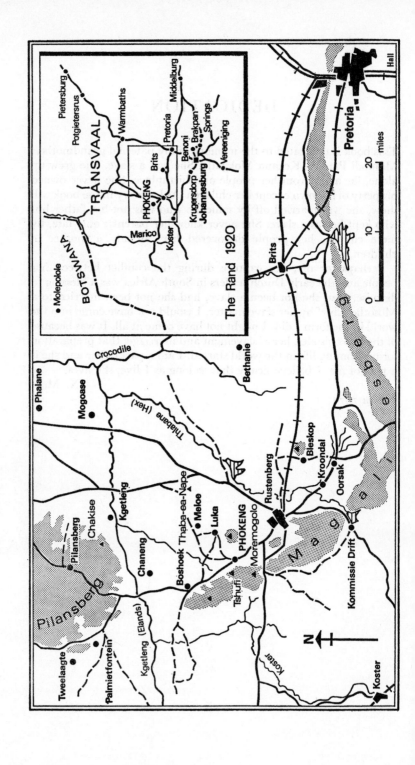

The Rand 1920

I Family

My name is Monyadioe Moreleba Naboth Mokgatle. I was born in a tribal village called Phokeng in the district of Rustenburg, Transvaal Province, South Africa, on the first of April nineteen-hundred and eleven. I was one of the three sons of Setlhare Hebron and Salome Mokgatle, and the last-born in the family. My parents had eight children, three boys and five girls. I do not know when they married, but my mother told me that in eighteen-ninety-six, at the time when the Bafokeng tribe lost most of their cattle through cattle sickness which swept the tribe and the surrounding tribal lands, their first child, a daughter called Nkatlholeng, was a baby of about nine or twelve months.

My mother was a Christian and my father was not. Because of that, their marriage was performed in both Christian and non-Christian traditions. The ceremony, according to my mother, was held in a Lutheran church at Hermannsburg Mission and at my father's home in the traditional way. My father's parents, like all African parents, paid *bogadi* (dowry) for their son's bride. Without the payment of *bogadi*, African law and tradition would not have recognised their union as a legal one.

Nkatlholeng, my parents' first-born, was followed by twin sons who, like her, died before they reached the age of three or four years old. My mother and father did not tell me why they died so early, but I am sure that they did not die because of lack of medicine but that those who claimed to know how to cure the sick tried to cure them.

My twin brothers were followed in nineteen-hundred by twin sisters who looked so much alike that many people in our village – close relatives, my parents' brothers and sisters as well as their children – could not tell which was which. Their names were Molebopi and Madira, but they were known by their Christian names Maria and Martha.

They grew up healthy and by the time Martha died in nineteen-twenty-four she was engaged to be married. Maria remained alone and was very lonely, but in nineteen-thirty-three, nine years after Martha's death, she got married.

In nineteen-hundred and four my mother gave birth to another daughter, named Majoni (soldiers), and her Christian name was Eva. She was born at the time when there were still movements of

British soldiers from the Anglo-Boer war in the country. She acquired the name of Soldiers because, according to my parents, on the day of her birth a large company of British soldiers passed through our village, from the north towards Rustenburg in the south, and some of them stopped to ask for water to drink. Majoni married before her sister Maria in nineteen-twenty-seven, and became the mother of six children. She died in nineteen-fifty-one, in Johannesburg, visiting her husband who was working there. She fell sick three days after her arrival, was taken to hospital, and five days later in hospital she died. I was living in Pretoria with my wife and two children, and one Thursday afternoon I received a telephone call from a friend informing me of my sister's death, which came to me as a surprise and a deep shock. I was at the time the general secretary of the African General Workers' Union in Pretoria. I left my office immediately and went first to an African location, called at the time Bantule or New Clare, on the south-west side of Pretoria, to tell my mother's cousin who lived there with her children, who were caring for her after her husband's death. From Bantule I hurried to where I lived, eight miles from the centre of Pretoria, at Atteridgeville, which the Africans called Phelindaba (the End of Worries), to tell my wife and to make preparations for both of us to leave for Johannesburg. We left our daughter and son, Keitumetse and Matshediso, with my wife's mother and left for Johannesburg. I was deeply worried, wondering why I did not know of my sister's sickness, only her death.

In nineteen-hundred and eight, my parents welcomed the birth of their fifth daughter and named her Phelloe; when she was christened she was named Sannie. At that time my parents' children were all girls, and the chance of ever having a male child was beginning to fade away. The most worried person was my father, because he knew that if there was to be no male child born into the family his name would eventually disappear.

Nevertheless, as time went on, my sister Phelloe became my father's favourite and that earned her jealousy and hatred from her sisters and myself when I joined them later. We suspected her as being father's spy and that she was at all times watching us, preparing a report for him. Our suspicion of her was strengthened by father's treatment of her, because on many occasions when we had all done something wrong, which demanded father's strong action, he would scold us firmly, and if our actions demanded punishment we would be punished, but Phelloe would be warned not to join in again in doing wrong with the wicked children, who were on purpose disobeying father and mother's orders. On many occasions when that happened, Phelloe would be taken away from us as we were accused, and would be standing at father's side or even leaning

2

against him. My father was a very strict disciplinarian and hated his orders being disobeyed.

My sister Phelloe was not as healthy as most of us were. She was slim and delicate and occasionally complained of being unwell. She was the first in my family to learn the English language at school, and during her school days she turned out to be very gifted in her studies. Each time they had competitions at school she never failed to bring a prize home with her. I remember the time when the head-master of her school came to see my father to suggest that he should try his utmost to send my sister to college, but my father turned it down on the grounds that she was a woman; back from college she would get married and forget everything she had learned.

My sisters were brought up in the old African tradition that the parents knew best and had a duty to marry their children into the families of the people they knew well and trusted, and where they were sure that their daughters would be well cared for and respected. My three sisters who eventually married all had their marriages arranged for them by father and mother. Equally, the men who married them were brought up in a similar way. They were from the Molefe, Petlele and Rakhudu families. The Molefes were not of our tribe, but were members of another tribe called Bamaake, living in a tribal village called Siga, far away to the extreme west of our tribe and lands. They were well known to my parents and reared many cattle, sheep and goats. They were also successful peasant farmers. My sister Majoni was married to them.

The Petleles were members of our tribe who, according to legend, had at one time in its history held high positions as Chief's advisers and councillors. They were still respected and were also successful peasant farmers with considerable means. Phelloe was married to them.

I was told that the father of Janki Petlele, my sister Phelloe's husband, was my father's best friend until he died, and left a wish that one of his sons be persuaded to marry one of my father's daughters. The last were the Rakhudus, who were also of high social standing, not very successful in their dealings with the soil and animals, but enjoying the privilege of being headmen of one of the clans in the tribe with a history of having produced in the long past poets and men who were learned in tribal laws and customs. My sister Molebopi (Maria) was married to them.

3

II Tribal Origins

My tribe, known in the Transvaal as the Bafokeng tribe, is Bosotho and its language is Sesotho. Like other tribes all over the Province, they call themselves Bosotho. Our tribal symbol is a crocodile (*kwena*) and we call ourselves and are know as Bakwena. Other tribes, too, have their tribal symbols, a baboon, a monkey, a black ox, or other animals or reptiles. These symbols are so sacred to them that whenever they sight them or come into contact with them, they must not kill them but only admire them, and recite poems of praise to them.

From what I have cited above it can be noted that our tribe, at a time unknown to me, perhaps long before the Europeans came to Africa, were part of the Basotho nation, who are today the inhabitants of Lesotho, formerly Basutoland. The language spoken in Lesotho is the same as the one spoken by my people, though some different pronunciations have been introduced, and anyone in Lesotho or in our tribe can understand each other.

The African people, not being writers in the past, kept no records of their movements, and therefore there are no dates as to what period my ancestors moved away from Lesotho and why they left. All I know because of the legend, which was handed down by the old to the young, is that from Lesotho my people went to Botswana (formerly Bechuanaland) and settled at the place still known today as kwa-Bokwena-ba-Sechele-sa-Motsoasele. Their headquarters was Molepolole, which remains the headquarters of the people of the tribe who remain there today. While my ancestors were at Bokwena-ba-Sechele-sa-Motsoasele, ruled from Molepolole, they moved away, led by a man called Tshukudu whom they made their Chief as they moved south-eastward, and crossed the Madikwe (Marico) River into the Transvaal. Again I do not know the reason why they left their people at Molepolole: I imagine it was before the arrival of the Europeans. Tshukudu and his people moved on until they reached the mountains known today as Pilansberg mountains, which Africans called Thaba tsa Bakgatla.

Having passed over Thaba tsa Bakgatla, under the leadership of Tshukudu, my ancestors found themselves against the barrier of noka ea Kgetleng (Elands River) flowing west to east. Instead of attempting to cross it, with its deep waters, they chose to move alongside it eastward on its northern side until they reached a place

4

called Mogoase. There they settled down and established their first independent village. Tshukudu was at that time well established as their Chief. They were a large group who constituted families, with possessions, owning cattle, sheep and goats.

There were no other tribes nearby; the land was open, roamed by wild animals and birds of all kinds, big and small. From there they began to set aside lands for cultivation, where they grew crops, and lands which they reserved for grazing animals. Tshukudu and other men went on to follow tradition and married more than one wife. They were far away from Molepolole in Botswana, and therefore saw no point in becoming a branch of Bakwena-ba-Sechele-sa-Motso-asele, but preferred to be an independent group of people who must make their own laws and determine their own future. From that time onward all the tributes were to be paid to Tshukudu and his successors. They followed traditions as they knew them, and Tshukudu's first male child became the Chief after his death and his elder son followed him, and all Tshukudu's descendants became Chiefs. Their livestock increased, and as new babies were born the tribe also increased. Tribal marriages took place and the Chief became the officiating figure, and with his blessing all marriages became legal and binding. The tradition was that any man could marry as many wives as he was able to support by building them homes and providing them with cattle to milk for their children. Polygamy, as they had known it at Molepolole, became part of life.

One of the things invented to discourage men from marrying many wives, just for the sake of marrying them, was *bogadi* (dowry) with cattle, and no man was allowed to marry a woman and take her away from her family without paying dowry to her parents. The Chief also was affected by this law. Naturally, rich men married more wives and less rich men married fewer wives. Many children found themselves having one father but many mothers. But each woman and her children had to have her own cattle.

One of the traditions and customs my ancestors inherited at Molepolole and perpetuated wherever they went and settled was circumcision. They practised circumcision for many years until some of them became Christians and the impact of Christianity made itself felt amongst them. Circumcised boys became men initiated into manhood and once they had been circumcised they could marry.

Boys were circumcised between the ages of twelve and sixteen. Once they reached those ages they were taken together in a large group away from their homes to the interior of the country, where only selected men knew where the ceremonies were held and only the circumcised could visit them. The circumcision periods were always in the cold months of winter and the boys lived there for a period of three months. It was said that at that period the boys

5

having been circumcised were in addition taught manhood, tribal laws, customs and traditions. It is also said that they were taught how to rear animals, hunting, war, as well as herbs and helpful remedies.

Their mothers and sisters were not allowed to know where they were or how they progressed. At circumcision times, the Chief's sons and those of the headmen of clans in the tribe were to be circumcised first, and the Chief's son heading the section with which he was circumcised became the leader of the section, or battalion. If the Chief had no son of his own to head the circumcised battalion, then one of his brothers' sons took over and became the head of the battalion. Each battalion was given a name by which it was known. Before a new battalion was formed and given a name, the one before it must have had five or six sections of circumcised boys added to it. The battalions of circumcised boys or men belonged in law to the Chief. If he desired to attack another tribe, so that he could add their lands to his tribe's and make them his subjects, he could call on any of the battalions to undertake the task. If he wished to have something done in the tribe for the tribe, or even for himself, which meant his family, he was free to call on any of those circumcised battalions to perform the task. They were, so to speak, soldiers of the tribe and the Chief was their commander-in-chief. Each time they were called upon to do something, the Chief's son, their leader, or his cousin, led them into action.

At the end of three months, after they had been circumcised, the boys returned home no longer boys but men who had graduated into the life of adults, and from that time onwards were expected to behave like adults, accountable for all their actions. While they were living away from home during the circumcision period, visited only by men already circumcised, strict secrecy was maintained about their lives, movements and whatever might happen to them. The area in which they lived and moved about was strictly prohibited to women and girls and young boys who had not reached the stage of circumcision. If one of the circumcised boys died, his death was kept from his mother and sisters. Only his father and uncles were informed, and they knew that they had to keep the secret until the boys returned home after three months.

When they returned, the first place they assembled at was the Chief's place, where mothers of boys who had been away from home for three months sat happily to welcome their sons. Mothers whose sons had been eaten by wolves (which was the term used to illustrate death at the circumcision camp) knew of their sons' death for the first time when their wooden dishes and spoons, broken into pieces, were thrown in front of them. When the boys paraded before the welcoming crowds, they all looked identical, smeared with red clay

6

to disguise them from recognition. Once broken dishes and spoons were thrown in front of a woman, she knew, and everyone else knew, that her son never left the circumcision area. She knew that she was there not to receive her son, but the news of his death. To inform the dead boy's sisters, who could not go with their parents to welcome their brother, the woman took the pieces of broken dish and spoons, to say to her daughters, this is what I went to collect. The legend is that mother and daughters would begin to weep, bitterly mourning the death of the member of the family.

Circumcised boys, having graduated into the new world of adults, became full members of the tribe and their battalions (*mophato*, plural *mephato*). I said that at that stage they had also reached marriageable stage. Since dates of births were not recorded and the exact ages of boys and girls were not known, how did my ancestors determine that a boy or girl could marry? Two methods were used. Men kept watch on the boy. The growing of beards was the determining factor. The boy was watched struggling with the problem of a beard for a year, and during the second year his parents knew they could marry him off at any time. Two factors determined a girl's womanhood: the rising of her breasts, and monthly periods, and both were watched by women, who gave reports to men that the girl was suitable to become a mother. Courting was unknown; the parents did that for their children. In some cases, the legend goes on, the fates of boys and girls were decided when they reached the ages of three and four. The parents on both sides could meet and decide that their children would become husband and wife when they had reached maturity.

At the age of twelve or thirteen, the girl was told by her mother who her husband was going to be and who her parents-in-law were going to be. Similarly, before the boy left for circumcision, his father told him whose daughter he was going to marry and the name of his future wife. Boys and girls were already engaged when they reached the ages of thirteen and fourteen. Before they got married, they saw each other, but were not allowed to be alone, or given time to ask one another whether they knew they were going to be husband and wife. At an appointed date and time, the girl would be sent to the boy's home to deliver a present or a message to the boy's parents. She would on certain occasions be sent to the boy's parents' home to perform certain tasks so that her future husband's parents could see that she was a hard-working girl who would make a good wife for their son. Similarly, the boy would at times be drafted to his future wife's parents' home to perform trying tasks in order to convince them that in him their daughter would find a protector and a hard-working husband.

Illegitimacy was very rare at the time of my ancestors' arrange-

7

ments of marriages. Where illegitimacy occurred it was amongst already married couples, where one party neglected the other, or the woman's husband had died. If a woman bore a child with a stranger, the child was regarded as illegitimate, but was allowed to use the name of the man her mother was married to, and the children of her mother were expected to treat it in the same way as their legitimate brothers and sisters. Illegitimacy also occurred with women whose sweethearts died at circumcision time and who found no one else to marry.

My ancestors' organisation was polygamous. Like most male-dominated social organisations, men were masters, made laws mostly in their own favour and to suit their needs, and made it appear that this was right, and being so, ought to be liked and obeyed. Women had no free choice in marriage. Law and custom allowed men to have more than one wife but women to have only one husband. This raises the question whether women were in fact happy under such a system. Men would argue that they were, but when in my early days I asked one old woman, who herself was born into such a setting, she could only remark, 'It was law and custom; women could not dream of arguing against it; it was part of life in those days; it happened everywhere in every family.'

The whole system was explained to me by one blind old man whose father was my father's half-brother; my father and his father had the same father but different mothers. The old man, whose name was Mogale (Christian name, Ananias) Mokgatle, was acknowledged as an authority on our tribal laws and customs. When I was old enough to understand some of the things he wanted me to know, I think I was fifteen or sixteen years of age and I was attending a village church school called Phokeng Preparatory School, and my parents' home was very near his. He became very fond of me. He could not go out for a walk because of his blindness, and therefore required help from someone to tell him where to walk and to lead him away from pitfalls and other things which would have caused him injuries. In the afternoon, when he knew that I was back from school, he would send for me to keep him company, or to lead him out for a walk. I didn't like him very much, because as a young man I thought he was denying me the chance of meeting my friends and playing with them. At times I used to put down my books quickly, when I didn't find either of my parents at home, and go away before a messenger arrived to call me. He was a highly respected man; he was third in line of our Chiefs. If the Chief who ruled the tribe at that time had died and his elder son had been too young to succeed him, the blind old man Mogale would have acted as regent over the tribe. So that he was at liberty to call any young man or boy near him, apart from his own grandchildren, to lead him for a walk. I

8

always complained to my mother, never to my father. 'Why is he always picking on me? I led him out quite recently, why call on me again?' My mother would say, 'You are doing nothing at present, it's your duty to go and lead your uncle.'

Sometimes, a day or two before Saturday, when he knew there would be no school, Mogale used to go to my parents to ask if he could have me on Saturday morning or afternoon if my parents did not specially require my services. Mother or father would readily agree if they had no need of me. Sometimes he would direct me to take him to the Chief's court, when he knew that there was a court case going on to which he would like to listen or wished to contribute his wisdom and knowledge of law and custom. That used to bring me into contact with high tribal legal debates, verdicts, and complaints of those who had lost legal battles. I used to sit there, waiting for him to direct me to take him back home, but listening to what was being said.

I remember listening to a case in which a man was suing his parents-in-law, demanding the return of his dowry, because his wife had left: he had tried for many months to get her back; she lived with another man; her parents and relatives made no efforts to help him to get her back; and while she was living away from home with another man she fell sick and died. The man was a member of the tribe but lived in another village, fifteen or more miles away from Phokeng, the headquarters. His case was dealt with first by the headman of his village, who agreed that he was entitled to his dowry back. His parents-in-law argued that they were not responsible for their daughter's actions, and therefore the question of returning the dowry did not arise. They appealed to the tribe's high court in Phokeng. When the appeal was heard I was at the court with old Mogale. After hearing the evidence presented, according to the custom the presiding judge had to ask any of the old men to speak for or against the appeal. My blind old man was asked to speak. He rose, spoke without seeing anyone present, only hearing their voices, and said that, according to the tribal law, dowry could be returned, but only to the one who paid it. The dowry, Mogale went on, was not paid by the man who demanded its return, but his parents. They paid it as a present to their son, to get him a wife. They made the arrangements and took part in the talks about the dowry and paid it to the woman's parents. If they were here, demanding the return of the dowry, the court would do nothing but grant that the dowry be returned to them as their property. The son had no right to demand the return of the dowry, only his parents.

Mogale Ananias Mokgatle was older than my father, but both were born into the polygamous system which my ancestors practised. Both their parents had more than one wife, but both got married at the time when the influence of Christianity had taken over in our tribe. Both my father and Mogale went to circumcision, but none of their children went because the church, which most of the tribe had joined, was against it. Circumcision therefore ended in our tribe with my father's battalion.

Mogale was a very interesting story-teller. He was not an educated man, he could not read or write, but he remembered many things and was also good at making riddles. I still remember one cold winter evening by the fireside in his fire house, which was also the kitchen of his family, when he told me and other young boys and girls who were enjoying the open fire with him, a story about how he himself got married to his wife of whom death had since deprived him. He was a practising Christian. He told us that, like all boys of his young days, when he returned from circumcision his uncle, acting on his father's instructions, told him the name of the girl he was going to marry. He knew the girl, who was about six years younger than himself, and when he got that message he knew that his marriage days were near. About a month later he was sent to the girl's home to observe her and also to give her a chance to observe him. He was welcomed by the girl's parents, who at the same time called the girl to greet him, so that for the first time they could exchange greetings and nothing more.

When they came face to face, the girl knew that she was greeting her future husband. A week or so later, he said, he left for the bush to join other boys of his age to herd their parents' cattle. That meant living with animals, away from home for an indefinite period. Two years later a man arrived at his parents' cattle post, sent to inform him of what had taken place at home in his absence. The messenger's name was Ranthuteng. A day after his arrival, Ranthuteng told him that he was sent to tell him that he was a married man and his marriage had already been celebrated at home, and he was to take him home to meet his wife.

I was, with the other young boys and girls who by the fireside made Mogale's audience, fascinated by the story of his marriage. Being born at the time when polygamy was no longer practised in our tribe, we were surprised that someone could be married in his absence. I asked him whether he didn't object to being married while away at the cattle post. He said, 'Whose son would I have been to object and go against my parents' wishes? I would not dare to do that. We were not like you children of today who can object and get your own way.' I did see some of the polygamy system in our tribe when I grew up. There were still a few families which had not become Christians and had more than one wife. Even my father's half-brother, who, though he never became a Christian, allowed his children to be baptised, had two wives. His name was Dikeledi.

Though Mogale was delighted with the system of Christianity, he said that it had brought with it liberal ideas which brought the breakdown of tribal discipline. He cited the fact that in the days of his boyhood we could not be sitting there with him listening to what he had to tell us. Boys, he said, would have been grouped together in the clan being told stories about discipline, respect for elders, tribal traditions, customs and all they were expected to know. He went on to say that when we grew up to be men and women we would have nothing to tell our children about our background and its things which kept our tribe together. I then asked him why he became a Christian, and he replied by making an illustration that when you swim in the river with other people, you must see which way they are swimming and swim the same way too. If, he explained, you decide to swim the opposite way, you will drown.

I, with my friends who listened with me, were enjoying what he was saying but not taking anything seriously. For us it was a mere story which had no connection with our life. We had no idea what the past meant to old Mogale. We were a new generation, and he represented the old world we didn't know and felt nothing about. Later, when I grew up – when I was away from him, working in Pretoria, struggling with the impact of Christianity and the European way of life and all we were getting from it – I realised that I made a mistake by not writing down all the old man told me.

III Split

I have already said that, after leaving Molepolole, in Botswana, my ancestors settled at Mogoase and that their first Chief was the man who led them, Tshukudu; also that, from that time onwards, every Chief who ruled the tribe was Tshukudu's descendant and was also named Tshukudu, and a long line of Tshukudu Chiefs followed. Being polygamous the Tshukudus married more than one wife and had many families. The tribe prospered, owned many cattle, sheep and goats, and also cultivated fields in which they grew food. Because men had many wives they found themselves embraced by the problems of satisfying their families, and they could not serve only one family, which would have started feuds and jealousies amongst their wives. They therefore devised a way out by making it a rule that each of their wives must cultivate her own fields, plant her own crops, and keep them.

As I pointed out before, each wife had her own house, a number of cattle, sheep and goats, and separate kraals of her own. As each wife's children grew, the girls usually became their mother's helpers in the fields; the boys herded their mother's animals. Men became inspectors of their wives' animals and took care that their sons were doing their work properly by herding the animals, as well as to see that their mothers had enough milk. Men's main tasks became tribal meetings – to decide cases brought to their attention and to settle feuding groups. Each wife had to see to it that in her home every evening there was a dish of food for her husband, although she was not sure that he would be visiting her that night. Husbands were at liberty to choose which of their wives they would visit each night, perhaps staying for a week or a month.

That arrangement was made in order to avoid wives' complaints that they were neglected, and that only one of them was loved and was visited more than others. But there was always a head wife, who was respected and regarded as mother of all the children of her husband's other wives. In the kraals of all his wives a man had animals which were earmarked as his own. Each time he desired to entertain his wives he would pick out any animal from whichever kraal he chose, slaughter it, and the meat of the slaughtered animal would be taken to his head wife's home, and the junior wives would gather there to take their shares, measured according to their ranks, from the mother of their children. Each wife had every right to do as she wished with her own crops and animals.

At Mogoase, my ancestors' first settlement as an independent tribe, they flourished and their wealth increased. They had the whole field open to them, their animals grazed anywhere they chose, and they hunted everywhere at will. Wild animals too were found everywhere, harmless as well as harmful ones. They travelled far afield without coming into contact with other tribes and therefore made the whole land they travelled theirs. Because of the polygamous system they practised the tribe grew, and they went on cherishing the crocodile symbol they adopted from their ancestors in Molepolole.

Women tilled the land and grew food, and men took care of the animals, the building of houses and the maintenance of law and order. They also developed and carried on the system of collective work, which they inherited at Molepolole. When one of them was building a home for his family, others came along to help, the man so helped being required only to provide them with food and drink. Also, women in the fields came to help other women to kill the weeds, similarly being provided with food and drink. At harvest time, too, they helped each other to get ripe crops away from the fields before heavy rains came to destroy them. In their homes also, with the help of others, women built grain storage containers called *sefala* (plural *difala*). Some such grain containers were built with grass by experts and lasted many years, keeping grain-eating insects out completely. Others were built with clay, also by experts and also lasted many years, keeping the grains fresh as they were brought from the fields.

Three types of grains were planted and preserved for generations and are still being planted and used in our tribe today. The first is *lebelebele*, a very thin grain from which they brew beer. The second is *lebele* (plural *mabele*) which is used for making porridge eaten with milk or meat. *Mabele* porridge, called *bogobe*, became and is still the staple food of my tribe. The third was *naoa* (plural *dinaoa*). These are African butter beans, which are found in many colours; yellow, red and white, and others with spots which make them pretty. These beans also provide cabbage, which can be boiled and eaten, or boiled, dried up in large quantities and stored away to be used later.

One of the crops my ancestors planted and used a great deal at Mogoase and have gone on planting, harvesting and eating until today is *tlhodi* (plural *ditlhodi*). These are African peas, green in colour and smaller than European peas. Like European peas and beans, they develop in pods, and when ripe get very hard, and the pods get dry and become easy to break open. They are harvested in large quantities, like beans, gathered together, heaped up and beaten

13

by women with special sticks called *mootloana* (plural *meotloana*). Then the women start searching the wind, to be sure which direction it blows, and with well-made grass dishes called *tlatla* or *tlatlana* (plural *ditlatlana*) start to throw the peas down from a standing position, to enable the wind to blow away the pods from the wanted *ditlhodi*. Like beans, *ditlhodi* take a long time (a hundred-and-twenty minutes) to get softened up when cooked. Unlike *dinaoa* (African beans), after cooking they stick together and are soft like mashed potatoes. They are very tasty and go well with milk. They stay a long time in the stomach before the body feels hungry again.

Before the introduction of maize by the Europeans, these were the three main crops my tribe planted and used. One other crop my ancestors handed down to their descendants is *ngoba* or sugar-cane, but this was not planted in large quantities. Sugar-cane is not easily differentiated from *mabele* until it is ready to be cut and sucked. But some people can tell it from corn plants even before it is ripe. It is very sweet and its juice is very nourishing. It has several joints, and to suck it they are broken apart, and either teeth or a small cutting object is used to peel off the outside and break off the inside. Then one grinds it with the teeth, sucking and swallowing the juice.

At Mogoase, while my ancestors were enjoying themselves, taking everything calmly, being ruled by one of Tshukudu the first's descendants, whose name was also Tshukudu, who like others before him was adhering to the system of polygamy, having many wives and children, there were three of the Chief's wives whom he loved more than others. Each time he visited one of the three, he promised her that after his death her son would become the Chief of the tribe. Like all mothers, each of Tshukudu's loved wives was thrilled to be told that one day her son would be a Chief and that she would one day be looked upon as the Chief's mother, so each made sure that the father would repeat in the presence of her son his promise that the boy would be Chief after his own death. But the tribal law was that the eldest son of the woman whose dowry was contributed by the clans would become the Chief after his father's death; his name was also Tshukudu and his mother was popularly called Matshukudu. As happens in most communities, there were some men who agreed with the Chief that, despite tribal law and customs, he had the right to delegate his chieftainship to any one of his sons if he was satisfied that it was in the interest of the tribe and that he would rule the tribe as he himself ruled it.

Old Tshukudu reigned over the tribe for a long period, during which he made sure that each of his sons to whom he had promised the chieftainship had supporters in the tribe. Though some people knew of his promises, they didn't bother about them but took them only as jokes. Finally he died peacefully in his sleep of old age, and the boy whose mother's dowry was contributed by the clans had a son by the name of Nape, who was destined to be called Tshukudu when he became Chief. One of the loved wives had a son named Ramokoka, and the other one had a son named Mogopa. After Tshukudu's death, when the tribe gathered to proclaim the new Chief, a new thing happened. My ancestors' tribe found itself torn into three hostile sections: one section adhering to the law and traditions of the tribe, and the other two sections putting their faces against the law and customs; some saying that the old Chief before he died left directions that Ramokoka should be proclaimed the Chief of the tribe; those who supported Mogopa, on the other hand, claiming that they had it from the late Chief that Mogopa should become the ruler of the tribe after his death. The traditionalists and upholders of the law insisted that Nape, whose mother's dowry was contributed by the clans, was unquestionably the successor.

The three mothers stood firm in opposition to each other, fighting for their sons, and the three boys also argued that they were given the power to succeed him by their late father. Nape and his mother contended that they were not for any arguments, their position was settled by the law of the tribe. That was the beginning of the split. For more than two years the tribe was without a crowned Chief, and the fierce arguments developed into hatred, suspicions, hostilities and mistrust. Warring sections began to call themselves by the mothers of the boys who claimed chieftainship. Thus Nape's supporters called themselves Bamanape (after Nape's mother), then there were Bamaramokoka (after Ramokoka's mother) and Bamamogopa (after Mogopa's mother). Because there could not be three bulls in the same kraal, my ancestors' tribe broke up into three, and as a result they had to be on the move again. They demolished the houses they had built at Mogoase, left the fields they had cultivated, but took their crops and animals with them. Those who chose to follow Ramokoka went east of Mogoase along the northern side of Noka-Ea-Kgetleng (Elands River) until they were sure they were no longer in sight of the other two sections. They settled at the place and called it Phalane. Their descendants are still there today. They began to call themselves Bakoena-Ba-Ramokoka and retained the crocodile as the symbol of their new tribe. The section from which I sprang crossed the Elands, went south-east and, when they were miles away from Mogoase, reached a huge mountain and decided to settle by it and named it after Nape, their Chief, Thaba-Ea-Nape, Mountain of Nape. The third section, which at first seemed to be following them, passed Thaba-Ea-Nape and went further to the south-east. These were the followers of Mogopa. They moved on until they reached a place where the town of Brits now stands, settled down and called it KoaMogopa (Mogopa's Place), and called themselves Bakoena-Ba-Mogopa. After the arrival of the Europeans, when the place became a European settlement, they moved further to the north of the area, where they still live today. When they became Christians the place was renamed Bethanie; this was now the headquarters of Bakoena-Ba-Mogopa. After leaving the site where Brits stands, some of them went further to the south-east and settled near Pretoria, and gave their place another biblical name, Hebron. Since there was no tribal dispute, those who settled at Hebron chose to remain the branch of those who settled at Bethanie. The Paramount Chief being at Bethanie, residents of Hebron kept being sent a Chief to rule them from Bethanie, and the practice still goes on today. There also began to develop other branches, which also looked to Bethanie as their headquarters, and they were satisfied to be ruled by headmen on behalf of the Paramount Chief.

The tribal symbol of the crocodile which they all inherited at Molepolole, and their ancestors perpetuated at Mogoase, has remained unaltered until today. My own section of ancestors, too, at Thaba-Ea-Nape, who became known as Bakoena Ba-Manape-Ea-Tshukudu, remained loyal to the tribal symbol of the crocodile, called *koena* in our language. Put together, Bamanape, Baramokoka and Bamogopa, we are all called Bakoena: of the crocodile. Those in Botswana, too, are called Bakoena Basechele-sa-Motsoasele. Their tribal home is called Koa-Mokoena, and their symbol is the crocodile.

Bakoena, Bamanape, Bamogopa and Baramokoka became independent of each other since the day they left Mogoase, because of the dispute as to who was to become Chief. It seems to me that our section, which stood for tribal law and custom at Mogoase at the time of the dispute, and followed Nape, whom they named Tshukudu when he became their Chief at Thaba-Ea-Nape, had more people than the other two sections. I base this belief upon the fact that our population has always outnumbered theirs; we occupied more land than they did, and were richer than they were. It seems to me also that they looked to us for guidance in some things; for instance, we adopted Christianity first and they followed and embraced the same denomination, the Lutherans of Hermannsberg.

The legend shows that, though they quarrelled at Mogoase and broke up, they never became bitter enemies. Thus, whenever there was a big social function taking place at Phalane, KoaMogopa, or at Thaba-Ea-Nape, whether it was a Chief's marriage, a Chief's death or tribal ceremonies, nothing could begin until all the Chiefs or their official representatives had arrived. Before the Christian days when there were no priests to perform the burials, Chiefs were buried by Chiefs from other sections. A new Chief would be crowned by one of the Chiefs from the two other sections by being wrapped in a leopard's skin, which they called tiger skin, though there are no tigers in Africa. The other Chief would, in public, address the crowned Chief, telling him of his responsibilities to his people and that, although he was their Chief from that day, he remained their child and must at all times consult them on whatever he thought should be done in the tribe.

To keep ties and friendships going, each section saw to it that its Chief must have amongst his wives one who came from the other two sections. That was also regarded as a safeguard, for when one of the sections was in need it could go to the others and ask for assistance. Because their daughter was married to the other, and their nephews and nieces were there, the requested assistance would not be hard to obtain. As a result, some of the Chiefs' children had grandparents, uncles and aunts in the other sections. Although the Bakoenas were tribes independent of each other, they have remained cousins and friends until today. Their feeling for each other is like that of Americans with English ancestors for England. They may have bitter criticisms of England and the English people, but there is nothing they hate like the thought of England being invaded or going through a troubled time. The Bakoenas even adopted a system of helping one another when they had tribal disputes which they could not solve themselves. For instance, if there was a dispute at Bethanie, and the Bamogopa could not solve it on their own, they could call upon those at Phalane or Phokeng, now our headquarters, to send their Chief and councillors to arbitrate. Their judgment would be accepted. Now, of course, all being under European rule, such disputes find their way into European courts.

To return to the crops my ancestors grew, one was called *marotse* (singular *lerotse*); these are African pumpkins, very tasty taken with milk. Another crop which my ancestors grew was similar to *marotse*, but was not eaten in the same way. From it they derived calabashes which are still being used today in my tribe in Phokeng. The crop produced hard containers, called *moduto* (plural *meduto*). Calabash is called *phafa* (plural *diphafa*). *Diphafa* are used for drinking beer and *meduto* are used for drawing water and for keeping water cool. Nowadays *meduto* are used when people are travelling in areas where there is not plenty of water, and to keep water cool when the tropical heat is too hot.

Before the introduction of European containers, steel tins and cooking pots, there were very artistic women in the tribes, and my father's half-sister was one of them. There were women experts in pottery who made pots from dark, soft clay called *letsopa*. The pots they made were of two different colours and some were artistically decorated with animals, birds, flowers, or other objects. Before I was

17

born and the cast-iron European cooking pots were introduced, I was told that clay pots made by women in the tribe were used for cooking. I did not see them used for that purpose, but I saw them made and fired in an oven dug in the ground to make them hard. When they had been fired they could stand any amount of heat and could hold water for many years without becoming soft. They keep water or beer cool and are still being used today. They are fragile and need careful handling. Nearly all the women who could make clay pots in my tribe have died out, and my tribe now gets clay pots from other tribes which still have women who can make them. To make them withstand fire, before they are fired they are painted outside only with paint derived from another earth called *letsoku*. *Letsoku* is dried, then ground into a powder, mixed with water and when in solution the pot is painted, either black or red. They are made in all sizes and shapes. There are big ones used to contain beer made from *mabele* or for holding large amounts of water when there are functions. The large ones are called *motsega* (plural *metsega*). All these things are still being used today, but younger people, because they can't make them, mostly use European containers. In my tribe today one can still find the past and present living side by side.

IV Emigration

After living at Thaba-Ea-Nape for generations – I have no knowledge for how many years – my ancestors emigrated from Thaba-Ea-Nape and moved south-westward. I do not know why they decided to emigrate. The legend is that at that time they were rich, had large herds of cattle, sheep and goats, large quantities of corn and other things people need wherever they go or settle. The land they occupied at Thaba-Ea-Nape remained theirs and the fields they cultivated there also remained their fields. In their movements they reached a middle-sized river which started from the mountains on the west and ran eastward, and its waters were clean and beautiful to look at. From the south-west of that river ran another one, much larger, with more water and full of crocodiles, watersnakes, fishes, and water animals like rhinos. The small river joined the large one and became one river flowing east. The legend goes that they settled in open land between some mountains in the east and the two rivers, spreading west and northwards of both of them, and used their waters for their animals as well as for themselves.

They called the large river Matsokubiane and the small one Tlhabane. I don't know who was their Chief at that time, but two names emerged when they were there and became famous, both Tshukudu's descendants. The first name, which is still being handed down in my tribe, is that of Sekete. He ruled my ancestors when they lived at Tlhabane, the place where Rustenburg, the European town, now stands. My tribe even today still calls Rustenburg Tlhabane. After Sekete comes another name of a famous Chief, who is still recalled with pride by my tribal people, although, strangely enough, I do not recall any child being named after this man in my tribe. His name was Makgongoana. During the reign of Makgongoana, before the arrival of the Europeans, the tribe moved again and went to settle ten miles away in the north-west, along the hill they named Direpotsane. This place they named Phokeng, our headquarters, where I was born and my parents before me. The first Chief who ruled my tribe at Phokeng was my grandfather, Mokgatle, popularly called Mokgatle-Oa-Makgongoana-Oa-Sekete.

My ancestors' departure from Thaba-Ea-Nape to Tlhabane, where the European town of Rustenburg stands, caused other members of the tribe to stop all along the route they travelled. Along the way to Tlhabane those who did not want to go to the new site established villages, but remained loyal to the Chief who led the emigration to Tlhabane. The villages they established became branches of the main tribe. The land they passed through to the new place became the property of the whole people, being owned by them collectively and the Chief being the trustee. The Chief's young brothers became sub-Chiefs or headmen to whom the Chief delegated his powers to preside over the branch villages' affairs and to report to him all the progress of the branches.

Once those branches were established the Chief was forbidden by law and tribal customs to interfere in matters the branches had decided, unless they asked for his help or advice. The laws and customs also, however, empowered the Chief to overrule, with the advice of his councillors, decisions made by the branches, if he thought they were not going to benefit the people in the branches or the tribe as a whole. The Chief was forbidden by law and custom to receive any complaint from any member of the branch at his court unless it was brought there by the sub-Chief or headman in the form of an appeal. The branches too, like the main tribe, have clans within them, with leaders who, before taking any dispute to the sub-Chief or headman, must try to settle it themselves. This procedure is still being followed today in our tribe, though, because of being ruled by Europeans, some disregard the tribal procedure and go straight to the European court.

These branches are found today, all of them to the eastern side of Rustenburg and along the mountains, called Maralla-a-Nape, not very far from Rustenburg. They are all in the east of Noka-Ea-Matsokubiane, which the Europeans named the Hex. They all still pay homage to the Chief at the headquarters, Phokeng. From Thaba-Ea-Nape, the first branch established was called Seruthube, the second Marekana, the third Tsitsing, part of which, after the introduction of Christianity, was named Kanana after Canaan, the fourth Thekoana, and the fifth Photsaneng, which the Europeans later called Bleskop and is now a mining area.

I mentioned earlier that calabashes, which my ancestors grew and handed down to their descendants, were used for drinking beer. My ancestors, like peoples of all nations, have always brewed their own beer. They drank it and enjoyed its flavour. Beer brewing from the days of my ancestors until today has been the occupation of women. Every woman in my tribe is expected to know how to brew good and nourishing beer, and before the arrival of Europeans, when all young women of marriageable age spent more time in the tribe with their mothers, they were taught the art of brewing. A woman found good at brewing beer is regarded as a copy of her mother, and the unfortunate one who cannot is also taken for granted as a copy of her upbringing. The reason given is that a woman must be in a position to entertain her husband and his guests. When men complain of hunger, they are understood to mean that they have had no beer for a long time. My mother was one of the fortunate ones who was always praised for being an expert in the art of brewing.

After harvest, men must be entertained by their womenfolk with beer, and, in the old days, men then entertained their womenfolk with meat by slaughtering beasts to show appreciation for the good work their women performed in the fields. These were customs and traditions, but present-day conditions have curtailed the one of slaughtering of beasts, but the one of beer still persists. When a woman starts beer preparations she takes *mabele*-corn, pours it into any size of *ngkgo* clay pot, depending on the amount of beer she wishes to brew, adds water, covers it up and leaves it for three or four days. After that she strains the water out, but leaves the corn in the pot for a period of a week or more to allow it to sprout. When that has taken place she takes out the contents of the pot, spreads it out on dry, well-worked ground which must be dustless. At this stage the corn is called by a new name, *momela*.

My people in the tribe, after building houses, erect round the house a circle of walls called *lapa*. They flatten the ground, smooth it evenly, first beating it flat with a well-made piece of wood made for the purpose called *kato*, and then, having mixed earth with water, pour this mud all over the ground. This piece of work is called *thitelo* and is performed by women. In the end the place is hard, smooth and dustless. Sprouted corn is spread on this ground to allow the sun to dry it up well. When *momela* is dried, young boys or girls are ordered to sit nearby all the time to see that birds and fowls do not help themselves to it. Any young boy or girl so ordered always feels that he or she is denied the pleasure of playing about with friends. My mother, too, used to order me to watch *momela*. I used to resent such assignments intensely.

After three days, when mother was sure that her *momela* was completely dry, she would gather it again and put it into a dry clay pot ready for grinding. Grinding of *momela* is done with a stone selected for the purpose called *lloala*, and a small stone called *tshiloana*, which mother held with her two hands, moving it backwards and forwards, crushing the sprouted corn between the two stones. After this performance, the corn is turned into flour and then is called *motlhaba*. After that, on her own chosen day, my mother would start brewing beer. The first act is that water is boiled and the ground sprouted corn *momela* is mixed with hot water. Beer yeast, which is always kept somewhere in a small clay pot, is added and the mixture is then called *tiing*. The mixture is left to ferment for one and a half days before it is cooked and turned into a soft, smooth porridge, which takes around two hours.

The porridge for brewing beer is called *serube* and can be eaten, though not in the same quantities as porridge cooked for eating purposes. *Serube* is then allowed to get cold, and when it has set hard but can be broken easily with human hands, water is added again, turning it into a solution. Then raw *momela* is added again. The water is carefully added so that it is not too much or too little. Here is where a good brewer shows her skill.

The mixture is left in a clay pot to ferment for one and a half days. At the end of the first day, experts in beer tasting can tell whether the fermentation stage has been passed or whether the beer is a strong and nourishing one. At any time after the fermentation stage has been reached, a woman or her friend, who could offer to assist her with the final stage, that of straining, could set themselves at work. The mixture itself when ready for straining begins to invite anyone who comes close to where it is placed. It begins to make sounds, shooting up bubbles on top and filling the room where it is kept with a strong beer smell.

The straining performance is done with a grass strainer, made by experts, either men or women. It is knitted like a woman's stocking, measuring about three-quarters of a yard, closed up at the bottom end. This act is called *gotlhotla* and the grass strainer is called *motlhotlo*. The unstrained liquid is poured into this *motlhotlo* and a woman, when she is sure she can operate it to her liking, closes the upper part of it with her hand, like trapping air in a balloon, the first hand holding the bottom part while the other hand holds the upper, and squeezing begins. While she squeezes the liquid runs out into an empty clay pot, leaving only bran inside the *motlhotlo*. Depending on the amount of beer brewed, the operation can take an hour or more. The bran left from the liquid is called *moroko*. Some of it, a small quantity, can be kept in a small container and be used again as yeast, but it is used largely for feeding pigs and fowls.

As a rule, women never allow their men to drink their beer immediately sifting has taken place; they say it is immature and they should wait until it has matured. After twenty-four hours it is a matured beer and therefore can be used for entertaining. Before it has reached maturing stage it is regarded as being unhealthy and liable to cause constipation. No woman would like her beer to cause anyone discomfort. When men enjoy a strong beer, which intoxicates more than a weak one, they are always found to be talking all at the same time. After enjoying a strong beer, they want to eat salty fried meat.

Every African man is expected to be a beer drinker. It sounds odd when a man declines beer that is offered to him. I heard many beer-drinking men in my tribe complain bitterly against other men, who had beer but did not offer it to them. Close friends always invite each other to their homes for beer drinking. Good and kind men or women are those who invite and offer friends beer when they have some in their homes. No function can be praised and regarded as a dignified one if there is no beer for men to drink. Men in my tribe go to functions to help work, so that in the end they could be given beer to drink and meat to eat.

Women can also become beer drinkers, but with a difference. It is regarded a disgrace for a young woman to be seen drinking beer, because it would intoxicate her and make her forget her honour, respect and character. Old women can drink if they wish, but are not encouraged to do so.

A teen-age girl is called *mothepha* or *moroetsana*, and as long as she is referred to by those two words she is very careful not to make mistakes in her dealings with other people. When she is referred to as the former, everyone is made to understand that she is of marriageable age. Women are called *mosadi* (plural *basadi*), which indicates the married state. Unmarried ones can be so referred to by those who are not familiar with their status, but once hearing them being referred to as *mothepha* or *methepha* the stranger would know that they were unmarried.

Boys in the old days were not permitted to drink before they were circumcised. On their return from circumcision they could drink, but were not permitted to drink with or amongst the older men who were all regarded to be of their parents' age and therefore required respect from all young men. Young men, like their elders, drank by themselves. As soon as a young man got married, then he passed on to the higher rank – that of older men. It was regarded as lack of discipline, and bad upbringing and character, if a young man still unmarried demanded the right to drink beer amongst the older men. He would put his parents to shame and many people would doubt whether he was sound in mind. Today things are not as they were. Because of new times and ideas, young men no longer feel it their duty to act in the same way as their fathers acted towards their older people.

My ancestors, like peoples in other parts of the world, had names and references which made people understand the meaning of things, places and people. A female child is called *mosetsana* (plural, *basetsana*). A male is called *mosimane* (plural, *basimane*), and as with females, there are references made which indicate whether he is a teenager below marriageable age or whether he has reached the stage where a feast can be staged for him as his marriage ceremony. When still a mere teenager, he is *lesogoana* (plural, *masogoana*). From the stage I mentioned until the day of his marriage he is called *lekoloane* (plural, *makoloane*). Thereafter he is a man, *monna* (plural, *banna*).

Old men also have references by which they are known. Either you say *monnamogolo* (plural, *bannabagolo*) or *mokgalabie* (*bakgalabie*). These indicate that they are grandfathers. Similarly, old women are referred to as *mosadimogolo* (plural, *basadibagolo*). All these convey the meaning that they are grandparents.

I do not know whether, before the introduction of Christianity, the names of the days of the week had any significant meanings; I don't know these names in my own language. But months of the year undoubtedly had meanings to them because all had names. My mother did her utmost to teach me the names of all the months, but I was not interested, because I thought that it would benefit me more if I knew them in English. Only now do I realise that I was foolish not to combine them in English and my own language. To my regret I can only remember the names of two months, the one in which I was born, April, which my ancestors called *moranang*, and the one during which dusty storms blow and rain begins to fall – August, called *phato*.

Seasons, too, had significant meaning. Autumn was called *dikgakologo*, summer *selemo*, spring *letlhabula*, and winter *mariga*. They had their own beliefs, right or wrong, that there were certain things you could do in one and not in others. Some of their beliefs undoubtedly hampered them, but others prevented them from acting in mischievous ways. The essential things are that they led organised lives in orderly communities. They had surveyors who mapped their territories and defined their boundaries. They had lawyers who framed their unwritten laws. Doctors of their own cured them when ill.

V Doctors

These colourful personalities became very controversial with the change-over from traditional life and customs to Christianity. Christianity primarily meant European rule. The church and government refused to accept them as men of medicine who could help the sick in any way. They gave them a new name, that of witchdoctors – men who, in their opinion, claimed to know something but really knew nothing about health and, instead of curing, could only kill the sick. These men of medicine, who have acquired the name of witchdoctors, are still found in my tribe today. They are in every place where African communities are found; also in every European city in South Africa where Africans work and live.

Their people refuse to be taken away from them. Accusations that they are killers, not healers, have not discouraged their people from patronising them. Personally, I have not been sick and required their cure, and therefore am not in a good position to say whether they help or not. But I can say that I did see people very sick being attended by them who recovered and claimed that they were cured by these men of African medicine. Unlike the Europeans, who claim that their medicine is better than in bygone days, the Africans say that their men of medicine of today are not as good as those of older generations. I think that it is right to pose a question here, whether the European church and government were right in refusing to accept African medicine men. I am a great admirer of scientific medicine and believe that doctors should be taught scientific methods of curing before they can attend the sick. But the African medicine man claims that he has been trained in the art of curing by his own men, but admits that Europeans refuse to accept him because he was not trained by them and suffers a disadvantage because there is no university building to which he can point and say, 'I was trained in this building.'

Europeans who have made Africa their home, and others who lived there, have a deep-rooted belief that the Africans fear and worship their medicine men. They say that everything the medicine man says goes without question. Therefore they believe that the only way to get the Africans away from believing in their medicine men is to discourage them by emphasising to them that their doctors, whom Europeans call witchdoctors, do not know what they are doing, and because they have not been trained in a scientific way cannot possibly know anything about curing the sick.

I myself think that the Europeans are wrong. The Africans do not worship their medicine men, but respect them. I admit that the Africans, even my own tribe which is largely Christian today, consult their medicine men more than European doctors and Africans trained by Europeans to be doctors. There are various reasons for this behaviour or attitude. In the tribes, in the villages far away from European towns or cities, the people for generations have known only one man whom they could consult when they were in pain or other difficulties, and this was their own medicine man. They saw his medicine help and saw him fail, and his predictions coming true and sometimes false. All this they took as inherent in human beings and unavoidable.

I admit, too, that an African can hardly go against his medicine man's advice. They have a deep-rooted belief that he knows what he is talking about. They doubt that he can tell them something he knows is not true. They not only respect him, but honour him as well. They believe that through his work and devotion they survived many tragedies. This is something deep-seated in their feelings, which even in this last half of the twentieth century still dominates the Africans, educated and uneducated alike. How does an African medicine man examine those who consult him? *Does* he know what he is talking about? How does he select his medicines, poisonous ones from unpoisonous ones?

They keep small bones from sheep, goats and other small animals in a small animal skin handbag, called *moraba*, and the bones are called *taola* (plural, *ditaola*). A person being examined is seated on a mat or skin on the floor, facing the doctor, who throws the bones on the floor and begins to speak, looking at the bones. After two or three throws, the doctor then asks his patient to throw *ditaola*, the examining bones, and blow his breath on to them, saying among other things, 'I am here sick, but I don't know what's wrong with me. Tell me, and choose the medicine which will cure me.' Thereafter the doctor will begin to read the bones, which he claims tell him what is wrong with his patient. But before he does that, he would ask the patient to agree or to disagree with the findings of his bones. He would emphasise that what he says is not from him, but what is conveyed to him by the bones. During the examination period, doctor and patient would agree and disagree.

At the end of agreements and disagreements the same procedure is followed, this time in search of the medicine which would cure the patient. Whether the *ditaola* do talk or not, I cannot tell, but what I can say is that very seldom have I heard of a medicine man giving his patients poisonous medicines during his work of trying to cure

26

them. Medicine men of my tribe have a saying that medicines do not cure everyone, only lucky ones.

What sort of medicine do the African medicine men use in treating their patients? They use herbs, some boiled and others ground into powder forms. These are usually taken with light, thin porridge, or beer. In the case of boiled ones, only the water or juice derived from them is drunk. Before he leaves his patient with his medicines, the doctor would boil them first and drink some of it in the presence of the patient and those who would nurse the sick person. Powdered ones he would mix with beer or porridge and take in full view of his patient and others.

African doctors in their own interests and reputation make it a rule to visit their patients every three days to see how the sick person progresses, or whether a change of medicine is necessary. In the old days fees were paid in the form of cattle, sheep or goats, depending on the seriousness of the sickness. They were never paid in advance, but after the sick person was cured. Today the pattern has changed: money plays a large part, and people pay for services, not for cure. That is why Africans say doctors of today are not like those of yesterday.

Medicine men of my tribe, in combination with those of other tribes in South Africa, stand firm in their claim that the accusation that they are witchdoctors who have no idea of what they are doing is baseless. They say they are being condemned without having been tested to see how they are able to help the sick. They have combined with others throughout the country and demand recognition from the state by way of registration. They ask that, before registration is effected, those who are in need of it should go through thorough testing by a group of doctors who have undergone the test before them and proved their skill and knowledge of medicine. For years they have said to the state: 'Test us; give us tasks; give us sick people in hospitals, mental hospitals and other institutions, to see whether we can help or not.' Their demands are refused and the accusations that they are not doctors but witchdoctors continue.

My people call a doctor *ngaka* (plural, *dingaka*). They are organised on a provincial as well as on a national basis. The name of their organisation is the African Dingaka Association. They say that if their request for registration can be effected the people will get a better and sounder service from the *dingaka*, because no *ngaka* who has not been tested will have the courage to say to a patient, 'I can help you', when he knows that he has not been tested or registered and has no authority to treat the sick. They point out further that, in the days of their forefathers, each year young doctors were called to the Chief's place to meet old ones, and the experienced tested the inexperienced in the presence of the Chief and the elders of the tribe.

They complain that since the Chief's powers have been taken away such gatherings are no longer taking place and people who are not well trained in the art of throwing *ditaola* and the use of medicine-herbs go about presenting themselves to the people as doctors.

VI Phokeng

From Tlhabane, where the town of Rustenburg now stands, to Phokeng, my birthplace and the headquarters of my tribe. . . . I said before that there are no records which could guide me in tracing the movements of my ancestors and the events which became part of them during the time of their movements from one place to another. Therefore I can only guess some of the events. I think that my tribe occupied the site of Phokeng and made it their permanent settlement towards the end of the eighteenth century, or in the early part of the nineteenth. I am not sure whether my grandfather Mokgatle was born there or at Tlhabane; his birth was not recorded. What I am sure of is that he was the first Paramount Chief of my tribe at Phokeng.

Mokgatle was the son of Makgongoana, the son of Sekete, the descendant of Tshukudu. I never knew the name of Mokgatle's mother, or where she came from: how many wives Makgongoana, Mokgatle's father had, or how many brothers and sisters Mokgatle had. What I can say with firmness is that he was a polygamist and had many wives. When they settled at Phokeng, Mokgatle's first name was Mokgatle and his surname was Sekete, after his father's father. When Mokgatle became the Paramount Chief, he cut out Sekete and called himself Mokgatle Mokgatle. All his children by his many wives followed their father and adopted the surname Mokgatle.

My father never told me much about his father; it was my mother who used to tell me something about Mokgatle into whose reign she was born and grew. She told me that he was feared and highly revered by his subjects, who were not only his subjects but his relatives and tribal people. My mother said that she did not know how Mokgatle was crowned Paramount Chief and by whom, as she was not born at the time. When Mokgatle took a walk amongst his people in the tribe, some people recited many and various praises of him. Others, she said, would hide away from his sight, because they could not bear fixing their eyes with his. When my grandfather assumed the paramountcy of the tribe the Europeans had not reached our part of Africa. They came when he was already the Paramount Chief.

My mother advanced a variety of reasons why my grandfather, Paramount Chief Mokgatle of the Bafokeng tribe, was revered and feared by his subjects with whom he was a member of the same tribe. She said that he was extremely just; he treated all the people in the same way, and intensely disliked injustice being done to some people because those who provoked them thought they were of the lower class in the tribal society. He loved children and would not like to hear that any children had no food to eat.

He was also a great entertainer and enjoyed seeing people having enough to eat. He stored large amounts of *mabele*-corn at his home, and when some people in the tribe were unfortunate and had had a poor harvest, and their stock of food could not carry them through to the next harvesting time, they could go and tell him that they were facing starvation, and he would not hesitate to give them *mabele*-corn, after ascertaining that they were in fact facing starvation. He was a very rich Chief, my mother would say with firmness. No one knew how many cattle, sheep, goats or other animals he owned. Many families in the tribe, which were not as fortunate as others, had large numbers of animals in their care, and very few people knew that they were Mokgatle's animals. The Paramount Chief, as my mother called him, gave them the right to use the animals in any way they wished, short of killing them, selling them or giving them away without his permission.

His subjects, my mother told me, regarded him as the father of the tribe. Every one of Mokgatle's wives had her own house and her own fields, which she cultivated with her children, and all controlled their animals, *mabele*-corn and other possessions. Mokgatle had his own fields, which were cultivated by all the clans in the tribe collectively and harvested in the same way. It was from such crops that the Paramount Chief entertained and helped unfortunate families. Mother used to say that there was no family without food and milk in Paramount Chief Mokgatle's time. To prove that they were telling the truth, people in litigation swore in his name.

My grandfather died many years before my parents married, but old people in my tribe still swear in his name when they testify to the truth. They cannot imagine anyone making a false statement in his name. They all agree that during his reign over the tribe, no one felt unjustly treated or unjustly judged. The people who are termed commoners, *mofo* (plural, *bafo*), felt more secure during his reign. When his relatives or any of his children were involved in disputes which required tribal court settlement, he always took the attitude that his relative or child who was a party in the disputes must have been the one who initiated the trouble because he was related to the Chief; he would emphasise that the commoners could not start trouble with any royal child or a relative of the royal house, but it was possible that his child or any relative could look down on a commoner and say, 'I can do what I like with you or your property, and when you take me before the tribal tribunal, they will side with me against you, because of my position in our society.'

They say he always encouraged those who dealt with court cases involving the commoners and his children or relatives to show more leniency towards the commoners than those who were related to him by blood. That, he said, would discourage his children or relatives from misbehaving towards the commoners. It would also encourage the commoners to stand up for their rights and to bring to the notice of the tribal authority their legitimate grievances. They say that he never spoke in singular form, but always in plural, never referring to 'my people', but 'our people'. When he disagreed with anything which concerned tribal laws or customs, he never said, 'I don't agree', but used the words, 'Our people would not like that or agree with such things'. Everything he did or said, he was doing it or saying it on behalf of the whole tribe. He said that everything he owned belonged to the tribe and therefore referred to them as our things, our cattle, or our *mabele*-corn. That was Mokgatle-Oa-Makgongo-ana, as they called him affectionately.

During my grandfather's reign there also lived in our tribe an outstanding figure who is also a legend. The legend is that he was grandfather's physician, a tribal judge and a man who had a great knowledge of tribal laws and customs. His name was Rasemathu Makgala. It is said that grandfather could not do anything concerning tribal affairs without consulting Rasemathu. What he advised grandfather to do was very seldom turned down. He was a man of great influence and others think that he ruled the tribe in grandfather's name. He was a commoner but, because he was a doctor and a man of wisdom, he gained grandfather's confidence completely. According to the legend, Rasemathu presided over nearly all appeal cases in the tribal court (*lekgotla*), and his knowledge of tribal laws, *molao* (plural, *melao*) and customs, *mokgoa* (plural, *mekgoa*) was highly respected by the inhabitants of the tribe.

Being the Paramount Chief's physician was also being the physician for the whole tribe. Yearly most acknowledged medicine men in the tribe and in the villages which formed the branches of the tribe were summoned to Phokeng and, under Rasemathu's directions and guidance, had to throw their bones in the presence of the Paramount Chief and some of his councillors, to predict what sort of a year it was going to be: a dry one with no rain; whether there was likely to be plenty of crops, or whether the tribe was likely to face an epidemic of some sort. When I asked my mother and others who told these stories whether their predictions came true, they all claimed that most of them came true.

My informers all agreed that during the time of the throwing of *ditaola*, which was meant to foretell the future, there was always conflict of opinion, but the accepted assertions were those of the majority. All these happened before my time and the arrival of Christianity with the Europeans. The ceremony of the throwing of bones no longer takes place in our tribe. But I was told by other Africans, from tribes in South Africa which have not adopted Christianity as part of their tribal lives, as in places like Bopedi in the eastern Transvaal, that the practice still goes on. This gave me the understanding that not only my tribe was doing it, but that it was an African custom generally speaking throughout South Africa.

Rasemathu, like all men of his times, was a polygamist with many wives and many children. To demonstrate how important and influential he was in the tribe, some of his sons married into grandfather's families and some of grandfather's sons married his daughters. As a result, even today in my tribe, those who bear the surnames Makgala and Mokgatle are cousins. Rasemathu and his fellow-doctors of grandfather's time are credited with many successes – whether true or not, it is beyond me to say, but I was told this by older people who knew the influential Rasemathu and saw him at work. The legend is that they could prevent an epidemic like small-pox (*sekongkonyane*) from coming into the tribe. Being interested to know how they could stop it, I was told that when the epidemic was reported somewhere in one tribe, Rasemathu and his fellow-doctors used to send out some of their men to the place to take samples of it, and on their return could mix the samples with their medicines and then begin to inject the people with it, making them immune from the epidemic, by making small cuts in parts of their bodies and then rubbing the mixture in. If the stories are true, to me it sounds like a high form of scientific work.

When I grew up there were still in our tribe men and women who were born during Rasemathu's time and I cannot recall seeing any one of them who had been a victim of smallpox; such people are recognisable. A claim is also advanced, by older people who saw Rasemathu and his men at work, that they could cure insanity. They could, they say, tame violent, insane persons by making them passive for the rest of their lives, if they could not restore their thinking power and reasoning abilities. That, they say, was done by injecting medicines into the person's body and by treating him with medicines for a certain period. When I grew up I found men and women in our tribe who were not in full control of their thinking and reasoning but who were passive and non-violent. They were not many, but were looked after by their relatives like helpless juveniles. Some of them would talk to themselves endlessly, as though engaged in conversation with another person, stopping only when asleep.

One of the achievements attributed to Rasemathu and fellow-doctors of his age concerns the good times when there was plenty of rain and there were bound to be good crops in the fields. In such a year when *mabele*-corn was ripe, or even when it was still young and green, not only did people like it, but swarms of locusts and hordes of corn-eating birds wanted to get at it before the people took it away from the fields. When the swarms of locusts (*tsiie*) were destroying grass and green plants wherever they could, Rasemathu and his fellow-medicine men used their medicine to drive them away from our tribal lands. All this sounded strange to me and I asked searching questions of those who told me the story, including my mother. 'How did they do it?' I asked, with a certain cynicism. They used to take one of the swarm of locusts, doctor it with their medicine, and leave it to fly back into the swarm, and the results were that it would lead the swarm away from our lands and our crops would be saved.

Similarly, I was told that when *mabele*-corn begins to get ripe, *thaga*, corn-eating birds, would come along in hordes to eat the corn away, unless people were assigned to live away from home at the fields, starting very early in the mornings, to chase the birds away. This occupation required people to do nothing else besides chasing birds the whole day. In this, too, I was told, Rasemathu and his men would put their skills at the disposal of the tribe. They would catch one of the birds, work their magic on it, let it fly back to the other birds, and when amongst them it would lead them away from our fields and our corn would be saved. All these, I repeat, were stories told to me; I never saw any of them happen. When Christianity arrived these things were discouraged as primitive, barbarous and the works of unbelievers in the power of God, and people began to shy away from practising them. Young people got discouraged from learning those methods, and when those who knew them died their knowledge died with them.

Europeans who live in Africa say that the Africans are superstitious people and false believers. I agree with the former, but contradict the latter. But I confess that superstition is very strong amongst the Africans I know in South Africa. However, it cannot in my opinion be dismissed as wholly bad; rather it is a mixture of good and bad. It can inspire people to do good and restrain them from doing bad things to their neighbours. It is not an easy thing to overcome because it is passed on to children as soon as they start being taught right and wrong in their society and environment.

One of the superstitions which still dominates the minds of Africans in the present time is witchcraft, which they find hard to disbelieve. Witchcraft is called *boloi*. A witch (*moloi*), the Africans believe, can poison a person even when he is a long distance away. They believe further that through witchcraft it is possible to force an evil-doer to confess. Similarly they believe that anyone who practises witchcraft can direct an animal to kill you, a reptile to bite you and can even send a fly to deliver a deadly poison to you, if he or she wishes to remove you from life.

The queerest thing is that they bitterly hate witchcraft. I would have thought that they would have welcomed it as an instrument for getting rid of people they disliked. One reason why Africans detest witchcraft and witches is that no one is free from being suspected of it. If neighbours quarrel, and, in the next few days, someone in the neighbouring family falls sick, meets misfortune, or dies, the family which was spared the affliction will be blamed for it not only by the suffering family but by all who heard the quarrel. This superstition is such a dominating factor in African minds that even when a man or a woman is a hard worker in his or her fields and manages to achieve great success in producing more crops, the less hard-working ones will cover up their weaknesses by accusing the successful one of having used witchcraft to achieve success. I asked my people why there are many people alive if witchcraft was so widely practised; the answer was, 'The protector is the doctor, the medicine man'.

The doctor, the helper – respected, not worshipped – plays two parts. With his medicine he can stop the witches from poisoning people and help to cure those who have been poisoned by the witches. Every African family therefore sees to it that it has a family doctor to fortify it against attacks by witches. Every African home is supposed to be so fortified. After the home has been built and before the owners occupy it, the family doctor is called upon to perform his magic. The magic is called *motheo* and the same word is used to mean the actual foundations of a house.

The doctor performs his magic at night when he is not being observed by the neighbours. He does it by mixing his medicines and spreading them all over the enclosure of the family; by planting four doctored wooden pegs in the four corners of the enclosure, called *lapa*, and finally by doctoring every member of the family. When this has been done the family feel protected, and if a witch wanted to poison any of them, his or her power would be ineffective. Witches are said to work more at night than during the day. They are the walkers of the night, when life has come to a stop. A doctored enclosure is meant to become a puzzle to the witches, so that when they come at night to poison the family they either lose their way in it or forget as soon as they get there what they came to do. It is also said that, though the witches are sure where the family lives because they see them every day, when they go at night to do harm they will find it puzzling, having been changed by magic into a vast area of water, or a place roamed by frightening reptiles and other deadly animals. These sound like high compliments towards medicine men, but, when I asked how the witches acquired their deadly poisons, then two types of medicine men are invented: bad ones who associate

34

with the witches and good ones who would never listen to them. The belief in and hatred of witchcraft is so deep-rooted in the minds of the Africans that it becomes almost impossible to draw the line. The doctor, *ngaka*, is divided in the middle, as a protector and in some instances as the aider of witches. They believe that a neighbour must not know the family doctor of the other neighbour for fear that, if known, the neighbour might go to him with bribes and influence him to relax his magic and thereby enable him to harm the family he is supposed to protect. *Ngaka* is also regarded as a fortune-teller.

Before embarking on a long journey an African would go to his *ngaka* and ask him to examine the success of his journey by throwing bones, to ascertain whether he was likely to meet danger on the journey, or whether the people he was going to visit or meet would be friendly to him. If *ngaka* expressed some doubt, or did not give him a clear bill of passage, the journey would be postponed. If, on the other hand, *ngaka* says, 'All is well, the journey is clear and smooth', the journey would be taken with great confidence. This process was followed in the days of my grandfather and Rasemathu, and is still being followed in the rural areas of South Africa where Africans live in tribal societies under their Chief.

When the Europeans came into contact with the Africans, they found them in this sort of spider's web; they thought that, since they hated witchcraft intensely, the best possible way they could discourage them from believing in their medicine and their doctor was to tell them that he was a wizard – from that sprang the term witchdoctor. To demonstrate to them that they reckoned nothing of him, the Europeans refrained even from asking him to show them what he knew and could do. The Africans listened, but carried on just the same old way.

The period before the arrival of Europeans is referred to by my tribal people as before literature (*pele-a-lekoallo*); after their arrival, after literature (*morago-a-lekoallo*). Before the arrival of literature my tribe believed in God. Rain, thunder, storm, droughts and the disasters they suffered to them were acts of God, whom they call *modimo*, meaning 'of the sky above'. They imagined that *modimo* was Mosotho like themselves but beyond their reach, and therefore that between them and *modimo*, whom they could not see and talk to, were their dead forefathers, whom they called *badimo*. Their dead forefathers, whom they could not see and talk to, could somehow meet *modimo* in mysterious ways and talk to him. They then decided to worship their dead forefathers and through them talk to God to ask him to forgive them if they had wronged him. They worshipped their *badimo* in many different ways, offering sacrifices of food which they imagined pleased them and gave them strength to plead to God for them.

35

They also believed in the second coming of their *badimo* in new forms. When a male baby was born it was imagined that his dead grandfather had come back to life, and so the child was given dead grandfather's name. The same thing applied to female children, in relation to their dead grandmothers. Until the arrival of Europeans the name of Jesus was not known in my tribe: I will accept that these ways of thinking were false.

My observations of other peoples have shown me that they too believed in falsehoods. For instance, some people would not do things on certain dates, days, weeks or months, for fear that disasters would fall upon them. Others refrained from eating certain types of food for the same reason. Some revered certain objects because they imagined that they brought them fortune, even health. Others will not eat pork, because they believe the pig to be evil and unclean. These are all false beliefs which are entertained by peoples of all nations.

VII Paternal Grandmother

My paternal grandmother was a slave. Her name was Matlhodi Kekana, but I do not know the date of her birth nor the names of her parents. She came from a small tribe in the north-eastern Transvaal who call themselves Matebele. She was born near a hill called Sefakaole and their tribal village is called KwaMukopani. According to legend, Mukopani was their ancestor who founded the tribe. It is said that they broke off from a body of Zulus who emigrated from Zululand under the leadership of Musilikazi, fleeing northwards from King Chaka the great, who sought to punish him for failing to defeat the Basotho in Lesotho, then ruled by King Moshoeshoe. Musilikazi, according to legend, was one of the most trusted of Chaka's army leaders.

My grandmother's people broke off and became an independent tribe and developed a language which can be described as diluted Zulu, or broken Zulu, which is a mixture of Zulu and Sesotho, today called Transvaal Sesotho. They called themselves Matebele and the language Setebele. In her tribe my grandmother was a princess, because she was the daughter of the Chief Kekana, like all Africans of his time a polygamist. My grandmother's birthplace is today called Piet Potgietersrust, or simply P.P.Rust. It lies between Pretoria and Pietersburg, in the north-eastern Transvaal. The Africans call Pretoria Tshoane, P.P.Rust KwaMukopani, and Pietersburg Polokwane. These names were used by the Africans before the arrival of the Europeans and are still in use today.

About the middle of the nineteenth century, when the Dutch settlers were fleeing from English rule in the western and eastern parts of South Africa (known today as the Cape Province and Natal), into the land of Barolongs (now called the Free State), and the lands they called the Transvaal after crossing Noka-Ea-Lekoe (now known as the Vaal River), the Dutch settlers, who today call themselves the Afrikaners and their language Afrikaans, were engaged in fighting with the Africans they encountered on the way. In the eastern Transvaal, in the places the Africans called Bopedi and other areas, the Dutch settlers were not welcomed and bitter and bloody battles resulted, the Africans stopping the fight each time when their Chiefs were captured.

Piet Potgieter's section of the Dutch settlers, who were moving northwards in search of a place to settle away from the English laws and influence in the south, reached KwaMukopani and came into contact with my grandmother's tribe; the latter had chosen the place when they broke away from Musilikazi's body of Zulus, who had gone farther north. My grandmother's people refused to allow Piet Potgieter and his people to occupy their lands without a fight. I have no records showing how long the war lasted, but the legend is that it developed into one of the bloodiest battles, and during the course of its progress the leader of the Dutch settlers, Piet Potgieter, was killed. The other story, which comes from the Dutch side, is that my grandmother's people showed frightening ruthlessness, that after killing Piet Potgieter they placed his dead body at the site where two roads met, so that from whatever direction his people might come they should see that he had been killed. This story is one of the stories which are told to the European children in South Africa which leave bitterness in their minds and a feeling that the Africans are ruthless people and in some ways ought to pay for their ancestors' cruelty.

In telling this story, which indeed sounds grim, they omit to tell their offspring and the world how they killed the Matebele people who opposed them. The Dutch claim to have won the war, but my grandmother's people dispute it by saying that they simply stopped fighting and left the Dutch where they were and continued to live where they had been before. Not very far from my grandmother's people's headquarters, Sefakaloala, the Dutch established their town which is called after their leader Piet Potgieter, P.P.Rust. On the western side of Sefakaloala runs a large river called by Matebele people Noka-ea-Mogale-a-Koena, River of Crocodiles.

The fighting which took place between my grandmother's tribe and the Dutch settlers under Piet Potgieter resulted in confusion and great distress. Cattle, sheep and goats were missed by the inhabitants of KwaMukopani, as well as men, women and children. No one knew whether they were killed during the fighting or whether they were merely missing. My grandmother, it is said, was still a child of about two or three years old, and was one of those missing when the fighting ended. As a daughter of the Chief, a great search for her was undertaken, but she was found nowhere. In the end, like many missing persons who could not be found, she was presumed dead. The people of KwaMukopani were sad because they did not see the dead body of their Chief's daughter, and no one could testify that he or she saw her dying.

The tribe's suspicion that she was not dead was true; she was alive, having been taken away by one of Potgieter's followers to the western end of the Transvaal province, in the Rustenburg district. With the Dutch family which took her away from her people, grandmother went to live in strange lands amongst strange people. They passed the town of Rustenburg, crossed the Magaliesberg mountains and settled to the south-west of them where the Dutch family began farming. The place was about twelve or fourteen miles from Phokeng, our headquarters, and my grandfather, Paramount Chief Mokgatle, was the ruler of the tribe. I tried hard to discover the name of the family or the man who took grandmother away and kept her as a slave, but failed. The only name I got was the nickname the Africans gave that man – KaMongoele, which means 'on the knees'. I shall therefore refer to that man as KaMongoele.

From his nickname, I guess that he was a deeply religious man, who must always have ordered his children and those who were under his care and guidance to go on their knees and pray. Every European, even today, who has daily dealings with the Africans has a nickname, and the Africans amongst themselves call him by that name. If he wears a beard he is nicknamed beard, if he is fat he will be called Mafutha, which means fat, if he is a man with a big nose he will be called Rangko, if he has large eyes, Ramatlho.

Although my grandmother grew up in the household of a Dutch farmer, working without pay as a slave, and had been taken away from her tribe at a very early age, she did not forget her language. She remembered well the names of her parents but did not know where she could find her people. She learned to speak Dutch, which is today called Afrikaans, but because there was no school for her could not read or write it. She remembered, too, that her tribal name was Matlhodi, the daughter of Chief Kekana of Kwamukopani.

I do not think that she was ill-treated, because that would not have been in the interest of KaMangoele and his family. KaMangoele and grandfather Paramount Chief Mokgatle became friends, paid each other visits and gave one another presents. According to legend, Mokgatle's greatest gifts to his friend KaMangoele were honey. Each time KaMangoele visited grandfather at Phokeng he returned to his farm with large quantities of honey and other gifts he liked very much. It is said that each time KaMangoele arrived at Phokeng he brought presents to his friend, and through those presents their friendship deepened. According to legend there was no feeling of a white man meeting a black man, one thinking that the other was not his equal, but man meeting another man and accepting him into his household.

Grandfather saw the young slave girl, who later became his wife, grow into a pretty young woman, but I wonder whether grandfather asked his friend where he got the little slave girl whom he saw working in his house. When grandmother was old enough to become a cook for KaMangoele's household, the task of working in the house and cooking for the family became her routine. She was not only the cook, but waited as well on her master's family and all friends who visited the family. KaMangoele's family gave grandmother a European name, Paulina. As a cook in a European house she learned a great deal about the art of preparing European food, and each time grandfather visited his friend he could not leave without a meal and expressing thanks to the one who did the preparations. For a long time grandfather thought that the cooking was done by his friend's wife or one of his daughters. It was only at KaMangoele's home that grandfather could enjoy European food, and he developed a liking for it, but to go to his friend's home meant that he had to be away from the tribe for the whole day.

I do not know precisely how many wives my grandfather Paramount Chief Mokgatle had. Some people said he had more than forty, others say less. Whatever the figure, like all polygamous Paramount Chiefs, he had many wives. At the head of his wives there were three top ones who were expected to provide the tribe with a ruler, in case one of them was childless. They were numbers one, two and three. Number one was the one expected to bear the future ruler of the tribe. The law and custom was that number one's male child should become Chief, his juniors following in succession if death or insanity deprived the elder one of the chance to become the ruler of the tribe. And so on with wives numbers two and three.

Wife number one is called Mohumagadi (queen, or mother of the tribe) and all the Chief's wives are under her and look to her for advice, and follow her lead whenever the women of the tribe were to do something which particularly concerned women. I do not know the name of my grandfather's number one wife, but I do know that in the tribe she was called by the name of her first son who became Paramount Chief after grandfather's death. The son's name was Dumagole and thus his mother was called Madumagole.

The name of wife number two, who was the closest to me, was Nkhubu, but like number one she was popularly known by her first son's name, Dikeledi (tears): I do not know why he was so named, but I can imagine that at the time of his birth there must have been something which saddened the grandfather or the whole tribe. One other thing which surprises me is why he was given the name Dikeledi, since the name belongs to females. Nkhubu was therefore called Madikeledi, Dikeledi's mother.

Grandfather's wife number three was also called by the name of her first son, who was named after grandfather's grandfather, Sekete. Sekete's mother was called Masekete. Those were grandfather's chief wives, who had great influence in our tribe. Their sons, too, became very powerful and influential during grandfather's reign and after his death. They called each other brother, one calling the other 'my elder brother' and referring to others as 'my younger brothers'. Dumagole led, Dikeledi followed him and Sekete followed both of them.

Other wives and their houses were important, but were referred to as minor wives or minor houses. Today in our tribe there are many families which bear the surname Mokgatle, and all are descendants of Paramount Chief Mokgatle. All of them know their positions in the tribal line and follow the rule as it was laid down for them by their grandfather. Dumagole too had several wives and his number one wife provided the tribe with the ruler after his death, and the procedure has been followed till today, when Dumagole's descendant Lebone (the lamp) is the Chief.

While grandfather and the Dutch farmer KaMangoele were great friends, offering each other gifts, receiving each other as equals in their households, and Paulina my grandmother cooked tasty European food which Mokgatle enjoyed enormously, grandfather asked his friend to allow him to marry Paulina, so that she could cook him European food at his headquarters, Phokeng. KaMangoele agreed but reminded grandfather that his marriage to Paulina must be performed according to his law and customs, so that Paulina could acquire social standing in his tribe. Grandfather readily consented, and this meant that grandfather must pay KaMangoele dowry (*bogadi*) which would make her grandfather's legal wife. On his return to the tribe, grandfather reported his intentions to the tribal Council and the negotiations he had had with KaMangoele. The tribal Council approved and later a number of messengers were sent to KaMangoele's home to ascertain what amount of dowry he required for Paulina's release, so that she could marry grandfather.

All the formalities were agreed to and finalised. A number of cattle were delivered to KaMangoele as dowry for my grandmother, and once delivered she was married to Mokgatle, and all that was left for Mokgatle to do was to take her to his tribe.

Grandmother, married to Mokgatle and given away by her master KaMangoele, began her second journey, that time from KaMangoele's farm to Phokeng to join the circle of Paramount Chief's wives. She was a young woman, beautiful, speaking the Dutch of that time and Sintebele, her tribal language. On arrival she found herself again in a strange land amongst strange people, with whom she had only the colour of her skin in common. She still did not know where her people were, and how she could get in touch with them. She had no choice; all that concerned her was that she was alive and married to a Paramount Chief.

At the time when her marriage was being negotiated, Mokgatle's second wife Madikeledi, Nkhubu, was sick, and immediately before grandmother arrived in the tribe she died, leaving three sons, Dikeledi, Dikeletsane (small tears) and Ramarata, and two daughters, Malengena and Theko, a name which indicates that she was born when grandmother's dowry was paid to Kamangoele. Theko means tariff or price. Dikeledi and his two brothers were still young and their sisters were very small, and all needed care. Instead of giving grandmother a home, fields and cattle of her own, like all married women in the tribe, grandfather decided that she should move into Nkhubu's house to care for the children who had lost their mother. That gave her the right to use Madikeledi's house and her fields, as well as her animals. Grandmother's four children were born in Nkhubu's house, and regarded Madikeledi's children as their true brothers and sisters. They looked upon Madikeledi's properties as their mother's properties. I think that grandmother's arrival, Nkhubu's death and the drafting of grandmother into the second main house in the tribe placed grandfather and the tribal councillors in a dilemma. Here was a woman, legally married, but also the last to be married, given the honour of living as, and caring for the children of, the second most important woman of the tribe. Was she replacing Nkhubu in status? What was her status in the tribe, the second or the last? What position would her children occupy in Kgotla (the royal court)? If these questions were asked, they were never settled. A vacuum existed and still exists.

My grandmother's position in the Bafokeng tribe was unique and most complicated. Her status was never defined to her nor to her children. And my father and Uncle Lazarus, who were both alive when I was born, did not know whether they belonged to the second or the last house. Their home was the second house, to which their mother's fields and the animals belonged. The true children of the second house claimed them as their brothers and they claimed them as their brothers and sisters.

Following the laws and customs of the tribe, grandmother was legally married, and it was not her fault that she had no house, cattle and fields of her own. I shall show later that grandmother had a stronger claim in the Bafokeng tribe than many of Mokgatle's wives. Her dowries were paid twice and her marriage was celebrated on two occasions. It was said in her time that she was the most expensive woman Mokgatle ever married. Perhaps, as she was a foreigner in the Bafokeng tribe, she had no one to take up her case for her. If Mokgatle's first marriage to her had been from her people, they would have demanded to know what position she was being married into in the Bafokeng tribe.

Grandmother, finding herself alone and at the same time being grateful that she was released from slavery and alive, allowed things to go on as they were. I was told that each time she was among Mokgatle's wives there were always divisions amongst them, some claiming that because they were married before her they were her seniors, and others again saying that, because she was drafted into the second house to care for its children, she replaced Mokgatle's second wife and occupied that rank. But grandfather and the elders of the tribe never bothered to remedy the situation, and after grandfather's death no attempt was made to define grandmother's rank – thus the situation was allowed to persist.

But when it comes to law and tribal customs, when any member of the tribe is in dispute with my grandmother's children, or any of her descendants, attempts to settle it will have to be made with the participation of Madikeledi's children or her descendants. Similarly, if any child of Nkhubu or any of her descendants is in dispute with anyone in the tribe, efforts to settle it will have to be made with the full participation of grandmother's children or descendants.

VIII Second Marriage

All the time that my grandmother's marriage to grandfather Paramount Chief Mokgatle was being arranged and performed by the man who had taken her away without consent from her people, and when she left the Dutch farmer's house for her new home in Phokeng, her people had no idea that their daughter was still alive somewhere in Africa, perhaps less than two hundred miles from her birthplace. They had given up hope that one day they would hear of her whereabouts, let alone see her, in possession of her body, flesh, blood and soul.

In Phokeng she gave birth to four children, her first-born being a daughter. When her birth was reported to grandfather he remarked, 'Keidumetse', and gave the child the name Keidumetse, which means 'I am pleased'. Keidumetse was the only daughter of my grandmother, but she could not withstand the impact of the world she was born into, and died at the age of two or three years. After her my uncle Segafi was born. Segafi is not a pleasant name for anyone to possess. I do not know why my uncle deserved such a name, but it was his name nevertheless. It means an insane one. Like his sister, Segafi passed away from this earth at an early age and his death broke grandmother's heart.

Then followed my father. As I said earlier, I do not know in which year any one of them was born. It is said that in grandfather's court, in front of the house in which he lived, there was a large tree which gave a very cooling shade, and when the sun was hot and the heat tormenting the tribe, grandfather would be found when not too busy under the shade of that tree conversing with his councillors or people who had come to see him on important matters. The legend is that when my father's birth was made known to him, he smiled, looked up at the tree and said his name shall be this tree (Setlhare). So my father's name was Setlhare-sa-Mokgatle.

My grandmother's last-born was also a male, Setlhatsana, which means a small tree. He was also given that name by his father when the birth was reported to him. These names were like those of Dikeledi and Dikeletsane, the sons of Nkhubu into whose house my grandmother was married.

After the discovery of diamonds in the Cape Province of South Africa at Kimberley in 1870, money became an attractive object in

44

the eyes of Africans, and with it they found that they could buy things they needed from the Europeans who introduced it. The claim owners at Kimberley needed labour and the only people who could provide them with it were the Africans. There was stiff competition for labour among the claim owners, which made them pay more.

African men from all parts of South Africa made their way to Kimberley, travelling days or weeks on foot to get there, to offer their services in return for money. Six months was a long period for men to be away from their homes. When they returned, they brought back with them large amounts of money which they used to buy themselves cattle and to buy presents or beautiful things for their wives, mothers, sisters or sweethearts. It became a source of pride for it to be known that a young man had been to Kimberley, and no one who had been to Kimberley was expected to be a poor man with no money or the other things needed to make life easier.

One man from my tribe whose name I do not know also reached Kimberley to search for riches. While he was there he met another man who was Ntebele, or Letebele, from my grandmother's tribe. Both worked for one claim owner and they got to know each other well. One day, the legend goes, the man from our tribe had an argument with the other, and for the first time he heard the language Sintebele spoken. It sounded to him like the way grandmother spoke when angry. Thus started a new chapter in grandmother's life. The man from our tribe told his friend that the language he spoke sounded like that spoken by one of his Paramount Chief's wives. During their time together they told each other stories about their people and tribes, and as a result the man from her tribe got to know that grandmother was alive.

The man from our tribe told the Ntebele one that when grandmother was annoyed by the people with whom she lived, she time and again reminded them that she was not a simple person as they thought, but the daughter of a Chief and her name was Matlhodi-a-Kekana. That cleared all the Ntebele man's doubts that the woman described by his friend was the one his people had been searching for and had presumed dead.

After a time, when both were satisfied that they had earned enough money to get some of the things they needed most, they returned to their respective tribes. Our tribesman thought that the story had ended at Kimberley, but the man from grandmother's people went back with a story to tell his people, that by sheer chance he had discovered the whereabouts of grandmother. After arriving home he passed on his information to the head of his clan (*induna*), who thereafter took him to the Chief's place so that he could relate the news himself. He had also gathered some information about our place

45

Phokeng, that it was to the west of them, though he lacked knowledge how many miles away it was.

His story was so convincing that his people began to prepare to send a group of men including himself to search for Phokeng, and to ascertain whether it was really true that Matlhodi was alive and a married woman. The story is that they travelled on foot through wild areas, asking people they met for directions to Phokeng. Eventually, after spending days on the way, they reached our capital. On arrival, the man who had brought the information from Kimberley asked where he could find his friend. Before long his friend was surprised to see him with a number of men calling on him at his home. After receiving the visitors our man reported them to the head of his clan, as was the procedure, and the next day they were taken to the Chief's place to be introduced, so that they could explain themselves thoroughly and why they were there.

As it was the rule in those days, once strangers were introduced to the Chief they became the Chief's visitors. For several days, the legend goes, they stayed at grandfather's place as his guests, being interviewed by councillors and others who were interested to find out who they were and the purpose of their visit. Their feet first had to be cooled off, since it was said, 'Never speak to a visitor while his feet are still hot; give him food, all hospitality, allow him a chance to relax and then ask him to open his bag', which meant, 'Give him strength to relate his story.' When the day had arrived for them to tell their tale, though grandfather, together with those who were close to him, knew the purpose of the Ntebeles' or Matebeles' visit, he called his councillors together to hear the news for themselves.

The leader of the Matebeles, who I understand was related to grandmother and was a man of high social standing in their tribe and was also a Kekana, told my people who they were and that they were searching for a lost child whom they had presumed dead. They were not sure, but had information that the person they were searching for was living with us. Eventually grandmother was produced before them and they were asked whether she was the person they were searching for. As she was no longer a child, but a woman with children, they had lost recognition of her and some members of their delegation had never seen her before, so they all said that they were not sure that she was the one they were looking for. Grandmother was asked whether she recognised any of the men who stood before her, but she shook her head, saying they were complete strangers to her. The leader of the delegation from Kwa-Mukopani then said that the only means by which they could identify her was by speaking to her in her own tribal language, Sintebele. That was allowed, and they began to talk to her in their own language, and were surprised that grandmother still spoke it

46

well. That cleared all the doubts and for the first time grandmother came face to face with her own people. At home her parents had died, but very close relatives were still alive. The delegation, being satisfied that they had found what they were sent out to search for, spent a week or two in Phokeng and they were given great honour and hospitality.

On the day of their departure, I learnt, they were given a dignified and exciting send-off, because both sides were satisfied that ever-lasting friendship between the two tribes had been established. No doubt grandmother became homesick when she saw the people she knew going back to her birthplace. There was nothing she could do, since she was already married to the Paramount Chief of the Bafokeng tribe. At that time my father was a young boy of about three or four years old.

On their return home the Matebele delegation, pleased with the results of their mission, reported to their Chief and people with pride that their presumed dead daughter Matlhodi-a-Kekana was alive, married and the mother of four children, two of whom died in infancy. The Matebele thereafter began discussions amongst themselves, whether or not they recognised her marriage to the Bafokeng tribe. Guided by their laws and customs, they agreed that since her marriage was not negotiated with them, they were not party to her marriage. They had not received dowry, or given her away to the Paramount Chief Mokgatle of the Bafokeng tribe. They were bound to declare that, according to their law and custom, grandmother was not legally married, therefore they did not recognise her marriage.

Two years after the delegation's return from Phokeng, another stronger delegation, led by grandmother's paternal uncle, was sent off to Phokeng, with a message to thank the Bafokeng tribe for having looked after and protected grandmother since she came to live amongst them, but to declare firmly that her marriage was not recognised by her people. In support of their argument, they cited a legal standpoint that the dowry the Bafokeng claimed to have paid was not paid to them but to a Dutch farmer, KaMangoele, who took her away from the people who gave birth to her without their knowledge and consent and had no legal right to keep her, demand dowry for her, and to give her away.

In addition, they were told to make it plain to the Bafokeng and their Chief that it was up to them, if they desired to keep her, to negotiate a new marriage. As for the dowry they paid to KaMango-ele, this was a matter which the Matebele could not discuss or go into, but one to be solved by the Bafokeng and their friend KaMan-goele, the Dutch farmer.

Apparently, at the time when the Dutch people arrived at KwaMukopani, the land of my grandmother's people, now called

47

Piet Potgietersrust, the lands were roamed by herds of elephant. Grandmother's people's tribal symbol was and is still an elephant, which I think they inherited from the main body of the Zulu nation, which they broke away from under the leadership of Musilikazi, the founder of the Matebele in Matebeleland in Rhodesia.

I was told that when the second delegation arrived in Phokeng to tell grandfather and his people that grandmother's marriage was not recognised at KwaMukopani, they brought with them large quantities of elephants' tusks and other gifts for grandfather. Again, the legend goes, they were received with great honour and dignity because at that time it was a visit not only of friends but of brothers-in-law. After resting for two days the delegation, led by grand-mother's uncle, opened its bag by breaking the news that the Matebeles of KwaMukopani did not regard their daughter as being legally married. They therefore proposed that if grandfather's people wished to start fresh marriage negotiations all over again, they were ready to talk. Before grandfather and his people had time to consider their proposal, which seemed astonishing to other people in our tribe, they gave a warning that if grandfather and his people did not agree to their proposal, there was no alternative but that, after their return home, another delegation would come to fetch her together with her children.

At that time, I was told, grandmother was in the family way, expecting Uncle Setlhatsana. Some councillors, without considering the proposal well, told the Matebele delegation that a second marriage was out of the question since, as far as they were concerned, grandmother was married and was their Paramount Chief's wife. It is said that grandfather reserved his views and made no comments. A few days later the Matabele delegation returned home to report how their proposal was received by the Bafokeng tribe. Several months elapsed, and after second thoughts and with grandfather's influence, a Bafokeng delegation left for KwaMukopani to say that they were willing to enter into marriage negotiations. Their arrival, I was told, was a colourful one. Before they opened their bag to say why they had come, the Matebeles could guess that they brought good news with them.

The arrival of the Bafokeng delegation at KwaMukopani, her birthplace, marked the beginning of grandmother's second marriage. The delegation was authorised to conclude all the arrangements so that the marriage could attain legal status. The Matebeles, knowing that they had the advantage over the people of my tribe, named the number of cattle they needed, so that my grandfather's people should know that, after all, grandmother had people who had the right to marry her off, and to give her away. The Bafokeng delega-tion agreed to the number of cattle demanded.

After spending several days in KwaMukopani they returned home, leaving a promise that before long the cattle demanded would come. This would bar grandmother's people from going to Phokeng to fetch her. Back in Phokeng, they reported the agreement they had reached with the Matebeles about their daughter. I do not know how many cattle went to KwaMukopani as grandmother's second dowry, but the name of the man who led the delegation which took the cattle to grandmother's people was Ramotsoagole Nameng. The cattle were exactly as the Matebeles had asked, and they became the stamp and seal of grandmother's legal marriage.

The celebrations for grandmother's marriage at her birthplace took place in her absence before the Bafokeng delegation left. Following the tribal customs, many beasts lost their lives to feed those who were still alive in her tribe as well as to provide the Bafokeng delegation with food to eat on their way back home. At Phokeng, too, the wedding was celebrated with the slaughter of many beasts to feed the people and to make known to them that from that day Matlhodi-a-Kekana was married to their tribe with the consent of her people and was the legal wife of their Paramount Chief. Grandmother's marriage established a friendship with the Matebele of KwaMukopani. It also gave her pride that the people to whom she had been married as a slave by KaMangoele, the Dutch farmer, now knew that she had people who could demand to know her fate should something unpleasant happen to her. She knew that those in our tribe who used to tell her that she ought to thank her lucky stars that she was married to their Chief, who had given her status in life, would not repeat their rudeness. The second dowry paid to her people earned her the nickname of the most expensive woman in the tribe.

When my own mother and father married, their first home was in the very house into which grandmother came to live, so my parents' first-born saw the light in Nkhubu's house. I am not certain whether my parents' first twins, both males, were born in the same house. Later, my parents built their own house in an area which came to be known in the Christian era as Saron. Before father was married, grandmother lived with Nkhubu's second daughter Theko, but later went to live with my parents in their home in Saron. There the rest of my parents' children were born. At that new home grandmother saw the birth of all my parents' children, but she was already old.

When my father's brother Setlhatsana was married, he and his wife Matlhobole went to live with my parents and grandmother until they built their own home. Grandmother also saw the first-born child of my uncle, a daughter called Mponena-Paulina, named after herself. At that time her sight was failing and later, due to old age, she lost it altogether. At the time of my birth she could only taste, feel and hear. Three days after my birth, although grandmother knew of the event, my mother reported it to the old woman, holding me in her arms and saying, 'Mother, I have given birth to a boy, hold out your arms, I am passing him on to you'. Grandmother did so and while she had me in her arms, but not seeing me, she laughed and said, 'He's heavy.' Mother then said, 'He has no name. Give him a name.' Grandmother laughed again and said, 'I name him after my maternal uncle. He shall be called Monyadioe.' Monyadioe was a Lentebele of KwaMukopani.

Although grandmother used to enjoy welcoming delegations from her people visiting Phokeng to see her, bringing with them elephants' tusks as gifts to grandfather, she never had the opportunity to see the land of her birth again. She lived in Phokeng from the day she arrived there from the Dutch farmer's place until she died totally blind.

When my father was at the age of twelve or fourteen, I was told a delegation was appointed in Phokeng and was sent out to Kwa-Mukopani, taking him to be introduced to his mother's people and they to him. The delegation was headed again by the same man who had led the delegation which took grandmother's second dowry to KwaMukopani, Ramotsoagole Nameng. By seeing my father, grandmother's people could see an offspring of their long-lost daughter whom they had thought dead. The only person father could find closely related to his mother was a man whose father was her brother. This man's name was Muretloa Kekana, and as he was father's closest cousin, a strong friendship developed between them. I do not know whether Muretloa ever visited Phokeng, but I understand that father developed the habit of visiting his mother's people whenever he could.

What I know is that Muretloa's son, Lekhalaka, Christian name Charlie, visited Phokeng after father's death in nineteen-thirty-five with a group of men from their tribe to offer my family condolences and to see father's grave. Lekhalaka was at that time a military policeman at Roberts Heights outside Pretoria. I was in Pretoria working, but neither of us knew that the other was nearby. While in Phokeng my sister Madira, who received them on behalf of the family, gave him my address in Pretoria. On his return Lekhalaka made it his duty to find me – I expected him because my sister had written to say that one day he would call. He arrived where I worked, dressed in his military police uniform, not knowing which one I was among the people there. He said that I was the person he was looking for, and while everyone was suspecting that I had done something wrong at the army camp, we embraced when we greeted each other.

50

From that day Lekhalaka and I became friends, calling each other cousins, claiming that we represented our fathers who were true cousins. I became a frequent visitor at his home and his family welcomed me as one of them. After I married, Lekhalaka, his wife and children became frequent visitors at my home. In nineteen-thirty-seven I made a journey from Pretoria to Potgietersrust, longing to see where my grandmother was born. I arrived at Sefakaole, the Matebeles' headquarters, and stayed two weeks with a family, also the Kekanas, recommended to me by Lekhalaka. It was a sentimental journey and I felt pleased when I arrived at what was and still is the place of my origin.

My Uncle Setlhatsana, unlike father, never reached the land of his mother's birth. While I lived in Pretoria, I took each of my uncle's children who visited me there to Lekhalaka's home to introduce them. I grew very fond of Lekhalaka and his family; I regarded them as the people who gave birth to my grandmother and the source of my being. From this it can be seen that, like many people of many nations, I am a mixture of two nations, the Zulus and the Basotho. I regard myself largely as a Mosotho, because my paternal and maternal grandparents were Basotho and I was born in their tribe.

Both my father and uncle married into two influential families of our tribe. Some people may wonder why I went so far back in tracing my background. My answer is that the birth of my ancestors and my grandparents after them ushered my coming, and therefore I am a continuation of them. As my mind develops, I increasingly believe that wherever I am, whatever I do, my ancestors play a leading part in my actions. I believe that they guide me and protect me. Some people say that, since I cannot prove it scientifically, it is false. My defence is that no one has been able to prove a belief.

IX Mother's Background

To paint my mother's background is a difficult task for me. I know very little of it compared with what I know about my father. During my youth in our tribal village in Phokeng I never felt a calm atmosphere with my father which would have enabled me to ask him questions about my mother's background. I feared my father, but nevertheless liked him very much. He was difficult to approach because at home he was quiet and always busy doing something. I got much information about his background from mother because I resented strongly the way some of Mokgatle's descendants wanted to relegate him, my mother, my sisters and myself to the last position in our tribal society.

I could not accept this, and felt that we were being cheated of our rightful position in the tribal order. I refused to accept it as being lawful that others whose grandmothers did not have the honour of being paid dowry twice, or the right of occupying the house of Paramount Chief Mokgatle's second wife, should feel that they occupied a higher position in the tribe than my father and myself. My resentment was supported by the fact that whenever there was a family dispute concerning the children of Nkhubu-Madikeledi, which was the second house in the line of succession to the tribal chieftaincy, the very people who claimed to have higher status than my father and myself would confess that they had no right to go into such matters; the person to approach was my father or myself.

Usually I felt at ease in my mother's company, she was an easy smiler and always gave time to explaining things I wanted to know. Because of being too obsessed with wanting to know the reasons why some Mokgatles adopted these attitudes towards us, I deprived myself of opportunities to ask mother her full background.

In nineteen-sixty-one, when I started writing, and was already resident in London, I started a correspondence home to my sister Pheloe (Christian name Sannie) Petlele, asking her to contact my only surviving aunt, my mother's youngest sister Madiseile (Christian name Magdelina) Mathuloe and ask her to give in detail my mother's family background. After waiting for several months my sister's letter arrived, telling me that she had done as I asked, but my aunt refused to give her the information I required because if she did so, she said, she would be encouraging me to stay and die abroad. I then wrote another letter direct to my aunt, explaining to her why I needed the information, and knowing that since she could not read or write herself, she would invite her daughter Ndube to help her. When the reply came back, Aunt Madiseile acknowledged both my request to my sister and the letter direct to her. Her reply was emphatic. 'Come home', she requested, 'I shall tell you everything you need to know. My reply through your sister is the same,' she said. 'If I send you the information you ask it would imply that I approve your living abroad and don't want to see you back in the land of your tribal fathers.'

I did not give up, I knew that as a person she was liable to changes of mind, and from that time, in each letter I wrote home to my sister, I conveyed greetings and best wishes to my aunt, at the same time asking my sister to remind her that we live in a changing world, and she should not rule out that I shall never come home again. Changes, I said, never give advance notice. My aunt remained emphatic in her replies, therefore my mother's background story will not be as bright as my father's. Her story begins with her parents who, unlike my father's mother, died before I was born. All I found were their properties and the houses they used and lived in.

My maternal grandparents were immigrants in Phokeng. They were not Bakoena but Bakgatla. They came to Phokeng from a tribe called Bakgatla, and their land lies north of ours, north of the mountains called Pilansberg after their Paramount Chief. Their provincial headquarters is called Moruleng and the chief headquarters is in Botswana and is called Motshudi. I do not know my mother's mother's African name nor Christian name. She was known and called by the name of her first-born child, whom they named Emma (I do not know her African name). My grandmother was therefore called MaEmma.

Grandfather, too, was mostly called by his daughter's name, as RaEmma, Emma's father. Unlike grandmother, I know his Christian name, Thomas, which was given to him when he was baptised in Phokeng. His surname was Mororo. As far as I know, their children were all born in Phokeng and were three daughters and three sons. I never knew my mother's African name, only her Christian one, Salome, and during the calm times I spent with her, it never occurred to me to ask her her parents' African names, her sister Emma's name or her own. After Emma came mother, and I was told she was followed by a brother, who died a very heartbreaking death, early in life, during the milking of one of his father's cows. The cow he was milking kicked him in the stomach and destroyed his liver, and he died an hour or more later.

He was followed by another son whose Christian name was Herman, and he died when I was thirteen years old. He was followed by a sister, who enjoyed both African and Christian names.

She survived them all and her names are Madiseile Magdelina. After her marriage her surname became Mathuloe. Their last boy had both African and Christian names, Rakgompana Kristof Mororo.

My aunt Madiseile Magdelina Mathuloe had only two children and her first-born was a male, Mmiga (Christian name Michael). After leaving home to face the world, he went to Durban in Natal, and for reasons known only to himself stopped writing to his parents, and all of us lost contact with him for a very long time. Unexpectedly one Christmas morning, he knocked at his parents' door; his father and mother rejoiced to see him, and his father, to show how pleased he was to have his son back with him, slaughtered an ox and invited his friends and relatives to come to celebrate his son's home-coming with him. Mmiga never married to the last day of life; his sister Ndubi married, but her marriage broke up and ended in divorce.

One day, I was told, a man arrived in our village and introduced himself as a missionary for the Dutch Reformed Church, and said that he wanted to start a mission station in the village. My grandfather, Paramount Chief Mokgatle, then asked the gentleman to call back in a few days time to meet him with his people and the tribe's councillors. As agreed, several days later the missionary arrived to find a large gathering of people, among them tribal elders and councillors. The missionary then, without wasting more time, began to explain in detail the message of Christianity he had brought to our people.

He told the gathering that what he was preaching was the word of God and that God could only be reached through his Son Jesus Christ, whom he went on to explain came into the earth to testify that there was a living God, the father of all peoples and nations on earth. He went on to say that Jesus gave his own life for the sake of all peoples because the people at the time of his birth were no longer obeying the commands of God who was angry and about to punish the people. He ended his talk, I was told, by saying that the only way people could speak to God, who made the earth, people and everything on earth, was by believing in God by first believing in Jesus Christ, the Son of God and the representative of God the Father to the people on earth.

Having explained the teaching of Christianity, which he keenly urged our people to embrace, he told them that in addition he was bringing a new system of learning and communication. But the first thing to do, he told them, was to give themselves to Jesus, by consenting to be baptised, and thereafter building a church in which they could meet to praise God through Christ, worship him and honour him. At the end of his lengthy talk, when he had explained everything he knew needed explaining at first, grandfather asked the

54

learned gentleman to give them time to consider alone what he had told them, but to return again in a few days' time to hear their detailed considered reply. The missionary readily agreed to their request and, after he had been entertained, he left. That was the first Christian message to my people.

When he returned to our tribe to hear what my people had decided, he received an answer which must undoubtedly have disappointed him. My grandfather, I was told, with the advice of his councillors and the elders of the tribe, said this to him: 'We thank you very much for the trouble you have taken to come here to introduce to us your religion and the church. We are sorry,' grandfather went on, 'we cannot accept your religion and the God you urge us to accept and believe in. We have our own way of worshipping God and the way we think we can reach him. We think that our dead ancestors are the way we can speak to God. Through them we firmly believe he can speak to us, by accepting our humble requests to him or rejecting them. We, therefore, think that it would serve no useful purpose for you or ourselves, to join together and worship the God you have spoken to us about. The best thing we think is that you pass on to try elsewhere.'

The gentleman waited after grandfather had spoken to see whether there were someone or other in the gathering who would rise to support what grandfather had said, or to say something contrary to it. No one rose and the missionary felt satisfied that grandfather's reply was a unanimous one. When he did stand up to speak he showed a respect for their decision and thanked them for having given him a chance to say what he had come to say to the tribe. He then asked them to permit him to leave and his request was honoured. Before his final departure he was entertained again, as it was the custom that when a guest was not given food when he arrived, he should not be permitted to leave with an empty stomach.

No doubt, though his invitation to my tribe to join the Dutch Reformed Church was fruitless, the words he left with them had built themselves houses in the hearts of some members of my tribe. Some of them had already become Christians in their hearts but were not courageous enough to say so at that time. They thought that if they did they would be regarded as men of weak faith, who were easily blown away from their faith in the power of their ancestors by something new and foreign to them. Christianity was indeed a new thing to them, they needed more time to think about it and everything that went with it.

The missionary left our tribe like a man who planted a seed in a dry soil, knowing well that one day rain would come to water the soil and the seed would grow and bear results. If that was what he had in mind when he said good-bye to my people, his judgment was correct. Afterwards, those who silently accepted the Christian message brought by the Dutch Reformed missionary began to express their feelings to their fellow-tribesmen. They said that it was wrong for the tribe to refuse the missionary permission to establish his church in the village so that those who agreed with his new system of worship could join him. Amongst these were some of grandfather's children.

Two or three years later, I was told, a message reached my tribe that a group of missionaries had arrived in the country from Germany, and were in Natal, at Durban, preparing themselves to move into the country with the declared aims of establishing Christian churches. They were the Lutherans of Hermannsburg Mission. How or by whom the message was brought to my people, I have not been able to ascertain. Those who had silently accepted the Dutch Reformed missionary's message immediately seized the news and said to themselves, 'This time we shall not repeat the mistakes we made when the Christian message first reached us.' They went to their Paramount Chief, my grandfather, and told him and the tribe's elders and councillors that they had decided to become Christians and would like the church to be built in the tribe. Grandfather and his councillors, because of what they had heard since the departure of the Dutch Reformed missionary, felt the right thing to do was to declare that they were not in opposition to those who felt that they would be happy to accept the Christian form of worship.

There being no opposition in the tribe, the Christians-to-be felt that it was their duty not to wait for the missionaries to come, but to go to Durban where they were and invite one of them to become their priest. The legend is that a group of ox wagons drawn by teams of oxen, with a large group of men and women, left our tribe for Durban, to interview the German missionaries. I have not been able to ascertain the name of the man who led the ox wagon delegation; however, to Durban they went and reached the Lutherans. When people seek something, language barriers become no problem.

In Durban, among the Lutheran missionaries, men from my tribe, like teen-age boys amongst teen-age girls looking for sweethearts to marry, made their choice. They picked one for themselves and asked him to consent to become their teacher of the Christian doctrine and priest. His name was Penzhorn. Having been chosen, Mr. Penzhorn and his family agreed to accompany my people on the long journey back to Phokeng. On arrival, they were given everything a strange family needed and a site on which to build their home. Since they were brought to the tribe, the building of a home for them became the tribe's duty.

While their home was under construction they lived at the Paramount Chief's home, and Mr. Penzhorn began his baptismal work to make sure that he had people in the tribe to join his church. At that time the whole tribe, as I said before, was polygamous. Men were free to marry as many wives as they could support. The legend is that the first man to be baptised – in the presence of a large crowd – was grandfather's son of his third wife, who was named after grandfather's father, Sekete. He was a polygamist himself. Mr. Penzhorn gave him the Christian name John, and from that day he was known amongst the first Christians as Johannes. He was followed by his brother, who was given the name of Peter and thereafter came to be known as Petrus. Peter had not become a polygamist at that time and the church he joined barred him from becoming one.

Since a prominent figure in the tribe had become a Christian, not only a prominent figure but the Paramount Chief's son of the third house, together with his brother Peter, the ordinary people of the tribe felt free to join the Lutheran Church of Hermannsburg Mission or to stay out of it. There is a proverb in our tribe which runs as a question and answer. It is said that a man once asked a worm, 'Worm, how did you manage to enter the large body of an ox and cause it to rot?' and the worm answered, 'Through a tiny piece of flesh.' That was how the Christian Church entered my tribe, not to cause it to rot, but to cause it to become Christian. That is the way the Christian teaching and following became part and parcel of life in my tribe. It would appear that the word went round like wild-fire that the Bakoena-ba-Phokeng had become Christians.

X Mother's Parents

My grandfather, Thomas Mororo, a Mokgatla of Bakgatla tribe, heard of the arrival in Phokeng of the Christian mission and decided to leave his tribe with his two wives to join the Christian Church in Phokeng. His own tribe had heard about the mission's coming and what went with it, and expressed opposition to it at all costs. Grandfather realised that there was no chance for him and his wives to become Christians if they remained with their tribe. He then took a heart-breaking decision, to leave the people who gave birth to him, his wives and his ancestors, to join the church in Phokeng. He was a very wealthy man. A man's wealth was measured by the number of cattle, sheep and goats he owned, and in addition by his corn and food.

My grandfather, with his two wives and his children, broke down his houses, dismantled his kraals of cattle, sheep and goats, loaded his corn on wagons and emigrated to Phokeng. Before first investigating what was in store for him in Phokeng, he burned his bridges behind him and said good-bye to his tribe. He arrived in Phokeng and asked for acceptance. The Bafokeng, following the tribal tradition that we welcome all who seek to join us, but regret the departure of those who leave us, opened their arms and said, 'Come in, Mororo, come in and join us.' After paying the number of cattle required of him to become a citizen of Phokeng, he attained the rights and privileges of citizenship.

Having become a Mofokeng, he approached the church requesting membership, and he was shocked at being told that he could only be accepted with one of his wives, not the two of them. Legally he was no longer a Mokgatla, but a Mofokeng. My grandfather's first wife had children already, but the second one, my mother's mother, had none at that time. Grandfather's first wife then, being disappointed, suggested they should return to their home in Kgatleng if they could not all be accepted into the church. It is said that she was uncompromising in her attitude and refused to accept that one of them should go into the church with Grandfather while the other remained outside. For a long time, I was told, Grandfather attempted to persuade her to change her mind, but failed.

I learnt from the stories my mother told me that her father, in his efforts to persuade his first wife to stay in Phokeng with the rest of his families, tried to strike a compromise with her that she should be the one to go into the church with him and that my grandmother should stay outside the church. Obviously life and people in Phokeng were not attractive to grandfather's first wife. She insisted, I was told, that if she had known in advance that things were going to turn out as they had done, she would not have consented to leave her people in Kgatleng and come to Phokeng. All she wanted, she told grandfather, was that they should tell the church people that they were disappointed, and felt justly treated by the people of Phokeng but unjustly treated by the church they had come to join, and therefore there was no point in them making Phokeng their permanent home. Grandfather tried to make her change her mind by pointing out to her that the church was not against any of them in particular, but that only one of them could join the church with him. She refused to alter her stand.

Eventually the man who brought them to Phokeng felt that you can give someone food but can't force him to eat it. As a last stand, grandfather left it entirely to her to decide what she desired to do. That obviously freed her to make her desires plain and clear. She chose to return home to her people with her children. Her decision was not an easy one for grandfather. In fact, it was a test for him. Grandfather at that time came face to face with the problem whether, for the sake of becoming a Christian, he was going to let his wife go away from him with his children whom no doubt he loved like any father. I do not know how grandfather felt, but I can guess that his first wife's decision must have broken his heart. Grandfather, too, had made up his mind that he had left his birth-place and people to become a Christian, and so he was going to join the Christian Church with or without his first wife.

Another problem grandfather had to deal with was whether he was going to allow his wife to go back with the children or whether he was going to keep the children in Phokeng with him without their mother. He then decided, my mother told me, that if he did that the children would be lonely, longing for their mother, and their feelings for her would create bitterness towards him and they would eventually turn against him. He then decided that they should go back with their mother.

Having made up his own mind, my grandfather was left with no alternative but to give some of his cattle, sheep, goats and corn to his first wife as the means by which she would keep herself and the children back in Kgatleng. The time for departure came and grandfather had to say good-bye to the woman he loved first and the children who were part of his flesh. I asked mother whether that meant that grandfather had divorced her, but mother said that it was not a divorce in the legal sense, but an agreement between them to separate. Mother then told me that if it was a divorce, it was grandfather's first wife who had divorced him, because she chose to leave him after accompanying him to Phokeng. I agreed.

Because grandfather had provided her and the children with all necessary means for living, she could not demand services from grandfather while she lived with her people in Kgatleng. 'But,' I said to mother, 'I blame the church for the break-up of that marriage.' Mother was surprised and asked, 'Why? The church was ready to welcome her into its ranks but she refused to go in.' I then said that my reason for blaming that church was that the church found an old institution working, polygamy. It should have recognised it at first, allowing people to join it as they were, but making it plain to them that if they became polygamous while they were members of the church, their institution would not be recognised by the church. If the church had adopted that line, grandfather would not have lost his first wife and the children.

Thomas Mororo, then, took his second wife, my grandmother, with him into the church and they became Christians. He had become a man with only one wife. The children of his second wife were all born into the Christian section of our tribe. Other polygamous men of Phokeng also faced the same problem, but because their wives were women of Phokeng, they did not have to see them go to live far from them. Others did not bother to join the church, but left the decisions to their grown-up children to join if they wished. Grandfather, having joined the church with other men of Phokeng, began to undergo baptismal ceremonies, and went to worship every Sunday twice a day.

They worshipped, I was told, under a large tree by the site where they eventually built the church, and it still stands there today. They were all rich but simple Africans, whose houses were built in African architecture, round with thatched roofs, known as rondavels. They were not built of bricks but of stones, timber and earth. There were houses for guests, children and parents, as well as ones for storing corn. Mr. Penzhorn, in addition to teaching them how to read the Bible, also taught them how to make bricks – and build with them – for the church. They did this first under Mr. Penzhorn's supervision and later on their own.

Grandfather, I was told, was one of the fast learners and later ended up being a highly skilled brick builder and a carpenter. In addition, he learned how to make doors and window frames, some of which I saw when I grew up. The original church built by grandfather and others is still there, a large building that imposes itself on the Phokeng scene and can be seen far away, painted with snow-white lime, with large windows, and with four entrances from the east, west, north and south. It has a large altar at which all confirmed new members kneel to receive their confirmation certificates.

I knelt there on the twentieth of December nineteen-twenty-eight, in the afternoon, after answering all the questions about Bible episodes put to me.

The floor of the church is laid with flat, smooth slates, which I was told grandfather went out with others to fetch from a slate quarry somewhere in our land and helped to lay down. The southern entrance of the church was solely used by the priest and those, grandfather Thomas Mororo amongst them, who held church services in his absence. Although grandfather was strictly speaking a foreigner in Phokeng, his wealth and his services in the church earned him great honour and respect amongst the people he had come to join.

I do not recall asking my mother whether, after grandfather's first wife's return to Kgatleng, their birthplace, they ever met again, or whether the children who returned with their mother (it never occurred to me to ask how many children there were) ever met their father again. When I think of it all I imagine that the longing of a father to see his children cannot possibly have escaped grandfather, and that their love and longing for their father must have tormented the children.

Mr. Penzhorn, the first Lutheran priest in our tribe, not only taught my people how to read the Bible, but transformed their lives entirely. He brought European architecture into their lives and new ideas. Houses built with bricks began to appear. Though many thatched roofs remained, they pushed rondavels out of the way and houses with European-type doors and windows spread all over the village. Old habits of building houses anywhere, anyhow, died out. Anyone in the tribe who wanted to build a house, particularly newly-married couples, had to go to the Chief's court to ask for a site. From the Chief's court they were sent out with three or four men to a place to cut a site for them and to see that it would be in a straight line with other houses built before theirs.

As a result of these new methods, which were due to the church and Mr. Penzhorn's influence, well-surveyed streets developed and houses faced each other, in a manner which was absent before the church came. Phokeng became a Europeanised tribal village. A man who played a great part in this transformation was my mother's father, Thomas Mororo. I found many houses built by him still standing when I grew up. Even the house of John Sekete Mokgatle, Paramount Chief Mokgatle's son by his third wife, who was first baptised in the Kgotla by Mr. Penzhorn and opened the tribal gates for the people to join the church, was built by my grandfather.

Other tribes nearby which later adopted Christianity were influenced by events in Phokeng. Some tribes did not become Lutherans, but joined the English, Dutch and French missionaries.

People of those tribes had strong grounds to argue that, if Christianity and the church was good for the Bafokeng tribe, it was good for them as well. Not only did they admire my people for adopting a new religion, they also copied their new methods of building houses. Today, Phokeng is being transformed again by the new generation, who are more Europeanised than their grandparents and parents. Now they have iron roofing on their houses.

When my people chose Mr. Penzhorn at Durban to be their priest, he had one child of less than a year old. I am not sure whether he was born in Germany or in Natal. His name was Ernest Penzhorn. His other children were born in Phokeng and therefore were Bafokeng. They grew up playing with Bafokeng children in the village and acquired the language of the Bafokeng, Sesotho, in the same way as the children of the tribe. There were seven children in all, five sons and two daughters.

Only when they reached school-going age did they leave Phokeng for boarding schools in Rustenburg and other towns to learn European languages. Ernest, the elder son, replaced his father when he died and became the priest in Phokeng, having been to Germany to study for the ministry. They spoke Sesotho so well that when any one of them spoke behind closed doors, no one would have known that there was a European speaking. When I grew up, the six of them had already left Phokeng, married, and were living in a place six or seven miles south of Rustenburg, which they had named Kroondal. All Lutheran missionaries of the Hermannsburg Mission in the Transvaal Province, whose children did not replace their fathers as priests in the African tribes they converted to Christianity, went to Kroondal to farm there. Kroondal was bought jointly by Hermannsburg missionaries.

In Kroondal they had their own church and brought a priest from Germany to be their minister. There, too, they built a private school, where they also brought a teacher from Germany whom they paid jointly, to teach their children their ancestors' language.

I heard them all speak Sesotho fluently, but I think their elder brother Ernest was more fluent than all of them. He spoke it, wrote it and gave all his sermons in Sesotho. I remember, when I was attending confirmation class with others under him, he taught us some Sesotho words we did not know. He called himself Mofokeng and a tribesman. He was a tall, well-built, handsome man with a very clear voice. Like his parents, he had seven children, four daughters and three sons, and all had African names after prominent men and women of our tribe. They too spoke Sesotho fluently, but in their home, a large house with a large yard and a thatched roof which was provided by the tribe, they spoke German.

Ernest Penzhorn, like his father before him, taught my people to read the Bible in their own language, and a few of them learned both reading and writing. Many of them, both men and women, knew nearly everything in the Bible by heart. Women especially became very keen on learning the episodes in the Bible. Later, a group of men and women was formed called *Kopano* (union), who sang and recited verses they learned by heart from the Bible about prophecies of the birth of Christ and the reasons why Jacob's children sold their brother Ismael to the Egyptians and why they went to live in the land of Egypt.

In the New Testament they were taught at great length about the birth of Christ, which introduced a new feature into their lives – the Christmas festival. Christmas became a day on which everybody had to try to go to a church service, and a day of enjoyment and entertainment of friends and relatives. They did not learn the art of sending messages of good wishes to friends or giving presents, but every household did its best to have enough food so that a friend or anyone who cared to visit them would be offered something to eat or drink. This resulted in ending the lives of many pigs, goats, sheep and birds. It also became a new tradition that on that day people should wear new clothes as a sign amongst the Christians that a new baby was born, the Baby who became their teacher and leader.

Other Christian festivals were introduced, and my people who became Christians felt it their duty to take part in them. The two weeks before Good Friday were declared silent weeks. During that time, every Christian family in our village was expected to gather, and most of them did, at a fellow-Christian's house in the evenings with their children, and there one of their well-informed men or women would read from the Bible and would then hold the floor in explaining to the children and new converts what their new religion was all about. On Good Friday itself work stopped amongst the Christians, and on their way to church no word was spoken. It was known as a day of sorrows, on which their teacher and leader died on the cross for the sins of Christians and non-Christians alike. Similarly, on their way from church no word was uttered.

The church taught the people that Sunday was a day of worship, not of work. During the six days before Sunday they were encouraged to ensure that they had enough time to do whatever they wished to do, and on Sunday the only things they could do were to cook their food and prepare themselves for church services three times a day. The morning and afternoon services every Christian was expected to attend, but those with young children to put to bed were not expected to attend in the evening.

When I was grown up, my tribal people had got used to adapting themselves to the church rule. Being peasants who grew their own food in fields which are a long way from homes, they mainly stopped work in the fields at noon on Saturdays and began to move home in order to be there the next day. Before I was born, I was told, parents very seldom went to church without their children accompanying them, because the parents wanted to be sure that their children grew with the new religion. It was also the business of church elders to see that people did go to church. If a member was not seen in church during morning service and in the afternoon, the church elder who was in charge of the area where that person lived would go round to find out what kept him away from church services.

If there were visitors in the family, even when they were not Christians, the Christian family was expected to invite them to accompany them to church. The other thing which, once people had become Christians, they were not expected to miss twice was taking part in holy communion. That was strictly instilled into the minds of the Christians – that by staying away from holy communion, they were staying away from eating the flesh of Christ and drinking His blood.

In the Lutheran Church, holy communion was not served every Sunday. It was a quarterly event. The Sunday before communion Sunday the priest gave notice that the following Sunday communion would be served. During that week, those who desired to take part would go to the priest's house to give in their names so that he knew how many members would be served.

On the Saturday afternoon preceding the communion Sunday they would all be in church with the priest to confess their sins and ask for forgiveness. Confession (in Sesotho, *boipobolo*) is not said aloud, but each member is expected to pray silently for forgiveness. Only the priest would preach a short sermon that afternoon and say a prayer. The next morning, forty-five minutes or an hour before the end of the normal church service, holy communion would be served. As the communicants receive communion the congregation sings hymns to make them feel more strong in their convictions.

Before I was born, I was told, the Christian rule was that no meal should be taken without a prayer being said. After meals, too, a prayer should be said, called *tebogo* (thanks). The first prayer was called *kopo* (request). Every Christian was expected to believe firmly that whatever he or she had, food or otherwise, were provided by God, therefore he should ask God to give him energy to enjoy them, and thank God later for having provided him with such essential things. Christian children were taught all those things by their parents, who were also expected to see that their children understood and observed them.

When I grew up I found those rules still being observed but with less strictness. Even when going to bed the Christians were expected to say prayers for peaceful nights, and before rising the next morning

64

they were expected to pray, thanking God for having protected them during the night and for having spent a restful night. I think that when there were non-Christian visitors, the Christians feared to offend their visitors and refrained from saying their prayers. As a result, I imagine, those fears encouraged them to move away from what their new religion required them to do. Until the time of my birth many families had non-Christian relatives who did not find it easy to throw over their old beliefs and habits and adopt the Christian way of life. Nearly every family before my birth found itself divided in the middle, into Christians and non-Christians. I am not sure that Paramount Chief Mokgatle, my grandfather, became a Christian, and that he was ever baptised. His picture and that of Ernest Penzhorn's father hang in the church. My paternal grandmother, Matlhodi Paulina, never became a Christian, nor did Dikeledi, Mokgatle's son by his second wife, Nkhubu.

I grew up to find that there were still in our tribe many Christians whose parents never became Christians. Because of that I imagine that the Christian tradition never found a strong hold on many of my people. They found themselves having to practise two kinds of religion, their ancestral religion which they could not altogether avoid because of their parents, and the new Christian religion they had adopted. For instance, my maternal grandparents became deeply religious, but their daughter's parents-in-law were not Christians. There was bound to be a conflict between them when religious matters came up. Again, my mother who was a Christian married my father who, like his mother and half-brother Dikeledi, was never a Christian. Only because of my maternal grandparents being staunch Christians was my parents' marriage performed in the Christian style. I never understood why my mother's father did not encourage his son-in-law, whom I was told he liked very much, to get baptised in order to join the Christian circles of Phokeng. I suppose that, because my father did not object to his children being baptised in church, my grandfather felt that he was a Christian. Or grandfather thought that later on mother would use her influence to make a Christian of him.

XI Other Churches

While the Lutheran Church under Ernest Penzhorn flourished in my tribe teaching my people the Bible solely in their own language, Sesotho, so enabling them to understand better and better the religion they had chosen, issuing pamphlets to make it easy for them to read catechisms, but not teaching them the art of writing; while all this was going on another man appeared on the scene. He was an American Negro, Mr. Morrison. He introduced himself as a representative of a Christian Church but of a different denomination; the church he was asking my tribe to allow him to establish was the African Methodist Episcopal Church (AME).

At first, I learnt, some people who were already members of the Lutheran Church argued that since there was already a Christian Church established in the tribe, there was no need for a second one. Others argued there were some who were not attracted by the Lutheran Church and might be attracted by Mr. Morrison's church, and therefore Mr. Morrison ought to be allowed to explain his church to the people to enable them to decide for themselves. Indeed, Mr. Morrison, like a young man seeking a young woman to marry amongst many married and unmarried, succeeded in getting recruits for his church. The church became popularly known as the church of Morrison.

In Phokeng itself, it seems, Mr. Morrison did not enjoy a large following, but he did establish his church. The English language was heard for the first time through Mr. Morrison, who found himself confronted with the problem of talking to people who did not understand what he was saying. The Lutherans had already laid the foundation; the first thing was to build a church, and the way to build it was already known. Those who chose to join Morrison's church began to make bricks with him, and asked the Chief to give them a site where they could build their church. Here, too, I have no record of the year in which this happened, but I think that Mokgatle's grandson, Paramount Chief Molotlegi (Christian name Augustus) was the ruler of the tribe. Molotlegi was the son of Dumagole, Mokgatle's son by his first wife.

Mr. Morrison established his AME Church not very far from the Paramount Chief's house, and three-quarters of a mile from the Lutheran Church. The AME Church did take some people away from the Lutherans; for instance the minister in charge of it when

I grew up was a man who was known by his son's name Israel – Raisraele. For his son to have had the name Israel, it is obvious that he was a Lutheran before Morrison arrived. But there were very few families who belonged to the AME Church. The congregation was so small that they never managed to acquire a proper church bell like the Lutherans. To remind their members that it was church time on Sundays, they waited for the Lutherans to ring their large and heavy bell, which could be heard very far away, and then rang their piece of iron and its sound went round as they beat it. Morrison's followers did not build him a house, but all the time he was in Phokeng he stayed with Raisraele's family, who encountered no difficulties in keeping him because they were wealthy. In Luka, one of our large villages, larger than Phokeng itself, Morrison found many converts. The Lutherans were not very successful in Luka, and their church there, like the AME in Phokeng, was a small, poor building with a thatched roof.

In Luka the AME built a very large and impressive church and a large priest's house. I think that what helped the AME in Luka was the fact that the Sub-Chief, who bore a Dutch name, Stuurman, by which he was popularly known and respected, although he did not become a Christian himself because of his many wives, allowed his children to join the AME and that inspired others to follow. Up to the time I left South Africa the AME was still weak in Phokeng and powerful in Luka.

In Phokeng Mr. Morrison started a day school for the children and taught them their first lessons in English. The English alphabet was studied and heard for the first time. Morrison's English day school attracted a good deal of attention among the people of my tribe. At that time (I do not know if Morrison left Phokeng before or after I was born) the people were aware that the white man's rule was spreading all over the country and therefore it was essential to get prepared and to learn his language. Those men of my tribe who had been to Kimberley to work for money in the claims had had contact with the English people there and were impressed by them and found them very clever; they found no comparison between them and the Dutch people they knew. Although the Anglo-Boer war had not broken out, they could sense that eventually the Englishman, with his cleverness, was bound to make an impact on the whole country.

To the amazement of Mr. Penzhorn, the Lutheran priest, leading Lutherans like Peter Mokgatle's children were sent to attend Morrison's day school to learn English. Mr. Morrison taught English largely to students whose parents were not members of his church, but Lutherans. By the time he returned to the United States, he had taught one man whose parents had become converts to his church to carry on with his work teaching English. That man's name was Pitso (Christian name Didrick), surname Senne. Pisto Didrick Senne carried on from where Mr. Morrison left off, but unfortunately when he died there was no one to replace him because, during Didrick's teaching period, no student was found amongst the members of the AME Church to be taught to take his place. The other students whose parents were Lutherans went there to learn English, not to carry on the work of the AME Church. The school died a natural death. Those who were fortunate to attend the classes started by Mr. Morrison spoke the English language as far as they were taught to speak, read and write, and they became the elite and the envy of others who had not been able to go there before Didrick's death.

So the Lutherans had a rival, but a weak one. They were not attracted by teaching English, and carried on teaching only Sesutho. For instance, those of my mother's generation, who were the first pupils in the Lutheran church school, learning through reading catechisms what was in the Bible, could read well-printed words but could not write or read hand-written letters at all. My mother taught me alphabets in Sesutho, but later when I wrote letters to her, she had to get someone to read them to her.

Rasemokana Rangaka was the influential and highly respected headman of one of the clans in our tribe. My mother's sister, Aunt Emma, married his son Tau (lion), Christian name Daniel, Rangaka. Dan Rangaka was one of the first teachers of catechism in the Lutheran Church Bible school. There were two others like him, of his generation, who also taught catechisms – Herman Pooe and Titus Mathuloe. The three of them, I was told, shared the preaching in the church on Sundays when the priest, Ernest Penzhorn, was away or unable to hold services. I am tempted to think that in addition to his brilliance and understanding of the verses in the Bible, Dan Rangaka had the particular advantage of being the son-in-law of Thomas Mororo, my grandfather, who was himself the second preacher in the Lutheran Church in the absence of the Minister.

Dan Rangaka's parents never became Christians, but allowed their children to choose Christianity. Dan was a tall, well-built man with a very dignified figure. His voice was clear, loud and powerful. Each time he spoke he smiled and showed his broad, snow-white teeth. As grandfather's first son-in-law, he was highly liked in my mother's family. Grandfather took a great interest in him and taught him how to make doors, door frames and window frames, so that in the end Dan was not only teacher and preacher but also a good carpenter. He also made benches and ox yokes. His skill brought him immense wealth and dignity. Just as Mr. Penzhorn's father, the first Lutheran church minister in our tribe, liked grandfather, so Ernest

68

Penzhorn worked with and liked Dan Rangaka. Most people in our village, when they needed a door or anything which went with the building of a house, thought first of Dan.

Later, as I grew up, I used to watch him working, and I began to note that he was a fast learner and a man with an abundance of energy. He did not smoke or drink beer. He was so highly trusted, I was told by the church minister, that he relied on him to help in holding confirmation classes. He also baptised babies on behalf of the priest when called upon. Only his close friends and members of his family called him by his African name Tau.

My Aunt Emma bore her husband, Dan Rangaka, nine children. They were six girls and three boys. Dan Rangaka was a loving man. I remember that each time he spoke to his wife he called her mother. They had a European-style house built for them, I was told, by our grandfather. It was a house of six rooms, with a passage which ran right through from the front door to the back door and led into the backyard. It was built with red bricks, but had a thatched roof with a wooden ceiling. All the doors of the rooms and the front and back doors were half wood and half glass. The panes on the doors were different colours – yellow, red, blue and white. The doors had large keys, called German keys.

At the back in the yard was built another house, called *sefala*, where grain was stored. Alongside it was another, but smaller one, which was used as a kitchen. In the yard there were peach and orange trees which produced sweet and nourishing fruits in spring and winter. These I used to enjoy very much. Aunt Emma, because of her upbringing and her husband, was very religious. She was a medium-sized woman, a healthy, hard-working peasant woman. Her complexion, like that of Uncle Dan Rangaka, was brownish, between dark and very light. She was an ever-ready smiler but firm in seeing that her orders were carried out.

I used Aunt Emma as my shield against my mother. Each time I was naughty, disobeyed mother, or wanted mother to toe my line, which mother never did but took strong action to force me to obey, I used to run away to Aunt Emma's house for protection. Once I was there, she would say, after listening to my story, 'Wait until your mother gets here, I shall put her in her place. She cannot treat our grandfather like that.' She never called me by my name, but always called me grandfather, because I was named after their grandfather Moreleba.

I was happy and completely at home at my Aunt Emma's house. I had the feeling that I was better treated there than at my own mother's house, because there I could pick and choose and was allowed to get away with it. Though Aunt Emma exercised strict discipline on her children, she was more tolerant with me and

69

always said that I did not know what I was doing, but that as I grew up I would learn how to behave in the right manner without being forced. Her children too, though their mother was strict with them, never resented the way I was treated. They all agreed that I was a mere child incapable of sorting out what was wrong and right.

When I search my mind to find reasons why I was so treated at my aunt's house, I always come up with the answer that because I was the youngest child, the last-born and the only son of my parents, I seemed fragile to my aunt and her children. There was not one among them who did not like me, or want to share with me anything nice they were given to eat. As the family was deeply religious, before bedtime, immediately after the evening meal, the children who were at home sat round the table with their parents and each had to read a verse from the Bible; thereafter a prayer for a comfortable and restful night would be said by their father or mother, or one of the children. Not a single one of the children was allowed to leave the circle while the praying was in progress.

But with me things were different. If I did not want to stay for the Bible reading or the prayer for the night, I was allowed to go to bed before anyone else. When I was young, I was allowed to sit on my aunt's lap without being disturbed until I fell asleep. My aunt's daughters, too, worked hard to make me happy when I was at their parents' home. When any one of them was sent to give their parents' friends something and it meant that they had to travel a distance to get there, if I had to accompany them they would carry me on their backs to and from the place. All I can say is that I grew up to find that I had two homes where I could eat and sleep. Aunt Emma was both aunt and mother to me.

Her elder children attended Bible classes at the Lutheran catechism school, and were either taught by their father or one of the other two, Titus Mathuloe or Herman Pooe. One thing I still cannot understand is how my father resisted persuasion to become a Christian, and yet I was told that Herman Pooe was one of his best friends. I was told that Father and Herman spent their leisure time together, at the home of one or the other. Herman Pooe belonged to the clan which my mother's parents had joined, and it was during one of father's frequent visits to his friend's home that he saw mother and asked his friend to introduce him to her. Father, like all young men and women of his early years, was not allowed to decide for himself who his future partner was going to be; his parents took care of that. While Father was enjoying Herman Pooe's company, there was already a young woman chosen for him by his parents to be his future wife. But before he was married to her, Father told his mother that he had seen another young woman in his friend's clan, and he could not resist a firm belief that she would be the best wife for him if only his parents would consent to change their minds about the first young woman. My grandparents became furious, but when they discovered that the girl father was attracted to was the daughter of Thomas Mororo, an immigrant in Phokeng, but nevertheless a wealthy, respected and influential figure amongst the Christians, they found no grounds to resist their son's request. I understand that father's half-brother's wife and others were entrusted with a mission to go secretly into my mother's clan to see whether the girl father had fallen in love with was worthy of being turned to instead of the first girl. Since these people were Christians, though they were not friends of my grandparents, they had grounds to enter Thomas Mororo's home, to talk about Christian matters and while doing that observe closely my mother's movements and appearance. Their reports were in favour of father's request and a decision was eventually reached that mother's parents should be approached. When that happened, mother's parents were surprised but felt honoured that it was proposed that their daughter become one of the wives of the Paramount Chief's son.

I was not only popular at Aunt Emma's home, but at my mother's younger sister, Madiseile Magdelina Mathuloe, I was also very much liked. My aunt, her husband Lekarapa (Christian name Eliphas) Mathuloe and their two children, Miga Michael and Ndubi his sister, treated me as though I was fragile. Aunt Magdelina, like her sisters, Aunt Emma and my mother, called me Grandfather and very seldom by my name. There, too, I picked and chose. At times I would just say to my mother, 'I want to go to Aunt Emma's place or Aunt Madiseile's place', and mother would grant me permission. My parents would wait for some days, satisfied that I was well cared for, until homesickness drove me back home. Aunt Magdelina's home was about a mile or two from our home, and a stone's throw from my Uncle Setlhatsana Lazarus, my father's brother; but I would never go to my uncle's home, though I saw them and played with his children every day when I was at Aunt Magdelina's place. When I was a boy of about three, four or five years old, I used to create trouble for other people. I liked cows very much and I was fascinated by them. At that time a boy by the name of Ramalana Ramokoka, who was second in line of chieftaincy at his tribe, Bakoena-Ba-Ramokaka, came to Phokeng to grow up with his mother's people. He was the grandson of Dikeledi Mokgatle, my father's half-brother. He lived at his uncle Lukas Mokgatle's home and was a cattleherd. Since he was very close to me, I used to run away from home to join him in the veld, so that I could help him and others turn the cattle the whole day. In the evening he was always in trouble when we arrived home with the cattle from grazing; he was accused of having enticed me to go with him so that during the day he could sit down under the cool shade of a tree, or play games with other boys, while I turned the cattle. Though poor Ramalana took pains to explain that he did no such thing and that in fact he did not see me until we were far away from home, and that I had run away to go with him, his explanations – which were nothing but the truth – did not help him. No attempts were ever made to make me feel that I was the one who ought to be scolded or punished so that in future I should refrain from disappearing without permission.

Not only Ramalana suffered such accusations. My cousin Miga Mathuloe, Aunt Madiseile's son, also found he was having to defend himself when I spent some days at his home. When I was there, every morning that I was unobserved I ran away to wait for him and the cattle at the place where I was sure it would not be easy for him to send me back home. At times when he wanted to beat me and then send me back home, I pleaded with him until he felt pity for me and allowed me to stay with him and the cattle that I enjoyed following and turning. There were other things, too, which attracted me to the veld. The older boys were good at trapping birds with a sticky paste called *boletsoa*. This paste grew from any tree; it came out of pods like pea pods, and it was like peas. The older boys could chew the grains of *boletsoa*, making it soft, constantly spitting out the bitter juice derived from it, and finally having their mouths full of the paste, which was deadly to the birds. Thereafter thin little sticks would be found, and every stick would be covered with that paste; many of them would be laid by a pond, where the poor birds would come thinking that they could enjoy drinking water without danger to their lives, but as soon as they settled on any one of those sticks they would be caught. While they struggled to free themselves they would be adding more paste to their feathers and flying would become impossible, and the poor birds would be caught alive. Good trappers would go home in the evening with some birds they had killed, and others alive, for the purposes of cooking and eating. Another attraction which made me run away was clay work. Some boys were artistic in working with clay. They made oxen, cows, dogs, men, horses, birds or anything they saw and were familiar with. It was always exciting for me to watch them.

XII New Method in Religion

Until I was two years old, Aunt Emma and her husband Dan (Tau) Rangaka were members of the Lutheran Church, Uncle Dan at all times prominent and active in the church of his father-in-law. No one suspected that Dan Rangaka was dissatisfied with the way in which baptism was being done in the Lutheran Church. In the Lutheran Church, children are baptised eighteen days after their birth. It seems that all the time Dan Rangaka felt that it was wrong to baptise children in church from a small dish of water, but did not say so openly. When he read how Christ was baptised in the river by John the Baptist, that system of baptism appealed to him more than the one practised in the Lutheran Church.

The year nineteen-thirteen came along like any other year, and no one, including Dan Rangaka himself, knew what was in store for the Lutheran Church and the Christians of my tribe. One day there was an old man, who like men of my tribe was mostly known by the name of his son (Abel), so he was called Rabele. He went out as usual with his sheep and goats for grazing in the veld. While he was keeping guard over his animals he saw a black man and woman like himself approaching him. They were strangers and their faces were new to him. They were walking, but the man was pushing a bicycle, on which they had a few belongings. When they reached him they greeted him in a strange tongue, but all Rabele could make of it was that the man and his woman were greeting him and he greeted them also. As it is when strangers meet, the stranger began to introduce himself and his woman, but old Rabele was unable to follow what he was saying to him, and only recognised that the language the man spoke was the language he had heard from Mr. Morrison, when he came to establish the AME Church in Phokeng.

Rabele then asked his newly-found people to stay with him until it was time to go home. Rabele and his family were at that time members of the African Methodist Episcopal Church of Mr. Morrison. As agreed, in the evening Rabele turned his animals and took the two strangers home with him.

The purpose for which the old man Rabele invited the strangers was to bring them into contact with the people who were taught by Mr. Morrison and his pupil Didrik Senne in the African Methodist Episcopal Church. They were the only people at that time in my

73

tribe who could understand and speak the English language, though in a limited sort of way. Following tribal tradition he took the strangers to his house for the night, but during the evening reported the arrival of the people he brought from the veld to the head of his clan so that the next day they could be taken to the Chief's house for formal presentation.

The man and woman who reached our tribe in nineteen-thirteen were Kenneth Spooner and his wife. I never got to know Mrs. Spooner's name because the Africans are quick at naming people their own way. They simply called her Maspunara – Mrs. Spooner or Spooner's mother. Kenneth Spooner, like Mr. Morrison before him, came from the United States of America. He was not bringing a new religion, it was the same as the one brought by Mr. Penzhorn of the Lutheran and Mr. Morrison of the AME Church, but his method of applying that religion was different. Mr. Spooner and his wife were received and allowed to tell the people who they were and the differences between his church and the other two already in Phokeng.

When Mr. Spooner unfolded his story there were, as always happens, some members of my tribe who were attracted right away by what he told them. It seems to me that two things appealed to them most: first, in his new church baptisms are held in the open in the rivers, lakes and ponds; parents do not make decisions for their children to be baptised, the children must grow up first and when they are over the age of sixteen they must ask for baptism themselves. He went on to explain that that was how Christ, whose servant and worker Mr. Spooner was, was baptised by John the Baptist in the river Jordan. That, I think, sunk deeply into the minds of those who later made up their minds to join Mr. Spooner's church.

The other point which I imagine also played a large part in recruiting members for Mr. Spooner was that in his church the priest did not have to pray for all the congregation; when the time for prayer came, everyone must make his or her own appeal to God.

Mr. Spooner gave the name of his church as the Pentecostal Holiness Church. It was Baptist in character and method and, like the Lutheran and the AME before it, it was against polygamy. There were two other elements which I imagine did not appeal strongly to those who listened to Mr. Spooner, even those who did join him in the Pentecostal Holiness Church. He said that medicines were not allowed in his church; prayer was more powerful than medicine. When a member was sick only prayers should be offered; if prayers could not heal the sick, nothing else could. Those medicine men and women who desired to join his church must first burn their medicine and on the day of their acceptance publicly confess in the church that they were no longer practising medicine, and declare that medicine has no power; only prayers and appeals to Jesus Christ can heal the sick.

The other rules which cut across the old customs and traditions were that members of his church must cease making and drinking beer. There was another old tradition which the Pentecostal Holiness Church did not allow, namely, that when a member of the family died, a beast must be killed and relatives and all who came to help in the burial must eat tasteless food and meat as sacrifice to the ancestors and a sign of mourning. Some people found it hard to agree with such alterations in their lives which both the Lutheran and the AME churches permitted. In spite of all that, Mr. Kenneth Spooner did manage to penetrate both the Lutheran and African Methodist Episcopal Churches.

Dan Rangaka's daughter Lenu, Aunt Emma's last-born, was the first victim of the 'No medicine for the sick only prayers' method of the Pentecostal Holiness Church. While she lay in her sick bed, prayers were offered twice a day for her recovery, but my cousin never recovered. My mother, Aunt Madiseile and close relatives said in their complaints, and I support their view, that when prayers showed no sign of helping, medicine people should have been called in. Her death left a question in our hearts; perhaps medicine would have helped and Lenu's death would not have come at such an early age.

From Rabele's house, Mr. Spooner and his wife were taken in by a very wealthy family to live with them. The wealthy man was called Raforedi Diale. But naturally Rabele Magano, the old man who had found them and brought them to Phokeng, became the first recruit and left the AME Church.

When all that happened I was only two years and a few months old. Raforedi Diale was the second recruit to the Pentecostal Holiness Church. With their joining, Mr. Spooner secured a foothold in Phokeng. Later they were followed by two Mokgatle families: Monnafela Mokgatle and his family and Hermanus Mokgatle and his family added their names to the list. They then asked the Chief for a site for their new church and this was granted. The news about the new church began to spread like wild-fire.

Without anyone suspecting it, something like lightning struck the Lutheran Church; news broke out that Dan Rangaka had left it to join the Pentecostal Holiness Church. His departure sounded like the Lutheran Church collapsing and its roof blowing off. Many people did not believe it until they missed him in church the Sunday after the news broke.

With his power of preaching and his prestige, Mr. Spooner had secured a powerful and influential man. Raforedi Diale's house, where Mr. Spooner and his wife lived, was in the same street in which my parents' house stood, where I was born. Their first church was built in the same street, about three blocks east of my home on the same side. On that site Uncle Dan Rangaka and other recruits were seen making bricks for their new church. Each time they passed on their way to their church's site they passed my home and my mother used to remark, 'I don't know what has become of my brother-in-law.' Many people, including my mother, did not believe that Uncle Dan Rangaka had really left the Lutherans, but that he would soon return to the church which made him famous. My father's friend, Herman Pooe, was dead, and Uncle Dan Rangaka's departure left the Lutheran Church with only Titus Mathuloe to hold the fort when Ernest Penzhorn the minister was away. Mr. Penzhorn himself was bitterly disappointed by the departure of the man he trusted, liked and respected highly. He also, I imagine, entertained the hope that Dan would come back to his first religious home. All waited in vain.

Dan Rangaka's departure was sealed off by the news that one Sunday afternoon he would be baptised by Mr. Spooner in the river called Legadigadi, which runs in the middle of Phokeng. That Sunday afternoon many people went to the river to see for themselves that Dan Rangaka was no longer a Lutheran. As he moved forward, following Mr. Spooner into the water, many of his admirers wept.

Dan Rangaka, the man who went through two baptisms in his lifetime, left the lake in which he was baptised by his new priest, Mr. Kenneth Spooner, wet from head to toe. He stood on dry sand, watched by the crowd which had gathered to see him baptised for the second time, dripping with water. He looked at the crowd motionless as though he was saying to them, 'Now I am satisfied that I have been baptised properly like Jesus Christ whom I have chosen to worship.' At that moment, doubts which were still lingering in the minds of his former fellow-Lutherans were banished by his actions; they now knew that Dan had left them in the Lutheran Church for ever. Before him was the future and he could not foretell what it had in store for him. He was starting all over again. On the day of his second baptism he was not alone. There were others, too, who were baptised for the second time but, as a man of high standing and an influential figure in Phokeng Christian circles, he had to go in first to give a lead. I did not understand anything at the time; I sympathised with my mother's complaint that he was wrong to leave the church which made him a Christian and in which his father-in-law was prominent and in which he himself became prominent, liked and highly respected. Later, as I grew older, I began to learn to respect him as a man of high principles and firm convictions. He knew that his departure would cost him friends in the Lutheran

Church, but had no doubts that he would make new ones in the Pentecostal Holiness Church. All that happened; his old friends in the Lutheran Church began to avoid him, perhaps fearing that he would influence them, or that people who saw them with him would lose confidence in them and begin to accuse them as double-dealers.

Mr. Spooner, having secured the help of Uncle Dan Rangaka and others who became members, built a one-roomed church with a grass thatched roof. From that little church everything started. To get his members used to his method of praying, services were held every day of the week in the evening. The tunes of the hymns were completely different from those Uncle Dan and others knew and sang at the Lutheran Church. When it was time for praying, every member knelt down and began to pray aloud, uttering words he or she thought would reach where they were meant to go. The whole church became so noisy that those who finished praying first kept saying 'Hallelujah', 'Amen', *Modimo a o bakoe*', 'Praise God' or 'Praise the Lord'. They could keep on that way until everyone in the church had finished praying. Not only *bona fide* members were allowed to attend those services.

As a result of that, many people got attracted to them for two reasons. First, some people went there to spend the early part of the night before going to bed. The second reason was that some people went for curiosity's sake, because people always get curious when new things take place in their midst. After the service some criticised the new form of prayer introduced by Mr. Spooner, and others admired it. The admirers began to feel that it was not enough just to admire, but they should take part. They began to ask to be admitted into the church, which meant that they too would be taken to the river to be baptised like Christ.

Men who were admitted into the church began to surprise their friends by telling them that they had stopped smoking and drinking beer. Some of them were men who could hardly allow two days to pass without enjoying a calabash of beer. Women who were noted for their skill in brewing good and strong beer before the Pentecostal Holiness Church arrived disappointed people who used to enjoy their brew by telling them that they had not known that they were engaged in an evil thing, beer-making, until they joined the Pentecostal Holiness Church, which opened their eyes.

Men and women who were praised for helping the sick with medicine, declined when approached, saying, 'I don't touch medicine any more, only God heals when you believe in him and pray to him for help.' The Pentecostal Holiness Church was at work and its message was spreading.

The little church house built by Mr. Spooner and his first recruits served two purposes. During the day, from morning until the afternoon, it was used as a school, where for the second time the children of Phokeng were taught English alphabets and to speak, read and write English. The children of those who had become adherents of the new denomination were the first to be enrolled, but children from the Lutheran and the African Episcopal Church were welcomed as well. Again the Lutherans, who were eager that their children should learn English, sent them to Mr. Spooner's school in large numbers.

What disturbed Mr. Penzhorn at the Lutheran Church was that leading members of his church, like Petrus Mokgatle, who was one of the first to join the Lutheran Church, repeated what he had done when Mr. Morrison opened the first English class at the African Methodist Episcopal Church, by sending his children to Mr. Spooner's English school. Mr. Penzhorn, I was told, tried to discourage them, but they told him there was a need for their children to learn English because, unlike their parents, the children were bound to have dealings with the English people who had established their rule in the country. Because there was no English school at the Lutheran Church Mr. Penzhorn's persuasions could not work. His line of argument was that since the people of my tribe were not English, it was pointless for them to be eager that their children should learn English, which, he imagined, would turn them into black English men and women.

He pointed out at great length that Mr. Spooner's school devoted most of its time to teaching the children a foreign language and little time to teaching them their own mother-tongue. Mr. Penzhorn saw in that a danger that in the end the children of my tribe would know only English, speak, read and write only English, and when they had reached that stage they would look down on their own parents, traditions, customs and language. When they ceased to read, speak and write their own language, Mr. Penzhorn said, they would cease to know themselves and their backgrounds and cease to be a nation.

I think that some of Mr. Penzhorn's arguments were sound, but he failed to realise that the time for the children of Phokeng to know only one language had passed. When they grew up they would have more to do with the white people who had come to South Africa and spoke English.

Mr. Spooner did not speak, read or write Sesotho. He was a stranger in a strange land among strange people. Mr. Penzhorn disliked him intensely. He nicknamed him Rabodiba (Man of Ponds) because he took people to ponds for baptism. In his efforts to discourage his members from sending their children to Mr. Spooner's English school, Mr. Penzhorn started a new rule in his church; that when the children of members of his church who went to the Pentecostal Holiness Church school sought confirmation, they should start

78

first at the Lutheran catechism school to prove that they understood Bible lessons in their own language and thereafter go to the confirmation classes which were held by himself. The Lutherans stood by that rule and did what their minister wanted them to do.

At the time Mr. Spooner opened his school, John Mokgatle (Sekete), Paramount Chief Mokgatle's first son by his third wife and the man who was the first to join the Lutheran Church, had sent his second son by his first wife to Kilnerton College, the African English teachers' training college conducted by the Wesleyans near Pretoria. John's son was called Jonathan Sekete Mokgatle. He was one of those who went to Mr. Morrison's English school before the arrival of the Pentecostal Holiness Church.

When Jonathan returned from Kilnerton training college, the Lutherans opened the first English school for the children of my tribe. That was meant to counteract Mr. Spooner's school and influence. The Lutherans did the same thing as Mr. Spooner, but the other way round. At the Lutheran English school most time was devoted to catechism teaching and little time to English teaching. As a result, children who went to Mr. Spooner's school spoke, wrote and read English quicker than those who went to the Lutheran school. The Lutherans who wanted their children to learn English found that, in order to avoid offending their priest, they could only send some of their children to Mr. Spooner's school. The boys were those who found their way into Mr. Spooner's school, while their sisters were sent to their church's school.

Boys and girls at Mr. Spooner's school who were fast learners became Mr. Spooner's assistants in teaching the beginners. To get them to speak English quicker, Mr. Spooner made a rule that at school the children should speak in English, and in their mother tongue after school. Those who were caught speaking their own language were punished.

One day towards the end of the week I was alone with my mother and she went into another room and took a long time to come out. I became suspicious and followed her to investigate what she was doing. To my disappointment I found her in distress, weeping. 'What's wrong, Mother,' I asked, but she went on. It was the first time I had seen her weeping. A few minutes later she wiped her tears away and said to me, 'Your Aunt Emma is going to be baptised on Sunday at the Pentecostal Holiness Church and I think that it is wrong; your Uncle Dan Rangaka should have left her in the church our parents left us in.'

I think that at that time I was about three years old, which was not an age at which I could advise my mother. To me it did not matter whether Aunt Emma remained a Lutheran or whether she followed her husband into the Pentecostal Holiness Church. Only

79

later I began to think about it and ask myself why mother thought it wrong for her sister to follow her husband into the church he had chosen. My mother and her younger sister, Aunt Madiseile Magdelina Mathuloe, were devoted to their elder sister Aunt Emma. They regarded her almost as their guardian or someone who replaced their mother when she died.

On the Sunday of that week, Mother took me and my sister Pheloe Sannie Petlele along with her to the river Legadigadi, where Aunt Emma underwent her second baptism in the pond, like her husband. From the river we followed the crowd, to see Aunt Emma made a full member of her new church. That day was the first and last time my mother entered the Pentecostal Holiness Church. Despite all that, mother's respect for her sister, and their friendship, never ended.

Aunt Emma Rangaka, having undergone Pentecostal Holiness Church baptism like her husband Dan Rangaka, became a full member of her new church, and any attempt to try to persuade them to return to the Lutheran Church was useless. What was left for their friends and relatives to do was just to take them as they were, Christians but non-Lutherans. The mother and father having joined the new church, the next to follow were their children. One after the other the elder children of Aunt Emma travelled the road to the ponds, in the rivers and lakes, identifying themselves with their parents.

Dan Rangaka became a very prominent figure in the Pentecostal Holiness Church community as he had been at the Lutheran Church, second only to Mr. Spooner. He was heard preaching in the church, and his loud and powerful voice was heard saying prayers, as it was the habit in their church, that each member should pray to God for him or herself individually. His friends, admirers and rivals got used to seeing him with Mr. Spooner in ponds and lakes, not only in Phokeng but in other tribes' lands as well, baptising new converts to the Pentecostal Holiness Church. But he was never forgotten in the place where he began. Stories about the Lutheran Church were never complete without his name being mentioned. I recall one Lutheran Church service which I attended, where during his preaching Mr. Penzhorn told the story of the working of his church, but could not finish without saying, 'At that time, we were with three sons of this church, the late Herman Pooe, one who is still with us, Titus Mathuloe, and the one still alive but lost to us, Dan Rangaka.'

Though Reverend Penzhorn was bitter that Dan Rangaka had left the Lutheran Church which taught him Christianity and made him a Christian, he never spoke about him in a hostile fashion, but only with regret. I recall also a story I was told, that during my sister Molebopi Martha's sickness, Aunt Emma asked that she should

80

be brought to her home, in case a change of surroundings might help in restoring her health. My sister, while at her aunt's home, requested that her priest Mr. Penzhorn should come and give her holy communion. Reverend Penzhorn went there, to the home of the man who left his church, and attended to the member of his church as though there were no bitterness in his heart about that house. Dan Rangaka himself was not there at the time but Aunt Emma was there. I heard that Mr. Penzhorn laughed and smiled.

Phokeng, the headquarters of my tribe, enjoyed the honour of being also the headquarters of the Pentecostal Holiness Church and the home of the Reverend Kenneth Spooner and his wife. From Phokeng a wagon train left for the north, carrying Mr. Spooner, his wife, Dan Rangaka, Raforedi, Hermanus Mokgatle, Monnafela Mokgatle and their wives. They left as new missionaries who had founded a new church. The wagons were owned by all the travellers except Reverend Spooner, who was the person to be introduced to the people who would be contacted on the way to the north. North of Phokeng lay the lands of tribes which call themselves Bakgatla, tribes from which my maternal grandparents had sprung and left when they heard of the arrival of the Christian religion in Phokeng.

After crossing the River Kgetleng (the Elands), they entered a small tribe, at the place called Mokoshele which the Dutch had named Pulmietfontein. There they established their first station. The people of that tribe called themselves Babididi. I have no information whether some of that tribe had already acquired the Christian religion or not. But judging by some of them, men like Mualefe and Lesolobe who became the first converts there and later came to Phokeng as leaders of delegations to the annual conferences of the Pentecostal Holiness Church, they were already members of the Dutch Reformed Church when Mr. Spooner and his people arrived there during the flames of the first world war, nineteen-fourteen or nineteen-fifteen.

By gaining converts there, Spooner and his men had established a foothold in the north. From there their message spread like wild-fire, so that when they moved further north they found people already knowing of their coming. The second tribe they penetrated in the north was at Kolobeng, Place of Pigs. The third was the Batlokoa tribe, the place called Tlokoeng. The fourth was the tribe called Bafurutshe; they called their place Kolontoaneng, or Lefurutshane. They are a branch of a large Bafurutshe tribe in the west of Phokeng which, like my tribe, had adopted the Lutheran Church. In the north the Pentecostal Holiness Church became very strong and that enabled it to spread all over South Africa, right up to Zululand. Most of their annual conferences were held in Phokeng, which for ten days became a meeting place of many tribes from all parts of the country, to some degrees speaking different languages, but sharing the same religion.

The north became so important to the Pentecostal Holiness Church and their activities were so large that Uncle Dan Rangaka exiled himself from Phokeng to live in the north without his family. Although his base was at Kolontoaneng, he travelled from place to place, from tribe to tribe, preaching the gospel and spreading the message of the Pentecostal Holiness Church. In some tribes, I heard him telling my mother, he was stoned, deported, and called names, but in others he was warmly received. He proudly told my mother that even in the tribes which refused to welcome him, he always left converts. He was already an old man now, but was full of spirit and determination. Aunt Emma, who had followed him into the north and lived there with him for several years, had died and was buried at Kolontoaneng. My mother tried to persuade him to return to Phokeng for the last part of his life, but he retorted, 'Salome,' as he called my mother, 'I am guided by the Word. The Word says when they drive you away from one place, go to another, you will be received.' Death reached Dan Rangaka at the same place as Aunt Emma and he was buried there. He had married a second time and left a widow and children.

During his lifetime many children of members and non-members of their church arrived in Phokeng to be educated in English at the school Spooner founded. The death of Spooner and his right hand Dan Rangaka brought disintegration into the church and disillusionment. New people from the United States came and took control of the church. Many people, including Dan Rangaka's own children, left it, some going back to their parents' old church, the Lutheran. Others joined other small groups, to continue as independents in the old spirit of the Pentecostal Holiness Church. The pillars and inspiring spirits were away; their hands were no longer in control. Later I met some of my cousins and asked them why they thought it not necessary for them to remain in the church their father worked hard to establish, and they told me that the principles, the spirit and methods introduced by the late Reverend Kenneth Spooner and followed by their father were no longer there, and even Mrs. Spooner was not given the due respect to which she was entitled as the wife of the founder.

Reverend Kenneth Spooner died in Rustenberg General Hospital, after undergoing an operation, in nineteen-thirty-six or 'thirty-seven. News of his death reached me in Johannesburg while I was there visiting my sick mother who was staying with my sister Majone and her husband Daniel Molefe in Sophiatown. After my father's death, my mother's health became very poor and my sister thought it wise for her to invite mother to Johannesburg, so that she could get in touch with the General Hospital Outpatients Department there, in an effort to restore her health. One of my tribesmen, Mogari Mokgatle, who knew that I was one of Kenneth Spooner's admirers, met me and asked me whether I had heard of his death. I had not heard and I was deeply grieved. When I reached my sister's place I broke the sad news to them, and they too shared my grief.

One thing we all did not understand was how it was that Kenneth Spooner died in hospital when his church's doctrine was that no medicine helped, only prayers were essential when anyone fell sick. Our queries did not help us much, Reverend Kenneth Spooner was no longer sharing life with us.

Afterwards I learned that, though all the time I knew Mr. Spooner as an American, nothing more or less, he was in fact born in the island of Barbados in the West Indies, and in his early days went to the United States, got himself educated there and joined one of the independent Baptist churches and met his wife. He chose to become a priest himself and, together with his wife, decided to start their church missionary work in the continent of their ancestors. His grave is in the Phokeng graveyard and he was buried alongside Paramount Chief Molotlegi Augustus Mokgatle, who received him and his wife when they arrived in Phokeng.

After Reverend Spooner's death, one of Dan Rangaka's sons, Foro Thomas Rangaka, returned to Phokeng from the Cape to teach in the school established by Mr. Spooner with the help of his father. While Thomas Rangaka was teaching there, in nineteen-thirty-eight or 'thirty-nine, a European woman, very famous in the Transvaal, especially in Phokeng, Miss Helen MacGregor, popularly known in Phokeng as Madi, got to know him. Madi, who owned and ran a large citrus farm west of Rustenburg and produced her own brand of orange marmalade, had become at that time a social worker, and one of her desires was to do something for the people of Phokeng, whom she had known for a long time. Madi MacGregor and Thomas Rangaka planned the establishment of a tribal secondary school for the children of my tribe. At that time the Paramount Chief was Manotshe James Molotlegi, who changed his surname from Mokgatle to Molotlegi after his father when he became the Paramount Chief.

Madi and Thomas approached the Chief and found him ready to accept their plan. It then became a joint enterprise, the Paramount Chief, Madi and Thomas being prime workers for the plan. The whole tribe became involved. One day, at one of the meetings where the plan was fully explained to the people in the presence of Miss MacGregor, the meeting was also attended by the Reverend Ernest Penzhorn of the Lutheran Church, and two unusual things happened. Reverend Penzhorn was asked to express his views, which he did. Miss MacGregor did not speak or understand Sesotho, in which Mr. Penzhorn was very fluent. In order that Madi should understand what Mr. Penzhorn was saying in Sestoho, Thomas Rangaka, son of the man who was Mr. Penzhorn's right-hand man before he went over to join Mr. Spooner, was asked to translate Mr. Penzhorn's speech into English. There Thomas Rangaka stood side by side with his father's former priest, speaking in English, while Mr. Penzhorn spoke in Thomas's tribal language. During Mr. Penzhorn's address, before he could finish a sad thing happened; he was struck by heart failure, collapsed and died. That was the end of the Penzhorns' life and activities in Phokeng. Reverend Penzhorn was a very handsome man, tall, well built, with heavy hands, blue eyes, and a loud, clear and frightening voice. He called himself a tribal man and a Mafokeng. I do not know which he spoke better, German or Sesotho. The secondary school was built and still stands in Phokeng.

XIII My Birth

My mother, her sister Aunt Madiseile Magdelina Mathuloe and their two brothers, did not follow their elder sister Aunt Emma into the Pentecostal Holiness Church. They remained Lutherans in the church which made their parents Christians. They were not deeply religious and went to church services very irregularly. They had all their children baptised in the Lutheran Church but did not make it a hard and fast rule for them to go to church, nor did they make sure that their children understood the lessons they were taught in the catechism.

My own mother, when she had time to spare, used to read the Bible to me and explained some things I did not understand. I can recall no occasion when I heard her press any of my sisters to go to church on Sundays. During their school days my sisters went to church regularly every Sunday because their catechism teachers were strict about their pupils being in church. In those days the teachers arrived first at church, standing by the door to see which child was absent. The next day they wanted to know why, and if a child simply stayed away without *bona fide* reasons, punishments followed.

Unlike her sisters, my mother very seldom asked us to pray before we had a bite at our meals. I recall complaining to her that each time I was at Aunt Emma's house they prayed too long and I got tired in the process. She agreed with me and added that God also may not like such long prayers, because he can hear and answer short prayers. But she insisted on discipline and said, 'When you are at your aunt's home, you must do as they say. That is the way they think their prayers can reach God. They may be right.'

My two aunts' children liked my mother and she in her turn liked them. Just as we could not leave any of our aunts' homes without having been offered something to eat, or to take home with us, none of my aunts' children could go away from mother without having been given something to eat or to take home. I was told that when my mother gave birth to her second twins, sisters Martha and Maria, Aunt Emma released her third daughter Ntina Rangaka to go to live with my mother at our home to help with the twins. Cousin Ntina didn't leave until my sisters were about five years old. Aunt Emma considered it her moral duty to her sister, and that was all there was to it.

It was on the first of April, on Saturday morning, my mother told me, round about the hours of eight and nine, in the year nineteen-eleven, in Phokeng, South Africa, in a place named by Lutheran Christians Saron, that I was born. I broke into my tribal scenery and increased the number of the Bafokeng tribe.

Naturally, my mother and those who shared in the event took a close look at me and found that I was a male. That was not what my parents were expecting because, since the birth of my twin sisters, only females had followed. A period of three years and several months had elapsed before I arrived. Not only had my parents lost the hope of ever having a male child, but any child at all after my sister Pheloe Sannie Petlele.

At the hour of my birth my father was away, as it was customary that new arrivals must only be witnessed by females, males to get a report when it was all over. On the day of my birth my father, like men of his time, was fulfilling a custom that grown-up males must each day witness the dawn by being at the Paramount Chief's house to pay him homage, or be at the animals' kraal to see whether or not anything had happened to them during the night. I do not know which one of these functions my father was fulfilling that morning. On his return, however, he found good news awaiting him. I do not know who told him that he was the father of a son, but I am sure it was not my mother, because tradition and custom did not allow him to see her and his newly-born baby. I was told that after receiving the good news that after all his name would not die with him, unless the new child died in infancy like his brothers before him, father went to one of his trusted friends who had consented to be the guardian of his sheep and goats in one of our villages, Luka, and picked out a big fat sheep to slaughter. My father's friend's name was Twekane, and I grew to know him well because each time he came to Phokeng out home was his first station. He was a medicine man and very colourful. He always carried a flute with him which he was fond of blowing.

There were two reasons for slaughtering a sheep or goat after a child was born. Meat was meant to strengthen the mother after the birth of her child, and the skin of the slaughtered animal was to be softened by the grandfather of the child, or a very close relative, to be used later as a *thari* (baby carrying skin) with which African mothers fasten their babies on their backs when they work in the fields or at home, or go on long journeys to visit friends or relatives. The *thari*, the skin my mother used for carrying me, was preserved so that I could see it. I was carried in the same way by my mother as African mothers still carry their babies today. I was never in a pram, nor were any of my children.

Eighteen days after the day on which I was born, I was told, I was wrapped in a snow-white shawl bought by father from a Dutch storekeeper trading in Phokeng called Raphalane, a nickname given him by the people of Phokeng. His real name was Mr. Strawie, and I grew up to find him very friendly to my father. On that day, when I was carried in a shawl, I was on my way to the Lutheran Church to be baptised by Reverend Ernest Penzhorn. That was done to me because of my mother, who was a Christian. Within those eighteen days, I was told, my father, who was not a Christian, went through most pages of the Old Testament in search of a Christian name for me, and came across the story of a Hebrew, in the first book of Kings, which fascinated him immensely. It was the story of Naboth, who got killed because he refused to give the king the vineyard he inherited from his father. The king wanted to give Naboth another one in exchange, but Naboth refused the deal. My father then ordered that I should be called Naboth.

I was told by my mother that fourteen months after my birth, when I was a promising child playing well with other children, I showed signs of unhappiness. Something had gone wrong with my health, but no one could make out what it was. When mother told father of my sickness, he became very worried and alarmed. Silently both of them tried to find out what had gone wrong with their only son, on whom they had pinned their hopes that they would at last watch a boy growing in their care into a teenager and ultimately into a strong tribesman.

A day or two later, when they saw no improvement, they told their relatives and friends that their boy had fallen sick and his sickness was of a puzzling nature. My mother's people, as well as father's, began to arrive at our home to see whether there was anything they could do to help. All my parents could do was to resort to medical men in the village and ask for help. One after another was called upon to see what was the matter with me, but they confessed that the sickness was so rare and new to them that they found it hard to get to the bottom of it. As they tested their skill in medicine on me, the sickness increased and I got worse day by day. Mrs. Penzhorn, the wife of the Lutheran minister, was noted for helping children and other people with European medicine when they fell sick; she, too, was called in, but her work could not bring relief. My parents and their relatives became desperate, fearing that I was only a temporary visitor on earth, and that my turn to follow my brothers who died in their infancy was drawing near.

One day father went away to attend to other tribal duties and on his return found the sickness had taken an alarming course. Mother told me that, as father stood above me looking down on me, tears began to roll out of his eyes. He remarked, 'I knew he would not live.'

I was told that my skin had wrinkles, like the skin of a very old person, and I was getting weaker and weaker. At that time mother's sisters, Aunts Emma and Madiseile, were taking turns in assisting mother to nurse me. Though men of medicine were still trying to help, hopes of my pulling through were sinking fast. One day, out of the blue, an old woman in our village was passing our home and saw my Aunt Madiseile leaving and remarked that she envied the way she and her two sisters were friendly to each other and wished them luck to carry on that way. Aunt Madiseile thanked the old woman but told her that her visit to her sister that day was not a pleasant one, her sister's only son was critically ill and they were waiting for the end at any time. The old woman asked if she could be allowed to see me. Aunt Madiseile invited the old woman in, and after listening to the tale of my sickness, she told them of an old Dutch woman living in a little settlement about twelve or less mile from our tribe, who she said helped children and sick people with old Dutch patent medicines and herbs. She suggested that my parents should go and try her.

This European woman was called Makurari, the African version of Mrs. Konradie. The next day mother, father and Aunt Madiseile were on their way to Mrs. Konradie at the place the Dutch settlers called Boshoek, north of Phokeng. They walked, taking turns to carry me on their backs. Mother told me that they arrived at Mrs. Konradie's place at lunch time, when she and her children and husband were busy having their lunch. They were told to wait until lunch was over. Because they were desperate they felt that Mrs. Konradie was not sympathetic; she saw they had a very sick child, but asked them to wait until she had finished eating. For them every minute was vital, as though by bringing me to Mrs. Konradie they had found a way to stop my death.

After lunch, as was customary with most Europeans in South Africa in those days, Mrs. Konradie went into her bedroom for an hour's afternoon sleep before she could see my parents and aunt to ask them what they wanted to see her about. I think that if they had not been tired, they might have left.

Mother never forgot to tell me that, to their amazement, when Mrs. Konradie came out of her house and found them still waiting, she ordered that they should be given food to eat before she talked to them. That was the custom they knew, but they were astonished to find Mrs. Konradie was also practising it. While they enjoyed Mrs. Konradie's food, she looked at me closely, held me up and spread her eyes all over my body. While she did that she called one of her daughters, told her to bring something in a glass and gave it to me herself to drink. When eating and drinking were all over, she asked father what was wrong with me. She was not a doctor but a herbalist.

After hearing the tale, she asked, 'Why did you not bring him before today?' Father answered that they had only heard of her two days before. She promised nothing remarkable but said, according to mother, that her observation of me gave her the impression that I was suffering from a blood disease. She went on to remark, according to mother, that if I had been brought to her earlier she might have helped. She noticed that her remark disappointed my parents and aunt, but quickly said, 'I am not saying that he is going to die. I think that it will take a longer time to overcome his sickness.' Those words of hers gave some relief to those who brought me to her.

Afterwards she went into the house and, according to mother's estimate, it might have been twenty or thirty minutes before she came out with a large bottle containing a mixture and ordered that I should be given its contents three times a day, in the morning, at lunch time and at bedtime in the evening. She ordered further that I should be fed with goat's milk and drink a cupful of it every day. She charged my parents seven shillings for her mixture and ordered that when it was finished I should be brought back for her to see whether there was any progress. Luckily father had some goats nearby, under the guardianship of his friend Sateraka Lesege. Every morning he went there to get goat's milk, as Mrs. Konradie ordered. The tale is that by the time Mrs. Konradie's bottle was empty I was beginning to play, the wrinkles on my skin were thinning out; Mrs. Konradie's work was showing good results. When I was taken back to Mrs. Konradie, only father and mother took me. They were laughing and full of hope. Mrs. Konradie herself was amazed to see how her mixture and goat's milk prescription worked. She was naturally proud of herself, and my parents were filled with praises for her.

Makurari had done something for them which they hardly believed at first would happen. Again, on the second occasion, she gave them a second bottle of mixture to treat me with. To their surprise and delight the charge for the second bottle was half-a-crown less than the previous one. That was the last visit to her. My mother used to tell me with delight that by the time I finished the second bottle I was happy and jumping about, and those who had not seen me before they took me to Mrs. Konradie could hardly believe that I had been on the verge of dying and they had lost hope that there was still someone alive who would help to restore my health.

When I had recovered I became once again a strong tribal youth, and my parents recovered confidence that I should grow into a young man who would perpetuate my father's name and, if possible, have sons of my own who in their turn would perpetuate it until the end of time. My parents never forgot Mrs. Konradie's help, or failed to acknowledge that it was her knowledge of herbs that postponed the death of their son.

In our yard in Saron, Phokeng, father had planted several orange trees, which he cared for very much. He used to soften the ground under them and build circles around each one of them, so that when rain came they could get enough water. He also used to get enough manure for them, so that the fruit they bore was not only large but sweet and soft. Many people in our village used to admire them and praised father for being the best orange-grower in the village. When they were ripe, father never forgot to pick out the ones he thought were largest, showing sweetness from outside, and take them to Mrs. Konradie while she was alive. By the time she died, my parents were friends of her family. Her death, of course, severed that friendship. Before that many people went to her for help when they were sick, because my parents advised them to go.

XIV After Sickness

My health having been restored, I began, I was told, to gather more flesh and grow strong again. My parents, particularly my mother, felt that they should treat me carefully so that I could grow up a happy boy. From that time I spent more time with mother than with father. Whenever she heard me cry, playing with other children, she always suspected and blamed others for having been the cause of my unhappiness without good reason. She would demand that my sister Pheloe Petlele should devote more attention to my happiness than to her own.

In the evening, before bedtime, mother would put me on her lap and make me sleep, gently, before she separated me from her. She developed a tendency of only refusing my demands when she was sure that what I demanded would harm me. During the first four years of my life father raised no objections to mother's treatment of me, but during the fifth year he began to object whenever he saw me sitting on her lap. He said that as a male child, according to tribal traditions and customs, I belonged to him more than to mother. He said, further, that mother had four girls to cope with, my sisters, who deserved to be taught domestic matters by her. He said that at that age it fell within his right to teach me things about the tribe, so that I would grow up with knowledge of tribal laws, traditions and customs.

Mother, though she did not mind father's assertions, still did not stop displaying her devotion to me. She was fond of quoting the judgment of Solomon, when the woman who refused that the child should be cut in half revealed herself the true mother of the child. Mother used to say, 'The mother of the child holds the sword by the sharp edge.' I am not suggesting that mother loved me more than her four daughters. But I think that as a male child, the only son alive in the family, whose death she nearly suffered, I appealed more to her motherly feelings than my sisters did. She treated me tenderly and, as I said before, she called me her grandfather. I was never separated from her until I was seven years old.

My father, unlike all the men of Phokeng, did not care for his animals himself. He scattered them amongst his friends and as a result did not have a kraal or kraals erected by him in which he kept his sheep, goats, cattle and donkeys, though he owned these animals. He seemed like a man who owned no animals at all. Some of them were in Phokeng, but because they were cared for by his friends no one knew that they were his. Some of them were entrusted to the care of friends in other villages of our tribe, and others were even entrusted to the care of members of other tribes who were father's trusted friends. I grew up like a son whose father was poor and owned no animals.

Mother used to complain that father did not care much about his property because he did not make time to visit his friends to see whether the number of his animals had increased or not. Whenever any of father's friends came along to report the loss of one of the animals, or the death of one, mother used to point out that it was impossible for father to know that the one reported lost or dead was his or not. She complained, further, that though father's friends used his animals for their own interests because they cared for them, they were not keen to report to him yearly how many had been added to his livestock. Father's reply used to be that he was too busy and the work he was engaged in would not permit him to care for his animals himself. In my early days I used to think that mother was unfair to father by urging him to be like others and care for his animals himself. But as I grew older I agreed with mother that father had too much confidence in his friends. Mother also used to point out that her fears that some of father's friends were earmarking some of his animals for themselves were strengthened by the fact that none of them ever complained that father was giving them no reward for caring for his animals. They all said that they were satisfied, because they used them without father's interference.

The story mother told me about father and animals was that, when they were married and immediately afterwards, father had a good number of cattle he was fond of. He cared for them himself. But later in their married life, South African animals were struck by foot and mouth disease, and many cattle and other animals were destroyed as a result. Father lost all his cattle and that broke his heart. He had nothing left and had to start all over again.

My maternal grandfather asked father to work with him so that he could teach him building and thatching. So the two men worked together and father learned a great deal about thatching. He was not keen on bricklaying but thatching attracted him. In addition, because grandfather was also a carpenter, father learned much about woodwork. Afterwards father became a professional thatcher and made it his life's work. Before money got a strong hold on the people of Phokeng, everyone who asked him to do thatching paid him with a cow, an ox, sheep or goats. That presented father with the problem of caring for them himself. If father had had to erect kraals for them and be close to them, he would have had to give up thatching. He chose not to do so, and therefore was left with no alternative but to ask a number of his friends to keep his animals for him. That was the reason why father was never seen, during his thatching career, erecting kraals or following his animals seeking good grazing fields for them like his contemporaries. He was not only good at thatching but at woodwork as well. He was good at making the stamping blocks and stamping sticks used even today for separating African corn from bran.

He also made ox yokes and the part called, in South Africa, Dutch *skeis*, used to hold firmly the neck of the ox. I used to watch him make them. He was also an expert at carving wooden spoons, large and small. I did not see him carve wooden dishes, but I found some which I was told were carved by him. I also watched him carve short sticks used by women for beating the earth flat, called kato.

Unlike other boys, I remained with my mother until I was seven or eight years old. Other boys left with their fathers' animals for grazing in the fields at the ages of five or six. When I was seven years old father and uncle, his brother, decided to group their sheep and goats together. Father took some of his sheep and goats from some of his friends and gave them to uncle to care for with his own. Uncle had already erected the kraal and all father had to do was to bring his animals to mix with uncle's. And in the absence of his brother, who was away from home for six days a week working in a tobacco factory in Rustenburg, father had no time to visit the animals.

Every week-end when uncle came home he had to visit the kraal to see whether everything was all right, and also to mend it if it needed mending. I think that uncle, though he did not complain much to his brother for whom he had a high respect, nevertheless felt unjustly treated. At that time I had to join uncle's children to care for the sheep and goats. Because of father's treatment of him, I think that uncle felt it right to revenge himself on me. Each time he came to inspect the animals and the kraal and found something wrong, he blamed me for it more than his daughter and son, who with me cared for the animals. When he felt it necessary to punish us, I got more than the others. I never complained to father about it but always to mother. Father and his brother's grouping of their animals lasted less than two years.

Father then talked to a relative named Samuel Mokua and asked him to take me, his sheep, goats, a few cows, oxen and four donkeys into his care. Samuel Mokua agreed, but said that he had to take me with the animals from Phokeng to his cattle post, which was twenty or more miles away on the borders of Bakgatla lands, near the Elands River, to live there with him and his children. I was nine or ten years old at that time, when I left Phokeng and my mother. I do not know how mother felt about it, but I was sorry to leave her and thought that I could not face the world without her and her care.

Father was the master, his orders had to be carried out. There were many cattle posts where I was posted, and so there were other boys and girls. The first few weeks away from mother were torment for me. From where I was I could only see two large mountains, Tshufi and Moremogolo, alongside which Phokeng stands.

Each time I stretched my eyes to those mountains I longed for Phokeng, much more for my mother, and became homesick. I was exiled from Phokeng and separated from the woman who gave birth to me, whom I loved dearly and knew that she had me in her thoughts all the time. Time and exile took a toll of my memories and strength. Before very long I adapted myself to the new life and conditions. The cries of jackals, hyenas, other animals and large birds like ostriches at night made me realise that life with my mother in Phokeng was behind me, but in front of me was the future. I was forced to accept that things had changed for me.

I was there for two years, during which I graduated into a cattle-post boy like the others. I learned many things, among them tribal dances, the riding of an ox, and the playing of a one-stringed instrument I learned to make there called *nkokoane*. To play it one needed practice. To make its music exciting to others, to make them dance, one had to be a good player indeed. To make its music loud and exciting, one had to place it on an empty tin or a large empty calabash and gently beat the one string with a thin stick, picking the string with the small finger of one's left hand if one is right-handed, placing one's cheek on the string. There were other boys who were better at it than I was, but there were also some who admired me and chose not to play in my presence.

Like other boys, I learned to hunt with dogs for rabbits and rock rabbits in the mountains. They taught me to eat wild fruits and roots, and how to produce fire, since we had no matches there. What we had in large quantities was milk, which we drank and treated friends from other cattle-posts with when they paid us visits to compete in playing *nkokoane* and dancing. For the most part we were left there without adults to face the world alone. When we received visitors they always brought with them their champion *nkokoane* players and dancers to show us how good they were at it. When they left for their cattle-posts, we took them halfway on ox- or donkey-back. The other things I learned there were bird trapping, and training dogs to chase and catch birds like guineafowl and partridges. All the dog had to do was to chase the shadow of the bird until it got tired of flying and came down.

During my stay at the cattle-post two things happened which I still vividly remember. Many people who had erected their cattle-posts there were very rich in livestock. They had hundreds and thousands of sheep and goats. We were close to a branch of my tribal village called Chaneng. Their cattle, sheep and goats, when they met ours, made a large number of livestock. It was in nineteen-twenty-one or 'twenty-two that the dipping of sheep and goats was introduced.

One day the dip inspector, Mr. Behrens, came to count all the sheep and goats our parents owned, in order to determine what quantity of dip was required. A few months later a large pond of dip was built and a day of dipping was announced. On the day of dipping we boys had to take our parents' sheep and goats to the pond. I shall never forget how difficult it became to identify ours from other peoples' because they looked so much alike dyed yellowish and all running about in all directions as they came out of the pond as though something was burning them. Thereafter for many weeks people were still looking for their missing animals. We were only able to identify ours after the yellowish stain had worn off and in some cases by markings.

We were told that our sheep and goats were not healthy and dipping would make them so. But what I experienced was the beginning of the impoverishment of my father and other tribesmen. Sheep and goats began to develop a strange cough which led them to their eventual deaths. People watched their sheep and goats dying but were helpless, since there was nothing they could do about it.

The other episode I still remember vividly is that I went with other boys to climb a large mountain nearby, to the north of the Elands River, called Chakise, to seek wild fruits and wild honey, called *semane*, found normally in the caves hanging on large rocks. While we were half-way to the top, about a half- or three-quarters of a mile below, we heard a strange sound. Looking down, we saw a wagon moving but not being pulled by oxen. Looking closely, we noticed inside it two white men. That was the first time I saw a motor-car. We ran away as if we had never seen a white person before.

In my young days, those of us who were in the tribes and lived far away from areas inhabited by white people seldom saw them. The surprising thing was that those like me who were born in Phokeng and nearby saw the Lutheran Church minister, Ernest Penzhorn, his wife and their children when they were at home for the school holidays, and at times played with them, chasing grasshoppers and birds; yet because they spoke our language so well, we never noticed the distinction between us in colour. We never noticed that they were white.

Whenever a strange white person came along we noticed that he or she was white, like the dip inspector, Mr. Behrens, at the cattle-post. I and others at once noticed the distinction and we small ones began to ask each other, 'Why is he not like us? His hair is longer than ours, straight like ox-tail hair, and he speaks a language we do not under-stand.' We wondered how the older men who were there at the time understood him. When we saw a motor-car for the first time, with white people in it, though we were in the mountain far away from them, hiding behind large rocks, we still thought that they could see us. Why we did not want them to see us I do not know, even today. I can only suspect that we were too young to understand these things because, had we been old enough to think, we would have under-stood that the white people we saw were like the Phokeng Church minister and his family whom we lived with and saw nearly every month. In those days, to me and others who shared my young days and thoughts, there was no other world outside the one we knew, no other countries outside our own, and we had no idea that many people did not speak Sesotho, which we took for granted was the language of all peoples. As youngsters, we had not gone to Mr. Penzhorn's house to hear them speak German, therefore it never occurred to us that they had learned to speak Sesotho.

At the cattle-post I also learned to milk cows, and swim in the Elands River which still flowed heavily eastwards. Later a dam was built at the extreme west of where we were, causing the river to dry up. Before I was born, I was told, in one of the heavy rainy seasons, the river was so heavily flooded that it broke its banks and drowned some people and weak animals.

While I was at Kgetleng cattle-post, my maternal Uncle Kristof was busy persuading mother and father that I should be brought back and placed under his guardianship with father's animals. At that time I was satisfied with life as it was at Kgetleng. I had made friends, I was liked by some and disliked by others, but that was how life worked in every community. Samuel Mokua had a brother-in-law, his wife's brother called David. David's parents were also, before I was born, leading figures in the Lutheran Church, and he, together with other children of his father's house, went to extensive catechism training, and I think he knew it well. David had cattle of his own, which we also cared for. He used to come down to the cattle-post to stay with us for two or three weeks. I resented his coming and so did others, because while he was with us we were not free to do what we liked. He was very strict and enforced iron discipline.

In the evenings while he was there, instead of letting us play our instruments and dance, he held a class, teaching us how to count up to a hundred, the alphabet in Sesotho, the Ten Commandments, stories about Egypt – the children of Israel, how they went there, Moses' leadership out of Egypt and other stories in the Old Testa-ment, as he had been taught. To find out whether we took in what he told us he used to test us the next day by asking us questions on what

96

he told us the previous day. Failures were punished by having to drink more milk than we wanted or by being made to go and carry firewood alone. Others were made to carry water from the river to fill all the containers there were. At times he resorted to beatings as well to make us take a keen interest in what he was teaching us. Each day while he was at the cattle-post I hated seeing the sun going down. He left us with a message whenever he returned home, 'Keep remembering all I told you, because when I come again I shall ask you everything I told you.' Within my heart it was always, 'Thanks for going'.

Looking back when I was at school, I thanked David for what he had done. By then he was already dead and I had no chance to say thank you.

After a little over two years at Kgetleng cattle-post, my father's animals having slightly increased in number, I left Kgetleng to join my uncle, my Aunt Madiseile's husband, and his two nephews. They had grouped their cattle together in an area called Meloe, not far from Kgetleng, a distance of about three hours' walk. There we were, three boys, and the name of the eldest – one of the two nephews – was Chaene Moketsi. His name meant 'Chinese'. I was told that he was born at the time when Chinese were brought to South Africa to work in the mines. When the Chinese workmen refused to work in the mines, some of them ran away and went into the country; one of them found himself in Phokeng, and on that day Chaene Moketsi was born and was given that name.

I was lonely at the time, always thinking of the friends I left at Kgetleng, but I soon settled down at Meloe. I was still far away from Phokeng and my mother. From Meloe I could see the white building towering on the hill – the Lutheran Church – but I never stopped wondering whether I should again see my mother, my sisters and Phokeng that I loved so much. I knew Chaene, though he was far older than I was, because he was born in the same street only three houses from my home. The other boy I did not know, his name was Medupe and he was a Mokgatla boy hired to my uncle's mother-in-law, working for one calf after completing twelve months.

There I found the same musical instrument I learned to play at Kgetleng, and my limited skill at it soon made me known and accepted as one of the players. My knowledge of trapping birds also made me famous and I soon found myself with a good deal of friends. I soon arranged for boys of Meloe and Kgetleng to meet and exchange visits, to compete in playing *nkokoane* and in dancing. Some evenings I found myself among those travelling on ox- or donkey-back to Kgetleng as visitors. On other occasions I was among those who received visitors from Kgetleng. At Meloe, as at Kgetleng, there were girls of about thirteen, fourteen and up to sixteen years of age, and boys of the same age, sharing the same enclosures, though living in separate huts, but no harm was ever done to the girls. Not a single girl went home pregnant because they lived with the boys alone, far away from home. Some of the boys were afraid of some girls and could be ordered about by them. Some girls came there to drink milk for a short time and others were there helping to care for their parents' animals.

While I was still exiled from my mother and my birthplace at the second cattle-post, Meloe, Aunt Madiseile's husband's nephew, called Raphiri, had a spotless black dog which he gave to me to look after. It was male and it seemed very clumsy indeed. When one looked at it one would hardly think that it could run and catch a hare. I gave it the name Monna-Motsho, which means 'the Black man' in Sesotho. The dog became my friend, and wherever I went during the day Monna-Motsho accompanied me. As it grew it became my defender as well. No one could fight me without the Black Man coming to my aid. I don't know whether Monna-Motsho was proud of me but I was proud of him.

The dog was born in Luka where Raphiri lived, but was brought later to the cattle-post. The dog was so clever that on its way to the cattle-post it studied very carefully the way back home. Whenever Monna-Motsho became homesick, he went back without asking my permission or telling me. He would wait until he was sure that I was fast asleep at night and then travel back home. The next morning I would find the Black Man gone. He would be away for a week or more, and in the same way he would leave home for the cattle-post. When I woke up I would find the Black Man ready to greet me by waving his tail, with his ears drawn back, as though he was also apologising for going away without telling me. Monna-Motsho would not do anything without my orders. If I ordered him to kill a sheep or goat, he would do it without mercy. Even if I wanted to catch an ox or a cow he would do so skilfully. He would run and catch it by its nose, making it stand still until I ordered its release.

When Monna-Motsho and I were travelling in the bush following the cattle as they grazed peacefully, if we ran into a hare, steenbok, springbok, guineafowl, partridge or any other bird or animal I wanted for Monna-Motsho and myself and the others who lived with us to make a feast of, all I had to do was to shout '*Motshoare*', pointing at the object. '*Motshoare*' means in Sesotho 'Catch him'. Monna-Motsho would go into action. All I had to do was to wait where he left me until his return to report the result. If he did not manage to catch the animal or bird, he would indicate this to me by coming to lie next to me. If he killed, he would stand looking at me, and when I moved towards him he would turn round and lead me to where he left the dead object.

While I was at Meloe cattle-post enjoying the company of friends and the Black Man, which I suspect was Sesotho because though he could not speak the language he understood it well when I spoke it, or gave orders in it to catch or kill anything, I noticed that Monna-Motsho was a heavy meat eater like all of us at the cattle-post. The only difference was that the Black Man disliked boiled meat and enjoyed raw meat. One other thing Monna-Motsho shared with me and the others was the drinking of fresh milk. There was always enough for all of us. The dog was really reliable. It would never eat anything unless it was given it. I knew that each time I felt hungry the dog must be in the same position. I realised that if I fed myself alone and ignored the Black Man, I would be inviting him to take things on his own accord before they were given to him. When that happened the one to deserve the blame would be myself, not the dog.

While Chaene, Medupe and myself were trying hard to be careful, one day we lost some of the cattle we were there to care for. After searching for them for several days we found some of them, but failed to find one ox which belonged to my uncle's mother-in-law. That ox was in the habit of leaving other animals to wander alone. It had done that on many occasions, but we always found it later. Sometimes, before we found it, it returned to the fold on its own. On that last occasion we searched for it while at the same time expecting it to return on its own. Days passed, and two weeks passed, without the ox coming back. We became restless and feared that, if it became known at home that we had lost that ox, the result would be serious trouble for all of us. We then decided that one of us should remain with the other cattle and two should go all out to search for the missing ox. Medupe was the one we chose to take charge of the other cattle, while Chaene and myself did the searching.

Still we failed to recover the missing animal. We never recovered it. What became of it is still a puzzle to me. We tried everywhere; we met many people and asked them, but none could help us with information. One morning I set out with the Black Man and went eastward to a pound which was twenty-five or thirty miles away, to see if it had been impounded by someone there. We got there, but found that no one had impounded it.

XV Return to Phokeng

When my dog and I went to the pound, it was immediately after the winter season, and the sun was bright and warm. Grass at that time was dry, the trees had lost their leaves but were beginning to show signs of getting new ones. It was early autumn, perhaps the end of July or the beginning of August, nineteen-twenty-two. I was eleven years old, but looked older. When the Black Man and I left the pound it was getting late in the afternoon and both of us were hungry because we had no lunch at all. I made a mistake when we left our cattle-post not taking food or something to eat. Earlier when I left the cattle-post I felt that I was not altogether well, but thought that as the day went by I would feel better and overcome the unpleasantness. That feeling, however, never left me. Coupled with hunger, when we left the pound I felt weaker than I expected. At that part of the year, wild fruits which might have helped were nowhere to be found. On the way between our cattle-post and the pound, almost half-way between the two, lived a family known as the Mareuma family. Mr. Mareuma was not a Mosutho but a Xhosa, whose people were in the Cape Province. How the family came to be in the north, in the Transvaal alone, I do not know. But they were members of our tribe by adoption.

Mr. Mareuma had a large number of cattle, sheep and goats. He established a cattle-post there, then decided to settle there with his family. The area where he chose to settle came to be known as Koa-Mareuma, the place of Mareuma. When I reached Mareuma area on my way from the pound I decided to stop there to ask for something to eat for myself and my companion, the Black Man. I found Mr. Mareuma away from home, but his wife and children were there. I introduced myself and told them the reason why I was in their area and also asked for something to eat. Mrs. Mareuma, as a mother, wasted no time, and shortly a calabash full of milk, some meat and porridge were in front of me. After I had expressed satisfaction, Black Man's turn to eat came. Though he did not eat inside the house as I did, he was nevertheless well fed.

The sun was near setting at the time, and Mrs. Mareuma suggested that I should spend the night there with them, but I said that my friends would be worried, wondering whether I had been eaten by the hungry African bush. Against Mamareuma's motherly persuasions, the Black Man and I left.

On our way back to the cattle-post from the pound, without the missing ox I had set out to find, and having been forced by hunger to stop at Mareuma's place, I began to regret having turned down Mamareuma's offer to spend the night at her home. The Black Man and I were still very far from our cattle-post. About a mile or more from Mareuma's place the sun went down as though it was saying, 'You have seen enough of me today, you will see me again tomorrow.' I kept on walking westwards towards our cattle-post. Before long, darkness overtook us. In front we could only see the road which led us back home. The sky was clear and soon stars, bright, big and small, began to appear all over the sky above us. I had no fears that we would be harmed by anything since our part of Africa was no longer inhabited by dangerous animals.

That day I still swear I saw a ghost. When we were about a mile or a little less from the cattle-post, far away ahead of us on the left-hand side I saw a big bright light, which convinced me that where the light appeared the area was on fire and the grass was burning. That did not surprise me, because at that time of the year it was common for some people to set areas alight, so that when the first rain came new grass could grow and animals could have green grass. The new grass which grew from an area which had been set alight is called in Sesotho *Pillo*. When cattle eat *Pillo*, they give more milk and grow fat and beautiful.

I moved on towards the burning area, which I could not avoid, suspecting nothing unusual and not frightened. By the time I reached it, the fire was very close to the road and the air was full of the smell of burned grass. The fire was covering a large area. When I reached the area on fire, the fire was so fierce and bright that the Black Man and I were covered by its brightness. Still suspecting nothing unusual, I walked on until I left the burning area behind me. When I arrived at the cattle-post I did not even talk about it because it was nothing unusual to me. I only reported to Chaene and Medupe that our missing ox was not at the pound.

Three days afterwards Chaene and I passed the area and there was no sign that the area had ever been touched by fire. I was shocked and frightened. I then began to tell Chaene of the fire I saw when I passed there three nights before. Chaene dismissed my story with ease.

My story that I saw an area burning but found later that the area was never touched by fire was not only rejected by Chaene, who heard it first, but by all who heard it later. They said that I was imagining it. I found myself at a disadvantage, because my dog, which was my companion at the time and shared the sight of the fire and the bright light which the fire threw upon us, could not, lacking the art of speech, support my story. At times Black Man was by my side when I tried to convince my friends that I was not imagining the story, that we did in fact see the area on fire and came very close to it. Black Man listened, heard what was said, but was unable to add anything to my story.

Although my story was not accepted by my friends, their rejection of it never altered my belief that on that night I did see a ghost. Afterwards I heard others say that they had similar experiences to mine. They told me that at some time in their lives, when they were travelling with friends, they saw objects or figures sharing journeys with them, but when they tried to show their friends the objects or figures they saw, their friends were unable to share their experiences and the results were that their friends accused them of imagining things and refused to believe their stories. I am leaving it to the reader of this story to pronounce judgment.

At the beginning of September nineteen-twenty-two, Uncle Kristof, Aunt Madiseile – Magdelina's husband Mr. Eliphas Mathuloe, and his nephew Mr. Raphiri Rapoo decided to separate. Their separation meant that Uncle Kristof had to take me, my father's animals, and his mother-in-law's and his own animals back to Phokeng, to get ready for ploughing, which starts at the end of October or very early in November. Before ploughing began young oxen had to be tamed and a team of oxen formed, so that when the work started there would be no time wasted struggling to tame young oxen. There were no quarrels between them; separation was agreed upon in a friendly manner. Before I left the cattle-post at Meloe with the animals for Phokeng, Uncle Kristof erected a kraal near Phokeng.

It was two or three weeks before the end of September that I arrived back in Phokeng with the animals, accompanied by Uncle Kristof. Though I was delighted to be back in Phokeng I was at the same time sorry that I had been taken away from Meloe and friends I had made there. I was like a newcomer in Phokeng; boys who had known me before I left four or five years before were as strange to me as I was to them.

I was pleased to be reunited with my mother and sisters whom I had not seen during the time I was exiled in the cattle-posts. My father, as usual, was busy thatching houses in Phokeng, which denied both of us a chance to work together as father and son. This I missed very much. I envied other boys who worked with their fathers. That lack of working together between father and me deprived me of his influence in my whole life. I saw him only in the evenings, but could not sit down with him to discuss our future together; that I missed very much. Only mother was always close to me.

My arrival in Phokeng with the animals from the cattle-post placed me entirely under Uncle Kristof's control and guardianship. I lived at home with my parents, but every morning when I left home to follow the animals into grazing fields, Uncle Kristof exercised undisputed control of me. Before this my uncle was very fond of me and I was also very fond of him. But when we became a team, working together daily, I noticed a change in his attitude.

During our time of taming young oxen, getting them ready for ploughing, my uncle became less and less tolerant towards me. He accused me of not learning fast enough and not listening to his orders. That was in October nineteen-twenty-two and I was about eleven years and a few months old. I was doing my utmost to please him but his mind was turned away from me at that time. He began to resort to beating me, in his own words to make me conform to his way of doing things. I kept his treatment of me from my father but told my mother everything. I think that mother found herself trapped between me and her brother but could not do anything about it. Uncle also accused me of not being clever like other boys. That accusation hurt me more than the beatings.

Ploughing time came, which meant that in addition to cultivating the fields we had to live away from home for weeks. It was customary to do that because very early each morning, before we started ploughing, we had to free the oxen so that they could graze for two hours. Because of the heat, which is always strong at that time of the year, we were bound to start work early when it was cool and stop at midday for two hours to enable the oxen to graze again and to take them to the river to drink. The afternoon session started late, when it was cool, and ended after dark; and then, again, the oxen had to be given time to graze for two or three hours before tying them on yokes so that we could go to bed. During the time of ploughing, if we ran short of seeds which had to be fetched from Phokeng, those were the only times that we could travel home at the week-end and return on Sunday with the seeds we needed. It was only on such occasions that I could see my parents and sisters again.

We had to cultivate uncle's fields, his mother-in-law's and my mother's, which were situated far from each other in different areas. If we were not hampered by anything beyond our control, we could finish them all in two months, November and December. If we lost some days because of sickness or heavy rain we would carry on until early January. After ploughing, the oxen joined the other animals, and at that time grazing pastures are green and there is plenty of grass everywhere because of the constant rain.

Nineteen-twenty-three. Ploughing was over and my duties were to follow the cattle every morning into the grazing fields and to see that they did not go into other people's fields and destroy their crops. At that time herd-boys like myself met in the veld, friendly ones mixed their herds and while keeping each other company compared their skills in playing herd-boys' games, trapping birds, working in clay, locating wild fruits and honey, hunting with dogs, and killing unfortunate animals. When the cattle were mixed during the day, elder people knew that the boys did that in order to be together. The elders hated that arrangement of the boys because they said the boys restricted the movements of the animals in order to allow themselves chances of doing what they liked.

Many fathers or elders used secretly to visit us in the veld, and when they found us mixing the animals, punished us heavily. When my uncle found me mixing our cattle with other boys' he punished me without sympathy. It was customary that anyone who visited the boys in the veld and found them mixing the animals must not only punish his boy but the other boys he found with him, so that next time the other boys would know that mixing the cattle led to trouble for all, regardless of whose father or elder paid the visit. We boys knew that as soon as we mixed our cattle we were inviting trouble for ourselves, but we never desisted from such practices. We were always taking chances that maybe that day no one would pay us a visit. Sometimes we got away with it and this encouraged us.

The more we were punished, the more we got together, as though we were defying our elders' instructions. Punishments by beating were very severe; we were ordered to strip naked, lie flat on our bellies, close our eyes and receive the punishment. Some lashes broke our skins open and for weeks we would be suffering from wounds which, when healed, would leave scars for ever on our bodies.

It is still beyond me to understand why other boys were so keen to be with me. Once they saw our cattle, they would drive theirs in the same direction, so that even when I tried hard to avoid them, I would eventually agree to mix our cattle with theirs and begin to play games. I, too, went to them when they tried to avoid me. One of the games which kept us together and even made us forget that we would be visited by an elder during the day we called *kuni*. We played it with buttons. We used sharp flat stones. We dug a not very deep hole in the ground and each one who participated in it contributed buttons. The buttons were given to one boy who was the thrower of the stone, aiming at one button which he must knock out from amongst the others without touching the other buttons. If he succeeded, he had won all the buttons and was crowned the Paramount Chief. That meant that that day he must be served by others; anything they managed to get like wild fruits or honey, anything he must eat first before others could do so.

The more buttons that were collected together, the more difficult it became to succeed in knocking out the button selected for you to knock out. The struggle to become a Paramount Chief would go on for hours, in many cases ending up without anyone having won the title. When we were engaged in it, we would even forget to be on the look-out for the elders. We used to be surprised to see one of them already standing among us saying, 'Are you still carrying on with this thing of restricting the movements of our cattle? Lie down all of you, I am going to punish you all.' In fact we were obedient, none of us would attempt to run away because that would not help. If you did run away your father would be told and he himself would give you the punishment you ought to have received in the veld during the day.

Kuni intensified my uncle's intolerance of me. In his efforts to make me stop playing it, he would punish me with other boys he found me with, and later when we were by ourselves, punish me again, and I would accuse myself of having been foolish in playing *kuni*. But the next day everything would be forgotten, and the struggle for Paramount Chieftaincy would go on as though nothing had happened. If it wasn't *kuni*, it was clay work. If not clay work, other things which kept us together and friendly.

Just as things have their beginning they also have their ending. People meet, work together happily, but the time for them to separate always follows. That happened to my uncle and myself. In April nineteen-twenty-three, on the Sunday following Good Friday, after milking the cows I expected that, as usual, my uncle would take the milk home; but I was wrong. Instead of going home, as I thought, uncle left the milk at the kraal and followed me as I followed the cattle into the grazing valleys, and about an hour later he found me mixing the cattle with other boys' busy playing *kuni*. It was a cloudless day and very warm. Uncle wanted to punish me first before he punished the other boys who were with me. Instead of going down on my belly, as uncle ordered, I ran away and returned to my parents. It was before midday. When I got home only mother was at home. I do not remember where my sisters had gone. I think they had gone to church. Father was not there, but I know that he had not gone to church, because he was not a churchman.

My mother was surprised to see me back so early and wanted to know whether I was sick. I reported to her that I had run away from her brother because he was beating me as was his new habit. Realising that it would have been of no use for her to send me back to uncle because I would have gone somewhere else, mother reluctantly ordered me to stay at home with her until father returned. An hour or two after midday father returned, and he too was surprised to see me home at that time of the day. Without asking me to account for my presence, he asked mother to explain. After he had heard mother's explanation, both of them agreed to wait for uncle's version of the story. Uncle could not follow me home because he had to look after the cattle until the evening.

In the evening, after milking the cattle again and putting them firmly in the kraal, he made his way home, but instead of going to his home, came first to our home, where he found me with my parents. After giving mother part of the milk he brought with him, he told them everything about my behaviour and why he resorted to beating me to make me conform to his orders. Mother and father did not ask me to say anything, as it was not customary to do so, but father spoke against me and scolded me, ordering that in future I must obey my uncle totally and do everything he ordered me to do; otherwise he, father, would join in beating me.

During father's scoldings, which were really forceful, mother remained silent from the beginning to the end. When my father had stopped, Uncle Kristof took over and said, 'You ran away and came back here because you thought that when you were with your parents I could not touch you. I,' said uncle, 'want to tell you that it is not because you are now with your parents that I can't beat you, it's only that I don't want to beat you. If I want to,' he went on, 'I can beat you more than I would have done away from your parents. Now you know,' uncle continued to say, 'that you have no shield here against me.'

Really, all the hopes I had entertained that my parents would warn uncle not to be harsh with me disappeared. I felt alone, with no protectors, completely at the mercy of my uncle. He and my parents left the matter there and began to talk about other things. As was customary, I left them alone to give them a chance to talk more freely, because children were not allowed to be amongst adults when they were in conversation. From that time, and throughout that night, I was deep in thought as to what was going to become of me since uncle had shown me that he was not afraid of my parents as I thought he was. I knew then that running back to them for protection was of no use to me.

The next day, Easter Monday, I left home as usual for the kraal to milk the cows and also to take the cattle into the grazing veld. On the way to the kraal uncle joined me and started to open the matter all over again. He began to tell me that he was still going to teach me a lesson I would never forget as long as I lived. I knew that he meant that he was going to beat me to satisfy himself, because he had not beaten me the day before. As we moved towards the kraal I began to understand the reason uncle did not beat me before my parents was not because he did not want to, but because he did not want to show disregard for them. Had he done so, he would have shown that he had no respect for them at all. It was customary that when one beat a child and it ran to an adult for protection, if one went on beating the child, one was no longer beating the child but the adult from whom the child sought protection. That adult would feel despised and could make a court case against the individual who punished the child. That moral precept kept my uncle from beating me in the presence of my parents.

At that time I knew of a number of Phokeng boys older than me who ran away from home and their parents and went away for a year or two to a German settlement I mentioned earlier called Kroondal, south of Rustenburg. Those boys came back with cows they earned in the years they were away in Kroondal hiring themselves to German farmers there. They talked of how easy it was to get oneself hired to German farmers because they needed herd-boys for their cattle, and at the end of twelve months they paid one with a female calf which later brings in other animals for you and puts you on the road to becoming rich. The Germans were all sons and daughters of missionaries who lived among African tribes and spoke Sesotho very well. Their treatment of the runaway boys was very good; some of them would even know your parents. I heard all those stories from the boys in the veld when we were following our fathers' cattle.

When uncle began to talk of teaching me a lesson, I said quietly to myself, 'Uncle, if you dare to do that we will have reached the end of the road together. I know what I shall do, I shall run away to Kroondal and that will be the end of your guardianship over me.' It was my secret. Uncle and I reached the kraal, milked the cows, and before we opened the kraal to let the cattle out uncle said, holding a rein (called *mokao* in Sesotho) which we used for tying a cow's hind legs while milking it, 'Lie down flat on your belly, close your eyes, I want to teach you that I am your uncle, that what I order you to do must be done.' I tried to plead with my uncle that I should obey him in future if he would forgive me for what took place the day before, but he refused. The cows were all looking on wondering what was wrong. Luckily for me, while we were arguing, in my case pleading for mercy, the mother of a friend of mine passed our kraal and I addressed my appeal to her, asking her to beg uncle to show mercy. After hearing his story about me she refused to persuade my uncle. While they were talking it provided me with an opportunity to escape. I slipped through the entrance and both of them saw me running away and disappearing.

I disappeared amongst the thorn bushes; they lost sight of me and I of them. It was Easter Monday, early in April nineteen-twenty-three, when I started my journey to Kroondal. I was just twelve years old on the first day of that month. I had no food to eat on the way, but I felt free to determine my own fate. Naturally I was sorry to leave my mother, whom I loved more than I can say. I moved southwards from Phokeng towards Rustenburg, which I had not seen before. I knew it was a village of white people, but nothing more. My destination was Kroondal. I estimate that I left my uncle at about eight o'clock in the morning.

There I left my uncle with the cattle on his hands and what he did with them that day I shall never know. That was my answer to his refusal to forgive me. I think that if he had listened and showed mercy I might not have taken that step. He forced me to take that vital decision and provided me with an opportunity to turn my back against Phokeng, my mother, father, sisters and everything I knew and loved in our tribe.

The advice I got from those who had been to Kroondal was that when you reach Rustenburg, avoid entering the town itself because the police might arrest you and after finding out where you came from, return you there. Rustenburg at that time was a small town amongst farms on the east, south and west, with a large area of African tribes in the south-east and the whole of the north. Rustenburg was as dark at night as Phokeng, because there were no electric lights and electricity was unknown.

When I left my mother and Phokeng, I had graduated from the fear that I could only live under my mother or parents' guardianship, protection and guidance. My exile to the cattle-posts a few years before had shown me that, away from parents, life goes on just the same. I knew then that wherever one went, one was bound to make friends and find help. I do not know how my parents felt that evening when uncle came back to tell them that I had run away again, and this time I was not to be found at home. I can imagine how my mother went to bed with no knowledge whether I was dead or alive.

I entered Rustenburg from the north, crossed the river at the eastern side of it near the African location, a place where Africans who had become urbanised lived away from the whites, though they worked for them and met them every day. That was my first encounter with the system of segregation, Apartheid, but I did not know it at the time. Before I crossed the river, feeling hungry, I knelt down and filled my stomach with its water, and into its water I dipped my feet and within a few seconds I reached the southern bank. When I passed near Bethlehem, the African location, no one noticed me, because many African children were playing about there.

I passed Rustenburg on the eastern side and I suppose that even the whites who saw me pass there thought I was a boy from Bethlehem. Having passed Rustenburg, something I was not expecting happened. It was after twelve o'clock that day, when I was pressing on southwards, moving away from Rustenburg, that I saw something completely new and strange to me coming from the south-east, making a great noise. There was thick black smoke coming from the front part of it. A huge black wagon was pulling other wagons, and when it was about to enter the town it whistled three times, warning those who were awaiting its arrival that it was about to enter. It passed me a good distance from its road as I stood wondering what it was. It entered Rustenburg and disappeared from sight with me still not knowing what it was. I had not seen a train in my life. I moved on, and when I reached the fence I saw two long irons on which it ran. At once I remembered the story my Uncle Kristof used to tell me when he still thought the world of me, that a train was a long wagon built of wood and iron. It had steel wheels and ran on steel lines built specially for it. It was pulled by another wagon on which fire was made. Boiling water and fire made it move and it moved very fast.

That story I remembered explained the mystery to me. It was a train. I put my head through the fence, climbed through, stood on one of the two iron bars to test it and went over. I reached the southern side, climbed through the second fence and then moved westwards towards the main road leading to Kroondal. I did not know till later that following that main road could take you to Pretoria and Johannesburg.

XVI My Arrival in Kroondal

Walking confidently southwards away from Rustenburg, firmly believing that I was in an area where no one knew me, I moved along the main road towards Kroondal. It was in the afternoon, the sun was still hot, but I began to feel signs of coolness. Because it was a public holiday, few people were to be seen moving about, and one could see anything coming a long distance away. Not very far from my destination, already in sight of a bridge over the river beyond which the Kroondal area began, I saw a trolley drawn by two mules coming from the opposite direction. I left the main road to walk on the footpath on the eastern side of the main road so as to avoid being run over by the trolley. The occupants of the vehicle were a man and a girl.

When the animal-drawn vehicle drew closer, I heard someone call me by my name loudly, saying, 'Nyadioe! *Oirang fa; Oea, kae?*' ('What are you doing here; where are you going to?') I looked at the trolley and came face to face with a Phokeng girl, my sister's friend called Mamashuku Makgale. I uttered no word in reply but kept on moving. After they had passed me I did not look back and I have no idea whether they looked back or not. Where I expected no one who knew me to see me, someone did see me that knew me. That day I learned never to think that you are alone and no one sees you.

I moved on, reached the bridge, crossed over into the Kroondal area, and at once I was beset by the problem; at which house was I going to start asking for employment? The farms were well cultivated, tobacco crops were beautiful, potato and other crops were equally attractive. The first house on my left, not very far from the main road, was owned by Phokeng-born attorney Kristof Penzhorn, the son of the man who brought Christianity to my tribe. Not far on the right was a large house, a mission house, occupied by their minister and his family. It was used also as board and lodging for German boys and girls sent there by their parents to learn German. Very close was a mill, owned by the Ottomann family, which provided the Kroondal people as well as the neighbouring farmers with their flour.

I kept walking along the main road and further away past the mill I saw two men and two women sitting down under the cool shade of a large tree. I went straight to them.

When I reached the people in the front garden of a beautiful house in Kroondal, one of them, a man who had settled himself on an armchair, filling it with his huge body, facing the direction from which I was approaching, said in clear, loud, faultless Sesotho, 'Boy, you have run away from your home, we don't want runaway boys here.' Those were the words and voice of Mr. Theodore Benholdt, who was born and had grown up in one of our branch villages called Kanana, in the east of Phokeng. He was the son of the Lutheran Church minister. His wife was born and grew up in Phokeng and was the daughter of the Reverend Penzhorn, the man who had converted my maternal grandparents to Christianity.

Obviously, they were not in need of a herd-boy. They did not even ask me where I came from. I have no doubt that if they had, my mention of Phokeng would have roused interest in his wife, who must have known my maternal grandfather, her father's right-hand man in the church. Shabbily dressed, bootless, hatless and hungry, I moved away from them and faced the world alone. I was carrying nothing, I was a traveller with no luggage.

I joined the main road again and continued moving southwards. Throwing my eyes far ahead of me, I saw a tall well-built old man coming towards me from the opposite direction. I stopped the old man, greeted him and spoke to him in Sesutho. I do not know what made me think that he knew my friend, but I asked him if he knew where I could find Ngatlhe Kgokong, a Phokeng boy who had also run away to Kroondal, who had already been there more than twelve months when I arrived. The old man replied in Dutch, because he could not speak a word in Sesotho. We at once found that we were miles apart in languages. The old man was Mr. Herbert Lange. He then invited me to follow him by waving a calling hand to me. I responded and he took me to the house which was formerly his own, but which he had given to his son Herman and daughter-in-law Ida. Herman and his wife Ida were Sesotho-speaking, but Herman was not as good at speaking the language as his wife. Herman made mistakes in conversation by treating persons in speech as though they were animals or things. Ida, on the other hand, was perfect, though she spoke a different accent from mine. At Herman and Ida's place I found a new home. My fears as to where I was going to sleep that night disappeared.

By the time I reached Kroondal I had already made up my mind to disguise myself. I was mindful of the fact that back in Phokeng my parents would do everything in their power to find me. The best thing to do, I said to myself, was to change my name. I convinced myself that a change of name would conceal me as though I was changing my looks at the same time. Though I had been seen by someone who knew me when I was about to enter the Kroondal area, I still thought that my parents would find it difficult to trace me. One thing did not leave my mind, and that was that as soon as my sister's friend Mamashuku Makgale arrived back in Phokeng, her first duty would be to tell my sister that she saw me near Kroondal.

Mr. Herbert Lange having brought me to his son and daughter-in-law, Herman and Ida, I hired myself to them for a period of a year for a female calf at the end of that period. When Herman Lange asked me what my name was I told him it was Johannes. I was never named Johannes. It was only an attempt on my part to avoid being traced by my parents. However, there it was, I named myself Johannes in Kroondal.

My first year with the Langes was a mixture of duties. At times I worked in the fields leading a team of oxen pulling the plough, cultivating the fields or pulling the farm rake levelling the earth the plough had turned upside down or inside out. On other occasions I went out with the cattle for grazing, leaving in the morning and returning shortly before sunset. All Kroondal farmers were using ox teams to cultivate their fields. All of them had large numbers of cattle from which they got milk and butter. I think that five or six weeks after I had hired myself to the Langes, one afternoon while I was leading a team of oxen driven by a man named Hendrik, I was called back to the house.

When I got to the house, I found my mother and sister Majone waiting to see me. Instead of greeting them with pleasure and a smiling face, I greeted them with tears rolling down my cheeks. I was appealing to them not to take me back with them to my uncle whom I was no longer inclined to work with. Mother, moved by my distress, waited until I had stopped weeping. After I had stopped, as though my head had no more tears to release, mother greeted me with motherly love and said, 'We are here sent by your father only to find out where you are, but not to take you away. Your father says that taking you away would be useless, because you would run away again and perhaps go farther than you have gone.' My employer, Mr. Herman Lange, and his wife Ida, were listening all the time. Mother thanked them for having looked after me until she came and said further that my appearance convinced her that they were looking after me well and would continue to do so.

Mother then told them that my name was not Johannes, but Naboth. Mr. Lange replied that since it was easy for them to call me Johannes, they would continue to call me by that name. Afterwards, mother and my sister left, saying that since the day was far spent they would spend the night at Bethlehem Location in Rustenburg with friends of my family. I stayed behind, relieved, knowing that I had permission from my parents to work for the Langes for a female calf to be given to me at the end of twelve months.

The hiring of myself to the Langes in Kroondal showed me two things which I did not know existed. The European way of life as practised in South Africa, and Segregation, Apartheid. At first, though I did not ask, I wondered why we, the black people who worked for the Langes, slept in a tobacco shed and wheat store which was next to the horse stable. There were no chairs for us to sit down on or tables in the place where we slept. I was an innocent tribal boy beginning to live in a different world from the one I was born into and knew. One evening, it was a warm evening, still light, but stars were beginning to appear in the sky, and Mr. Herman Lange called his older men together to give them orders about the next day's work and to get reports from others as to how they performed the tasks he had set them in the morning. They all sat on the ground.

While Mr. Herman Lange's workmen sat on the ground, he sat on a bench alone giving the instructions about the next day's work in the fields and talking to others whom he had not found time to visit in the fields where they worked that day. Innocently, I joined them and went straight to the bench and sat next to Mr. Lange. All the older men and others who were already accustomed to the European way of life in South Africa became breathless. They had not seen anything like that before. An old man who drove the team of oxen I led that day tried to take me away from the bench, but Mr. Lange spoke to him in Dutch, saying, 'Leave him, he is still stupid. Talk to him afterwards; make him understand.'

Later, when the meeting was over, the old man, whose name was Hendrik, took me aside and said, 'Boy, you mustn't sit where a white man sits; you can't sit on the chairs they use, drink from the cups they use, eat from their plates, or sleep in the same house with them. Don't do it again,' he said. 'Didn't you see us all sitting on the ground? You are lucky,' Hendrik continued, 'he didn't push you off or beat you, to teach you that you can't sit on the same bench as a white man.' I did not ask why, or say anything. I only listened to what Hendrik told me. That was the day on which I came into contact with colour segregation. I was twelve years old. At first, when I began to work for the Langes, I wondered why we were not sharing the house with them, or why there was no house built for us to sleep in. Hendrik explained all to me in a short time. I learned and never repeated my mistake.

As time went by I noticed that we at the Langes were not the only ones who slept in the shed or in buildings which were not built for people to sleep in. It was the same throughout Kroondal. Only female servants slept in rooms built specially for them very close to the masters' houses, so that a watch could be kept over them. Kroondal farmers and their wives were very strict with their female servants. I cannot recall a single case of a girl who worked for them and returned to her parents pregnant. I am sure that the reason Mr.

113

Lange did not push me off the bench was that he was not a rough, violent man. During the two years I spent with him I did not once hear him swear or beat anyone, although he was strict.

Herman Lange and his wife Ida, though they practised segregation like other farmers of Kroondal and the rest of the Europeans in South Africa, were good and kind people. Like the rest of the Kroondal farmers, they cared very much for their workmen and women. Farmers' wives baked and cooked for all of us. Everyone who worked for them had enough to eat. They grew peas, potatoes, wheat, maize, fruits of many varieties, but not oranges. They were not for the market, but for domestic use. Only tobacco was grown for the market. The maize porridge which was eaten by African workmen was cooked by female servants, who were found in every Kroondal home.

There was plenty of meat, mostly pork. Every winter season, pigs were reared, fed well three times a day, and by the time the next winter set in they were fat and some could hardly move. Then the slaughtering of the pigs began, providing everybody with fresh pork to enjoy. In every Kroondal home at that time, everybody ate and enjoyed tasty home-made pork sausages, and some polonies made of pigs' blood mixed with small pieces of pork. Milk, too, was produced for domestic use, though work people had to wait for it a day or so until the cream for butter-making had been taken from it. Pigs too enjoyed a good deal of it. No one who was at Kroondal at the time could complain of want of food.

Breakfast consisted of a large slice of white or brown bread baked by the farmer's wife and a large mug of coffee. The mug was made out of a jam tin by a Scotch plumber and blacksmith who lived in Kroondal mending farmers' ploughs, pots and everything requiring mending. The Scotch plumber was not married and lived alone in one room behind his workshop. He was a short man with bushy eyebrows. He may have understood everything spoken in German, but I doubt whether he spoke the language, because he was spoken to only in his own language. I saw him on two occasions playing his pipes at a wedding. On the whole he seemed a lonely man, because on Sundays, when he was free from his hammers and fires, he was always sitting alone by his workshop or taking long walks enjoying the weather and fresh air. Kroondal was a lovely place, especially when crops and plants in the farmlands were green. The farms were well worked and well irrigated. As a Christian community, Kroondal farmers ceased work on Sundays and so did their work people.

On my arrival at the Langes I found them with only one child, a daughter Elizabeth who was eighteen months old. There were no other children of her age nearby, so Elizabeth had no one to play with and spent most of the time with her mother. Although Kroondal farmers as I have already said, spoke Sesotho perhaps better than I could do in my young days, in addition they spoke Dutch – known today in South Africa as Afrikaans. I do not know how well they spoke English. But they saw to it that they spoke to their children in German and encouraged them to feel that they were Germans.

There were in other Kroondal homes children of both sexes who were born there and never lived in African tribal villages as had their parents, who spoke very fluent Sesotho: these were children of families like the Penzhorns, the Benholdts, the Millers, the Bakebergs and the family of Hendrik Jorde. Parents of those families were born in African tribal villages and their children were born in Kroondal, but the children spoke Sesotho as fluently as their parents. I still do not know how they acquired the language, because all the time I was there their parents spoke to them only in German.

When they spoke Sesotho, one would never have imagined that they spoke German as well. I think that speaking the same language draws people together. The white children of Kroondal of my age were very fond of the people who worked for their parents. In school holidays or on Saturdays, when they were free from school, the boys wanted to go out with us into the grazing fields with their fathers' cattle and to be there the whole day playing games with us. Their parents were dead against their going out with the cattle, but some boys used to run away from home to join us. On many occasions we were found with them swimming naked in the dams. Only when they were at school did their parents know that they were not with African boys in the grazing fields. I had no such boy at the Langes. Some boys told me that their boss's sons stole things for them that they thought their parents were not giving them.

I have no knowledge whether Elizabeth Lange ever managed to speak Sesotho, the language her mother spoke so well. I last saw her in nineteen-twenty-five, in the middle of May, when I returned to Phokeng. When I left South Africa twenty-nine years later, she must have grown into a woman of thirty years old, perhaps married with children of her own. One day when I was already a resident of Pretoria, amongst crowds in busy Church Street, I found myself standing next to her mother, Ida Lange, and a well-built young woman who was talking to her. I recognised Ida Lange and convinced myself that the young woman must be her daughter Elizabeth. To avoid embarrassing them, with great sorrow in my heart and regret, I refrained from saying 'Hello' to them. I did that because in South Africa, where a non-white and a white are forbidden by law to fraternise, I was not sure that they would have welcomed it. They might have welcomed it somewhere else where they would not have been seen shaking hands with a black man, laughing and reminding each other of the past, but I doubt if it would have been the case in Church Street, Pretoria, amongst crowds of Europeans.

I am sure also that Elizabeth had heard a lot about me from her parents; she might have been pleased to meet me and to know someone who had at one time lived on her parents' property and seen her every day for two years. But things which were not of my making, nor Elizabeth's, stood in our way. Later, when I thought of it all, I at times blamed myself for not having taken a risk, taken the bull by the horns and said 'Hello' to the woman who for two years looked on me as though I was a real member of her family, who on many occasions sat next to me in a horse-drawn cart, being driven to her mother's home. As they moved away from me in Pretoria, I stepped aside on the pavement, looked at them disappearing from my sight and said, 'If anyone asked me where I thought Hell was situated, I would say, "Where I stand now". Hell is where people are denied meeting because they differ in colour.'

I saw in Pretoria many young men and women I knew in Kroondal; the Penzhorns, the Benholdts, the Millers and others, but I could not reveal to them that I knew them because of the same fears that they might have felt offended, or that their friends might think that they fraternised with someone of my colour.

The Lange family and others in Kroondal claimed that they were God-fearing and loving Christians. They were Lutherans with a lovely church, to which they went at least once every Sunday. I recognised its beauty from outside, though I never saw its interior. The farmers went to worship in it with their wives and children but with no one else. They were not the only families of Christians in Kroondal. Every farmer's family had African families living as squatters on their land who must work for the right to live there each time the farmer wanted them to. The Langes had such families. Every farmer had such families. The man Hendrik who talked to me about black and white relationships was the father of such a family of squatters.

There were two squatters' villages in Kroondal when I arrived there. The first village was very near the houses of the farmers on the southern side of the farmlands; it was a stone's throw from the Jordes', the Millers' and the Scotch plumber's houses. The second village was a mile or three-quarters of a mile to the south-east. Both villages were inhabited by Sesotho-speaking people. They were all Christians and Lutherans. There were two Lutheran churches in Kroondal. Each had its own priest. The Europeans' minister lived in Kroondal and the Africans' minister lived in Rustenburg and had an assistant African minister living in one of Phokeng's villages, Luka, many miles away. Black and white Lutheran congregations did not mix. They sang the same-sounding hymns and had church

116

services conducted in the same Lutheran ways, but they worshipped separately. The church for African worship was also beautiful but, like the European one, I saw it only from outside. The minister from Rustenburg and the Reverend Koos Khunou from Luka-Phokeng rarely came to Kroondal.

During my first year with the Langes, due to the fact that their daughter Elizabeth spoke only German, I listened very carefully to her mother as she told her the names of various objects and silently, on my own, repeated them so that next time I could communicate with Elizabeth. Within a few months her parents and other people were surprised that Elizabeth and I could talk to each other, though in a small way. Visitors to the Langes also began to wonder at how quickly I was able to learn a few things in German. Many people who had been in Kroondal before me complained that the German people did not want their language to be known because they never spoke to them in German. I found that when the German people of Kroondal heard me speak German, instead of being angry they were pleased, laughed, and were eager to know how I picked it up. Some who heard me, even when they met me in the street, spoke to me in their language, and where they found that I did not follow, explained to me in Sesotho.

There was no school for African squatters' children when I got there, although there was a church for them. In the absence of the minister, there was in the area an African church elder who held services every Sunday. For several months, boys and girls who had reached confirmation age attended catechism classes under him. Before I left Kroondal, due to the squatters' demands, a day school was started for their children. An African teacher came along; I do not know who paid for his services, or what subjects he taught, but I heard from some that in addition to Sesotho he taught them English. Some farmers disliked their being taught English but did not object to Sesotho.

Amongst the things I learned in Kroondal was catching and eating fish, swimming and diving in the deep waters of the dams and playing the three-stringed guitars we made ourselves out of one-gallon paraffin tins and pieces of plank. I was good at playing the instrument, but there were others who played much better than I did and went on to learn to play six-stringed guitars, but I never managed. I learned, too, how to catch live frogs; we then killed them and used them as a bait to trap fishes in the nearby River Oorsak, south of Kroondal. The River Oorsak had some deep spots where we used to swim if we were not near any of the three big, deep dams which the river supplied with water. The Oorsak started from huge mountains called the Magaliesberg, ran westwards, and when it reached Kroondal the farmers diverted its water to fill their dams, which they used to irrigate their cultivated lands. The river had endless movement of shellfish, big and small, as well as other varieties of fishes. The water was so clean and clear that at times we used to sit down and admire fishes which passed by, swimming beautifully up and down the river, big ones chasing small ones.

We would trap fishes, end their lives, make a fire to fry them and then eat them saltless. We did this so often that in the end we got used to eating them without salt. They tasted nice and we liked quarrelling amongst ourselves that others were cheating by taking bigger portions. The Oorsak area was one of Kroondal's cattle-grazing fields. The farmers did not object to us mixing their cattle as long as we did not restrict their movements. The Oorsak had an endless flow of water and herds could drink and still leave the Oorsak flowing and filling the Kroondal dams. When we were not busy trapping the fishes, or when we could not eat any more of the fishes we caught and fried, we taught each other tunes on the three-stringed instruments, or danced while someone entertained us with music. I made many friends amongst squatters' boys and others, who like me were in Kroondal to earn themselves cows, which were regarded as the means by which later on in life one would become a rich and respected man in his community.

Most of us were under sixteen years of age. With plenty of tobacco around us, we began to roll cigarettes with any paper we could lay hands on, and as a result most of the boys became permanent smokers. I followed others, but never became a permanent smoker, and looking back I cannot trace anyone on either side of my family being a smoker. My father took snuff. He was the only one I knew who carried a tobacco product with him. Otherwise tobacco had no place in our family. I like to feel that was the reason why I never became a permanent smoker in Kroondal. Each of the boys who went out with the cattle carried with him a large slice of bread as his lunch. With fried fishes we used to make it a big feast.

XVII The Langes' Second Child

Towards the end of my first year with the Langes, Ida, Mrs. Lange, began to expect her second child, who turned out to be a boy. Ida developed a liking for me and pressed her husband Herman to allow her to make me her houseboy. That meant that I would have to cease going out with the animals, or being used to lead teams of oxen during the cultivation of farmlands. She said that she needed someone to send about, someone she could use without disrupting any of her husband's plans. The husband at first tried to resist her demands by offering to get a young African girl from one of the squatters' families to be at her disposal, but Ida refused, saying that the girl her husband was suggesting would not chop wood for her, would not carry bread-pans, would not empty flour bags into the bath at the time of baking, would not make fire for her in the oven, clear fire from it, put pans of bread into it and take them out when the bread was ready. Herman again offered to give her a man to help her when she needed one, but Ida put her foot down.

They also owned a horse called Baby. Before she became pregnant Ida used to harness the horse herself, inspan it and drive herself and Elizabeth to her mother who lived alone on an estate three or four miles south of Kroondal. Ida argued further that she could no longer be expected to harness the horse herself and drive herself to her mother. Herman had no answer to that, so he gave in. From that day I became Ida's houseboy. Other boys and other people who were already there became very jealous, but there was nothing they could do about it. I began my second year having a soft and easy life with the Langes. Everything Ida ate, she shared with me and Elizabeth.

I did not clean the house because there was Rosina, an African female servant working in place of her father who was in ill-health. My duties were to gather eggs, to harness the horse whenever Ida wanted to travel to her mother, and to do all the other things I have mentioned. I was also charged with wheelbarrowing a bag of wheat to the Ottomanns' mill to be ground into flour and to fetch it when ready. During that period, I learned more and more German words from both Elizabeth and her mother. Ida began to speak to me in German and corrected me where I went wrong.

During my second year I was frequently to be seen in the afternoons leaving the Langes' yard, driving Ida and her daughter to her mother's place, the little girl sitting between me and her mother. On our return I was equally frequently to be seen leading Baby the horse round the yard, softening its feet before I put it into the stable and fed it. I arrived at the Langes with no boots, having never worn them before, and left without having seen my feet inside a pair of them. I was not the only one, only adult Europeans wore shoes or boots. Their children, boys and girls, moved about and went to school barefoot.

One day Ida was not as I usually knew her; she was quiet and seemed worried. I just could not make out what disturbed her mind. In the afternoon, after lunch, she ordered me to harness the horse while she wrote a letter. When I was ready I told her that I was waiting in front of the house with the cart, hoping that I was taking her to see her mother. She gave me the letter and said, 'Take it to my mother.' That day I went alone. After my arrival there I waited, and within twenty or more minutes, Ida's mother went to the next door farm-house to ask them to look after her dogs, fowls, the house itself and her orange trees. She left her house with suitcases containing her belongings and I drove her back to Kroondal. She had a horse and cart of her own, but left them in the care of her neighbours.

We arrived back after sunset, it was already getting dark, and found that Ida had given birth to a son, assisted by her sister-in-law, Mrs. Jorde, who was the only midwife I knew in Kroondal at the time. I did not know what had happened until I heard laughter and the cry of the newly-born baby. The first to break the news to me was Elizabeth, who was enchanted by the event. Later, when I was in the stable feeding the horse, Mr. Herman Lange came along and said to me, 'Missis has a baby'. He was speaking in Sesotho ('*Missis o filoe ngoana*'). The baby boy was named after his paternal grandfather, Heinrich Herbert. Dutch-speaking people called him Hendrik. He became one of my duties. I worked my second and last year with the Langes looking after Heinrich, and saw him grow to like me. At times I dropped him, hurt him, gave him wrong things to eat which made him uncomfortable, and taught him to understand signs when I wanted him to stop crying. We became such friends that sometimes when I was leaving him with his mother he cried for me.

Amongst various domesticated pets, birds, cattle and others there was a black dog called Nero and a female cat which seemed to have the stamina to give birth to a good number of kittens twice yearly at the Langes. Nero the dog developed an intense liking for me and influenced me to like him. On many occasions when I went out of the yard Nero saw no reason not to accompany me. At times, he would let me go, and when I was a good distance from home would use his power at running to catch up with me before I disappeared from his sight.

One day Ida Lange asked me to take a bag of wheat on a two-wheel push-truck to the Ottomanns' mill to be turned into flour, and to collect it that afternoon. Immediately after I had left the yard, I noticed Nero walking by my side, but not helping me to push the truck. The bag of wheat was heavy for me and all along the way to the mill I kept stopping to gather more strength. Sometimes Nero walked ahead of me, as if he was saying, 'Come along, the bag is not all that heavy.' We reached the mill eventually and I delivered the bag and asked the Ottomanns whether we could fetch the flour in the afternoon, and they told me to fetch it any time after lunch. In order to avoid pushing the empty truck back, I left it at the mill. Nero and I began our walk back home. That was an unfortunate day for Nero, because his life ended that day.

As we walked along the main road we saw a black motor-car approaching us from the back, from the north, moving southwards as we were. I was walking ahead of Nero, but did not look back to see where he was or what he was doing. He had decided to walk on the opposite side of the road from me, and when he heard the noise of the motor-car, he decided to cross over to my side, but the vehicle was too close and moving fast. Nero, unfortunately, could not out-run it; the machine ran him over. All I heard was Nero crying in agony under the vehicle, and when he managed to get out great damage had been caused to his health and body. When Nero reached my side of the road, he was in great pain and unable to move. The vehicle stopped a few feet away and out of it emerged a well-dressed European man who began to speak to me in a language I was unable to follow. I am sure he spoke in English, asking me whose dog Nero was, but I replied in German, crying, asking him why he killed Nero. We failed to communicate, there was no one in sight, the man went back into his vehicle and drove off.

In a few minutes Nero was dead. I moved his dead body into a ditch near the main road, and left, with tears still dropping from my eyes, to report his death to Ida Lange. On my arrival Ida did not notice Nero's absence, but the grimness of my face convinced her that there was something wrong with me. 'What's wrong?' she asked. 'Why have you been crying?' 'Nero got killed,' I replied. 'Where? By whom?' she asked again with forceful voice. I explained that he was run over by a motor-car and the man who drove it spoke words I did not understand and drove away afterwards. Knowing that I knew nothing about taking registration numbers of a motor-car, she did not even ask me whether I could remember the numbers of the motor-car which killed Nero. Both of us only wondered what Mr. Lange would say when he heard the news of Nero's death. My feelings were put at rest. Mrs. Lange did not scold me or promise to urge her husband to beat me. I knew that whatever Mr. Lange would say his wife would be on my side. When he came back from the fields for lunch his wife told him all about it, and defended me at the same time, saying that the fault was of the man who drove the motor-car.

After lunch I was told to take the wheelbarrow to fetch Nero's dead body to be buried in the Langes' area somewhere in the fields. This I did and on my return I found that a hole had been dug near the river which ran very close to the Langes' home, and under a large peach tree the remains of Nero were put to rest. Later I was on my way again to the Ottomanns' mill to fetch the flour, which was ready by then. When I left them, the Langes had not bothered to get another dog.

Towards the beginning of the summer of nineteen-twenty-four, disturbing news from Phokeng reached me through a message to Ida Lange. She received a telephone call at the Kroondal post office in Mr. Augustus Behrens' store (the only place in the town with a telephone) from Reverend Ernest Penzhorn in Phokeng, saying that my twin sister Martha was sick and I should be told of her sickness. When I got the news I became very sad, wondering what was going to happen to my sister, because the message Ida received emphasised that her survival was very much in doubt.

I think that two or three weeks later, another message came by telephone from Phokeng, again from Mr. Penzhorn, this time wanting to speak to Mr. Herman Lange himself. My parents had asked Mr. Penzhorn to use his influence on the Langes and ask them to permit me to return to Phokeng because my sister was critically sick and had asked to see me. On his return Mr. Lange told his wife why he was called to the telephone, and they agreed at once, before they told me of the message, that I should be on my way to Phokeng the next morning. They then called me and told me to get ready for the journey.

The next morning, as arranged, I left for Phokeng, which I had not seen for over a year. That time I passed through Rustenburg because I was armed with a special travelling pass, in case I met the police on the way and they wanted to check on me. I walked all the way from Kroondal to Phokeng and reached my birthplace after sunset. My parents, my sisters, and those relatives who had come to help nurse my sister were delighted to see me. According to them I had grown and changed. The news of my arrival was kept from my sister until the next day. She slept, still thinking that I was in Kroondal. The following day my presence was revealed to her, and she asked that I should be allowed to come to where she was at that time, being unable to rise on her own. She was so happy to see me that she asked that she should be given some food and that I should feed her. While I fed her, she talked to me at length, telling me that she had been afraid that she would die before seeing me. She said, among other things, that I should not be worried like our parents about her, because nothing unusual was going to happen to her.

While I was feeding my sick sister, she stressed firmly to me that I should remember at all times that I was the only living son of our parents and that Father and Mother would require my assistance and care later in their lives. She said, 'You must not go away from them. You must know that without your help and care when they are old they will be helpless. If,' she went on, 'during your lifetime and theirs you find that you live away from them, you must make it your duty to go where they are to see what help they need and, if you can provide it, you must do so with an open heart.' She kept coming to the point that I should not worry about her as she would get well one day and nothing unknown or unusual was going to happen to her. She was really very ill, and her voice, though clear, was weak. Mother and others who were nearby at the time felt that she was tired, and that to enable her to rest I should be taken away from her. I went away and she stopped talking.

Two days after my arrival in Phokeng from Kroondal my sister reached the end of her life. She died on a Saturday morning and her funeral took place the next day, Sunday afternoon, in Phokeng graveyard, very close to the Lutheran Church. Before the burial, a service was held in the Lutheran Church, conducted by Reverend Ernest Penzhorn. Because of it, Aunt Emma Rangaka entered her former church for the first time since she had left it with her husband Tau Daniel Rangaka. On that occasion I saw my father in church for the first time.

I spent ten days in Phokeng after my sister's death before returning to Kroondal. My Uncle Kristof Mororo, whom I ran away from, was there, but he never asked me why I chose to desert him. On my second Sunday in Phokeng, a brass band from Rustenburg came along to entertain the Paramount Chief Molotlegi Augustus Mokgatle and the people of his tribe. The men who played in the brass band were urbanised, but still regarded themselves as his people.

The brass band which performed at the Chief's place under the conductorship of a man called Antoni, who was also the band's drummer, attracted large crowds, and being a Sunday it seemed as though most of the inhabitants of Phokeng were at the Chief's place. I went to join the crowds and like everyone present enjoyed the music which was pouring out of Antoni's band's trumpets. During the performance the band played a tune or song, the name of which I cannot remember, and everyone there was enchanted by it. When the band ended the tune, a man called Rangkokoropane Mokgatle, who had been sitting down during the performance, jumped to his feet and, waving his hat, shouted three times, 'Again, Again, Again'. Members of the band, who had sat down, rose to play the same tune again. When they had finished there was great applause and whistling from the crowd. I caught up that word 'again', memorised it many times thereafter and carried it with me back to Kroondal. I understood what it meant, but I had no idea that it was an English word.

Back in Kroondal, where drinking water was pumped from closed wells by hand pumps, I used the word at the Langes one afternoon. Elizabeth Lange, their daughter, said to me that she was thirsty and wanted water to drink. She took her mug, I took mine, and both of us started operating the hand pump. First Elizabeth held her mug near the mouth of the pump and I pumped water into it. The mug was filled and I stopped to enable her to drink her water. Afterwards it was Elizabeth's turn to pump water for me. The pump was not easy to operate and young people like Elizabeth found it hard. She operated it by jumping up to the handle and with the weight of her body pulled it down again. Not enough water came out to fill my mug and I said to her 'Again', and Elizabeth stopped, wondering what I was saying. I repeated 'Again', and she moved away from the pump. I pointed to the handle and said 'Again'. The young girl still did not move. She spoke only German, as I have already said. Her mother Ida then said to me, 'Speak German, she knows no English. You are speaking English to her.' Only from that moment did I know that 'again' was an English word. Mrs. Lange did not ask me where I learned the word although she had never heard me speak English before.

I was doing my second year, working for a second cow. It was customary with German farmers of Kroondal, at the end of the first year and subsequent years, to invite an African boy who had hired himself to them for a cow a year to choose for himself the one he liked from amongst the young calves to be earmarked for him. I did not get such treatment from the Langes. I was doing my second year, but still did not know the calf I was going to get or its colour. It was not because there were no calves from which I could have chosen, but Mr. Herman Lange had made up his mind to go to Rustenburg market at the end of my second year to buy cows for me. Like other boys who worked for other farmers, I disliked cows chosen for me. We were told by those who knew more about animals than we did that when one accepted a cow that one wanted to rear, and expected to breed from and milk, one should know its history. If its mother was a cow which produced plenty of milk and was a good breeder, the calf was bound to be as good as its mother. It was also said that if a person to whom one had hired oneself for a cow allowed one to choose for oneself, that person wished the one who worked for him good luck and expected the cow to make the one who received it a wealthy person in the future.

Though generally speaking I was happy with the Langes, I was nevertheless disappointed that I was not allowed to pick out a cow from the Langes' herds, from the cows I knew well. Although I did not say so to anyone, I had a bitter complaint that I was going to be given cows I didn't know, cows which I would not be able to talk about. It was a pleasure to talk to people about your cow and its background. I felt that I was deprived of that right. Though eventually Mr. Lange did go to the market and bought me two cows at the end of two years and there was no complaint that he did not reward me for my services, I never liked them. I took them because I had no choice.

In addition to introducing me to the English language by saying that I was speaking English by saying 'again' to Elizabeth, Mrs. Ida Lange taught me other things as well. For three weeks in winter after the killing of pigs, I had to make a smoke fire in the room called the smoke-room, in which pork was stored. Every day during the first week I had to gather sawdust or very small pieces of wood, make a fire on a piece of zinc and add pieces of paper, grass and wood, or spread sawdust to produce dense smoke. The smokeroom had only one door but no windows which would allow air to come in or smoke to escape. Thereafter I would close the door tightly, so that the room could be filled with thick smoke for the whole day. The smoke would darken the pork or other meat in the room. Once that had been done worms would never get a chance to get into the meat to cause rottenness. The second week I used to make a fire in the smoke-room only twice, and the third week only once.

Once the pork or meat had been darkened in the smoke-room it remained fresh inside as long as it hung there. Each time it was cut for cooking, it was as fresh as ever. That was how Kroondal farmers got their meat supply. They had birds, too, but the Langes very rarely slaughtered one of their fowls. They used to sell their eggs to Mr. Augustus Behrens, the storekeeper, who in turn sold them to hotels in Rustenburg, grocery stores, boarding houses and restaurants. With the proceeds they got from selling eggs, they bought whatever things they needed from Mr. Behren's store. Many farms had many peach trees which yielded large amounts of peaches each year. When they were ripe, they were picked, peeled and preserved in jars to be eaten whenever they were needed. The surplus were dried, to be eaten as dried fruits or cooked for jam making. All the farmers' wives I knew were very good at making such things. When the fruit was ripe, we were allowed to eat it when we wanted to but not to waste it. Things like potatoes, which as I have already pointed out were not for the market, were part of daily meals.

I can remember nothing the working people were not allowed to eat in Kroondal, except for butter, which was kept away from them and was only for the farmers and their families. That was my life in Kroondal, which I shall never cease to remember.

XVIII My Departure

At the end of two years and three months I left the Langes and
Kroondal, accompanied by another tribal boy from Phokeng called
Chianyana Rathebe. He had joined me at the Langes at the beginning of my second year. We had three cows between us which Mr.
Herman Lange bought us at Rustenburg cattle market. Chianyana
was two years older than I was and we were born in the same street
in the part of Phokeng called Saron. It was in the middle of July
nineteen-twenty-five when we said good-bye to Kroondal. Many
months before my departure Mrs. Ida Lange did her utmost to
persuade me to stay another year, because she liked me and their son
Hendrik was so used to me looking after him. I was so homesick
that, though I had no complaint against the Langes' treatment of
me, Ida's appeals got into my right ear and got out through the left
ear.

It was because of homesickness that I left, and my father's call that
I should return to Phokeng because he wanted me to go to school.
I was fourteen years of age and my father was worried that if he
allowed me to stay away much longer, I would never go to school
and would die a man who could not read or write. He had not gone
to school himself, but since my four sisters had been to school, I, his
only living son and the one who would perpetuate his name, should
also go to school. Ida suspected that it was not because I was homesick that I wanted to leave. She complained that I was hiding from
her that I felt unjustly treated. On more than one occasion she
begged me to be frank with her and tell her the real truth why I was
leaving. When I mentioned homesickness and my father's call she
offered to ask my father to allow me to stay another year, and for the
cure of homesickness, she said they could let me go back to Phokeng
for three weeks. But, as I have already said, a third year was too
much for me.

I noticed that Mr. Herman Lange did not co-operate with his wife
in urging me to stay. Though I did not tell Ida, there was also inside
me a suspicion that her husband was not keen to keep me on because
he could not use me as he did the other boys. What discouraged me
was that one day one of the men said I was leaving because I wanted
to go to school, and when Mr. Lange heard this he laughed and asked,
'What would a monkey do with education?' His remark went deep

into my feelings. I did not resent what he said about education or school, but the fact that he compared me to a monkey.

I am not suggesting that Herman Lange was not a kind man to me, but rather that he seemed to think that I was not contributing enough for the cows he was going to pay me with. I do not know whether if I had not been taken away from him against his will to become his wife's boy and enjoy an easy life at the house, he would have given me cows from his own herds. I still think that Chianyana got a cow bought from the cattle market in Rustenburg because of me, and that if he had decided to stay on for the second year and leave after I had left, he would have been given the chance of selecting his second cow from the Langes' herds. Even the day before my departure Mrs. Lange was still urging me to change my mind. I shall never forget the question she asked me on the morning of my departure, which I did not answer. She asked me, 'Are you really going away from me, Hendrik, Elizabeth and everything I have done for you since you came here?' I looked at her and saw tears in her eyes. I moved away from her and Hendrik in her arms, and from my eyes, too, tears began to fall.

My two cows were tied together in the kraal at that time, and when the other cows were released to go out for grazing, they were left with Chianyana's cow in the kraal so that we could move them out easily. After breakfast, reluctantly, Ida gave us a big piece of bread to take with us to eat on our way to Phokeng. I do not know whether Hendrik and his sister Elizabeth knew what was happening. Herman Lange left for the fields after he had wished us a smooth journey. When Chianyana released our cows from the kraal, I tried in vain to say good-bye to Ida and her children. She had made it clear to me before that she could not bear seeing me going away. She only said good-bye to me by word of mouth. She locked herself and the children in the room to avoid seeing me moving away from them.

Armed with permits for our cows to leave Kroondal for Phokeng, Chianyana Rathebe and myself said good-bye to the farmers, the friends we had made there and everything we liked and hated there. By the time I left Kroondal it was not as I had found it in nineteen-twenty-three. The farmers during that time had decided to divide their land into separate camps, each having his own camp where his African farm squatters could build their homes and others where their cattle could graze. The African villages had been demolished and there were fenced camps even where the villages had stood. Only the Lutheran Church was still standing where I found it. Since the villages were scattered about in the camps, the school for African children was no longer there and the teacher had left. I do not know whether after my departure a new one was built.

We arrived late the same day that we had left Kroondal, and

found that Phokeng cattle were already in their kraals. During the time I was in Kroondal, Father and his brother-in-law, Uncle Kristof Mororo, had separated, and Father had given his cattle to one of his friends called Dikobe to look after for him. They were not in Phokeng but far away at a cattle-post. One of the Mokgatles, Rabali, had some of his cattle and oxen in Phokeng and father asked him for permission to put my cows in his kraal while he was making plans to take them to Dikobe's cattle-post. Rabali agreed, but said that I had to go out with them every morning to see that they did not get lost, because they were new in Phokeng and were not used to his cattle. Harvesting of winter crops was in full force and instead of enjoying Phokeng, which I had not seen for more than two years, I was going out daily with the cattle as I had done before I ran away to Kroondal. None of the boys of my age was any longer about going out with animals, and I was therefore the only one over the age of fourteen still following the animals. I knew not a single one of the young boys and they did not know me.

Three weeks after my return, Mr. Dikobe arrived to take my cows to his cattle-post. The Phokeng schools were on holiday until the beginning of September, and I then asked my parents for permission to go and seek work for three weeks on the orange farms beyond Kroondal, south-west of Rustenburg and west of Kroondal. It was orange-picking time and father reluctantly agreed after I promised that I would come back in time to start school.

I set out from Phokeng with Chianyana Rathebe for the citrus farms to pick oranges at the place called by the Africans Njedimane, by the Europeans Kommissiedrift, alongside the huge mountains called the Magaliesberg. At Kommissiedrift we got jobs on a farm owned by a man called William Rex, who ran the farm jointly with his brother Jack.

In the same area were other citrus farms owned by their other three brothers. Before their time it was all one farm owned by their father, John Rex. After their father's death, as always happens, the five sons divided the farm, each running his own part, but still growing oranges for export and sale in South African markets. William and Jack Rex engaged us for thirty shillings a month each, providing us with board and lodging. Every tree was carrying red, well-ripened navel oranges, big and small, sweet and bitter. We found that there were other boys and girls from Phokeng who had gone there to work for wages during the school holidays. I did not know most of them, but there was one who was much older than I was called Kaleb Molose.

As soon as I got there I recognised my father's work on the thatched roofs of the packing houses. Kaleb, Chianyana and myself were drafted to work with the men picking oranges, while other

Phokeng boys and girls worked in the packing houses, sorting oranges into grades, the girls wrapping them in thin white or pink paper with written on them 'Navel oranges by W. Rex' and the name of the farm, in the district of Rustenburg. I was the weakest one amongst the pickers, and I used to find it difficult to carry my step-ladder around the tree or from tree to tree. As a result I was slower than the others. The stronger ones used to feel it unfair for them to carry their own ladders and then carry mine. I used to beg them to help me.

Some flatly refused, saying, 'You have come to work for yourself, why ask for a job when you are not strong enough for it?' Most of them were from other tribes and lacked sympathy for me. Tribal feelings worked on Chianyana and Kaleb. Chianyana would help me carry the ladder round, or Kaleb, who was older and stronger, used to do it on his own for me. It was due to my tribal men that Mr. Rex never discovered my weakness. I heard later that before I came, when the Rexes heard that some of the boys and girls they employed were from Phokeng, they asked them if they knew my father, but since they called him by a European name, Hebron, none of them said they knew him.

A good deal of time had passed since my father was there to thatch packing sheds for their father, but they still remembered him well and the good work he did. There was a man there who chose to go with William and Jack when their father died, called Piet. He was a fairly old man when I got there, but when father was there he was young and remembered well working with him and how well father treated him. Oom Piet (Uncle Piet), as we called him, was a coloured man in the South African sense, who had in his veins both African and European blood. He spoke only Dutch and none of the African languages. He had never been to school in his entire life.

One evening Oom Piet was sharing an open fire with us and he began telling us that the roof of the *banhuis*, under which we were enjoying the warmth, was done by one of our tribal men. He said that he had always wished that one day he would meet that man again. Oom Piet then mentioned father by his European name, Hebron, but could not remember his surname. I think that I was in my second week there. I told him that the man was my father. He remarked in Dutch: 'What? You are his son?' Others then supported my claim saying, 'It is true, his father is the best thatcher in our tribe.' Oom Piet looked at me carefully and remarked, 'I begin to see resemblance to him in you.' Oom Piet, as though he saw me for the first time, expressed great delight at meeting the offspring of the man he always wished to meet.

The next morning Oom Piet broke the news to both William and Jack Rex. Similarly they expressed surprise. They called me to look at me carefully, and both agreed that I resembled my father, but remarked, 'You do not seem as clever and active as your father.' To that I had no answer. The boys and girls of my tribe suspected that I would be treated better than themselves, but their fears did not materialise as far as work was concerned. I carried on doing the same work until my return to Phokeng. Jack did not care much whose son I was, but William began to develop a liking for me. When I arrived there, I told them my right name, Naboth, but William refused to call me by that name and gave me a name of his own. He said, 'Here we shall call you Jappie.' Though the Rexes had English names, their home language was Afrikaans. William was a man full of jokes and was easier to get on with than his brother Jack, who liked to enforce the fact that he was the master. Jack was in charge of people working in the *banhuise*, while William controlled those of us who picked oranges.

William was fond of calling me '*Jappie met drie vrouwe, sonder kind*', 'Jappie with three wives and no children'. In Kroondal with the Langes I was called Johannes, with the Rexes at Kommissiedrift I was Jappie. As far as both families were concerned, no one called Naboth ever worked for them. Food at the Rexes was not as good as at the Langes. At the Rexes we had no bread or coffee, but *mealie-pap* (maize porridge) three times a day; meat once a month. William used to go to Rustenburg once a month to sign papers and get payments for oranges already sold. On his return he brought with him ox offal and ox head from the butchers, and that was our meat.

After knowing that I was the son of the man who once did thatching for their father, William used to call me after work in the evenings to go into the fields with him carrying a rifle. Poor hares used to come out of their hiding places at that time in search of something to eat. William was a very good marksman and we would return carrying more than one hare. He would take one for his household and the rest were for me to enjoy with the others. On Sundays he called, 'Jappie, come here,' and took me with him to the mountains to search for rock rabbits. We would return carrying a collection of them. One was for him, the rest for me and the others. All he wanted of the rock rabbits were the skins.

Oom Piet used to remark, 'You see, he thinks of your father; he likes you, he never did all that before.' I do not know what William told his three sons about me. They too began to take a keen interest in me, especially the elder ones Lulu and Jan, who were already at school. I had learned to kick a football at that time; other boys from Phokeng and myself used to play football, using a tennis ball, with Lulu and Jan. At times their father used to come and force them to leave our open fires in the evenings. After lunch on Sundays both

131

Lulu and Jan used to disappear with us into the mountains to chase baboons or monkeys, or search for birds' nests or wild honey.

Jan and Lulu used to steal bread for me from their mother's pantry and made sure that I ate it alone without the other boys seeing it. We knew that if others knew they would give away our secret. Oom Piet too, who mostly worked in Mrs. Rex's house and looked after the cows and milked them, used to give me coffee. That, too, was done in secret. He would call me to his room saying, 'Drink quickly and say nothing to the others, they will be jealous.' We were forbidden to eat large first-grade oranges, but there were no restrictions on medium and small ones. Once they were in the *banhuise*, to be seen taking one was regarded as stealing. Very small ones and bitter ones were dumped, and we used to squeeze out their juice into mugs and fill our bellies with the juice which we used when eating *mealiepap* with no meat.

I did not know that Chianyana had no permission from his father to go with me to Kommissiedrift. His father, like mine, was keen that he should go to school. When he asked for permission it was refused, but he left with me nonetheless. His father searched for him and in the end found out where we were. One day he arrived at the Rexes' farm. He told William Rex that he had come to take away his son, and William raised no objections but led him to the field where we were picking that day. We did not see him coming, we were busy talking; all we heard was Chianyana screaming in agony. His father was beating him with a stick and thereafter took him to Mr. Rex to collect what was due to him and his belongings. They left for Phokeng afterwards.

In the evening of that same day Chianyana returned to the Rexes' farm. The story he told us was that half-way between Rustenburg and Kommissiedrift his father met someone he knew and excitement made them stand and talk. While they did the talking, he carried on walking and that provided him with a chance to escape. When he was a good distance from them, he told us, he dropped a bundle of his belongings he was carrying, went through the fence into another large citrus farm owned by a Scotsman called Mr. MacKenzie, disappeared into the orange trees and made his way back to Kommissiedrift.

His poor father then realised that he had wasted his precious time collecting him, and returned to Phokeng. Five weeks later, at the end of the second week in September nineteen-twenty-five, I left the Rexes with Chianyana for our tribal place Phokeng. Kaleb and others had left long before as they had to be in time for the reopening of schools. On my arrival home, I found Father worried, wondering whether I was going to be a boy of my word. Both Father and Mother were relieved when they saw me. I had spent all the money

Mr. William Rex paid me by buying myself some clothes, including a pair of black boots, when we passed through Rustenburg. When I showed them the things I bought I apologised to my parents that I had no money left, but both of them said that what was important to them was that I came back, as I promised. But within me I was ashamed that I did not buy either of my parents anything with the money I earned.

The pair of boots I bought were the first in my whole life. I was fascinated by them. I wore them only once a week on Sundays. Schools had reopened two weeks before and our parents wasted no time enrolling us. Chianyana went to the Lutheran Church school, where his father was an elder, but my father was keen that I should learn English. He went to see Reverend Kenneth Spooner of the Pentecostal Holiness Church, to ask him to accept me in his school. Mr. Spooner agreed, but said that since we were not members of his church and did not help to build his school, father should pay a pound for my enrolment.

On the Tuesday, Father took me along to Mr. Spooner's home and there paid the required pound. Then father asked what I required to start school within the form of books and other things. Mr. Spooner got up from his armchair, opened a big, dark-brown cupboard, and from it brought out a small flat book, a slate and slate pencil. Smiling, he told father that those were the things I needed as a beginner. At that time Reverend Spooner had lived for twelve years in Phokeng, and could well make himself understood in the broken Sesotho he spoke. When he arrived with his wife in nineteen-thirteen, neither of them spoke a word of Sesotho. Because they spoke only English, Phokeng people nicknamed them black Europeans.

Father armed me with the book, slate and pencil, and the three of us left Mr. Spooner's office for the school which was just across the street. When we entered, the three teachers, Mr. Ramphomane, the principal, Mr. Koos Mokgatle and Mr. Enoch Moamoge, interrupted the lessons they were engaged in and called on the children to stand in respect for the two adults who were with me. Mr. Spooner led us to the principal to introduce me. Shortly afterwards, father and Mr. Spooner left and I was handed over to Mr. Enoch Moamoge, who was good at softening raw material.

Reverend Kenneth Spooner and his congregation had built two schools, the large one, painted white, opposite Mr. Spooner's house, was used for two purposes. During the day it was a school, and every Friday night it was turned into a church, as well as on Sundays. The other one, which was built first, with a thatch roof, was used for the beginners' and other lower classes. It was in the old thatched house that for the first time I saw the inside of a classroom.

The beginners' class was larger than the other classes. Mr. Moamoge divided it into two sections, 'A' and 'A senior'. The former was for those like me, whose tasks were to learn the English alphabet, as well as struggling with the task of writing on the slates. The latter was for those who were beginning to read and to pronounce words. From the 'A senior' class, the pupils graduated into Standard 1. The three classes were under Mr. Enoch Moamoge.

In the larger building, the principal, Mr. Ramphomane, held classes with Mr. Koos Mokgatle. The principal was in charge of the most advanced standards, four, five and six, and Mr. Mokgatle was teaching two and three, which were also fairly well advanced. After a long campaign Mr. Spooner had obtained recognition for his schools by the Transvaal provincial authorities, but only for classes from 'A' to standard five. That recognition meant that the authorities agreed to pay the three teachers every three months and in addition to send school inspectors once a year to examine the pupils. Those in standard six were never examined by the inspectors when they came. Our school was called Phokeng Preparatory School (PPS).

To the west of our school, the Lutheran schools were given full recognition by the authorities. Although these introduced English classes as a counter to Mr. Spooner's school, they enjoyed recognition which meant that the pupils there, though they paid school fees of one shilling a month like pupils at Mr. Spooner's school, were supplied with free slates and other materials until they left school.

My family, like most families in Phokeng, had children at both the Lutheran and Phokeng preparatory schools. At the time I started school, only one of my sisters, Pheloe-Sannie, was a pupil at the Lutheran school. She was such a bright pupil that her teachers kept coming to our home urging father to do his utmost to get her to a college. All of them emphasised that she would do well in teaching and our tribe would benefit from her services. Father was never impressed by their advice, countering it by saying that he was grateful to them for the keen interest they were showing in the future of his daughter, but each time telling them that in his opinion it was unwise to spend a lot of money educating a female child who would, after marriage, cease to make use of what she had been taught.

My sister was in standard five at the Lutheran school. She was studying both English and Sesotho. For her and all the pupils at the Lutheran school, scripture and Sesotho took most time during lessons and left lean time for English classes. The result was that she was a student of scripture and Sesotho rather than the English language. At first, when I was a beginner learning the alphabet in English, she helped me a great deal. At home she was the family's cook and helped mother with house-work. In the evening, when we studied,

I used to beg her to teach me the English alphabet while she was heavily engaged in studying herself, or doing her homework, which she rarely came home without. She would go through it with me from A to Z, sometimes three times, but when she left me alone to remember them, I quickly forgot some of them. When I appealed to her to help me with the ones I had forgotten, she used to rage with anger, saying that I did not pay enough attention to what she told me, therefore she was wasting her time trying to help me. But she would eventually come to my aid, and because I knew that Mr. Moamoge would be waiting with a lash the next morning I learned fast.

XIX Progress

Towards the end of nineteen-twenty-five, at the end of the second week of November when schools broke up for holidays, I had made such progress in learning the English alphabet, counting and writing, that Mr. Spooner and the teachers felt that I should be moved up to 'A senior'. They did not say anything to me at the time, but I could see that when schools reopened I was going to be promoted. It was midsummer and also time for ploughing and planting new crops in the fields.

Before we dispersed altogether one of the men in my tribe called Ramadoko Katane approached my parents to ask them for permission to have me with him during the whole of the ploughing time, since he had no son of his own, only two daughters. He said that he would provide his team of oxen for ploughing my parents' fields as well as his own; all he needed was me to work with him. My parents agreed and three days after our school broke up I joined Ramadoko and his team to start ploughing. Our tribal fields are a long distance from Phokeng, and to do the work well we had, like many others, to sleep for weeks near the fields in the grass huts built for that purpose. My contact with Phokeng was suspended again, though for a short time. When we ran short of food or seeds, Ramadoko went home to fetch them while I remained with the animals at the fields.

Although Phokeng itself is built on a soft red or yellow earth called *motlhaba*, meaning sand, the fields where we grew our tribal crops are in black earth called *seloko*. When wet this earth becomes sticky, muddy and very heavy. When it rains, ploughing stops completely until the sun has dried it up again. Though dry on the surface, beneath *seloko* remains wet for a very long time. Even during periods of severe dryness, when rain had not fallen for a considerable time, crops in such soil take a long time to die from lack of water. Crops in *motlhaba* soil need rain nearly every week, otherwise they die quickly. Ploughing in Phokeng starts at the end of October every year, and lasts until the end of December. Those who are late with their ploughing sometimes go on for the first two weeks of the following year. At ploughing time Phokeng is only inhabited by old people, women and children.

For two months I worked with Ramadoko, ploughing his as well as my parents' fields. We were lucky, nothing beyond our control hampered us, and we finished ploughing at the end of December after Christmas. Schools at that time closed for two months and two weeks to enable children to help their parents in the fields. Similarly, at harvest time in winter, schools broke up for six weeks during the months of July and August to enable the children to help their parents with the gathering of the crops. At the end of ploughing I found that I had to wait for two weeks with very little to do before the schools reopened. I then decided to ask father for permission to go to Rustenburg for two weeks to seek work at the factory, known at that time as the United Tobacco Corporation. It was easy to get work there for two weeks, working in the factory packing tobacco or doing other odd jobs for seven, eight or nine shillings a week. Father, after thinking carefully about my request, reluctantly granted me the permission after I had promised him that I would come back in time to start school again.

It was nineteen-twenty-six and I was approaching my fifteenth birthday. At that age I was covered by the South African government's pass laws. To leave my tribal birthplace to go to Rustenburg I was required to carry a pass, a note authorising me to travel to a European town to seek work. The person authorised to issue me with such a travelling document was my Paramount Chief, Molotlegi Augustus Mokgatle. One Monday morning I went to the Chief's place to seek a pass. After hearing me, the Chief said that he had had requests from the United Tobacco Corporation for boys like me, but to go and work at their factory in a town called Brits, east of Rustenburg. Brits is halfway between Pretoria and Rustenburg. I declined the Chief's offer and he also declined to issue me with a pass to Rustenburg. I moved away from the Chief's place and went to my cousin's home nearby. While there, thinking what to do next, I saw the Chief leaving his place to take a walk in the village. I hurriedly went back and found his secretary alone. Unaware that the Chief had refused me a pass, he issued me with one.

That same day I left for Rustenburg and arrived there at lunch time. While I walked in the town's main street, which was also its shopping centre, admiring the shops and everything which came my way, a European man came towards me. He asked me in Dutch, which I understood but spoke very little, whether I was looking for work. I replied in the affirmative, and his next question was whether I could milk a cow. I assured him that I could, whereupon he asked me to wait there for him until he came back. He cycled home for lunch. Sixty minutes later he returned and took me along with him to the nearby office where he worked. He was Mr. Paul Coetzee, chief clerk in the firm of solicitors, Messrs. Penzhorn, Olivier and Coetzee. Mr. Penzhorn was Kristof Penzhorn, the son of the man who brought the Lutheran Church and Christianity to my tribe. He was born in Phokeng and spoke my language as I did, if not better.

Their office was opposite the charge office, which was also the main police station. After reporting to the office Paul Coetzee took me along with him to the native affairs commissioner's office to register me in his employment.

Before that time, I had no idea that such a place as the native affairs commissioner's office existed. I did not know that, although I had agreed that Mr. Paul Coetzee could employ me, Mr. Coetzee still had to get the native commissioner's permission to employ me. That was my first introduction to the pass system and the pass laws as they operated on the Africans in South Africa. If the native commissioner, a European, had withheld his permission, my agreement and that of Mr. Paul Coetzee would have been of no value. The African male's right to get work, or to be employed, is at the mercy of the native affairs departments and the native commissioners in South Africa.

However, Mr. Paul Coetzee took me into the office of the native commissioner for registration. It could not be for two weeks but had to be for thirty days as the law required. Mr. Coetzee registered me as we agreed, at twenty-five shillings a month, plus board and lodging. While registration was going on, I did not realise that I had my hands in my trouser pockets. The Chief Registrar, Daniel Branke, shouted to me in Dutch saying, 'Kaffir, take your hands out of your trouser pockets, you are in a white man's place now, not in your tribal village where you can do as you like.' That was my introduction to the hard relationships between black and white.

Those harsh words of Mr. Dan Branke, whom I later came to know, built themselves an everlasting house in my heart. Dan Branke was introducing the white man's power in South Africa to me. I was an innocent tribal boy who was there with no intention of defying his authority. If he had merely scolded me for having my hands in trouser pockets while talking to adults, I think that I would have apologised to him, but his forceful words, 'You are in the white man's place where you can't do as you like', surprised me and angered me. Instead of apologising, I defiantly remained silent and left his office without having uttered a word. I never forgot his rude words.

Outside Dan Branke's office, after I had been registered, Mr. Paul Coetzee directed me to his home where his wife Marie and invalid daughter Johanna were waiting for me. When I arrived there I found that they had in their employ an African girl from one of the Bakgatla tribes, north of Phokeng. Her duties were to clean the house and to help Mrs. Coetzee with Johanna, as well as cooking. My duties were to work with a spade and rake in the garden, cut the hedges, and water the flowers and other plants in the afternoons. In the mornings, before milking the cow at seven o'clock, I had to clean the pantry and kitchen floors, and both the back and front stoeps. After milking and taking the cow out to an open place for grazing, the female servant and I sat down to our breakfast, given us by Mrs. Marie Coetzee.

After breakfast my place was in the garden until half past ten, when I took tea or coffee to Mr. Coetzee and all who worked with him in the offices of Messrs. Penzhorn, Olivier and Coetzee, Attorneys. They paid Mrs. Marie Coetzee for the tea and coffee she sent them and the rusks baked by her mother-in-law, Mrs. Coetzee senior, who was their neighbour. It was at the offices of the Attorneys that I saw typewriters for the first time. I remember seeing one of the women there typing so fast that I wondered how she knew where the letters were that she had to hit. Mrs. Marie Coetzee seemed not to like me very much. She used to complain to her husband that I was not working hard enough, that I took a long time to return from taking him tea or coffee. But Paul only listened, and never acted.

Rustenburg in nineteen-twenty-five, when I worked for Mr. Paul Coetzee, was a complete farm town with no dairies, three butcher shops, one bakery, two first-class hotels, one second-grade hotel, numerous boarding-houses, houses with large gardens in which they grew their own vegetables, fruit and flowers. Almost every household had one or two cows for the family's milk needs. Wherever one went, one saw cows grazing about in the town and outside its borders. There were a few fruit shops which served also as restaurants or cafés. Streets were not tarred, and the main street was watered twice a day to keep the dust down. There was one printing press which produced a newspaper twice a month called *The Rustenburg Herald* owned by Mr. Wolfe. There was no cinema. In the centre of the town was a Dutch Reformed Church, where at Easter time Dutch families came from all corners of the district to attend church services there for ten days. The ox wagons, with huge tents, served as homes for the families while they were there.

Paul Coetzee was a fine and liberal man who refused to let his wife influence him against me. When his wife accused me of not working hard enough, he used to visit the area where I worked to see for himself. He would say, 'You have done it well here, but not too good here. Do it again tomorrow.' His mother, who lived next to them with her other children, was a good-looking old Dutch woman who could not free herself from the bitter feelings she acquired during the Anglo-Boer war of eighteen-ninety-nine to nineteen-o-two. She hated the English and the English language. I remember her ordering her African garden workman to dig out a tree which she said stood in her yard like a drunk Englishman. She was uncompromising in her belief that black people were inferior, therefore should be kept apart from white people.

It was when I was in the employ of Mr. Paul Coetzee that I learned to ride a bicycle. On Sundays he allowed me to use his bicycle for the purpose. His mother used to scold him for allowing a kaffir to sit on the same saddle as himself. Paul listened but always gave me his bicycle to practise on. Paul took after his father, Jan Coetzee, who lived away on his farm to the west of Rustenburg. I once heard him say to the gardener, 'Come along, son.' His wife scolded him saying, 'He's not son, don't call him son, he's a kaffir.' The old man gave no reply.

Mr. Paul Coetzee used to accompany me to the cow's enclosure to watch me milk the animal. It was a beautiful brown cow, with its calf, and gave enough milk to satisfy all the family's needs. Paul's mother also had her own cow. When the time came for me to leave I had no option but to say 'Good-bye' to the Coetzees. In those days, twenty-five shillings a month seemed a lot of money. I left on a Saturday, to be in Phokeng on Sunday, to prepare myself for school on Monday. With the money I earned from the Coetzees I bought myself a pair of khaki shorts, a khaki shirt, a set of underwear, a pair of white tennis shoes and a pair of socks. In the end I found that I had seven shillings left to take home with me to show my parents. It was an improvement on what happened when I came back from the Rexes the previous winter.

I was eager to learn and my parents were pleased to see me back determined to start school again. I was two weeks late but my teachers and school friends were glad to see me back. On Monday I left home dressed in my new clothes and my feet in white tennis shoes looking very smart. I had only three things with me, the slate, pencil and book father bought me when I started school. After drilling, which was the first performance we underwent each morning, we marched into the grass-roofed school. Before we settled down on wooden benches our teacher Mr. Enoch Moamoge offered a prayer, then he said in English, 'Sit down, children.' That stage having been passed, he read the register, and then asked those whose names had not been called to stand. Within a few seconds I was on my feet, whereupon he invited me to his table to write my name down. Before I could return to where I had sat before he took me to the other side of the passage which led from the door to his table.

My crossing the passage meant that I had been promoted to 'A senior' class. That meant a good deal of studying, reading, spelling, dictation, writing, learning tables, measurements and going into the difficult world of arithmetic. I could still use my slate and pencil but had to acquire a new book, which contained no alphabet. Since I came two weeks late, I had to catch up with those who had studied two weeks in the 'A senior' class. In that class I found two girls who put pressure on me to study hard. They were Dilli Pooe and Annie

Kgoadikgoadi. The former was a Phokeng girl; her father was Herman Pooe, my father's greatest friend who became a prominent figure in the Lutheran Church but never turned my father into a Christian. The latter was a girl from one of the Bapedi tribes in the eastern Transvaal, sent to Phokeng with her elder sister Wilhelmina and young brother Abraham to learn English. They had no relatives in Phokeng to live with and were living with Reverend Kenneth Spooner and his wife.

They and two young boys who were far younger than I was, put pressure on me to spend two or more hours before going to bed each night by my mother's paraffin lamp, cramming words, memorising tables and trying hard to remember everything we heard at school each day. The girls did not worry me much because they were of the same age as myself, but I could not stomach the two boys beating me at lessons. At times they did and put me to shame. I knew that when I was beaten by them, it was not that they were much brighter than I was, but that I did not study hard enough. As I went on I found that in many cases I managed to beat the two girls, but perhaps one of the boys or both of them beat me, making me number three. That I hated intensely. The only way I could pass them was by hard work.

When Mr. Spooner came with his quarterly internal tests I found the girls could beat me only at scripture because they attended Sunday school regularly every Sunday, which I never did. That did not worry me because I knew that when the inspectors came in six months' time in June, scripture would not find a place in the examinations. My battle became against the two boys. As we pushed through towards examination time, I noticed that one of them, Samuel Ramaboa, was beginning to feel weighed down but still forcing me to take note of him. I think that homesickness was taking too much out of him, because at first he was cheerful, but had taken a turn to silence and showed a good deal of loneliness.

In June of that year when the inspectors came – Mr. Johns a European and Mr. Mathabathe an African – the five of us passed with others into standard one. That ended the slate period and we entered the period of ink and exercise books, more studying, reading and advanced sums. Our parents paid our school fees and for our books and writing materials. After the examinations, schools broke up for the winter holidays to enable children to help their parents with the harvest. We were free for two months, from July to the end of August. That year my parents needed my help for only one month. By the end of July, with my parents' permission, I left for William Rex's farm in Kommissiedrift to pick oranges. I left knowing that there would be a place for me. I arrived to find that William and his brother Jack had separated and divided the farm, but William took me on for thirty days at thirty shillings, which represented one shilling a day. I had expected him to employ me in the *banhuis*, amongst those sorting or wrapping oranges for export, but the trees in the field were still the place for me. That time there were few people from my tribe; most were workmen and women from other tribes, whom I had to get to know. Oom Piet was still there, but older than when I first saw him.

None of the foreign people I found there became hostile to me, but there was one man, Phalane Mojapelo, from a Batlokoa tribe in the Pietersburg district of the Transvaal, who developed a great liking for me because I became an asset to him. He had never been to school, had two wives and children at home and was keen to know how things were getting on at home. At that time I was good at writing Sesotho letters.

Time was short, I was there for only thirty days. Every Sunday, when we were free from orange trees, he would take me away from the others into the mountains nearby, or some lonely spot, to write letters home. While I wrote, he would lie on his back, facing the blue sky avoiding the brightness of the sun, and dictate to me what to write to his wives. In the end he would kindly ask me to read to him what I had written to make sure that I had left nothing out or he had forgotten nothing.

When letters arrived from home at lunch time, we would move away from the others to read the letters. It was not because he did not want others to know that he could not read or write himself, but because he did not want his secrets to be known by others. There were others like him, but he was the only one who had chosen me to be his secretary. He trusted me with his secrets. I on my part promised him that in me his secrets were as though inside a dead boy.

Phalane Mojapelo in his turn was an asset to me. Every day when we went into the field to pick oranges he made sure that I took a row next to his. When I needed my ladder to be shifted, and they were fairly heavy, he moved mine for me. He could not eat anything he thought sweet or nice without seeing that I had a share of it. Mr. William Rex, too, carried on his liking for me. I remained his old 'Jappie with three wives'. Hares in the evening and rock rabbits on Sundays felt the pain of bullets going through their bodies so that I could enjoy their flesh.

When the day of my departure drew nearer, Mr. Rex made an effort to persuade me to drop the idea of going back to school. He began by condemning school and education, telling me that he was good to me, he would be good to me in future, if I stayed. I tried to convince him that my father would be angry with me and would come and fetch me. He laughed and said, 'Your father? He knows that you are well looked after here. If he did come, I would talk to him myself and he would let you stay.' I knew my father would be furious; I was afraid of him and did not want to disappoint him. When he observed that I was keen to return to school, he said, 'If you stay I shall give you five shillings more and, unlike at school, you would earn every month, so that you would become a rich man. You are losing by going to school, here you gain,' said Mr. Rex.

'What will you do with your education?' Mr. Rex asked me. 'You are wasting your time,' he continued. 'Here you are not wasting your time, you are working for yourself, making yourself a rich man of the future. Jappie,' he said, 'I like you, you are a good boy. If you agree to stay, you may end up being a foreman on my farm.' I had tasted school and had gained something from it, namely reading and writing. I was determined to go on, knowing that if I did I would know more about English, which I envied others being able to speak when I could not.

In reply to Mr. Rex's efforts, I asked him why, if he thought it was a waste of time to go to school, he allowed his three sons to go to school. At once he realised that his efforts were in vain; no word came out of him, he left me silently and never tried again. Special treatment of me also came to an end. He did not become hostile, but treated me like anyone else. I suspect that Phalane Mojapelo would have liked to persuade me to stay, but he knew that one day he would have to return to his home and would see to it that his children went to school, so that when they reached his age they could write letters for themselves.

The end of my time came and I was careful not to be late again at school. I left Kommissiedrift on a Saturday, two days before the schools reopened. I was in Phokeng on Sunday. On Tuesday morning father noticed me not making preparations to leave home for school. I had expected him to go to Mr. Spooner's place on Monday to buy my books, but he had not done so. I thought that it was useless for me to go to school without books. Father asked me why I was not getting ready to leave and I replied that I had no books to take to school with me. He forcefully ordered me to leave at once. I had already washed so I went on my way to school, bookless.

While I sat among other pupils wondering what was going to happen during the day, since I had brought no books to use in my new class, I saw my father pass the door of our school on his way to Reverend Kenneth Spooner's house. I was at once relieved, for I knew that the only purpose for his going there was to buy the books I needed. Before a real start was made in sorting us out according to the way our teacher, Mr. Enoch Moamoge, desired, father knocked at the door carrying all the books Mr. Spooner told him I required.

Mr. Moamoge invited him in, and being accustomed to the standing order that when an elderly person or a visitor entered the room we must stand, father passed through the passage to Mr. Moamoge's table while we were all on our feet. I can only remember a few of the books: a Rustica reading book, Blackie and Sons dictionary, an atlas and history of South Africa.

Corporal punishment was not forbidden in our school. Teachers were allowed to punish us by beating and our parents encouraged it. They said that it increased discipline at home and at school. Even at home when I did something which my parents disliked, if they did not want to punish me themselves, they used to say, 'We will bring this to the notice of your teacher.' Then the teacher would say, 'I understand that you have turned yourself into a bully at home and think nothing of your parents. I shall teach you that you owe your parents respect and obedience.' The teacher would punish a child by beating, until the child promised that he or she would obey the elders. Girls got beatings on the hands, but boys got them on the buttocks as well as on the hands.

We were punished in the same fashion for coming late to school, fighting, being dirty, or swearing.

In standard one at Phokeng Preparatory School we were taught almost every subject children sent to school ought to know. It was hard going for me and others who were in that class with me. Our teacher, Mr. Enoch Moamoge, was a very strict man but a good teacher at the same time. He was gifted at explaining things. He hated lazy pupils and those he called blockheads. None of us was sure where we stood with him. He would joke with us and, while we enjoyed his jokes, spring on us to find out whether we did in fact study what he had given us to study, or whether we could remember what we had studied.

Subjects we were ordered to learn and to know by heart were geography, history, spelling, arithmetic and above all historical dates. Since our teacher taught the beginners who required more attention, he kept us very busy. While he was busy opening the eyes and minds of the beginners, he used to pile work on the blackboards for us. He would give us sums to start with; when we had finished them, an object to draw, and then he would order us to struggle with writing letters to friends in English, telling them about things around us. While we expected him to correct us the same day he would switch on to something he had ordered us to study a week or two ago. Our work for that day would be left over for the next day.

Those of us whose memories were weak, or those Mr. Moamoge called blockheads, would find themselves sorted out from the rest, to wait punishment. I was seldom found among those sorted out for punishment for having not studied what we were ordered to study, or failing to remember what I had studied. My main weakness was in coming late to school. For that I was frequently found among those who had to pay with pains for late-coming. In geography we had to know the main cities of South Africa, the main railway stations, junctions, and halts in the Transvaal Province. There was not a single day that we went home from school with no homework. Even when school broke up we were still given subjects to study, to be corrected when schools reopened.

During the period of my studies in standard one, two important things came my way. Many games were played at the school. Girls were taught to play basket-ball and hockey, which were completely foreign to the people of my tribe, and never seen in our village until Mr. Spooner and his wife arrived in nineteen-thirteen. Though Reverend Penzhorn of the Lutheran Church intensely disliked Mr. Spooner and his church and school, to avoid many of his church's children going to Phokeng Preparatory School he encouraged his teachers too to introduce the same games the children enjoyed there. For girls there were hockey and basket-ball, while boys were taught the art of playing soccer. When I arrived there the games were played with keen interest by both boys and girls. I joined in the excitement and tried my feet at the ball, which was nicknamed the egg. I became one of the best young players and I was drafted into the youngsters' team which was called the Zebras. Our uniform was of white and black stripes and so were the stockings.

The elder boys' team was called the Home Defenders and their uniform was yellow with a white collar. Most of the youngsters played without boots. Before I went to the school, one of the boys whose parents were well known to my parents was kicked by another while playing, strained his ankle and was unable to walk for a long time. Because of that episode my father hated football and was against me playing it. For that reason I could not ask him to buy me football boots. I liked the game intensely. I played it, but without telling father, who was often away from home thatching. I remember that once he came home to find that I was away at the football ground enjoying myself. Angrily he fetched me, and when we got home he beat me.

Also I could not ask my father to buy me football clothes, the jersey and stockings. My aunt's son, Didrik Rangaka, gave me the jersey and stockings he used when he was in the Zebra team. He kept them at his home for me and brought them to school with him when he knew that I was going to play. Father had no idea that I had such clothes. The Lutherans, too, had their soccer football clubs. Their first team was called the Swallows and the second team was called Young Vultures. Mostly we played on our ground against our senior team, but there were times when excitement took control of the children of our village. Before a big clash came about, announcements would be made at both our school and the Lutheran that the two first teams would meet in a match, either at the Lutheran ground or at our ground. In the afternoon of the big clash most of the school children from both sides would be at the ground to cheer and encourage their side to win.

There were also times when a visiting team would come from Rustenburg to play Phokeng. On such an occasion the best players would be picked from our side and the Lutherans to form a Phokeng team. On the day of such a match, Phokeng would be full of excitement. Matches of such a nature were played on Sundays or public holidays. Visitors always brought their supporters to cheer them. I can't recall any match amongst the ones I witnessed won by the Phokeng team. Our team consisted of scholars and the visitors' team was of workmen. Our players were good at the game but the Rustenburg players were more experienced and they always returned home the victors.

The second teams from our school and the Lutherans also used to meet, and because I was good at the game I was usually picked to play. But to my regret and disappointment, at times my team had to play without my aid, because father knew about the match in advance and gave me orders that I must not go to a game he hated so from the bottom of his heart. To make sure that I should not get a chance to join my fellow Zebras, father used to give me something to do which would keep me busy the whole afternoon until the match was over. I used to be tortured by the cheering I heard from our ground, which was not far away.

My period in standard one at school was also a period of letter writing. Though my English grammar was still far from perfect, I was nevertheless trying my hand at it, like others who shared the class with me. There was great competition amongst us as to who was best at writing English letters. That led me into writing to girls as well. I fell in love with a pretty girl, Laki-Lucy Thipe, who was a year younger than myself, but because she had gone to school before me she was already in standard two. Her teacher was at that time Mr. Koos Mokgatle and they were in the larger building, away from the one I was housed in. Like me, her parents were not members of Mr. Spooner's church, but Lutherans. Her father was an ex-catechism teacher at a Lutheran school. My love for Lucy grew deeper than I had expected. I loved her very much, and I hoped that she had the same feelings towards me. She was my first girl friend.

Our meetings were harmless ones. I was only too pleased to hold her hand and to kiss her whenever we had a chance to do so. We made appointments to meet in the evenings, by letter, since we could not do so openly during the day at school. Other boys, too, had girl friends and used the same methods of communication as I did. The Pentecostal Holiness Church held two evening prayer services a week, on Fridays and Sundays. Those church services gave us a chance to meet after the service and walk home together in the dark streets of Phokeng unrecognised. My duty was to take her up to her home and then, after making sure that no one observed us, kiss her good-bye and leave. That was as far as we could get in our friendship.

I used two messengers who delivered my letters to Lucy and she used them to deliver hers to me: a younger boy who was in the same class with me, Senataila Ramasodi, who was also Lucy's closest relative, and a girl called Gamongoe Mokgatle, a relative of mine and Lucy's. Everything was done in secret. If we had been found out by our teachers or parents we would have undergone severe punishments. So we were very careful.

Winter of nineteen-twenty-seven came and it was time for examinations. The inspectors came and I passed into standard two with very high marks. My friendship with Laki was solid and I was enjoying it. Schools broke up after that for the winter holidays, and as usual most of us went into the fields with our parents to help with the harvest. Laki and I were separated for a period of two months and I longed for it to be time to return to Phokeng so that we could resume our secret meetings. We returned to school at the end of August and our friendship blossomed again. I was in standard two and she was in standard three, always ahead of me.

We carried on as before our harmless meetings on Fridays and Sundays. The year was drawing to a close, time for ploughing was getting near. Two months later, at the end of October, schools broke up again. Again separation; I went to plough, and our schools were set to reopen at the end of January. I finished ploughing a week before Christmas; that gave me chance to see Laki during the Christmas activities. We met several times and there were no signs that our time to break up was in sight. After Christmas I left Phokeng to seek work in Rustenburg for the whole month of January. That took me away from Laki, or Laki from me. In Rustenburg I did not go to my previous employer, Mr. Paul Coetzee, though earlier it had been my intention to do so. At that time my father was working in Rustenburg, thatching a large house for the manager of an insurance company, Mr. Dorse. On arrival I went to see my father, and he told me that my cousin Silas Mokgatle, who was employed by Barclays Bank as a messenger, would like to see me. After spending an hour with father, I went to cousin Silas and he told me that one of the European clerks in the bank had asked him to find him someone to work in the garden at his home. I agreed to meet the man, Mr. Gabriel Vermeulen, who, after seeing me, agreed to employ me at a wage of thirty shillings a month. He gave me a letter to the Native Commissioner's office for registration and one to his wife Maria.

I found on arrival at the Vermeulens that they employed as a domestic worker a Phokeng girl whose home was in the same street as mine, an old friend of my sister by the name of Nkefe Molefe. She was older than I was and had been confirmed in the Lutheran Church the same day as my sister Sannie. Another thing I found was that the Vermeulens had bought one of Paul Coetzee's houses, a house I knew well, because when I was employed by Mr. Coetzee a year before I had worked in the garden of that house. The Vermeulens had no cow for me to milk, but got their milk from a dairy in the town. My duties at the Vermeulens were to work in the garden I used to tidy before, to polish the floors of the house, and to clean and polish its stoeps.

First thing in the morning before breakfast I had to crawl on my knees with a hard brush and a cleaning rag over the large front stoep (Dutch for verandah) and the smaller one at the back, to make them shine. Twice a week I had to smear them with red stoep polish and rub them until they shone with the brush and rag. It took a lot out of my strength, and I hated Wednesday and Friday mornings, they were the days I would be wet with perspiration before breakfast. Every day before I made a start in the garden, I used to go through every room in the house with a brush and rag to make them clean while Nkefe Molefe was making beds, dusting the furniture and preparing lunch. The Vermeulens had two board-lodgers who also worked at Barclays Bank, Messrs. Prinsloo and le Roux. English was never spoken in that house, only Dutch and Sesutho. Nkefe and I spoke to each other in Sesutho and to the others in Dutch.

There was no municipal water supply in the town and every house operated a hand pump which drew water from the well. Richer ones had installed electric machines which pumped water out of the wells, but the Vermeulens were not among them. In the afternoons, for half an hour or more, I had to pump water out of the well by hand to fill a large tank from which the house got its water supply.

I hated hearing people in the house having a bath, because it was emptying the tank, which took a lot of my strength to fill. At times, to avoid it getting empty, I used to pump it full in the evening instead of having a rest. Sundays were the days on which the tank water went down, because in the afternoons I went out to enjoy myself with friends and there was no water pumping into the tank. By Monday mornings it would be at its lowest ebb. I would sweat on Monday afternoons.

At the Vermeulens, as at the Coetzees, twice a day I carried a tray of tea or coffee to Barclays Bank for Gabriel Vermeulen, Prinsloo and le Roux. I liked doing that because it gave me a chance to get away from the spade, scissors, hedge-cutting or digging out of unwanted trees in the garden. I also used to visit my father where he was doing thatching work for Mr. Dorse. He was careful to see that at the end of my contract with the Vermeulens I should return without waste of time to school. Gabriel Vermeulen, unlike Paul Coetzee, left me entirely to his wife. He gave me no orders. She was the daughter of one of the successful farmers in the district whom the Africans had nicknamed '*Gayeatsena*' (It didn't get in). His nickname was linked with a story that during the Anglo-Boer war of eighteen-ninety-nine to nineteen-o-two, he narrowly missed death and pretended to be dead from a bullet shot, but when his men reached him his first words were, 'It didn't get in', meaning that the bullet didn't hit him. He liked his African nickname and his daughter was proud to tell the Africans that her father was 'It didn't get in'.

Maria Vermeulen told me that before she met her husband she was a teacher in the girls' school in the town. She liked giving me pencil and paper to write down orders to the butcher and a list of groceries needed in the house. She would correct wrong spellings, but on the whole she knew the butcher would understand and so would the grocer. Once a week her brother or father came to town and brought them fresh vegetables from the farm. The day I left the Vermeulens, father went home with me by country railway bus. On the way, in the afternoon, it rained heavily and when we got out of the bus, the stop was some distance from our home and we got very wet.

XX End of Friendship with Laki

While the cat is away mice get a chance to enjoy themselves. While I was in Rustenburg working for the Vermeulens, a best friend of mine whose name and surname were the same, Moagi Moagi – the boy I could not afford to spend two weeks without seeing, one of the brightest in English at the Lutheran school – befriended Lucy and made her fall in love with him. On Sunday before I met Lucy, I went to Moagi's place to see him and to find out how things had gone in Phokeng during my absence. At once I noticed he wasn't the Moagi I knew before. He was not hostile but cool. I asked him about Lucy; he said she was all right but he had not seen her for a few days – when in fact they were together on the Friday night before I left Rustenburg.

From him, a bit disappointed, I went to Gamongoe Mokgatle's place, and there Gamongoe told me that my friendship with Lucy was sour, and the boy responsible was my friend Moagi Moagi. Gamongoe, being my relative, was against Moagi's friendship with Lucy. She had tried, she told me, to break it up, but failed. In the evening I went to Mr. Spooner's prayer service to meet Lucy. Moagi stayed away by agreement with Lucy. After the service Lucy tried to avoid me, but Gamongoe made it possible for us to meet. Lucy was a changed girl; she told me that she was not well and wanted to get home quickly. I pretended to be ignorant of her friendship with Moagi and, as though disappointed, accompanied her home. When we parted I was the only one to initiate the good-bye kissing. That was the last kiss I got from Lucy, my first girl friend. During the week I registered at the school, but observed that Lucy was unhappy and did everything possible to avoid me. When I looked at her, she looked down. My love for her was at its height, but I realised that on her side the sack was on the ground and I was the only one trying to lift it from the ground.

Before the Friday of that week Senataila Ramasodi delivered a letter to me from Lucy telling me that our friendship had come to an end. After reading it, Phokeng was empty of girls for me. There was only one girl in the whole village – Lucy Thipe. With weak knees, I went to Moagi's place to ask him why he did such a thing to me.

My friend tried his utmost to convince me that at first he did not want to take Lucy from me, that he only tried to keep her company while I was away but eventually fell deeply in love with her. I took

everything he told me with a pinch of salt but saw no point in breaking off my friendship with him. I kept it up, and at times, though
with bitterness in my heart, said 'Hello' or 'Good-bye' to him in
Lucy's company. My love for Lucy never came to an end. Even
after her break with Moagi, I wanted to go back to her, but I felt
that she would think that I was not popular with other girls. I
remained friendly towards her but never proposed love to her again.
Later, when both of us had reached adulthood, I observed that she
was ready to accept me in any way I cared to suggest, but I withheld my feelings as though I had no love feelings towards her.

When my friendship with Lucy Thipe broke, I had no notion that
other girls cheered and saw a chance for them to lay their fingers on
me. Not a single girl in Phokeng that I proposed love friendship to
objected. I formed friendships with Mashadi Mokgatle, Mpompo
Ramaidi, Shadi Magano, Dora Mutle, Basetsana Magano and
others, who were all pretty and pleasant girls, but none of them penetrated my heart and feelings like Lucy Thipe. It was only then that I
realised that I had always underestimated my influence on the
members of the opposite sex; it was more powerful than I imagined.

With them, too, my relations were harmless. We held hands, met
at tribal dances in the evenings after weddings, at Mr. Spooner's
evening prayers services, but went no further than goodbye kisses.
Some of them got married before I left South Africa; unfortunate
ones had died; Lucy herself married a man of another tribe she met
in Johannesburg, but divorced him before my departure to England.

My friendship with Moagi Moagi, who took my first girl friend
away from me, went on into our adult lives. He left Phokeng before
me for Johannesburg, where he went to seek his fortune. He got a
job there in a picture-framing firm and learned to become a first
class picture-framer. In addition he learnt to play the violin, and
tennis. He lived in the centre of the City of Gold in the Municipal
African males' hostel called Mai Mai. The one unfortunate thing
he did was to couple his leisure with drinking. He formed associations
with people who thought that the best thing one could do with
leisure was to drink and to go on drinking until the power of what
was taken into the stomach took possession of the man and his movements. He was a man who liked to be seen clean and well-dressed. I
remember a story, told me by one of our friends, that at one of their
drinking meetings Moagi arrived well dressed but drank too much,
and when he left the room he could not see a wash-bath filled with
water. He went into it with his shoes on and got himself so wet that
they realised what had happened when a young woman screamed
for help.

Whenever I was in Johannesburg, on Sundays or public holidays,
and I had the time, I used to visit him at Mai Mai. I remember one

occasion – he was happy to see me but remarked that I was an awkward visitor because he could not entertain me as he would have liked since I did not drink beer or other drinks which make people happy. He pulled his wallet out and showed me a few pound notes and said, 'If you had grown out of pretending to be a juvenile, into the life of adults, I was going to spend all these on you today. The best I can do,' he said, 'is to take you to a restaurant, get you a good meal and a cup of tea or coffee, and you expect me to feel that I have entertained a good friend I have not seen for months.' I was living in Pretoria, more than thirty miles away. I thanked him and said that the fact that he showed me the money should make him feel that he gave me everything he would have liked to give. He was a good-natured fellow.

I think the other mistake he made was to choose not to get married. Each time I put the marriage question to him, his reply was, 'I am still searching for Miss Right. I haven't found her yet. I may one day.' He was still unmarried when I left South Africa. We drifted apart when I devoted my entire life to African politics, about which I shall have more to say later. Like many of my friends, he said I was heading for total destruction.

From the winter of nineteen-twenty-seven to the next winter, I was in standard two at Phokeng Preparatory School. I was in good form and those who watched me said they could see a tribal intellectual developing, if only he adopted the method of persistence in remaining at school and studying hard. But time was running out. Most of my friends who started school years before me were nearing the end of their school days, preparing themselves to return to the Lutheran school to wait for their selection for confirmation. To reach standard six, if I passed every year, I faced another four years at preparatory school. That meant that in a year or two I would be left amongst pupils all younger than me. All the girls with whom I would form friendships were also leaving, giving way to younger ones.

I was not sure what I was going to do, to leave or to carry on. Father was eager that I should carry on. He had his own plans laid down for my future, which I did not know about. When the inspectors came in the winter of nineteen-twenty-eight I passed into standard three with high marks again. As usual, after that schools broke up for harvesting, I went into the fields with mother and two sisters; father was again busy, outside Rustenburg, thatching a large house for a man who was at one time a minister of justice in J. B. M. Hertzog's government, Mr. Dielman Roos. During that period with mother and my sisters in the fields I went through a mental revolution. First my sisters wanted to know whether I was still returning to school, to continue in standard three. I was willing to have a go for another year, but my sisters hammered into me that I had passed the time for remaining at school. 'All pupils of your age are leaving,' they argued. 'You are seventeen years old, you went to school late. It is time to go out to work for youself, in preparation for marriage.' That was the picture my sisters displayed in front of me.

Mother at first supported me that I should return to school at least for one year, but my sisters accused her of having not stood up for me when Father kept me with the animals, which made me go to school late. Their arguments overpowered mother and she resorted to letting me argue with my sisters without her help. I was frightened, I did not know how to approach father about what my sisters said. I asked mother to do it for me but she declined, saying that father would think that she had influenced me against returning to school.

My sisters' arguments were attractive and they won. I never read a standard three book. One Sunday, at the end of his sermon, Reverend Ernest Penzhorn gave out that in three weeks' time he would announce the names of the boys and girls he had selected for confirmation and they would be of the ages of sixteen, seventeen and over. They would be required to attend confirmation classes for three months under him from the first week of September to the end of November. That was meant to afford the parents whose children were not in the Lutheran schools a chance to approach the priest on behalf of their children, if they desired them to get confirmed.

My sisters' victory was complete, but they were not prepared to approach father for me. They were not seeking confirmation, they were confirmed already; it was me, the influenced, who must do the talking to the father, who was not a Christian, and in whose life confirmation played no part. Confirmation classes were held at the Lutheran Church at intervals of three or four years. My sisters kept knocking into my head that I was seventeen, when the next one came I would be twenty-one or twenty-two years old. An old man seeking confirmation. That had a strong psychological effect on me. The Lion of the family, father, was away; he was surely coming one day, but we did not know when. My sisters were so desperate, they said that if father did not come the following week-end I should go to him to lay my cards on the table. I waited for mother's support, but she withheld it from me. At times she did say to my sisters, 'Leave him alone; allow him to make up his own mind.'

Father, as though he knew what was going on, arrived the following week-end after an absence of several weeks. After hearing that I had crossed the barrier of standard two, he congratulated me and, as though he knew, withheld further comment. The whole evening my sisters waited anxiously for me to move into the Lion's den, but I was too frightened; the tribal Lion was about, moving, crunching bones, moving everything out of its way, getting ready to return to the work of roofing a house with grass. The next morning my two

F

sisters pushed me from behind into the Lion's den, saying, 'Come on. Tell father. He won't eat you.'

Father was leaving in the afternoon and after breakfast, as was his habit, he sat on a small reim stool (he was expert in making such stools) and waited for anything or anyone who cared to visit him. Reluctantly, frightened, I forced my weak legs to carry me to him. I took one of the stools with me and, when I reached him, asked for permission to sit down. Having sat down, with trembling voice I said, 'Father, I want to talk to you.' Without uttering a word or looking at me he waited for what I wanted to talk to him about. I said, 'I am asking for permission to go to the Lutheran confirmation classes next month.' With a harsh voice he asked, 'What?' I was satisfied that he got the message. He called for my mother and, when she reached us, asked her, 'Salome, what have you done to him? Do you want him to end the same way as the girls?' He repeated to mother what I told him and asked mother if she knew about it. Mother admitted that she did, but said that she told me that it was something to be settled between him and me.

As was his habit, he did not go further with it, only said, 'I am going to think about it. I want you to think deeply about it, but I want you to know that you are throwing yourself and your future away.' We left it at that, but at least I was glad that I left the Lion's den unscratched. My sisters were waiting to welcome their hero. Father was shaken and disturbed but felt that he should settle it quickly. The following Saturday he returned home specially to talk to me about my intentions. When we began to talk he was calm, not hostile. He said to me, 'Your future is yours. You are going to suffer or live happily depending on what you do now.' As an old timer he realised that my mind was made up, but suggested a compromise, that after confirmation I should return to preparatory school, to struggle for my standard six examination. I agreed. He then unfolded his plan to me for the first time. He said, 'I want you to be independent, like me. I want you to set a price for your work and accept the price from the other side as a compromise, not in desperation. After standard six,' he said, 'I want to send you to industrial college in the Cape to study building.' The college was called Tigerkloof Institution, where non-European pupils were taught trades. 'That is why,' father continued, 'I want you to return to school.' I agreed.

At the end of the agreement I reminded my father that he had to take me to Mr. Penzhorn about being confirmed. He retorted, 'Oh, that can be done by your mother.' I reminded him that for candidates like me from Phokeng Preparatory School, Mr. Penzhorn wanted the asking to be done by fathers. He then said, seeming in a changed mood, 'I can't leave my work just to ask Mr. Penzhorn to confirm you into his church. If he wants you, he ought to take what your mother says.' I replied and said, 'Father, you won't have to leave your work, we can go to see him on Sunday after morning service.' I had trapped him, he could find no way out. He agreed and we arranged it for the following Sunday.

For three week-ends in succession, father came home to settle domestic matters. That Sunday we waited until we were sure that Mr. Penzhorn had finished his lunch and went to see him. Mr. Penzhorn knew father very well, because though he was not a member of his church they were friends, and because he used to do thatching for him. When he saw father with me he knew what the visit was all about. After exchanging greetings, Mr. Penzhorn uttered two Dutch words, '*Ja Ja*', which are also German, and in Sesotho said, 'Hebron, have you come?' Father replied, 'I am bringing him to you, his priest.' Mr. Penzhorn invited us to sit down. Father at once said, 'He wants to get confirmed.' Mr. Penzhorn said, 'I know where you sent him to school. Can he read Sesotho, or is he a black Englishman?' Father said, 'Yes, he can,' and thereupon Mr. Penzhorn opened a Sesotho Bible which was on his desk and asked me to read to him two verses he had selected. I read three instead of two to impress him, and he was impressed. He then said, 'I don't want children like him who have been denied their mother tongue to waste the time of other children in confirmation classes.' Mr. Penzhorn then went on, 'Hebron, since you married one of our daughters in our church you have never paid your church dues, you have never been seen in church. Only your wife brought the children to baptism and confirmation.'

In reply to Mr. Penzhorn's complaint Father smiled and said, 'I had no reason to do that. I never joined the church, I am not a member so I owe no dues.' Mr. Penzhorn said, 'Unless you pay dues like everyone else I shall not confirm him.' Father again replied, 'I don't want him to get confirmed; he wants it and wants it done by you his priest. I am here with him because he asked me to come and talk to you for him. If you don't want to confirm him, all is right by me,' said father with a broad smile. Inside me I was filled with anger against father, that he was not being nice to Reverend Penzhorn. His words, I thought, were too cruel; they would force Mr. Penzhorn to reject me. If I had not been frightened of my father I would have argued with him in Mr. Penzhorn's presence. 'Why can't he apologise?' I asked myself silently, but very bitter against my father.

Without allowing Mr. Penzhorn to say anything, father proceeded further to say, 'When I was a young man I went to work in Pretoria and there I met the Wesleyans. They ran a night school and I joined it. They were the ones who taught me how to read and write. During that time I used to go to their church services on Sundays whenever I was free. Ever since that time,' father went on, 'I have always felt that if I was asked which was my church, I would say the Wesleyan Church.' It was on that occasion that I learnt for the first time that my father at one time in his life went to school at night and attended church services.

Mr. Ernest Penzhorn then told us that he would take me into his confirmation class, but warned father that if he did not pay something towards the dues, on the confirmation day I would not be among those whose parents had settled their duties to the church. He warned father again that, like all parents of children who attend the confirmation class, he must take me to church every Sunday. To that father said nothing, but he knew that he had won the argument.

As father and I left Mr. Penzhorn's office, my die was cast; the fear that I might not be taken on for confirmation class was removed from my mind. Mr. Penzhorn had not acted the way I expected when my father plainly refused to pay him church dues. Harvesting was not over, there was still a lot to be done in the fields in the way of gathering crops. It was an unpleasantly cold winter Sunday, but the sun was bright and the sky was deep blue and completely cloudless.

As we walked back home I had no way of knowing whether father believed my promise that after confirmation I would return to Phokeng Preparatory School to start where I left off and struggle hard until I had passed standard six, which would have paved my way to Tigerkloof Industrial College in the Cape Province.

I was now going to a school which had a strong influence on the children of my tribe; once they had gone through that school, been confirmed and issued with confirmation certificates, they were no longer boys and girls but men and women who had reached adult stage from which they must prepare themselves for a higher stage of becoming fathers and mothers. I too became the victim of that influence. My father knew the likely impact of that influence, but left the decisions for my own future to be cut and dried by me. He had done his duty as a parent, but realised that he could not make me do things I was not willing to do.

A week before the schools started I went to Phokeng Preparatory School to tell Mr. Spooner and my teachers, that I was not going back to school to begin standard three. I arrived at his house and found him in his office. I think that he thought I had come to order my standard three books, but when I broke the news of my leaving to him he doubted whether he had heard me clearly enough. He remained silent for a while and then invited me to repeat what I had told him.

Reverend Spooner took pains to try to persuade me to change my mind, telling me that he knew that one day I would leave to go to the Lutheran Church, but he never thought it would be so soon when I was right in the middle of my studies and making good progress. He looked right into my face, said that he had observed my progress closely and was convinced that I would reach standard six without difficulty. He said, further, that if I took his advice and stayed, I would thank him in the future, and myself for having listened. He went on to say that from his close observation of me he saw a boy who would develop into a man who would help his people in the years that lay ahead. When he observed that my mind was poisoned and there was no way of changing it, he drew a picture in words for me to see. He said, 'You are like a man who starts eating a huge ox, beginning with its head, horns, neck, shoulders, front legs and stomach, and when left with only the tail and hind legs wants to leave off, saying he can't finish it. Finish the ox,' he appealed to me, 'eat it all, you have already eaten the larger part of it.' As I did with father, I promised to return.

Before I left him I promised him that I would always remember his kind words and I would try to make them my guide during the period I spent in the confirmation school. 'Don't be afraid to come here to see me if you need advice, I shall always do what I can for you,' said Mr. Spooner. His words moved me and my eyes began to fill with tears, which I failed to stop running down my face. I shall never forget his last words to me: 'I shall always be your friend.'

From Mr. Spooner's house I went to see the principal, Mr. Mpeche Motaung, who had also developed a liking for me. It was in the afternoon, the sun was nearing setting, and Mr. Motaung welcomed me with both open heart and hands, expecting that I was paying him a purely social visit. After spending several minutes with him and his wife, I broke the news to them that I was not returning to PPS but going the way most Phokeng boys and girls were going, to attend confirmation school and eventually to get confirmed. Mr. Motaung, like my father and Mr. Spooner, tried his best to make me see that confirmation would make me feel that I was no longer a schoolboy, but a grown-up man who must go out to work for himself like others. He tried to make me change, to pursue my studies at PPS. He told me for the first time that it was his intention to approach my parents during the course of my standard six studies to suggest to them that I should be sent to Lovedale African teachers' training college in the Cape Province to study to become a teacher. He said that his judgment was that I could become a good teacher, to help my tribe and other people.

Although highly disappointed by my decision to go to confirmation school, Mr. Mpeche Motaung nevertheless made every effort to make me understand the importance of education. He told me first a story of a man who was born in a very humble family in the United States of America who eventually became the President of that country. I had not heard of that man before, but Mr. Motaung gave me his name as Abraham Lincoln. He told me that Abraham Lincoln's parents would have liked to educate him, but had no means to do so. Abraham, he told me, struggled on his own against great odds and educated himself. In the end he became a wise man and the Americans elected him their leader and President.

From Abraham Lincoln he moved on to another American, but of African descent, Booker T. Washington. He too was born in very humble circumstances, but loved education and made everything possible for himself to acquire it. Booker T. Washington, he said, worked and studied. Because he wanted to become an educated man he persevered, and after long, hard years of struggle he became the educated man he wanted to be. He then turned to his people, to pass on to them the knowledge he had acquired by becoming their educator, leader and adviser. He founded one of the famous places of learning in the United States of America, the Tuskegee Institute. If, said Mr. Mpeche Motaung, Lincoln and Washington could do it, you too can do it.

Something else which Mr. Motaung taught me always lives in my mind. One morning, when I was in standard two, he took us for a scripture lesson. It was a story in the Bible about the children of Israel in the land of Egypt, their sufferings there, the birth of Moses, and the way he grew up in the royal house of Egypt. He said the Egyptian royal house were satisfied that they had made Moses an Egyptian prince. The education they gave him, the honour and privileges of a prince, must have made him feel that he was no longer an Israelite but an Egyptian. Moses, on his own side, never lost the knowledge that he was an Israelite, the sufferings the Children of Israel went through were his and he had to share them with the people who brought him into life. All that, he went on, happened in Africa. The African people thought that they could bribe an Israelite with privileges, but they were utterly wrong. He then posed a question to all of us: where is Africa? how can you get to Africa? The trick nature of the question caught all of us unawares and none of us knew the answer. He repeated the question but no hand went up. He looked at us with amazement and asked, 'Don't you know where Africa is?' Angrily he said, 'You stupid children, stand up.' He lined us up against the wall, ordered us to stretch out our hands, and each one of us got a beating with a stick. Afterwards he stamped hard with his foot on the floor and said, 'This is Africa you are standing on.' He made us stamp hard three times on the floor shouting, 'This is Africa'.

From that day I never forgot that Egypt was in Africa, not elsewhere as the Bible seemed to suggest to us. Most of us when we read the stories in the Bible about the River Jordan, Jerusalem, Egypt,

Jericho, Sinai and other places mentioned in the Bible, were left with the impression that all those places were in Heaven. It had never occurred to us either that the Israelites were the ancestors of the Jewish people, some of whom were the traders in our village whom we knew so well and liked.

The next day I went to another teacher who was going to see me through standard three, Koos Mokgatle. He was a relative, sometimes my part-time employer. In addition to being a teacher he was also a butcher. Sometimes in the afternoons or on Saturdays when my parents did not need my services, I used to work for him in his butcher shop selling meat, or take some already cut, weighed and parcelled into the village to sell to people in their homes. On Saturdays, especially, I used to go to other villages outside Phokeng shouting '*dinama*' (meat) and those interested used to come and buy.

Before he knew of my intentions, Mr. Mokgatle, too, was looking forward to helping me through my education up to standard six. I went to his shop and broke the news to him. At that time he was following his parents who had joined the Pentecostal Holiness Church. He was not a Lutheran and therefore was never confirmed. He was astonished by the news I brought him and, like the others, did his utmost to persuade me to rethink what I had decided by telling me that he had faith in me that I was going to go on with my education to standard six and then if possible go on to a teachers' training institution to train to become a teacher in Phokeng. He said that most of the teachers in Phokeng were from other tribes and their being in Phokeng deprived their own people of teachers. If their people demanded their return, Phokeng would be left with no teachers. Though we must thank them for having come here, we must also recognise that their tribes educated them for themselves, not for the people of Phokeng. 'The people of Phokeng,' Mr. Mokgatle went on, 'need teachers from their own children, but if boys like you only think of going to confirmation school, which means leaving school afterwards, Phokeng will always borrow teachers from other people.'

His words were excellent, encouraging words meant to open my eyes, but it was too late. Perhaps if I had heard such moving words before I went with my father to see Mr. Penzhorn, I might have altered my feelings. I was already committed to going to confirmation school and my name was in Mr. Penzhorn's book. All I could do was to promise Mr. Mokgatle, as I did the others, that after confirmation I should come back to school; but Mr. Mokgatle took that with a pinch of salt. He didn't believe it at all. The stage was set for me; envy for those already working was also there.

I was seventeen years old and the year was nineteen-twenty-eight. I was not good at speaking English but I could make myself understood. Phokeng Preparatory School had brought the language into my life and created the urge in me to know English. There were others who spoke the language better than I did, wrote it better, and I envied them immensely. There was no doubt in my mind that envying them was not enough: the right thing to do was to be like them. The stories of Abraham Lincoln and Booker T. Washington had opened up new ideas in me, that even if I did not return to school, I could work and educate myself at the same time. Promises to my father and others were still there; the question was whether I was going to be a boy of my word or going to let down my father and those who wished me well.

During the year I had spent in standard two, in their efforts to teach us expressions in English, our teachers started a debating class which was held once a week in the evening for two hours. Our teachers took it in turns to be with us while we tried to express ourselves and to show others how well we could speak the language. At the end of the debate, the teacher in attendance would correct us, showing each how she or he misused the words, or how we had repeated ourselves. Each one of us was given the task of going home to think up the next topic to be debated at the next meeting. The topic was announced at the end of the debate to enable us to prepare something to say on the next Tuesday.

When my turn came to introduce what I thought should be debated I came up with a political topic, unaware that it was political. My subject was: should the Europeans leave Africa and go back to Europe or should they stay? My task was to open the debate, and my line was that they should go and leave us alone, since they are not friendly towards us. The subject roused great interest and was debated on three consecutive weeks. Those who supported my contention and those who opposed it remained evenly divided all along until the teachers stopped it because it had been debated long enough. All along I had no idea that I had introduced a political topic until years later when I was right in the middle of African politics in South Africa.

Three episodes had influenced me into thinking that Europeans were not friendly towards the Africans. The three of them followed each other and I resented them all. The first was at Kroondal with the Langes, when I found that I could not sit on the same chair eat from the same plate, drink from the same cup or mug, and sleep in the same house with them. The second was at Kommissiedrift, when Mr. William Rex tried to discourage me from going to school. The third was in Rustenburg, in the native commissioner's office, when Mr. Daniel Branke shouted at me with a brutal voice ordering me to take my hands out of my trouser pockets, telling me that I was in the white man's place. The three episodes left undying memories with me. All the Europeans I worked for earlier treated me well, as I have already stated, but their nice treatment never managed to remove those memories until later, when I was in politics and had more to do with other Europeans.

Until I was in politics I thought that Europeans needed us only as long as they could make use of us, to create pleasures for themselves and nothing more. I thought that they looked upon us as a man would look upon his cow or ox; as long as it could provide him with the milk he needed or pull his plough, he would look after that animal, but as soon as it ceased to provide for his needs his liking for it would cease.

Before these experiences I had never known that South Africa was occupied by people who thought of men not as equals, but as superiors and inferiors. To me the African saying that to grow is to see and to learn became a reality. As I grew I saw, learnt and started to think. Though I knew of another African saying, 'Don't judge all by the weaknesses and faults of some', the feeling that Europeans were unfriendly dominated my feelings all along. Before my entry into politics I suspected everything they said or did. My mind was poisoned. The fact that in Kroondal I found that they could not go into the same church with the Africans who worked and lived with them made me question their sincerity. I repeat, that at that time I knew nothing of what politics were about. I was only a tribal boy entering the new world inhabited by Europeans in South Africa.

XXI Confirmation Class

In the second week of August nineteen-twenty-nine I started confirmation classes. We were a hundred when we started; there were two of us from Phokeng Preparatory School and both of us shared the same surname. The other boy was Phokeng Sitwell Mokgatle, who had passed his standard six there and had been to an African teachers' college run by the Anglican Church, called Khaiso, in the Pietersburg district of the eastern Transvaal. I arrived at the confirmation class carrying a new Bible and a new hymn book my father bought me. It was four days a week from Mondays to Thursdays; we were free on Fridays and Saturdays.

From the beginning to the end we were under Mr. Ernest Penzhorn himself. We did no writing or taking of notes, but we read a lot from the Bible and the hymn books and we were to know most of the things we learned by heart. It took us four months to get confirmed. We started school at half-past nine in the morning and finished off at half-past two in the afternoon. Every day when we broke off Mr. Penzhorn gave us homework to learn at home and to repeat to him by heart the next day. We went through both the Old and New Testaments and the Hermannsburg Lutheran Church hymn book, as well as the prayer book. In addition, we learned the history of the Lutheran Church, its methods and differences from other churches. More important, we learned about the founder of the church, Dr. Martin Luther, his quarrel with the Church of Rome and why he left it. We learned, further, that through its founder the Lutheran Church was the pioneer in the Reformation movement. We were also taught a bit about other religions, Islam, Buddhism and Judaism.

We were all prepared to become good Lutherans and devout Christians. I do not know about the others but I was full of doubts, which forced me in the middle of our course, when I had become accustomed to Mr. Penzhorn, to ask him lots of questions. I remember asking him why, as a Christian with such a good message to love your neighbour as you love yourself, he had such an intense dislike for Mr. Spooner and his church. His reply was that he disliked Mr. Spooner's coming to people already converted. 'My father,' said Mr. Penzhorn, 'cultivated this field and Mr. Spooner comes along to reap where he did not plough. There are still many places in Africa,' said Mr. Penzhorn, 'where Mr. Spooner could go to start his church, but he chose to come here where the ground has been softened.' That, he said, was the main reason why he was intensely against the Pentecostal Holiness Church and its founder.

Although Mr. Penzhorn on more than one occasion ordered me to stop asking him questions, like why there was such rivalry between the churches of different denominations and yet all said that they were the armies of Jesus Christ and all were out to spread his message of peace and love, he did in fact inwardly recognise that I was searching for a solution to the problem which had beset the Christian Church. As we went along my persistence in asking searching questions increased. I remember well one day at playtime he asked all to leave the church where our confirmation classes were held, but ordered me to stay because he had something to say to me. When the other children had left the church he asked me to come to him and to kneel down between his feet, and while I was on my knees facing him took hold of me by the ears and pulled me backwards and forwards, which was very painful, and when he thought that I had had enough, he said, 'You give me too much trouble, I hope this will make you stop.' I answered, 'Moruti-Reverend, I want to know.' He replied, 'You will know more later, you are going to be a priest in this church; you will be ordained a priest.' In reply I said, 'I shall never be a priest, in this church or in any other church.' He said, 'I know you will be; your mother's father used to preach in this church, from that altar,' pointing to it. He said in a harsh voice, 'Get away from me, go and play.' I left.

The other children outside were wondering what was happening to me, and as soon as I emerged from the church most of them, especially the boys, gathered around me to find out why I was kept back. I told them of the events which took place between me and our Moruti-Reverend and all laughed, but one of them asked why I did not cry to make him feel that he was hurting me. On the whole we liked our priest, he was a nice old man who sometimes joked with us. He was so good at our language that he knew a hundred proverbs in it and their fundamental meanings. He used to laugh at us when we did not know the names of things in Sesotho, and after telling us what they were called he would say, 'You call yourselves Basotho, I am the only Mosotho here.'

During our confirmation class I made a bet with two friends of mine, Phokeng Sitwell Mokgatle and Nudu Elias Maithufi, that during the duration of the class none of us would fail to answer a question correctly, or fail to say correctly what we were asked to learn by heart in the Bible or hymn book. I did not know Nudu Maithufi until we met at the confirmation school, but we became very close friends. Phokeng Mokgatle was more than a friend as he was a relative as well. At the end of three months Nudu Maithufi fell by failing to remember some parts of the chapter we were asked to learn in the Bible. Phokeng and I remained the contestants, but unfortunately for Phokeng Mokgatle, two weeks before we were due for confirmation he failed in the Bible too and I won the contest.

On the first of December, nineteen-twenty-nine, there was great excitement in our villages, as was the habit on such occasions. It was our confirmation day. We, the boys, were dressed in white trousers, black waistcoats, black jackets, white shirts, black ties, white panama or straw hats, and with white handkerchiefs in our jacket pockets. Shoes were black or brown. The girls wore white dresses with small black spots, blue kerchiefs, white handkerchiefs in their hands and black or brown shoes. We were following a tradition which had been followed since church confirmations began in our tribe in eighteen-sixty-seven. Our parents went to great lengths to get the outfits for the confirmation day. It was also a day for feasting. Wealthier parents on that day killed sheep or goats to entertain their children and friends.

On that day we gathered at our priest's house, lined up there in pairs, a boy and a girl, and waited for the church service to begin. When the service was in full session, led by our teacher and priest we started moving to the church which is a distance away from the priest's house, singing a hymn always sung on such occasions. All the boys' panama or straw hats were fastened on their jacket lapels by thin silk elastic strings to enable us to throw them off as we entered the church door. As we went into the church our hats hung on our backs, held tight by the elastic silk cord. As soon as we entered the church the congregation rose to their feet as an honour to us. On that day the parents of every one who was getting confirmed were expected to be in church to welcome their children into the full membership of the Christian community. My mother was there, but not my father.

The man who declined to pay church dues because he was not a member stuck to his beliefs and principles. He never went to church, and saw no reason why he should on that occasion. But he had ended the life of one of his sheep so that I could invite my friends to celebrate with me. On such a day there was no preaching. The morning session was devoted to the ceremony of handing out confirmation certificates, showing the day on which the receiver was born, baptised and confirmed. My Christian name was entirely unknown to many people, only those who went to school with me knew it. We who were getting confirmed occupied the altar with our priests, who had our certificates in alphabetical order. We knelt in groups of four to receive the certificates. First the priest read out the name of the recipient and then read words he had chosen from any chapter or verse in the Bible which he thought suited the recipient,

When my name was read out many people wondered who I was, but those who were able to see my face recognised me.

In the afternoon there was still no preaching, but the church was packed with the congregation come to listen to the questions and answers put to each of those being confirmed. Parents whose children answered all the questions correctly were the most proud. My mother was one of them, because not a single question passed me. By that time people who had not known my name in the morning were well informed.

December the first came and went, schools were on holiday and were reopening in January nineteen-thirty. I had promised my father and teachers that I would return to school to get to standard six, and I was in a dilemma whether I was going to return to school, knowing full well that not a single one of those who got confirmed with me was doing so. It was still ploughing time and I joined a relative of mine called David Makgala, mixed our oxen and went out to plough his fields as well as my mother's fields, and on the eighteenth of the same month I returned to Phokeng to join others in receiving our first communion. We went to church in the afternoon of the previous day for a service of confession and asking for forgiveness.

That was the first and last communion I received. It was customary that those who received communion for the first time must make every effort to be at the second, which was held three months later. When most of my friends assembled for their second I was not among them, and I learned later that in his sermon Reverend Penzhorn remarked, 'All my children have come back, but I miss one and I suspected that he would not return with the others.' Everybody knew that he meant me. Faced with my father's expectation that I was returning to school as I promised after ploughing was over, I confronted him again. I had been thinking most of the time how I could get round him with another excuse. As though he knew what was in my mind, he waited for me to break the ice.

One day after I had armed myself with a pretext, I went to him. He was busy thatching in the village. That was in January, after we had been to the Chief's house to express our loyalty and to be given a group name Mangana-a-Sekete. Earlier I mentioned that Sekete was the man who became the first Christian in our tribe and was Mokgatle's son by his third wife. Before Christianity came he was the head of the tribal group known as Mangana and our group was named after his group and his grandson Phokeng Mokgatle became the head of our group.

'Father,' I said, 'I am not returning to school, I have lost interest in studies. If I do return,' I said, 'it would only be to please you but I would fail every year.'

My father received the news of my not going back to school with reluctance and disappointment. He sat down, looked at me and in a broken voice said, 'I knew this would happen. No one has come out of that confirmation but he imagines that he has reached adulthood. Therefore the only thing to do is to go away to work. You know what my wishes are, what I planned for you. I wanted to send you to Tigerkloof Industrial College to learn building, so that in future you could set up on your own. Perhaps,' he continued sadly, 'someone has told you that there is something nice waiting for you in the future, but take my warning, there is nothing nice waiting for you except a hard life if you depend on going from place to place seeking employment.'

'There is one thing which pleases me in all this,' Father said. 'In future you will not blame me when you lead a rough life and see some of your friends who took their fathers' advice have an easier life than yours. I am glad that you will say, "If I had listened to my father and had gone back to school I would not be living like this." You will tell the truth, "My father wanted to educate me but I refused." You will not come to my grave after my death, to cry over it and say, "You didn't care about me. Look how I live today." You will come there to say, "Had I listened, I would be a better man today." You are the only son I have, therefore I felt that I should use everything I have to get what I think you deserve.'

Those fatherly words of my father never left my memories. Everything he said I have silently repeated when I met great odds. I have never blamed him, as he foresaw, but myself for not having listened to his advice. From that day my love for my father grew and grew. His frankness left me in no doubt that he wanted to give me something he himself did not have: education. To cool him off, I told him that wherever I settled to work I should educate myself by correspondence. There were places, I told him, where one could educate oneself while working. Father then said that he hoped I meant what I said, but remarked that he had no control over that; everything depended entirely on me.

A few days later Mr. Penzhorn approached him with a proposal that I should be sent to the Lutheran Church African teachers' training college in the western Transvaal, but father rejected it, and advised me against it.

My father refused the offer for me to go to the college because Mr. Penzhorn told him that he need not worry about paying for my training, board and lodging, the church would provide all that; but after the completion of my training course, when I started teaching, the church would deduct from my salary an agreed amount until what the church had spent was paid off. My father saw that I would not be free to do what I liked, go where I wished, or choose

166

the nature of my employment, and that for a very long time I would be at the mercy of the church. Father liked freedom of action and movement, and complete individual independence. To him Mr. Penzhorn's offer seemed like imprisonment for me in the early part of my life. Though he desired to see me an educated man, at the same time he wanted to see me master of my fate and captain of my soul. On these principles he could not compromise.

At the beginning of February nineteen-thirty, carrying a small suitcase containing my confirmation clothes, two shirts and two blankets, I left my parents, tribe and Phokeng – the place I loved very much – for Rustenburg, to begin to face the world alone without my parents' guidance and protection. Unlike in nineteen-twenty-three, when I ran away to Kroondal, and a few years later to Kommissiedrift, my departure from Phokeng and my parents was permanent. In the world I was facing, I was also going to search for a new home. Before I said good-bye to my birthplace a friend of mine Ntebeng Rasetlola, who was already working in Rustenburg in a bottle-store, invited me to come to take his job because at the end of the second week of February he was leaving for Johannesburg to join his two brothers. He promised that he would tell his employers that he was only going away for a month and would like me to hold down his job for him until his return. When in Johannesburg he would write to say that he was not returning and that would induce his employers to keep me on.

When he told his employers of his intention to visit his brothers in Johannesburg, although they agreed they could not let him go until the end of February. When I arrived I found that I had to wait for two weeks before I could take on his job. He nevertheless introduced me to his employers; they agreed to our arrangement, but asked me to call back at the end of the month. There was no question of my returning to Phokeng. I had to seek two weeks' temporary employment. At that time I still did not know that I had no right to work without the native commissioner's consent. Another friend Ngatlhe Kgokong, the boy I had looked for when I arrived in Kroondal, was working in the Grand Hotel. My friend urged his employers to take me on trial and this was done. They had no right to keep me in their employ without obtaining the native commissioner's permission, which would have meant registering me for thirty days – which is the only basis on which all African workmen are employed in South Africa even today. They took the risk of keeping me with no registration. The agreement was that if they decided to keep me and I wanted to work for them, they would report their error to the commissioner and apologise and then ask for permission to employ me. I worked in the Grand Hotel for two weeks until I went to take Ntebeng Rasetlola's job.

The Grand Hotel management drafted me into the kitchen to assist the chef, who was a woman. I knew nothing about cooking and had not worked in a kitchen before. The chef was a kind and a patient European woman who wanted to teach me the art of cooking. Her main wish was to make me her second chef, but for the two weeks I worked there with her I learned nothing and left the place as I went into it. Perhaps I ought to say that I learned to fry chips, which were used in the bar as snacks. In addition I learned how to clear ashes from a large coal stove and to make a fresh fire.

Early in the morning at four o'clock I got up to make the fire and fill all the kettles with water, so that by half-past five when the cook came in to make breakfast, tea and coffee, everything would be ready and the kitchen itself would be as hot as an oven. In the afternoons, immediately after lunch was served, I cleared the stove of the ashes, cleaned it thoroughly, left it for an hour to cool off and then made a fire again, for chip-frying, tea- and coffee-making and for preparation of the evening meal. The same operation went on day after day. Breakfast, lunch and dinner times were torment for me. Each time the hour for those meals drew near I got frightened and worried to the depths of my heart. The chef was really determined to make me her assistant. The things used in cooking I could not get into my head. When the kitchen was quiet, when only the two of us were there, she used to take out all the plates used in the kitchen to tell me what they were for, but I could not remember any of them. Knives, forks and spoons were explained to me in the same fashion by her, but when the time came for me to remember them all and to pass to her when she was dishing up at the rush hour, I got mixed up and was of no help. She put all the plates, not once but many times, on long tables in the kitchen, saying patiently that these were soup, dinner, fish, bread and sweet plates. Cutlery, too, she laid on the tables and explained to me as she did with the plates, and asked, 'Do you think that you will remember them now?' And I would say, 'Yes, I will remember now.' But when she called for them at the busy time, I remembered none of them.

In the middle of the third week I left the Grand Hotel kitchen, and the chef was nearly in tears to see me leave. Despite all the trouble I had caused her she was still willing to work with me and to teach me cooking in its highest form. But domestic work was not for me. I hated working on Sundays and public holidays. I knew that if I chose to become a domestic worker, I would never get a chance to play soccer which I loved to play, or be with my friends whenever I wished.

I left the Grand Hotel to start at the Masonic Hotel, not first-class, owned by a German, Josef Setzer, and his wife. The hotel had a bar like the two first-class ones but, unlike them, also had a bottle store. Mr. Josef Setzer took me on to work in the bottle store at the wage of forty-five shillings a month with board and lodging, five shillings more than I was paid at the Grand Hotel. The Masonic Hotel, unlike the Grand Hotel, had very few residents and few who came to have their meals there. The chef at the Masonic Hotel was an Englishwoman called Jane North. There was no second chef. There were two African girls working there, and an African by the name of Bogatsu Pilane who became my best friend. He was not of my tribe but a Mokgatla from a tribe north of my own. Another African worked in the bar. As with my friend who gave me the job, my duties in the bottle store were to sweep the shop every morning and then wash the floor with a bucket of water and a rag.

My other duties were to wash dirty bottles and twice a week fill them with wine, brandy and other drinks sold in the bottle store. I worked with a young man, Egmond Behrens, whose parents had come from Germany to settle in South Africa. His parents were farming alongside the Magaliesberg mountains, west of Kroondal. Like many Germans in Kroondal he spoke my language very well. I handled the European liquor daily but South African European law forbade me, as it did all Africans throughout the country, to drink it, and to be left alone in the bottle store without a European being present.

Another duty was to deliver the liquor on a bicycle to the customers. The town Rustenburg was in fact a village, with houses and streets, but the houses were not numbered. To deliver the parcels one had to know the names of the people and where they lived. Each time I went out on the bicycle to deliver liquor I had to be given a special pass by the employer authorising me to be in possession of liquor, the number and brands of liquor I was carrying and the names of the customers I was sent to deliver liquor to. It was a criminal offence for an African to be found in possession of European liquor without a permit. The Masonic Hotel was right opposite the town's charge office and the police station. The police saw me working there every day, so that when they saw me on the bicycle carrying bottles they never bothered to stop me.

The bottle store closed at twelve o'clock on Wednesdays. For an hour until one o'clock I had to work inside, cleaning and dusting the bottles and the shelves. Since I was not working in the hotel, I was entitled to be free from the time we closed until the next day. Egmond was free to do what he liked. Mrs. Setzer thought that it was a waste for me to be allowed a free afternoon. She persuaded her husband to order me to help in the hotel, sweep the yard and to wash and comb their dog. That was meant to occupy me the whole afternoon.

I considered Wednesday afternoons as my free time, that it was beyond Mrs. Setzer to make me work in the hotel, sweep the yard or wash and comb her dog. In order to preserve peace and harmony I did perform such tasks, though I detested them. I was also forced to help with scrubbing the bar floors with brush, water and rag on Sunday mornings. Mrs. Setzer took the attitude that I was in their employ, therefore it was within their right to make me work wherever they chose. I, on the other hand, argued that I was employed to work in the bottle store, that as soon as its doors closed on Wednesdays the afternoon belonged entirely to me. I was therefore determined to stand firm for my freedom.

With some boys from my tribe and others, we formed a soccer football team and called it the Matopo Hills Football Club. I was selected club secretary. We met in the evenings to plan our activities and practices. The only times we had to practise were on Wednesday afternoons, and we played matches with rival teams on Sundays. There were no other days on which we could engage in that game, which I was very fond of. As it was the official policy of the authorities in the country, our team was purely African. No European boy could join us, even if he wanted to or we wanted him. But other non-Africans could join us; for instance, the coloureds, or Indian boys, but there were so few of them in town that there was no one to offer his services to us.

There were other teams too with whom we played. We practised in the open place outside the town, near Bethlehem, the African residential area. There were two playing fields, one of which we could use if we were the first to apply for it. Though we called our matches friendly games we did play for money. The amounts laid down by each side varied; the winning side gained from the beaten one. We were at times out of luck, and when our funds were at their lowest ebb we taxed ourselves, so that we could challenge or accept a challenge from other teams.

XII Journey to Pretoria

At the beginning of August nineteen-thirty I gave the Setzers notice that I was going to leave their employ. A friend of mine and a relative at the same time, Nchotlho Diale, was already in Pretoria working, and nearly every week I received a letter from him urging me to join him. Pretoria, being bigger than our home farm town, was more interesting and one could enjoy and learn more things there. Mr. Josef Setzer, assisted by Egmond Behrens, tried hard to persuade me to stay but the news in my friend's letters was too attractive and prevented me from changing my mind. 'I am here,' said the contents of Nchotlho Diale's letters, 'there will be no need for you to be in need of anything except find a new job. In the task of seeking a job,' the letters said, 'I shall do my best to help you.'

Egmond Behrens especially was disappointed, and promised that a month later it would be his turn to leave. I was also fond of Behrens. If he had not been a European I think that we would have established a strong friendship. I remember more than once hearing Mr. Setzer warn him in German, which he did not know that I understood, that he should not be too friendly towards me. All the time I worked for the Setzers in the Masonic Bottle Store it was on a monthly basis as required by law. That was uniform throughout the country, under the Native Urban Areas Act of nineteen-twenty-three, framed and passed by the Smuts' government.

When employed, an African went to the native commissioner's office with the employer's letter to enter into a monthly contract of employment which binds both sides to a month's notice to terminate the contract. It was a document with a duplicate. The original was kept by the worker, the duplicate by the employer, who renewed it by paying one shilling each month for it and by signing his name on the original kept by the worker. If the police found me with an unsigned one they could arrest me for being unemployed.

At the end of the month Mr. Setzer signed off my monthly contract and gave me the one he had in his possession to show that he needed no renewal. At the native commissioner's office I was left with the choice of asking for another permit to seek work or for a travelling permit to enable me to leave Rustenburg for Pretoria. Without the commissioner's permission to leave I could not leave. Without his consent to take up employment, I could not take it up. That was how

I faced the South African Europeans' world, and that paved my way into politics, about which I shall have more to say later.

On the second of September, for the first time I saw myself inside a train carriage, third-class, with hard wooden benches, leaving Rustenburg for Pretoria, where I settled until my departure from South Africa. I arrived in Pretoria after five o'clock in the afternoon. My friend knew of my arrival, but as it was a working day he could not be at the station to welcome me. I had not been in a European city as large as Pretoria before and it seemed very confusing to me. Armed with my friend's address, with a travelling pass to Pretoria, but without a permit to seek work in Pretoria, I hailed an African taxi outside the main station and asked the taxi man to take me to the hardware merchant at 129 Church Street where Nchotlho Diale worked. On arrival I found he was out with deliveries, but inside the shop I was assured that he would be coming back to stable the horse. I was delighted that I had found him, that the only thing I had to do was to wait for his return. It had astonished me how the taxi man found the place because I was not used to houses or places with numbers on.

When the shop closed I was still waiting for my friend outside, and although assured of his return, beginning to entertain doubts. Tribal and rural life was behind me, and before me was a long period of urban life with complications, trials, webs of pass law restrictions, colour discrimination and uncertainties in this home of the South African European that I heard about first from Mr. Daniel Branke, native commissioner in Rustenburg. Darkness began to set in before my friend returned to find me worried to the bones. I was a stranger in a strange city.

I did not see him arrive, but from the other side of the street I heard him shouting with joy at me, saying, 'I bet you don't know where you are.' It was true.

I was greatly relieved to see my friend and a sense of security took possession of me. He entered his employer's yard, released the horse from the harness, led it round the yard for a few minutes loosening its legs before he took it into the stable for the night. I was hungry, looking forward to going to where he stayed so that we could have something to eat.

The Urban Areas Act forbids Africans in the urban areas from making or brewing beer to their own natural tastes, to drink it or possess it in their homes without the permission of the municipality under which they live. When I arrived in Pretoria I knew nothing about this, I had no idea that it placed me and my life at the mercy of the European native commissioners. We walked to where my friend lived. When we got near the place I began to see a large concentration of Africans moving about. We were in the area of 'Pretoria

Municipal Unmarried' compounds, for men without their wives in Pretoria. There were three large buildings, all of them compounds. The street was called Proes Street, in the area called Pretoria West. It was not outside Pretoria, but in the centre, towards the south, next to the old European grave-yard and next to a location for coloured people and Indians called the Cape Location or Reserve, or the Indian Bazaar.

On the northern side of Proes Street was the Municipal African Workmen's Hostel, where men were housed rent-free and women were not allowed. Next to it was a large block consisting of rooms let out to Africans employed in Pretoria paying monthly rents. Non-residents and women were not allowed, especially women. Male visitors could go in provided they obtained a permit at the office which was at the entrance. All the rooms were communal; tenants only hired a concrete bunk and they lived twelve in a room, six sleeping on each side. At the end of the room facing the door were large steel cabinets where they stored their belongings.

There was also a communal kitchen where they cooked their meals. At night the municipal police had to go round to see that no strangers were being given shelter in the rooms. On the west side of Proes Street right opposite was another large building, the reception depot. Strangers to Pretoria like myself were required to sleep there until they had found jobs and obtained places for themselves. I knew nothing about all that. My friend was an occupant of the hostel, where he paid rent. He occupied a room with two other tribesmen of ours, both my close relatives, whom I did not know were in Pretoria. They were Godfrey Mokgatle and his brother Mafito. The three of them took me in as their guest and obtained a permit for me to be with them for several hours. They gave me a tasty meal but before ten o'clock, the time when both the gates of the hostel and the reception depot were shut, they told me that they had to take me to the reception depot.

I was disheartened but I had no choice. At the reception depot, where they took me, the man in charge was from another tribe married to a girl of our tribe and friendly to everyone from our tribe because of his wife. His name was Mogotsi. He was not employed by Pretoria Municipality but by the Native Commissioner's Department. He was a policeman. They introduced me to Mogotsi and left. After taking me in he asked me if I knew his wife's people, which I did. He then took me to a room, showed me an empty concrete bunk in a room full of completely strange men from nearly all the tribes in the country. He then warned me to be careful with my belongings because others might help themselves to them. The building was double-storeyed and full of men seeking work. Mogotsi instructed me to be early at the reception office next morning with my blankets and other things neatly folded for safe keeping, and for a rubber stamp showing that I had spent the night at the reception depot as required by law. Without such a stamp on my travelling pass or on my native commissioner's permit to seek work, the police could arrest me and get me charged for not having spent the night at the reception depot.

That was an eye-opener for me. At last I began to realise that I was in the white man's place, as Dan Branke had remarked earlier in my adult life.

Municipal hostels and reception depots for unmarried African workmen, the direct results of the Native Urban Areas Act of nineteen-twenty-three, are instruments designed purely to put into operation the doctrine of Apartheid. Before its introduction, African workmen – who are largely migrants from tribes – who went into towns and cities to seek work, leaving their families behind, were housed by their employers close to their places of work. They lived in the centre of cities and towns, but the authorities, who are always the first to incite the European population into thinking that Africans living next to them are a menace and ought to be removed far away from the areas defined as European areas, began to make a law by which they could compel the municipalities to build such hostels and reception depots. They then arrested Africans if they failed to sleep there, or for trespassing into European residential areas.

Nineteen-thirty was a year of depression. Many Africans were out of work and could not find any; some of them were thrown out of their jobs to make room for European workers. Hard manual jobs like working on the railways, road making, digging trenches and sweeping streets, which were considered suitable for Africans only, were taken away from them and given to the Europeans. In cities like Pretoria where I lived, the authorities were even inciting European families to boycott factories, bakeries, butcher shops, laundries and others which kept on employing African labour instead of European labour. Notices appeared in the windows of many places stating that the work done there was only by white labour.

Being placed in such a situation, I was faced along with many others with the dilemma of being arrested for being in a European city without work. An African seeking work was allowed fourteen days within which to find it, and after that the local native commissioner was entitled to refuse him another chance to try his luck. Once your pass was stamped with a refusal stamp you knew that your next home would be the police cell. The next morning you would be before the same native commissioner who refused you a chance, and you would be sent to prison if you could not pay the fine.

The next morning, after depositing my belongings with Mogotsi

174

at the reception depot office and obtaining a stamp that I spent the night there, I set out for the native commissioner's office to ask for permission to seek work. I found the place in Church Street, a large flat building, next to the house which had been Paul Kruger's.

There, behind the building in a large yard, I found hundreds of Africans in long queues waiting to be served. There were four queues: one for those who had come to pay their poll tax, one for those who had been arrested the previous day on pass offences, one for those who came to ask for another chance to seek work and the last for newcomers like myself who were there for the first time. There was an old man, a European by the name of Malherbe, who was the head of that section and in charge of granting or refusing permission. As always happens, some were laughing because their requests were granted and others were looking at the blue sky above their heads wondering how they could disappear into it. It was very rare for newcomers, if their travelling passes were in order, to be refused a chance to try their luck.

I was about to celebrate my twentieth birthday, but when I left Rustenburg the native commissioner's official, without asking my age, stamped my travelling pass 'Not Liable for Tax'. When Mr. Malherbe in Pretoria issued me with a permit to seek work, he also stamped my pass with his large stamp 'Not Liable for Tax'. In fact I ought to have been liable when I was eighteen, but because of that stamp I did not pay poll tax until I was twenty-three. Armed with a permit to seek work I went to Nchotlho Diale's place for lunch and to start my future in Pretoria. I didn't know that one of my school friends from another tribe who had been sent to Phokeng by his parents to learn English was also in Pretoria working. Diale told me of him, gave me his address and told me how to get there. After lunch I set out to find my friend Titus Diphoko. I found him working for a butcher in Esselen Street, Sunnyside. He was out collecting orders but I was told to wait, that he would arrive at any time.

I did not wait long before Titus Diphoko arrived to find me, leaning against his master's shop. Surprise was coupled with happiness. After laughs and warm handshakes he invited me into the yard to introduce me to his fellow workers who were all from tribes far away from Rustenburg. Their master, Mr. Herbert George How, was having an afternoon sleep and was due to get up at four o'clock to see that everything was in order for the next day. Mr. How was a fairly old man who, I was told, came to South Africa during the Anglo-Boer war, decided to stay, married a Dutch woman, but never bothered to learn the language. He understood everything said in it but always replied in English. Titus and Phoshoko Thsetla were the only two who spoke English among the African workers, who numbered more than fifteen. Both Titus and Phoshoko agreed to introduce me to their master to see if he could give me a job. When he got up and found me amongst his men he asked what I was doing there. Titus explained that I was looking for a job. 'Can he speak English?' Mr. How asked. I replied, 'Yes, sir, I can.' That was enough.

He demanded to see my pass, and after seeing it he took it back to the house, signed it, came back, gave it back to me with a shilling and said, 'Be here tomorrow to start work.' I was employed and that was my first job in Pretoria. After giving me the evening meal which was supplied by their master, mealie meal porridge with tasty beef or mutton, Titus accompanied me to the reception depot which was far away in Pretoria West. In the evening I reported to my friend and relatives, who had given me hospitality when I arrived, that I had got the job and all were happy about it. I spent the second night at the reception depot and told Mogotsi, who also congratulated me on being so lucky so quickly. The next day I was in front of Mr. Malherbe again, that time for my monthly contract pass. I was carrying my belongings with me. It was not until after lunch that I arrived at Mr. How's butcher shop. I found some of them making sausages and others cooking dripping. Mr. How ordered that I should be shown how sausages and dripping were made. He asked me to write on a piece of paper to see my handwriting, and that satisfied him too. We were housed in his back-yard, in one large room with no beds. Not all slept there; he had three butcher shops, one not very far away, also in Esselen Street, which was under the management of his brother, and the other one far off in one of Pretoria's sophisticated residential areas near the University, called Hatfield. Some slept at Hatfield, others at the other shop. We started work at four o'clock in the morning, first cutting orders and wrapping them.

By six o'clock deliveries began, but as a newcomer I stayed in the shop the first day. Mr. How told his daughter Queenie to draw up the list of all the customers I was going to be drafted to. In the afternoon I was handed a list of names and addresses to go to and collect the order books which had been left with the parcels in the morning for customers to write their needs for the next day. I took the bicycle with a cane basket in front and rode into Sunnyside. I did not come back until after five o'clock, but I had managed to collect all the books. Mr. How thought that was excellent. The next morning things had changed for me; I was to go out delivering. Some customers got their meat late that day, but when they telephoned Mr. How he told them that a new boy was on the round and he would be there at any time. When I did arrive the customers already knew that my being a stranger was the cause of their trouble.

When I returned I was nervous, thinking that Mr. How would

say, 'You are no good, you delivered my customers' meat too late.'
But the contrary was the case. In the afternoon I went out again to
collect orders, but I had gained a little experience and my troubles
were fewer than on the day before. I was engaged at a wage of fifty
shillings a month and it was an enormous improvement in my earnings. Food was always the same, mealie meal porridge and meat once
a day in the evening. Some customers were kind; they knew we
started work very early, and when we reached their homes they told
their African servants to give us something to eat or tea or coffee to
drink.

Delivering parcels into so many homes with so many female
servants was bound to introduce relationships with some of them.
They were girls from many tribes but most were Sesotho-speaking.
Arrangements started being made for dates and selection of meeting
places to talk matters over. At that time relationships did not end in
hand-holdings and good-bye kissings as they had when I was at
school with my first girl friend, Lucy Thipe, and others; they went
beyond that. I was careful not to promise marriage, because I knew
that my parents were waiting to suggest a wife for me. Nevertheless, I
kept my girl friends company in Pretoria and they in turn kept me
company. Some of them would have liked to marry me but they too
knew that their parents might have objected since they did not know
me and my history.

Mr. How grew fond of me and always wanted to travel with me to
Hatfield in the mornings. On Friday mornings we went there to do
orders. Sometimes I was left alone in the main shop in Esselen
Street, which was the head office. Some men who had worked for
Mr. How for years, far longer than I had, did not like it. Why
should this young boy, a newcomer, be treated so? Mr. How said it
was because I understood him and he understood me. That could
hardly convince anyone, because long before I appeared on the
scene Mr. How and his workmen got on well together. To be liked
is good, but it was not long before I found out that it has its dis-
advantages as well. Mr. How developed a habit of piling responsibilities on my shoulders. At times when I had a date with a girl friend
for the afternoon I would find that he wanted me to wait for the
wholesale meat sellers to deliver meat, to check it and sign for it.
Most of them came very late in the afternoon when my girl friend
had returned to her duties. That annoyed me immensely. When I
argued, 'Why always pick on me?' he replied, 'Because you do it
better than the others.' I always felt that I was deprived of my afternoon's freedom and to that I objected most strongly. My girl friends
always accused me of making dates when I knew I would not keep
them. The other thing which annoyed me very much with Mr. How
was that he relieved others of making dripping and shifted it on to

me. His reasons were always the same, 'You know how to make it better than others.' When I argued that dripping-making did not begin when he employed me, he used to shout at me with a harsh voice, 'Shut up, do as you are told, or else I'll call the police.' It was the habit of the police when called to listen to what the master had to say.

Mr. How did not stop there. He had a tennis court in his yard where he sometimes played with his friends or his son Denis or his daughter Queenie. They usually played on Sunday mornings before lunch. He used to wake me up early in the morning to water the court and afterwards pull a roller over it to make it level, and then draw white lines to make it a real tennis court. I hated doing it on Sunday when others were sleeping, having a rest. In the house they had an African male worker. When he was not well, I was the one to take his place. Mrs. How was a person never satisfied with the work done.

I worked ten months for Mr. How, but his insistence that I should wait for the wholesalers and cook dripping while others went freely where they liked, and do the Sunday work in the tennis court, forced me to give him notice to leave his employ at the end of July nineteen-thirty-one. It seems to me, looking back, that August was a month of movements for me. I left Mr. How's employ at the beginning of the month after struggling for my release for four days. I refused to change my mind when he urged me to, saying that in future he would see that we took turns in cooking the dripping. I was, in addition, tired of getting up early in the mornings and hoped to find a job where I could get up later than four o'clock. Reluctantly, after first refusing to sign off my pass, he did so and threw it at me, saying, 'Don't come here again.'

During November nineteen-thirty, when I had been in Pretoria two months, I undertook a journey one Sunday to find my mother's cousin who lived in one of Pretoria's African locations, Bantule. When I left home Mother had told me to search for her so that when I experienced difficulties I could call on her for help. From Sunnyside to Bantule was a long walk, and as we were not allowed to use delivery bicycles on Sundays I had to start early to get there, find her and stay with her before returning to my place of work.

I did not reach Bantule that day as I intended to. On the way, walking westward through the old and famous African location Marabastad and the Indian Bazaar (on open ground at the end of Boom Street) at about two o'clock in the afternoon, I saw a large gathering of people with police nearby, some standing next to their motor-cycles. I went to see what was taking place. For the first time I attended a political meeting, but I had no idea that was what it was. I found four groups holding a joint open-air meeting. They

178

were the African National Congress, the ICU (the Industrial and Commercial Workers' Union of Africa), the Radicals and the Garveyites. The speakers were taking turns delivering their addresses. The ICU were represented by Ismael Moroe, the Radicals by George Daniels, the Garveyites by a man whose name was also Garvey, a follower and admirer of Marcus Garvey, and the Congress by Simon Peter Matseke, who later became President of Congress in the Transvaal.

Their theme was the burning of passes by Africans on the sixteenth of December nineteen-thirty, Dingaan's day. Such agitation against the passes was in full swing in all major cities of the country. The emphasis was that on that day all Africans must burn their passes and never carry them again. The police were taking notes, and the speakers were speaking in very high tones charged with high emotions. I was surprised by the bravery displayed in the presence of the police. The speech which impressed me most was made by the Radical, George Daniel.

Hertzog's government was in power at the time and his minister of justice was Oswald Pirow, the man who prosecuted in the famous treason trial of nineteen-fifty-six. During his speech Daniels said, and repeated it three times, 'Pirow, Pirow, Pirow, I am not going to call him Minister of Justice, but Minister of Injustice.' He went on to attack Hertzog, his government, Pirow and the whole system of pass laws, urging every African present to respond to the call to burn the passes on the day. While he went on I expected the police to rush to arrest him for saying such things against the government and those who were running it. Nothing of the kind happened. Daniels' speech and attacks inspired me greatly and I did not leave the meeting until darkness had fallen and everyone dispersed. Bantule was not far away, I could see it on the hill to the north-west of where I attended the meeting, but I returned without having reached it.

The day on which the passes were to be burnt remained in my memory, and I made sure that I remembered it, so that I too should be there to throw my pass into the flames. I did not attend further meetings after that but on the sixteenth of December I left my place of work, telling the others that I was going to visit my aunt. I listened to my fellow-workers discussing the burning of passes, but all warned that if you burn your pass the police will arrest you and those who urged you to burn it will do nothing for you. But I remained convinced that if I did burn my pass I would have freed myself from the pass system. I never told my friends that I was going to burn my pass on that day. Dingaan's Day was a public holiday in South Africa at that time and I went carrying my monthly contract pass with me but forgetting that its duplicate was with Mr. How. I got there in good time before the ceremony and a large number of

Africans turned up, but I think that the majority were the unemployed and those who were refused a chance to seek work who were eager to get rid of their passes because they were exposing them to the police. The meeting started with singing the African national anthem, Nkosi-Sekele-Africa, and thereafter the burning started in the presence of the police. As I threw my pass into the flames with the others, Hertzog and Pirow's effigies were also held in the flames. Compared with the number of Africans employed and living in Pretoria those of us who performed the burning were like a tiny drop in the ocean.

After the burning, columns of passless Africans were rounded up by the police in the streets, arrested, brought before the native commissioner's court, charged for being without lawful documents, and some spent days and weeks in prison. All pleaded the loss of their passes, including myself. With me it was easy because of the duplicate which Mr. How held, and I got another one. Some who went to prison came back with prison documents and the lucky ones got permits to search for work once more. Some had a very hard time and had to go back to their tribal homes to go through the old procedure of making their way back to Pretoria and other cities and towns. I never told my friends or Mr. How that I was a pass-burner.

It may be said that it was a useless effort, but I have always held the view that, though the burning did not in any way mean the ending of the pass system, if only the Africans had made a gesture by burning some of their papers they would have demonstrated their hatred for the badge of slavery, the pass, which restricted their movements since its inception. The pass denies the African privacy, choice, dignity, movement and everything which makes a man.

I went back to Phokeng on Christmas Day to see my parents. My mother wanted to know whether I had found her cousin. My reply was that I worked so hard that at the end of the day rest was the only course. I did not reveal to her or my father that nine days before I had burnt my pass.

It was nice to go back home again, to see my birthplace, relatives, friends and former school girl-friends. I was delighted to see them, and they were delighted to know that I was still intact, trying to become part of Pretoria and its life. Some were already married with children, and others were still like me, wondering what would happen on the day they got married. In the afternoon on Christmas Day I went to visit the man and his wife who made it possible for me to speak and write the English language though in a limited fashion, without which I wonder if I would have held my candle burning in the political storms of South Africa which followed later. That Christmas at home I found that I was in great demand. Relatives on both sides of my family were eager that they should see me before my return to Pretoria. I managed to visit some but asked my parents to apologise for me to those time prevented me seeing. I was dressed in a brown three-piece suit I bought ready-made for two pounds nineteen and sixpence from a Pretoria men's outfitters in Pretorius Street.

XXIII Second Employment

I was unemployed for a week in September nineteen-thirty-one. After leaving Sunnyside Butchery it was a week before I stood in front of Mr. Malberbe asking for a permit to seek work. With my contract with Mr. How having been ended lawfully I had no difficulty in getting the permit. Though I knew that I had to sleep at the reception depot while not working, I took a chance and did not go there. I was given shelter by a tribal boy, Moagi Mokoe, whose mother came from Phokeng and had married a man in one of our branch villages. He was working for a chemist in Church Street East, Arcadia, and his employer provided him with a room not far away in his yard. He was a delivery boy, cleaner and washer of bottles.

The way one could find a job was through friends or by going from door to door asking for work and if lucky getting it. Many employers did not insist on references; if they needed workers they took them. I started one morning from Arcadia and moved westward along Church Street towards the city's main shopping centre and the square. I did not get far. I went into a soft drinks factory called Shilling's Minerals and got a job. My work was to examine the bottles as they passed on a conveyor belt, to spot ones with something undesirable inside and pick them out. I missed some and those who were putting them into wooden cases noticed them. My errors came to the notice of the manager, who wanted to move me from there into another section. I did not like the job and after three days I said that I was unwilling to go on. Luckily they had not taken me to the native commissioner for a monthly contract. Without a fuss, they paid me off for the three days and I left in the afternoon. Three doors from there in a firm called the Ryall Trading Company I got a temporary job because one of their workmen was away ill. By that time my pass was showing that I had been unemployed for a week, that I had not reported myself to the commissioner and that I was not spending nights at the reception depot.

I started work at once; by then I knew many Pretoria streets and was good at delivering parcels. I came back before the shop shut to ask the manager, Mr. Percy Robert Preece, to give me a special pass that I was in their employ temporarily. The next day, to my surprise and joy, the management of the Ryall Trading Company decided to keep me. Mr. Preece gave me a letter and money to sign a monthly contract with them. When I got to the native commissioner's office I was brought before Mr. Malherbe as one who did not report himself to the office immediately he lost his previous employment. Mr. Malherbe asked me with a harsh voice where I had been all the time. I made up a story that I was sick, staying with a friend and could not come sooner. He warned me that he knew I was not telling the truth. If I repeated it he would refuse me a permit and send me back to Rustenburg where I came from. I promised to come next time as soon as I was out of a job. Without writing out a new permit he simply made out a new contract with the Ryall Trading Company.

When the sick man came back we were all kept on. My work was to deliver parcels, clean the premises with others, and do general work in the shop as well as making tea twice a day. To the disappointment of those who worked there before me, I was also sent out to pay some of the firm's accounts and sometimes sent to the post office to buy stamps, and to Barclays Bank to deposit the firm's money. The Ryall Trading Company dealt in hardware, selling among other things electric appliances, electric stoves made in Canada, electric heaters, irons, and electrical supplies for the building industry. They also carried out installations of electricity in houses all over Pretoria. There were three electricians working for the firm. One of them, Mr. Campbell, did repairs at the shop and helped with jobs outside when needed. When there was extra work outside, I went out with him. My work was to carry the tools, to carry the ladder about and to drill the walls when switchboards were erected. Like all Africans, I was forbidden to work with tools, only to carry them.

Campbell liked me and wanted me to know something about electricity. When we were out together he used to show me how the work was done and what to give him without being told. I picked up a little bit about electricity while I worked with Campbell. I remember one day when we were working in a house, the lady of the house wanted to give him tea, leaving me out, but he refused it.

The Ryall Trading Company was opposite the Pretoria Technical College, for Europeans only. Each day when the college was in session I kept asking myself why it was called Pretoria Technical College when because of colour discrimination not all the children of Pretoria were admitted into it. I was young, not politically minded by any means, but I kept asking myself that question and could not find the answer. At playtime I used to see the students buy boiled sweet potatoes, monkey nuts, mealies (what the Americans call sweet corn), and other things to eat from African women who went there to sell. That convinced me that the European children of South Africa were not against the Africans but were taught by the government and their parents to look down on them and to regard them as no equals of theirs. There was nothing wrong below but everything wrong above; the incitement came from the top.

In the office of the firm were two European women, who were both very kind to me. They brought sandwiches with them to work, which they both always shared with me. When they asked me to pay accounts for them, which was a secret arrangement, of course, they always gave me tips from the change they got back. I noticed there that I was lucky with womenfolk. I don't know what it was but I think they always felt sorry for me. There was no way of testing because a black man and a European woman were not allowed to talk apart from when she gave him orders. One evening when the shop closed the manager, Mr. Preece, called me and said, 'To-morrow morning, don't come here, come to my house. I want to see you there.' I obeyed the order and when I got there in the morning he said, 'My wife wants you to help a little. She'll tell you what to do.' From eight o'clock until eleven I was on my knees polishing her floors, ending up with the front step. I was very annoyed, but did nothing to offend her. I vowed to myself that I should never do that again. I had learned the hard way.

Mrs. Preece, like all European women in South Africa, wanted servants, but she could not keep them. Her complaint was that most of them spoke no English. The three hours I spent in her house gave me the reason why she could not keep her servants. She wanted her floors to look like mirrors; more than once she called me back to point out a spot that was not shining brightly enough for me to go over it again.

Two weeks later Mr. Preece called me into his office to tell me that his wife was pleased with the work I did for her; she was impressed by my English, I was the first servant she could understand and get on well with since her arrival in South Africa and, therefore, he was going to transfer me to his house to work for her as a domestic servant. I listened to his flatterings, but it was as though he was pumping air into me which caused an explosion. I lost my temper, forgot that he was the manager and said, 'Look, Mr. Preece, if I wanted to be a domestic worker I would not have looked for work in the shops but in Sunnyside or Arcadia.' Those were residential areas for the rich and well-off. My outburst astonished Mr. Preece. With a harsh, forceful voice he said, 'Get out, go and do your work.' I was glad I got it off my chest.

In the Ryall Trading Company there was also a young European working called Leslie Grant, the son of the Presbyterian minister in Pretoria. Leslie disliked me intensely, but I had no idea why. I do not think I had offended him in any way. He used to accuse me of being lazy, dodging work, spending a long time in the toilet and always running away as soon as I saw railway wagons coming in. I also developed a hatred for Leslie, but tried hard to avoid him. I knew that he was leading me into trouble. I was the tea-maker, and one afternoon when I was beginning to make tea, a railway trolley pulled in with a load. The other workmen went to meet it, but Leslie found that I was not with them. He called out for me. I answered that I was washing cups in the small room where I made tea and that I had switched on the kettle. He came along and ordered me to leave tea-making to off-load the trolley with the others. I said, 'As soon as I am finished here, I shall come.' Whereupon Leslie said, 'When I say now I mean now.' I ignored him and went on doing what I was engaged in. The next thing I felt was a hard kick on the buttocks.

When I turned round, there was Leslie pointing and saying, 'Come on, lazy.' Without uttering a word, without thinking what would happen, I threw my whole weight into my bare fists, burst into Leslie's face and caused damage to his eyes and lips. With blood streaming from the cuts, he ran to Mr. Preece to display the damage to his good-looking face. I was called in, Cliff French, the director's son, was called in, and Leslie unfolded his story that just because he asked me to help the others to off-load the railway trolley I caused that damage to his face. I was asked why I did it. I replied, 'He kicked me and I did it in self-defence.' Both Mr. Preece and Cliff looked at him, still bleeding, looked at me and Mr. Preece said, 'Leslie, why didn't you bring him to me when he refused to obey you? He must have been very cross to do this.' He then turned to me and said, 'You know you have no right to do this to a white man, why didn't you come to me when he kicked you?' He asked Cliff: 'Shall we call the police?' Cliff said his father should know about it. I was ordered out of the room. Outside in the yard I waited for the police to arrive.

I saw Leslie leave for home after one of the two European women had applied first aid to his face. I then expected one of two things to happen to me: to be arrested, which would have meant going to jail to learn the lesson that the inferior cannot sit on the superior, or to be sacked on the spot. My fellow Africans were nervous, saying, 'Why were you so stupid? You know whites stand together, they are never wrong, now you are going to suffer.' I said, 'It is too late now. I lost my head.' I was beginning to blame myself that I had failed to control my temper.

Nothing happened, the shop closed and I went home convinced that the next day I was going to collect my monthly control pass and the money due to me. I knew that they had not informed the police, because they would not have allowed Leslie to go home if the police had been coming. We were paid fortnightly and I was getting fifteen shillings a week, a big advance on Sunnyside butchery and

Shilling's mineral factory. The news spread in the firm and all waited to see what was going to happen. Three days after that the electricians made a stand. They went to see Mr. Preece to find out what he was doing about it. They put forward a demand that I should be sacked or they would go. Mr. Preece had to make a choice, the electricians or me. He took the obvious line, and I got the sack. I was not sorry, but glad that the police had not been called.

It was all over and I was back on the street among the unemployed. I had worked ten months for the Ryall Trading Company. Remembering Mr. Malherbe's caution, I was in the queue next day at the native commissioner's office for a permit to seek a new job. I got it, but made up my mind not to go and sleep at the reception depot. Friends put me up while I was unemployed.

I moved westward along Church Street towards Church Square. A relative of mine, Godfrey Mokgatle, was working for a grocer, Mr. Solomon Price. The firm was called Prices Limited, in Andries Street opposite the Methodist church for Europeans only, next to the public library for Europeans only. Godfrey asked Mr. Price to give me a job as a delivery boy and I got it. I was now working in the centre of the Pretoria shopping area, near the famous Church Square, not very far from Pretoria Supreme Court Palace of Justice, where, later, I was frequently tried and conducted my own case against Pretoria City Council.

While I was at the Ryall Trading Company I met with other boys, some home boys, others from other tribes, and formed a soccer football club. We named it Matopo Hills, reviving the name of the team I formed and played for at Rustenburg. Again I was elected secretary of the club. The colours were the same as those of Rustenburg Matopo Hills, blue and white with one stripe across the chest, and stockings of the same colour. There were several teams in Pretoria against which we played friendly matches or for money. We lost and won. We were not amongst the best, but there were others worse.

In nineteen-thirty-one something which thrilled me and others came to South Africa. The Scottish soccer football team, Motherwell, arrived in the country on tour. It was the first time I had seen an overseas team play in the country. They took South Africa by storm immediately they landed at Cape Town. Their first match was won by a good number of goals, and the northern newspapers praised their skill in high terms and we looked forward to seeing them when they arrived in our city, the administrative capital of South Africa. They were playing Europeans only.

If politics could be removed from the playing fields, Europeans would not refuse to play with or against non-Europeans. Other countries like New Zealand, who have non-Europeans in their rugby teams, always argue when they send teams to tour South Africa, and the politics of South Africa require them to exclude their non-European members, that they do not want to impose their will on South Africa. But they never tell those they want to convince that they allow South African politics to be imposed on them.

For Motherwell it was victory all the way with high scores. As they advanced northwards, their popularity grew and excitement took control of us. They were highly skilled footballers. Their methods were new and fascinating. Perhaps if Motherwell had found real South African teams, not tribal ones, they might have lost one match or drawn others. Wherever they went they met European tribal teams and won. Black teams wished them to win, because of being forced to remain tribal teams themselves. Wherever Motherwell arrived and played, non-Europeans, though denied by politics to talk to them or shake hands with them, went to see and admire them.

When they played on the Wanderers' ground in Johannesburg, we in Pretoria grew impatient. 'When will they come here?', as though we didn't know. When the local paper informed us that they had arrived in the capital and were staying at Polley's Hotel, some of us went to pass by the hotel just to see them as though we had not seen Europeans before. Pretoria was full of excitement. On the Wednesday they played we got the afternoon off to see them. I had saved half-a-crown to be sure that I was in the ground when the referee signalled to them to start the egg rolling. They won, and the memory remained with me for a very long time.

XXIV Turning Point

I reached a turning point in my life when I worked for Prices Limited in nineteen-thirty-two. I was still not politically-minded, but merely a working boy still hoping that one day, after making enough money to get married, I should go back to my tribe, find a girl to marry and settle down as a true tribesman. I thought that the best way to get away from the Europeans' web of pass laws and curfews was to go back to the tribe. The country was under Hertzog's government, as I have already mentioned, and Smuts was leading the Opposition party in the Parliament comprised of European tribes only.

Hertzog and Smuts, though they both belonged to the European Dutch-speaking tribe, were leading rival sections of it. Hertzog was heading the Nationalist section and Smuts a section known at that time as the Unionists, which comprised the English-speakers as well. In that year they decided to come together to form one party, as they said, for the best interests of the country. That meant dissolving the parties they led to form a new one to be called the United party. The late Dr. Daniel François Malan, a former priest in the Dutch Reformed Church who had been a keen follower of Hertzog, refused to follow him into the United party because he and others of his Dutch-speaking tribe thought that their aspiration to dominate the whole political scene in the country would be hampered. Malan became a leader of the Dutch-speaking tribe in what they then called the pure Nationalist party.

Africans who were already politically minded realised that 'the best interests of the country' Hertzog and Smuts said they were coming together for meant more and ruthless oppression for the African people. They were guided by past experience, the pass laws framed and passed by Smuts, the Native Urban Areas Act framed and passed by Smuts and amended by Hertzog in nineteen-twenty-five, adding more restrictions and denials to the Africans. They knew that more denials and deprivations were to follow.

At that time the African National Congress was no longer heard of, and the African people in the country were completely leaderless and without political spokesmen. A group of former Congressmen in Johannesburg came together and decided to revive Congress. They were R. V. Selope-Thema, Mbavasa, Sikota, Kumalo and others.

Immediately after that a newspaper appeared, published in and distributed from Johannesburg, written in African languages and English. It was called *Bantu World*, the Africans' Newspaper, and the editor was R. V. Selope-Thema. I do not know who owned the paper but according to those who said they knew the inside story, it was owned by the Chamber of Mines in Johannesburg. However, *Bantu World* set me off along the road to becoming a regular newspaper reader. My pages of it were the Sesutho section which I read with keenness and understood best. It came out once a week and reached Pretoria readers on Fridays. I became a subscriber.

Mr. Price, my employer, was Russian born; he came to South Africa alone and had no relatives or friends in the country. However, he married into one of Pretoria's old Jewish families, the Lauries. Mr. Price was a hard-working man. He left home without breakfast in the morning and one of us had to go and fetch his breakfast from home. Mrs. Price made an order that I should be the one to fetch it. Each day I had a good breakfast there, and Mrs. Price saw to it that when there was something to be sent to her home from the shop I was the one to take it there.

Her husband was a good-natured man who seldom sacked his workers. I worked two years for Prices Limited as delivery-man on a bicycle, covering the entire area of Pretoria. I got to know the city very well and nearly all the beautiful African girls in domestic service. I still played soccer football.

I was earning fifteen shillings a week, paid on Saturdays. Our half-day was Wednesday and that gave me and the others a chance to go and practise, because our matches were played on Sundays. I was happy and very popular with the girls. When I was not in football uniform, I was always smartly dressed and clean. I do not know why, one Saturday, without the week's notice which I was entitled to, Mr. Price handed me my contract monthly pass, the week's wages and another week's pay instead of notice and said, 'Sorry, I don't need you any more.' I asked why and he said, 'That's all', and walked away from me. I was alone with him in the shop. The others had already left and the rest had not come back from deliveries. No one knew that I was sacked, not even Mrs. Price. Some of my fellow-workers knew about it when I met them on Sunday, but most, including Mrs. Price, only knew on Monday when I did not turn up for work. I was told that Mrs. Price wanted me back and told the others to tell me to come back to the shop when they met me, but I thought that it was no good going back when Mr. Price did not want me. I did not go to the native commissioner's office on Monday but only on Tuesday for a permit to seek work. Still I vowed not to go to the reception depot. I was unemployed for a week, but in the second week, again by sheer chance, I got a temporary job in the

Pretoria branch of Messrs. W. M. Cuthbert and Company, a large boot and shoe dealer throughout the country.

One of their workers at a Sunday drinking party was involved in fighting, got arrested and was imprisoned for two weeks, but his friends made a mistake and told the firm that he was in hospital sick, unaware that the firm's manager, Mr. MacDonald, would check with the hospital. When Mr. MacDonald checked, Cornelius was nowhere to be found in hospital but was traced in prison, and the reason for his being there was discovered. I was taken on permanently. At Cuthberts I was a pavement away from Church Square and the Palace of Justice. I delivered shoes on a bicycle and that took me almost into the homes of most of the rich Europeans in Pretoria. Libertas, the home of the European tribe's prime ministers, was one of the places I entered carrying boxes of shoes or boots. At that time, nineteen-thirty-four, my enthusiasm for soccer football had waned and I was reading a lot, beginning to see things which deprived me of pleasure. I was sad and worried.

That year *Bantu World* was bringing news which broke my heart, about the plight of the Jewish people in Germany. What I read there happening to them was my own story, the story of the African people in South Africa. When I read that they were deprived of freedom of movement in the land of their birth, that they were segregated, denied education, dismissed from their jobs, forced into concentration camps, some of them dying without their relatives' knowledge, hunted, persecuted, their intellectuals despised, barred from practising medicine, carrying cards to identify them as Jews, their dignity destroyed, their homes no longer their castles raided at any time of the day or night, that was a description of the Africans' life in the country of their birth.

Columns of Africans were seen daily, arrested, handcuffed, marched to police stations all over South African cities and towns for being in areas declared European with no permits, or without work which they could not get because they were thrown out of jobs. Sometimes I feel like dropping dead when I hear people say that South Africa is almost becoming a police state. For the African people it became a total police state in nineteen-eleven when Smuts passed the Master and Servant Act and later the Native Urban Areas Act of nineteen-twenty-three, amended by Hertzog in nineteen-twenty-five, with the notorious section seventeen which sends scores of Africans to concentration camp prisons where they die without their parents, wives or relatives knowing. Those were the happenings in Germany under Hitler, and in South Africa under Smuts and Hertzog in nineteen-thirty-three.

In nineteen-thirty-four I decided to emigrate to the United States of America. I had managed to save thirty pounds in the post office.

My intentions were that in America I should work, study and after obtaining a degree, I did not know in what, return to South Africa. I told a friend of mine, Mr. Larius Motshepe, of my aims. He worked for a law firm, and he offered to introduce me to a young lawyer there, Mr. Noach, who he said would help me with my plans. One Wednesday afternoon I climbed the twisting steps of the building.

I unfolded my story to Mr. Noach, whereupon he offered his services to help me to obtain a passport and a visa to enter the United States. For his services, he said he required seven guineas, but estimated that the sea voyage to America would cost forty or fifty pounds single. He advised me to go and fetch seven guineas so that he could start working, and also to try to raise sixty pounds for the journey. I assured him that I would call on him again, but that was the last we saw of each other. After a little time I began to think of my parents who were still alive; that I would be betraying them if I left them and went to America. I told my friend Motshepe to tell Mr. Noach that I was trying to raise money and as soon as I was ready I would call on him. That was as far as I could go on my journey to America.

At that time I was still not aware that I was moving near to the political arena. Every Friday at lunch-time, after receiving my copy of *Bantu World*, I sat alone in the back-yard which Cuthberts shared with other firms which had stores in the same block and read with absorbing interest. I had no idea that someone nearby was noticing me. There were many other African workers in the yard, but at the end of their lunch they began to play cards or an African game called *morabara* which caused excitement, and sometimes quarrels and exchange of fists. When I was waiting for my *Bantu World* earlier in the week, I read all the old papers I could lay my hands on, always saying to myself news is never old. Reading all that, the old papers and any other reading material I could find, broadened my knowledge of events in the country and far away.

One Friday I saw a European moving towards me. I stopped reading my *Bantu World* and got ready for him, thinking that he was going to ask me who I thought I was reading a newspaper. There was a mood in the country at that time that some Europeans disliked Africans who read newspapers. When that man came to where I was sitting he said, 'I always see you reading papers, do you like reading much?' I said, 'Yes. Why?' He replied, 'I just wanted to know.' He left me. I wondered why he asked. I knew his face very well, I saw him every day but he never spoke to me and I never spoke to him. He was young, I think in his twenties at the time. He was a chemist's apprentice in Tudor Pharmacy, three doors from Cuthbert's Church Street entrance. His name was Archie Levitan. I did not meet Archie

Levitan again until the following week, when he approached me at lunch-time to ask me what time I finished my deliveries in the evening. I told him there was no particular time; as soon as I finished the parcels. He invited me to his flat which he shared with another European man who owned a petrol-filling station near Marabastad in Boom Street. The other man was Mr. Chekonovsky, a short man with one leg shorter than the other. Their flat was in Church Street East below Prinsloo Street, where later I was heard addressing open-air public meetings between the hours of one and two in the afternoons. That same evening after delivering all the shoes I went to see what Mr. Archie Levitan wanted to talk to me about. I found him with Mr. Chekonovsky. On entering the room I saw a large attractive picture on the wall before me. They said it was of Lenin the man who led and organised the Russian Revolution of nineteen-seventeen. I knew nothing about him or the Russian Revolution. It was the year nineteen-thirty-five.

They told me that they were members of the Communist party of South Africa in Johannesburg, and asked whether I had heard anything about the Communists or the Communist party. I replied that I sometimes read about them in newspapers and that was all. They further asked me whether I knew anything about trade unions or trade unionism and I confessed ignorance. They said that if African workers had trade unions they could work for the improvement of their wages and working conditions. That was strange talk to me, I just did not understand what they were trying to tell me. Noticing that I was beginning to get bored because of lack of understanding, they asked me if I knew of any Africans who would like to attend night classes to learn reading and writing, and that attracted me very much. I promised to see if I could find some. I was interested myself because I wanted to learn more.

I left their flat wondering whether they meant what they said. For me it was the first time I had heard Europeans saying they were willing to hold night classes for Africans in Pretoria. I went away to try to find Africans who like me desired to learn reading and writing. A link between me and Mr. Levitan was established; each time we saw each other we smiled, avoiding people noticing it, because of the laws about black and white relationships in the country.

A few months before my meeting with Archie Levitan and Chekonovsky, friends of mine including Moagi Mokoe told me that there were two Europeans, a man and a woman, who came to Pretoria twice weekly from Johannesburg to hold talks, and were interested to meet Africans who wished to find out anything. They said they had already attended several meetings held by them and found them very interesting people. They urged me to attend with them, but I was very suspicious of Europeans, having decided in my own mind that they needed us only to use for their own benefit. I promised to come, but on the day of the meeting stayed away and made excuses afterwards that I had forgotten all about the meeting. At that time I had convinced myself that nothing good for the Africans could come from a European, no matter how sweetly he might talk.

My friends found my excuses vague and one day one of them made it his duty to collect me and take me to the meeting. I went, and in a room at the back of one of the Indian shops in Prinsloo Street we met the two Europeans from Johannesburg. My friends introduced me to them as Mr. Lee and Miss Kahn. There were a good number of us and the meeting began at eight o'clock sharp. The first speaker was Mr. Lee, who dwelled at length on the formation of the Socialist party in South Africa which would admit into its ranks all people regardless of their colour, sex or religion. He went on to develop the point that non-Europeans in the country were segregated, denied the right to vote and paid low wages because they were not organised. If, Mr. Lee went on, there was a strong Socialist party in the country backed by non-Europeans, a great change would result. All the people in the country would have the right to vote for a government which would rule for the benefit of all instead of the few rich ones, as was the case at that time. He went on to explain that the Africans were suffering under the pass laws because they lacked an organisation to lead them in the struggle against the passes. He showed that the failure of the pass-burning campaign in nineteen-thirty had been because there was no Socialist party to lead and guide them. He said further that some Africans thought that Europeans oppressed them because they were black, but that was not true. He said that in Europe and in England there are no black people, but the rich white people had oppressed poor white people, before they organised themselves into trade unions and strong socialist parties which later led the poor and got them improved conditions.

At the end of Mr. Lee's talk Miss Kahn took over, but merely filled in points she thought Mr. Lee left out. She talked mainly about the struggle of the Indian Congress in India under the leadership of Mahatma Gandhi, and went on to point out that Gandhi began his leadership in South Africa when Smuts and others wanted to force the Indians to carry passes, and won because the Indians united and followed Gandhi's advice and leadership. In India, too, Miss Kahn pointed out, the Indians would eventually win because they had formed a strong body, Congress, and were following Gandhi without hesitation. The Africans too needed such a leader as Gandhi and a strong and determined organisation like the Indian Congress in India. Unfortunately, Miss Kahn said, the African National Congress was badly organised, the men in it were not willing to build it strong enough and to suffer for their cause like Mahatma Gandhi in India.

There was still time, she went on, for the Africans and the other non-Europeans in the country to organise themselves into a powerful movement which would guide them in the struggle for democracy in South Africa. There were many Europeans in the country like themselves who were prepared to join hands with the Africans and all non-Europeans to work for a better life. In Johannesburg, she went on, were people ready to help to form the Socialist party, which would have no colour bar and which would work for the ending of all forms of colour bar and oppression in South Africa. I listened with all eagerness but my suspicions refused to leave me. All this, I said to myself, is sweet talk with nothing behind it. I never attended their meetings again. I cut myself away from them. After trying for several weeks Mr. Lee and Miss Kahn failed and ceased to come to Pretoria.

Following my meeting with Chekonovsky and Archie Levitan, I went about talking to my friends, telling them of the offer they made to run night classes to help Africans who like myself were eager to improve their English and those who were keen to learn the art of reading and writing. Pretoria was full of such Africans who had never seen the inside of a class-room in their tribal villages. They wanted to communicate with their families back home, with friends far away, but were unable to do so. I managed to find a good number like me who had seen the inside of class-rooms but were not good enough to express themselves in English, could not understand most of the things they read in English and could not write it in a way they could be proud of.

The response was fantastic. I informed Archie Levitan of the results of my recruiting, and he asked me to tell them that they were seeking a place where the class could be held. As soon as they found one I would be told the place and the date on which the fight against illiteracy would begin. I went round spreading the news and everyone interested got ready. A few weeks later Archie asked me to meet him and others after work at 150 Struben Street, to see the place they had found. That evening I met seven persons, five men and two women, all Europeans. They were Archie, Chekonovsky, George Findlay, his wife Joan, Samuel Woolf, his wife Ethel, and a Dutch-speaking man called Retief. I was introduced to them and they welcomed me with warm handshakes. The place had been used as a butcher's shop before and was owned by a man called Mr. Massey. There was a large room in front and a smaller one at the back big enough to hold a good number of people. A week later we met there again to start classes.

All except Retief became our teachers. As the classes progressed, new faces also came in to help. The people who started the classes were Communists attached to the Johannesburg district committee of the Communist Party of South Africa. Apart from basic things like reading, writing and counting, we were taught, those of us who could already read and write, many things like politics, trade unionism, the formation of organisations, the running of such organisations, the reasons why trade unions were necessary to industry, and the reasons for the low wages and bad conditions experienced by the workers, particularly the Africans, in South Africa. The explanations I had heard from Mr. Lee and Miss Kahn were repeated by our teachers, who also said that without organisation higher wages and better conditions of work were unattainable. They, too, referred to England and other European countries. If, they said, the workers of those countries could help themselves by forming and supporting strong trade unions, the Africans could do the same in South Africa.

They told us that the pass laws were designed and maintained by those who ruled the country to control the movement of the Africans and force them, by arresting them for not working, to accept low wages in desperation to avoid going to prison. They opened our eyes, particularly mine, telling us that the passes were never meant to be means of identification for poor Africans who would get lost and never be traced, but to beat them into submission and to make them a permanent source of cheap labour in the industries of the country. They did not hide their political identity from us, they told us frankly that they were Communists and their party recognised no colour bar. They went on to say that their party was not promising anyone an easy passage in the struggle for equality and the abolition of segregation in South Africa, but that it did say that people could achieve equality before the law if they stood together.

They advised us strongly that as Africans we should belong to the African liberatory organisation, the African National Congress, work in it, make it strong and turn it into a fighting force for the African people. They said that it was no good for us to complain that Congress was not doing anything for us, the right thing was to say, what am I doing in Congress, am I playing a leading role in its activities, am I seeing to it that it becomes a powerful force with determined leadership, dedicated to the cause of gaining equality for the Africans in the country, the abolition of the pass laws and the ending of all forms of colour discrimination in the country?

The Communist party will welcome you into its ranks, but you will be expected to work hard, be dedicated, honest and willing to take on tasks assigned to you, they told us. If you like, you can belong to both Congress and the Communist party, but at least belong to Congress. The Communist party is dedicated to two stages, they said, the first to work for complete equality for all the people of this country regardless of their colour, sex, creed, or former place of origin, the second to achieve in this country a socialist form of republic within which all the people would have complete equal opportunities to improve themselves and to advance.

As time went by I found myself being attracted to their ideas, particularly since they did not promise us anything by waiting for it to come. Their frankness that we would have to do things ourselves if we wanted wrongs ended appealed to me most. They built within me a feeling of being someone who could do something with others to achieve something for ourselves. The suspicions which I still entertained, even when I agreed to attend classes organised and run by them, began gradually to melt away. They made me see that Europeans are not our enemies. What impressed me most was that they spoke against things done to us by their own people.

The classes ran for a few months, and many of us benefited from them. Not only Communists taught at the classes, but others volunteered and came along to help in the fight against illiteracy. They charged their pupils nothing and in most cases spent their own money buying stationery for their pupils. Those who came to help were lawyers, book-keepers, chemists and teachers. All of them felt that they were passing on what they had been fortunate to acquire to those less fortunate. I began to ask myself, what sincerity do I still need from them? Here they come, suspend their pleasures, leave their homes, come here to pass on what they know to us free of charge. I began to apologise silently for the views I used to hold that they were all our enemies by nature.

Our classes began to grow, especially the beginners' class. Men and women of all ages were seen in them. After several months I suspect that someone, possibly the police, began to frighten the landlord, Mr. Massey, saying that his place was being used to spread communism. Some of the people like Sam Woolf, George Findlay and their wives were well-known Communists in Pretoria, though there was no Communist party there. At the beginning of one month Mr. Massey gave us notice under the pretext that he wanted the place for his own use. That meant the break-up of our school. After trying hard to find another place and failing, we had reached the end. This caused great regret to us all, but we were powerless to do anything. We could have found a place in Marabastad, or anywhere that non-Europeans lived, but this would have meant that each day our teachers would have been required to ask for permits to enter the area, which would have been impossible. Without a home people scatter, and we were not the exception to the rule. We scattered and lost touch with each other. For me, it had been an introduction to another world, of reading books, books and more books, and politics. I became a Communist at heart, but not officially; I carried no card.

I don't know how long our Struben Street school would have lasted

196

if Mr. Massey had not closed it down. It had shaped my political future and made up my mind as to how I was to spend the rest of my adult life. I had begun to read about events in other countries, trying to relate them to the events at home. I had become convinced that the way South Africa was ruled was influenced by events abroad.

I read about the events in Italy at the time I had run away from home to Kroondal in nineteen twenty-two, when the fascist Benito Mussolini marched on Rome and established himself as sole ruler of Italy. I learned what resulted from that; the destruction of the Italian trade unions and the Socialist movement, the preparation of Italy for war, and the breaking of the League of Nations, which was supposed to make nations settle their quarrels by words rather than by guns. The school had taught me that the Communist movement was the utter enemy of fascism and that fascism was equally the enemy of the Communist movement. My assessment of the rule in my own country left me in no doubt that we were under fascism.

And there were the events in Germany in nineteen thirty-three, the taking over of power there by Adolf Hitler, the rule of the Nazi party, which launched a vicious attack on the Jewish people, eliminated all opposition, and destroyed the trade unions, the Communist party and the entire Left movement; deeds which were admired by the Nationalist party of the European tribe of my own country. All this confirmed my assessment that my country had been turned into a police state and was ruled by fascists. Smuts and Hertzog believed deeply in race purity, in the master race theory, segregation, denial of human rights and the keeping down of non-Europeans, particularly Africans. In that they belonged to the same school as Hitler and Mussolini.

I also took part in witnessing the flames of the Reichstag which Hitler burnt but cast the blame on the German Communists, to enable himself and those who endorsed him to justify his vicious actions; the ending of civil liberties in Germany. I was fascinated by the way one world-famous Communist, a Bulgarian, Georgi Dimitrov, whom Hitler attempted to make a scapegoat, fought the Lion in its own den, tore the mask off its face and left it bare for everybody to see that it was out to plunge the world into the destructive flames of the second world war. Reading Georgi Dimitrov's bold attacks on fascism in its nest convinced me of what a man can do for the people and the cause he holds dear, whether others agree with him or not. The courage of Communists in South Africa and abroad inspired me immensely, though I did not join them at once.

The attack by Mussolini's Italy on Ethiopia in nineteen-thirty-five, and the way influential members of the League of Nations refused to aid unarmed Ethiopia against the aggressor, refortified my waning suspicions that throughout the world a case was judged by the colour of those who were engaged in litigation rather than by its merits. In it I could see nothing different from South Africa. Those were the conflicts which were tearing my mind and causing me great uneasiness. I could not find the way out of them. When I was about to fall down there were other things which picked me up. The stand taken by Russia and Mexico demanding the upholding of the principles of the League of Nations restored me to the right thinking that all white people were not our enemies. The fact that they were in a minority but took a firm stand taught me that one must not throw up one's hands and say, 'It's no use doing anything, they won't agree.' Their arguments at the League of Nations further taught me that, though they spoke to a small circle of men, they were in fact addressing a world-wide audience. The Spanish civil war also influenced me greatly.

In those years between nineteen-thirty-five and nineteen-thirty-nine I frequently visited the Left Book Club run by the Pretoria Communists and others of Left opinions, first at Gresham Buildings and later at Hamilton Chambers, both in St. Andries Street. There I read Left books which I could not find anywhere else, since there was no library in the city where non-Europeans could obtain books to read. There was also a second-hand book shop which sold Left Book Club books owned by a Mr. van Leer in Paul Kruger Street, which connects Church Square and the main railway station. At the Left Book Club or at Mr. van Leer's shop I could find books to read or buy to read at home. At first none of them was easy for me to understand, with the little school education that I had, but because I was interested I worked hard to understand them, though it took a very long time.

The history of British trade unionism, Keir Hardie's life and works and the founding of the British Labour party were amongst the things I enjoyed struggling to read about and understand. On the South African scene I studied the causes of the Anglo-Boer war, its end and the peace negotiations from nineteen-o-two to the founding of the Union of South Africa, matters from which the Africans were excluded by the Boers and the British. Hard books to understand I I found were Lenin's *Selected Works*, but later, after a long time, they began to inspire me. Lenin's determination against great odds, his strength to carry on even when in exile, built faith in me. The *History of the Communist Party of the Soviet Union* by Joseph Stalin, and his *Problems of Leninism*, added more strength and faith in me.

Joseph Stalin's capacity to influence such a vast country as Russia and the whole Communist movement throughout the entire world amazed me and inspired me more than I could explain. When I heard his critics say that he was using secret police to force his influence on the Russian people, I asked, 'Is everyone in Russia a member of his secret police? If your assertions are correct, then he must have a secret policeman or woman in every family or every group of people.'

Sometimes in the evenings when my deliveries of shoes were finished I used to attend lectures on trade unionism, politics, and social subjects at the Left Book Club by Sam Woolf, George Findlay, Franz Boshoff and others. *Moscow News* was one of the papers I used to read there, and from that came into contact with the Communist International Organisation's activities and its reports. They too widened my knowledge of world affairs. Through it I knew the names of most leaders of the Communist parties throughout the world. In the United States of America I admired figures like John Z. Foster, Earl Browder, Eugene Dennis and others; in France, Maurice Thorez and Jacques Duclos; in Italy, Palmiro Togliatti; in Spain, Madame Dolores Ibaruri; in Germany, Ernest Thaelmann; in Brazil, Prestos; in Britain, Willie Gallagher, Palme Dutt and Harry Pollitt; in China, Mao Tse Tung and Dr. Sun Yat Sen, though he was not a Communist; in India, P. Joshi; in Indo-China, as it was called, Ho Chi Minh; and at home veteran trade unionist and founder of the Communist party of South Africa, William Henry Andrews. I came late, when one who will always live in the history of work for better relationship between black and white was no longer in the scene, Sidney Percival Bunting. Dr. Edward Roux, famous for organising Mayiboye night schools for Africans in Johannesburg, was no longer active when I came into contact with the party. I shall be failing if I miss the names of Dr. Max Joffee and his brother who helped to organise African mine workers along the Reef, a man I never missed at any meeting I attended in Johannesburg.

None of them could have done more for better relationships between the inhabitants of South Africa of all colours. Those I met built me up and gave me courage to carry on to the day I left the country which I shall never stop loving, together with its inhabitants of all colours. It is easy to accuse South Africans, but I know that they are incited by those who rule them to distrust each other and some to follow a myth that they are superior to the others and as such are performing an ordained mission to rule and have all the best while the rest live in hunger and frightful poverty.

XXV Father's Death

From the day I arrived in Pretoria I never spent a single Christmas Day without enjoying it with my parents in Phokeng. Every Christmas Eve night I took the train from Pretoria main railway station. On the Christmas of nineteen-thirty-four I arrived to find my father away doing thatching for another tribe to the north of our place. He had many engagements there and thatched nearly the entire village. He was so good at his work that before he finished a house there were already two, three or more in the queue waiting for him. He did not come to Phokeng for Christmas, and since I had not seen him for twelve months I missed him. I returned to Pretoria dissatisfied that I had not seen him or exchanged greetings and best wishes with him.

In March nineteen-thirty-five I felt compelled to go and see the man who brought me into life. Knowing that there was no train from Phokeng to where he was thatching, I bought a brand new Hercules bicycle from Pretoria Cycle House and travelled by it to Phokeng and from there to where my father was working. I had not written to mother to tell her that I was coming, nor to father. Mother was surprised to see me so early in the year, but was relieved when I told her the reason. I spent three days in the tribe seeing friends and relatives and on the fourth day I was in the saddle cycling to my father. I left mother early in the morning at half-past seven and arrived at Bobididi, Tweelaagte, at five in the afternoon. I knew that without asking anyone I would spot father on the roof of a house busy thatching. I was right. When I entered the village, right at the edge of it there I saw my father on top of a house in bright sunshine. He did not see me coming; those who did had no idea that I was his son.

I found him with the man who helped him. The owners of the place were away, but coming back later. He heard a voice – I doubt whether he recognised it – and as he looked down he saw me standing there with my teeth shining bright with joy that I had found him. 'Oh,' he shouted in surprise, 'is that you, where do you come from?' 'I have come to see you,' I replied. At once he came down to introduce me to his helper, saying, 'This is my only son.' That took place after we had embraced, both with great emotion. From that time Father stopped work and waited for the owners to come back. They came and he introduced me to them.

The next day father told the people he was thatching for that the following day he was leaving with me for Phokeng. There were things for both of us to discuss there before I returned to Pretoria. They were disappointed when he told them that he had no idea when he would be back to resume his work. I could read that in their faces, though they did not openly say it in words. As arranged, we left for Phokeng and we spent ten days with mother before I returned to Pretoria, again by bicycle. I shall never forget my father's last words to me when we parted. On the day of my departure he took a long walk with me, telling me to take great care of myself, also reminding me that I had reached a marrying age and that I should think seriously about getting married, at the same time trying to take me back to his early days and suggesting that he and mother should look for a good wife for me amongst the people they knew and trusted.

When we shook hands he said, 'Think seriously about what I have been saying, this may well be our last meeting and words together. We may not meet and talk again.' He turned back, we waved good-bye and turned our backs on one another. I disappeared from him and similarly he disappeared from me. Indeed, it was our last meeting and our last words. Back in Pretoria one day at the beginning of August, when I returned from delivering shoes I saw a fellow-tribes-man standing by Cuthberts', where I worked. He was our Para-mount Chief's son-in-law, a man who could not have cared less about tribal men in Pretoria, but I guessed that he was waiting for me and wondered why, since we were not friends. When I reached him he handed me a telegram he had received from Phokeng, requesting him to let me know that my father was seriously ill and I should come home at once as he wished to talk to me. I thanked him for the information and he left. I told my manager, Mr. MacDonald, and asked him for permission to leave the next day. He agreed. He was kind and ordered the office to give me two weeks' pay, two pounds.

During the train journey to Phokeng on Wednesday, I was worried that I would find my father already dead. My fears were based on the fact that, since I had known him, he had never spent one day confined to bed sick. To hear of his being ill was a completely new thing for me. I grew so used to not seeing him sick that it never occurred to me that one day he would fall sick like anyone else. Even when he used to warn me to take things seriously and not to depend so much on him or mother, saying one day we shall be dead and you will find yourself alone with nobody to expect help from, I never really believed that he would die one day. He used himself and mother as an example: they had their parents, they died and left them alone. That, too, never sank deep into my mind.

I arrived in the afternoon and more worries were added when I found my three married sisters already there, father's two half-sisters, two men cousins and other relatives and neighbours. I thought that he was already dead. He was still alive. Having arrived I waited outside for forty-five minutes, and during that short time one of father's half-sisters gave me an account of his sickness. She told me that he was away, as usual, back at the village where I went to fetch him in March, and a week ago mother had received news that he was sick. Mother, like all of us, being unaccustomed to him falling sick, hurriedly went to fetch him back to Phokeng. She found him sick but not as I found him. Since his arrival back in Phokeng, my aunt told me, his sickness had grown worse. She said to me, 'Unfortunately for you, since this morning he has ceased speaking. His last words this morning,' she told me, 'were to ask whether you had been called from Pretoria. From that time he uttered no word.'

Having heard that from my aunt I went into the house and into the room where he was laid. I found him critically sick, but his eyes were open as though he saw me and everything around him. I sat down by his bed and greeted him, expecting a reply because his eyes were fixed on me, but not a word passed through his lips. I shook his hand several times, moving my left hand over his forehead, trying to make him feel that I was with him, but what I wanted from his lips, words of welcome, never came. Night fell and I went to bed still waiting. The next day, Thursday, I went to greet him, expecting some improvement, but that day was worse than the previous one. His eyes were still bright as though he could talk.

That morning at ten or eleven o'clock he spoke but I was not by his bedside. I was walking in the yard, sad, wondering what was going to happen at any time. I was deeply worried, like the moon right in the centre of the sky about to be deserted by the clouds which had hidden it for a long time. My mother's sister who was there at the time called me in hurriedly, saying, 'Your father wants to speak to you.' Inside I held his hand and tried to get words out of him by saying to him, 'Father, it's me, I am here.' He kept his eyes fixed on me but said nothing. Everyone who was there, including mother, was surprised. They told me that he had said, 'Has Nyadioe arrived from Pretoria?' When they said yes, he asked, 'Where is he?' Those were his last words. I did not hear them.

I spent the day not moving far away, hoping that he might speak again. It was all in vain. Night fell, we all went to bed, but my father's hours to live were numbered. The next morning, like everyone else, I tried to make him speak to me but things were the same as the day before. Word had spread in the village that the end was near. Many people had gathered to find out how he was getting on; some were leaving after hearing the news, others were delaying their departures to talk to me and my sisters to strengthen our morale.

At eight or nine o'clock that morning, Friday, my father ceased to live. My aunt, father's half-sister, came out of the house to announce the end by carrying water in a calabash. She dropped it and said, 'The sun has set, the cradle is broken.' All the older people who were there stood up with their heads hanging, looking down for one minute, and that conveyed the news to me that my father was dead. Another old man, a relative, took me away from the rest for a walk, during which he consoled me by telling me that though he was my father, he was also his brother and tribesman. He went on to ask me not to imagine that the loss was mine alone, it was suffered by the whole tribe and many people who knew him and many more who were entertaining the hope that one day he would do thatching for them. He asked me to consider myself fortunate because he died when I was already grown up and could look after myself. Many children, he told me, lose their fathers when they are very young; others, their fathers die when their mothers are pregnant and they grow to know only their names.

In African tribal villages at that time we had no undertakers, but we had good carpenters who were expert at making coffins. We would go to the hardware store to purchase planks, together with everything else needed. All the stores in the villages stocked such equipment. Near our home was an Indian store-keeper, Ismael Bokaria. He had known father well and they were great friends; he knew he was sick and he too used to call to hear how he was getting on. When we went to him for coffin equipment he charged for the planks and nails but contributed the other materials free as a gift to his old friend. My father's death revealed to me that he was a very famous man. He was buried on Sunday and crowds of people came along to bury him. What surprised me was that when Mr. Penzhorn, the Lutheran Church minister, was told of his death he said, 'He was not a Christian, but he allowed his wife and children to belong to the church. He never refused to come to help me when I needed thatching to be done on my house and the schools, and he was a friend. I am going to give him a Christian burial.'

That Sunday afternoon service was my father's service in the Lutheran Church. Mr. Penzhorn conducted it himself. Many people were surprised and I was also surprised. My father's coffin was laid on the altar, as though he had frequently been seen in the church amongst its congregation. I was so overtaken by grief that when the carpenters were busy at home making the coffin I nearly went to them to order them to stop; my father was not dead, they were only wishing that he was dead. Even at the graveyard when men began to lower father's coffin into the grave I nearly shouted to them to stop, they were putting a living man into the hole. One of my relatives, an old man, had noticed that I was in that state; he held me all the time. It was because of him that I did not jump into the grave to stop the men when they began to cover the coffin with earth. Only when I got back home, I was free, laughing and joking with other people. Only then was I convinced that my father was dead.

I spent two weeks at home sorting out things and after that returned to Pretoria. I was still left with the task of gathering all father's animals which were scattered amongst many of his friends.

Having buried my father I vowed that I was no longer going to worry about politics but would become a true tribesman and care for my mother and the animals father left us. Many of my friends and tribesmen were not in Pretoria but in Johannesburg. They had tried hard to pull me to Johannesburg and offered to help me to find a job there. I loved Pretoria so for many years I had refused. While I was in Phokeng I realised that if I returned to Pretoria it would be difficult to carry out my vow. The way to enable myself to carry it out was to go to Johannesburg. I wrote to Cuthberts' manager to say that I needed two more weeks to settle things after my father's death. At the same time I wrote to friends in Johannesburg that at last I was coming to join them. They replied saying, you are welcome, come any time.

I had more than twenty pounds in the post office. I left home without a travelling pass and took a chance and went to Johannesburg. Diale, the boy who had received me in Pretoria five years before, was now in Johannesburg working for Roman Catholic monks as their cook and housekeeper. He promised me that shelter and food would be no problem, all I needed was to land in the City of Gold. The rules were the same, on arrival go first to the native commissioner's office for a permit to seek work. I knew that without a travelling pass it was useless going there and decided that if I got a job I would go there to say that I had lost all my documents and place myself at their mercy. Cuthberts' manager believed I was in Phokeng, yet I was in Johannesburg seeking a job, eating and sleeping in the monastery.

I tried everything to find a job, my friends tried as well, but my luck was out for two weeks. There was in Johannesburg a man well known to the Africans and hated by them, Mr. Du Preez, a European, head of the police squad whose task it was to clean the city of Africans who were not working and without valid documents, and arrest them under section seventeen of the Native Urban Areas Act as vagrants. Thousands of Africans had been sent to the prison colony called Blue Sky, a hell where brutality was at its highest. Many went there and never returned. Du Preez was nicknamed 'Sporting' by the Africans because he wore a sports coat all the time. Every African male who went to Johannesburg at that time to seek work was warned by others to look out for Sporting and his men.

Du Preez started his work of arresting Africans and sending them to Blue Sky in nineteen-twenty-five after Hertzog's government had inserted section seventeen. By the time of my arrival he was still active but old and tired. He was still arresting hundreds of Africans a day. At Marshall Square, the main police station, he got rid of many by persuading them to plead guilty, and collected ten shillings from each for admission of guilt. He even sent others out to friends to see if they could get ten shillings to pay their fines.

On the Wednesday of my seond week in the City of Gold I went out to try my luck job hunting in the shopping centre. In Church Street, at about ten or eleven o'clock while I was admiring things in the window of a men's shop, I felt someone tapping me on the shoulder. When I looked at him he asked me where I was working. I said I was looking for work. Thereupon he demanded to see my passes. I realised that I was in Sporting's net. I tried to escape by running away from him. He chased me along Church Street westwards, appealing to people to stop me. In the end two men, Europeans, came to his assistance and caught me for him. When he arrived he handcuffed my hands behind my back and took me to the corner of Harrison Street, where I found a large number of arrested Africans being looked after by his men.

We were marched to Marshall Square, all handcuffed, and there Sporting asked each one of us whether we pleaded guilty or not. Following the example of the others, I pleaded guilty, but said that I had no money on me. He asked me if I knew someone nearby who could help me with ten shillings. I remembered that not far from there one of my friends worked in a garage. He sent me out there still handcuffed with one of his men. Luckily for me my friend gave me ten shillings, which released me from Sporting's net. From there I went straight back to the monastery to tell my friend that on Saturday I was returning to Pretoria. Thursday and Friday I did not leave the yard. I drew a pound from the post office, repaid my friend's ten shillings and used the balance for fares to Pretoria. I left at ten o'clock and at half-past eleven I reported at Cuthberts' as though I was only just arriving from Phokeng. I wanted to start work on Monday, but Mr. MacDonald said, 'You start now; go and get your bicycle from the shed to deliver parcels.' When the shop shut at one o'clock, I was on the saddle on the way to do deliveries. Johannesburg was not for me.

Some of the barriers I wanted to erect between me and politics from nineteen-thirty-seven to 'thirty-nine were girl friends. In that period I had five of them, three in Pretoria and two in Johannesburg. I used to travel at weekends to visit those in the City of Gold, but none of them knew that I was there seeing the other. They were in different parts of the city; and didn't know of each other's existence.

They were Mpona Sepato and Mmeme Raleru. Mpona Sepato was a girl from my tribe, from Luka, a branch of Phokeng, whom I met in Pretoria before she went to Johannesburg. Mmeme Raleru was from another tribe, but had lived in Phokeng with relatives, sent there by her parents to go to school and learn English. She was much more beautiful than Mpona Sepato.

I was in love with both of them, but Mpona Sepato was so deeply in love with me that one weekend I wrote to her telling her that I would not visit her, but suddenly changed my mind, and late on Saturday took a train to the City of Gold to surprise her. I was taking the chance that if I did not find her in I would go to Mmeme Raleru to surprise her as well. But when I got out of the train at Park Station, the city's main railway station, I found her waiting at the part of the platform where she knew I would alight from Pretoria. I asked her whether she had come to meet someone, but she told me that she felt that I was coming and she had to be there to welcome me.

I found myself torn between them all, not knowing which one to marry. They were all very kind and gave me all the comfort I needed. I was always happy when I was with any of them. Parental influence in marriage was still very strong; though we were in love there were still bridges we had to cross before we could marry. Our parents had to agree and approve. Marrying without parents' approval was considered scandalous. While my friendship with Mpona Sepato was at its height, she was called home, to be told by her parents that they had arranged for her to marry a local boy. Everything was at an advanced stage and she had to do as she was told. She was not in love with the boy. She wrote me a heart-breaking letter requesting me to send her money. She wanted to run away before she was tied to a boy she did not love.

Fearing that if I did send her money news would spread and eventually reach my parents that I broke someone's daughter's marriage, I wrote to her regretting what had happened but advised her to respect her parents' wishes. She wrote three letters, still insisting that she would marry no one but me and I should send her money to run away. I replied to the second letter repeating what I said in my first letter. Other letters after that I did not reply to and Mpona married her parents' man. The man was much older than she was. They were a married couple for two years, but one day I got the sad news that her husband killed her and then hanged himself. That was how my friendship with Mpona Sepato ended.

Mmeme Raleru was in fact engaged through her parents to a relative of mine, Seth Mokgatle, who was working far away in Cape Town. Seth heard about our friendship going on all the years he was in Cape Town. On his return he told her that he had had no objection because we were relatives, but said that since he had returned the friendship had to stop. Mmeme admitted the friendship. Seth then requested her to give him all my letters to read, promising her that he would send them all back to me to make me realise that he knew about the friendship and that I should break it up. Mmeme was trapped and handed all my letters to Seth. Seth took the letters to show his parents that Mmeme was unreliable, and that if they got married we would continue our friendship in secret. He was wounded that I could do such a thing to him, knowing well that Mmeme was his girl friend and they were engaged to get married. The engagement was broken off, since my letters were evidence that Mmeme had been carrying on a friendship with me for a number of years. Her parents hated me, and so did Seth and his parents, though as relatives they did not show it openly. My parents, too, disapproved of my actions strongly and blamed me for having done a friend and relative an injustice. Mmeme and I became enemies; I blamed her for giving my letters away and she blamed me for having caused her engagement to break up. We lost contact with each other, but as time went by I heard that she married another man and they settled in Cape Town. Some years later I heard that Mmeme was in Pretoria staying with her cousin. I asked her cousin to ask her if I could see her to apologise, but she said that she had decided to keep me out of her sight for ever.

In Pretoria I was visiting Ntobana Kgamphe, Nana More and Matlhapi Sekgothe. They were all pretty, and I took great care that they knew nothing of each other. I was very strict that my girl friends should never visit me at my room in Marabastad. I knew that if I allowed that to happen my secrets would be revealed. I was deeply in love with the three of them but much more with Nana More. While I went on seeing her she got engaged through her parents to a boy at her home in the tribal village of Hebron, not far from Pretoria. Like Mpona Sepato, she attempted to resist, but knowing that I would not marry her, I encouraged her to obey and respect her parents' wishes, promising her that each time she came to Pretoria I would always be ready to see her and give her whatever I was able to give.

Matlhapi Sekgothe was so in love with me that one day when her father was in Pretoria she arranged a meeting for me and her father. I could see that her father did not fancy me, though he pretended to have no objections. That year she went home to spend Christmas with her parents. She did not return to Pretoria but went to visit her aunt in Johannesburg. I think that she was ordered to forget me. She got a job in the City of Gold. She knew my address; I did not know hers but she never wrote to me so that we could meet. That ended our friendship.

Ntobana Kgamphe became the centre of my attraction and we planned to bring our friendship to the attention of our parents and seek permission to get married. Because of that I made her pregnant, and in nineteen-thirty-eight she gave birth to a baby girl whom she named Peggy, and I was the father. When Christmas of that year drew near, I wrote asking her to request her mother to permit me to visit her and the baby Peggy at her home at Christmas. Her mother was a widow, and she granted the permission. I went to spend Christmas with them. The custom was that if I went to people to whose daughter I was not engaged they should treat me just as a plain visitor, and not discuss with me the damage I had caused them and their daughter. That custom was strictly observed while I was there. All they were waiting for was for my mother or her representative to come to apologise and to admit that their son had caused damage for which they accepted the responsibility. My mother was also a widow. I was well treated at the Kgamphes and I enjoyed the little girl I hoped to raise.

Having been forced to return to Pretoria by Sporting arresting me in Johannesburg, I decided to turn the other way. I was still not a Communist but greatly inspired by the party's teachings. I was unwilling to go firmly into politics but events at home and abroad forced me. On Sundays I reluctantly used to attend the open-air meetings of Africans outside Marabastad to listen to what radicals, the ICU and Congress speakers had to say about many things which were happening daily in Pretoria and elsewhere. The main topics, as usual, were the effects of the passes and police raids in Marabastad and other African locations which were mainly carried out on Saturdays for passes and beer. In such raids, not only men but women were arrested for being in possession of beer in their homes and for brewing.

At the end of that year, nineteen-thirty-five, I did not go to Phokeng to spend Christmas with my mother because I had been there in August to attend my father's funeral. I was invited by a young woman friend, Selina Mogomotsi, to spend the festival with her family in an African village not very far from Pretoria called Rantailane-de Wildt, a branch of the Makau tribe. That was the first Christmas I spent away from home. My mind was made up to turn my face against politics.

Nineteen-thirty-six came along with its troubles and found me wavering, unsettled, trying to forget about going to the Left Book Club, or to attend lectures there. The Smuts-Hertzog government launched an attack on the African people by framing and passing the law disenfranchising the Africans in the Cape Province who had been able to vote since nineteen-ten. The law came to be known as the Native Representation Act of nineteen-thirty-six. Before it the

Native Urban Areas Act of nineteen-twenty-three, amended by Hertzog's government in nineteen-twenty-five, had created advisory boards in all African locations in the country. This meant that Africans who had become urbanised must elect their own men into bodies called Native Advisory Boards to advise municipalities of their needs, as though Africans were strange people in the country whose needs were not known by those who ruled them. Advisory boards could only advise. Municipalities were free to reject their recommendations.

The nineteen-thirty-six Act was creating a larger advisory board for the whole country which would also, it was said, advise the government on the needs of the African people.

That national advisory body was called the Native Representative Council, to be elected by the Africans through the urban advisory boards and in rural areas by the Chiefs through electoral colleges. Instead of the Africans being enabled to vote for or against those who made laws for the country, they were given advisory boards to recommend what was needed for them or by them. The same rule was applied; the government was free to reject the recommendations of the Native Representative Council. I could not hold myself back from attending the first meeting of the Chiefs and leaders of the Africans from the Free State and the Transvaal held in the Methodist Central Hall, Vermeulen Street. Here they were to be told of the new law by which they were made to believe that at last the government was going to allow them to choose their own men to tell it of their needs and get improvements for them. I was glad when Africans all over the country rejected the idea and demanded the right to vote in the same way as Europeans. The Africans' rejection was blamed on the Communists who, it was said, were standing in the way of African progress.

The same year, in December, the African leaders met in Bloemfontein to debate and consider the implications of the situation created by the Hertzog-Smuts government. At that time they were heavily divided, some saying that they should accept the offer and others insisting on rejection. At the Bloemfontein conference, after fierce debates, one of the highly respected leaders, Professor T. Jabavu, came along with a recommendation that half a loaf was better than no bread, which meant that though they were not happy with what was offered it was better to have something through which they could work for improvements. The Native Representation Act was accepted and the newspapers hailed the decision as a victory for African progress. I was for total rejection because I was guided by the example of the advisory boards, which were at the mercy of municipalities and whose recommendations were in many cases rejected on the grounds that they were recommending the impossible.

I continued reading newspapers and Left Book Club books, but very seldom went to the Left Book Club for lectures. I decided that what would take me away from politics completely was to become a man interested solely in social events, dances, parties and girl friends. I was frequently at the Orient Hall or the Empire Hall, Boom Street, dancing, or at parties.

The social life I had chosen as an alternative to politics used to take me as far afield as Johannesburg on some nights to dance in the Inchcape Hall at Mai Mai, Wemmer, dancing with African beauties working in the City of Gold. At times I went with others to places like Benoni, Brakpan and Springs to dance. That was an expensive business; we went by taxi and had to pay to get into the hall and for refreshments inside to show the girls that one was kind and generous. I was always broke, owing friends money and finding it difficult to settle my debts. Once seen in a dance hall or at parties, you always got invitations because you had shown yourself to be interested.

During the week it was always the same, reading old newspapers or new ones if I could get them, or reading books at home, struggling to understand the contents. On Sundays, when I had nowhere to go, I would reluctantly visit open-air meetings. I liked to meet my girl friends, but preferred to see them in the evenings when I was free. At heart, I called myself a Communist, though I was not a member of the Communist party of South Africa. The war in Ethiopia was raging; my sympathies were with Ethiopia. The Spanish war was on; my sympathies were with the Republicans. In the United States of America the trial of the Scottsborough boys was going from court to court. Africans were going to prison in large numbers in my country merely for pass offences. Stories about Jewish persecution in Hitler's Germany were not missing on newspaper pages. I was seeing unpleasant things near and far. Could I last long away from politics under those circumstances, I asked myself? I tried to read about them but not be influenced by them.

Expenses forced me to withdraw from dances and parties. Friends began to see me getting lonely, retreating into my room in Maraba-stad at Mr. Madisha's house, 41 Third Avenue. I was sharing a room with a friend, Rampai Madiba, who was very much interested in girls. Most of the time he was away visiting girl friends and that gave me a chance to read more in his absence. Rampai Madiba was a very good singer, good looking, with a beautiful voice and girls could not resist him. He was singing in a group called the Roaring Forties which used to win prizes in African Eisteddfods.

It was there at Marabastad that I decided to engage in politics. Many heart-breaking episodes were taking place around me. Not a single month passed without the police raiding Marabastad and other African locations searching for beer and passes. As a result many African men and women were arrested. There was also agitation going on that Marabastad was too close to Europeans and must be demolished. In fact the place was a slum and unhealthy. It was built of corrugated iron sheets, with electric lights in the streets but not in the houses. The streets were dusty and the water supply was poor. If it had not been that its demolition was to be on the grounds of being close to European residential areas, many people like myself would not have protested. We protested because we were said not to be fit to be near Europeans' homes though we were with them in the factories, in the shops and working in their homes, cooking their food and minding their children.

Near Marabastad across the river to the east was another African location, Schonplaats. It was mainly a place of religious people whose language was Afrikaans. There was a large church belonging to the Lutherans of the Berlin Mission. Their head priest was Mr. Sachs, but services were conducted by an African priest called Mr. Motau. Schonplaats was the first on the list to be demolished and the inhabitants were given notice to leave and find themselves places to go to. They resisted the order to move for several months on the grounds that they had nowhere to go. It was said that the place belonged to the church and Mr. Sachs had sold it to Pretoria City Council. One day I witnessed a sight which broke my heart and which I have never been able to forget. I saw the City Council's workmen brought in to demolish Schonplaats, and as they did so to throw the inhabitants and their belongings out. That drove me into politics never to return. It was the end of Schonplaats. In its place was built a football ground and playing fields for European children. Schonplaats was a slum, and many unpleasant things were reported from there, but that was not why it was demolished.

While I was hesitating whether I should apply for membership of the Communist party, newspapers came along with reports that the Communist party of the Soviet Union was being purged of its best and leading figures who had brought it into being and many were being arrested to stand trial. That was nineteen-thirty-seven. Leading figures among them were Radek, Kamenev, Bukharin, army leaders and many others which newspapers said were the cream of the party. The newspapers also said that they were arrested because they opposed Stalin and those who supported him.

Some were sentenced to death by firing squads. After reading the verdicts I remember asking myself, how can I join the party which destroys its cream, the party with no future because its leadership is destroyed? I convinced myself that it was just a matter of time before the Communist party of the Soviet Union would cease to exist and all the arguments for a World Communist Movement would collapse. I found myself overtaken by fear, wondering what was going to happen, because among the Communists in South Africa was the only voice I could hear which demanded equal opportunities and education for non-Europeans. There was nothing else in the country demanding that for *all* non-Europeans. Congress was asking for better treatment for the Africans, the Indian Congress was doing the same for the Indians, the African Peoples' Organisation working in Cape Town was saying the same thing for the Coloured people. The whole field was open to the Hertzog-Smuts government to do as they saw fit. All I could do was wait and see.

One day on a public holiday I went out of Pretoria with a number of Africans who were not interested in politics, invited by one to his home where his father was opening a new house for which he had worked for a long time. He wanted to open it with a ceremony because it was indeed a large house and most modern. I spent two days there with the others, and while enjoying ourselves I suggested to them that we should form ourselves into a body called the Bantu Men's Society. They agreed, and back in Pretoria we met on several occasions, formed the Society and I was elected secretary. There were more than ten of us. We contributed a pound each every month and banked the money in a building society.

Our sole aim was to raise money to buy plots of land and eventually build on the properties, which could bring us enough income to become rich men. The money was banked in the name of the society and the interest from it was to be shared each year. I was all the time a Communist at heart, though disagreeing with what was happening in the Soviet Union. Unfortunately our original aims did not blossom into the fruits we intended, but the money helped in many other ways. As time went by some of us died. The first one to die was Nka Malope, a great friend of mine, whom I missed for a long time. We had to withdraw his money and gave it to his parents.

As we grew older and desired to get married, each member luckily could fall back on what he had saved in the society. The money we saved founded many families, including my own. Nineteen-thirty-nine came along and the Communist party I had thought would collapse was still there in the Soviet Union and in South Africa and other parts of the world. I was about to ask for a form to apply for membership when another storm came along to blow me off. It was the arrival of Molotov in Berlin to sign a non-aggression pact with Ribbentrop. Fascism joining hands with Communism, enemies becoming friends: 'No,' I said, 'not for me.' At that time the man who introduced me to the Communist movement, Archie Levitan, was in Krugersdorp. I wrote him a long letter asking him to explain how it could be possible for communism and fascism to become friends. What grounds were there for them to have a common goal? I was bitter and disappointed. Was the Soviet Union endorsing fascism, were they approving Hitler's deeds against the Jewish people? I asked myself and Mr. Levitan in my letter.

A week later I got a more than ten-page letter from Levitan explaining at great length the purpose of the pact. I remained unconvinced. One of the passages I remember in Levitan's letter was the difference he wished me to see between the government and the party; they were not the same. The Soviet Union, he explained, was not the Communist party and Germany was not the Nazi party of Adolf Hitler. The pact was not between the parties, but between the governments. The Soviet government was aiming at avoiding a conflict with the German people whose minds had been poisoned by propaganda. Communism and fascism were still bitter enemies, Levitan explained, but that does not mean that the Soviet Union must send the Russian peoples' army into Germany to destroy it. For the destruction of fascism in Germany, he went on to explain, it was for the German people to recognise its danger and turn against the Nazi party and its leader Hitler. If there was going to be war one day between the Soviet Union and Germany it would come from Hitler's fascist Germany, not from the Soviet Union.

Still unable to see all he was trying to make me see, I put the letter in my suitcase and forgot it. I did not reply, but simply said to myself I am finished with you and your Communist party as though I was a member of it. The year the war broke out I saw a meeting advertised and I went to the Left Book Club to listen. At the meeting I was disappointed to hear that Communists all over the world, including the Soviet Union, were not supporting the war, that it was not a people's war, not a just war, but an imperialists' war quarrelling for possession of the world. That could not go down my throat; here they are again supporting fascism, giving it a chance to win. One of the leading members of the Communist party in Johannesburg, Maurice Basner, disagreed with the party's stand and was either expelled or he resigned. I decided to stay away from them and support the war, though I hated the South African army because Africans were not allowed to join as real soldiers, not allowed to be trained or to carry arms. I was sure that if Hitler won, fascism in South Africa would have won. To me Smuts was nothing but another Hitler in a different form. He hated Hitlerism in Europe but liked it when he practised it in South Africa himself.

At the beginning of nineteen-thirty-eight I began to get disturbing news from home that my mother was not well. She was alone, as my three sisters were married, none of them in our tribal capital Phokeng; two were in Luka, our main branch village, the other one far away in another tribe, in a village called Siga, near Koster in the western Transvaal. When I went to spend Christmas with Ntobana Kgamphe and the baby Peggy, mother was away from Phokeng, taken to Siga by my sister to try to help her regain her health. There was no news of her getting better when I left Pretoria for Christmas.

I returned to Pretoria still hoping that my mother would one day go to the Kgamphes to apologise for the damage I had done to their daughter so that Ntobana and I could start preparing for our future life together. Our hopes never materialised and there was nothing I could do for myself, and there was nothing the Kgamphes could do with me alone. As time went by my sister realised that mother was not getting better, and mother herself asked to be returned to Phokeng to see whether in her own house her health could be restored. Back in Phokeng more disturbing news began to reach me, that instead of regaining her health she was fast losing it. In June of that year I received a letter that my sister had arrived in Phokeng from Siga and that our elder sister had joined her to try to help in caring for and nursing their sick mother. I then realised that time was getting short, it was time I went to see mother before anything happened. I was still working for Cuthbert and Company. I asked for and was given three weeks' unpaid leave to go and visit my sick mother. I went home to find her really ill. Everything had been tried, but doctors were still trying to rescue her for us up to the last day. However, she was pleased to see me and I was pleased to see her still able to speak to me. At the beginning of my last week she advised me to return to Pretoria to take things easy, my sisters would keep me informed of developments, for better or for worse. On Saturday of that week I returned as mother suggested.

One Sunday afternoon, the eighteenth of August, I was at my place in Marabastad getting ready to go out to attend an open-air meeting, but I kept delaying. When I was about to leave I heard a knock on our door. I said, 'Come in,' and there appeared two boys from my tribe whom I knew were in Johannesburg and very seldom came to Pretoria. I welcomed them with a joke, saying, 'What the hell are you doing here? Pretoria is no city for you.' They laughed, settled down; we laughed and when I suggested making tea for them, one said, 'Don't worry, we are not staying. We are from Phokeng. We are sent to fetch you. Your mother died yesterday and her funeral is today.' I did not utter a word but took what I thought I would need and together we went out to their car and drove to Phokeng more than eighty miles away.

On the way they told me that they left Phokeng early that day but the car gave them trouble with punctures, also they had not noticed that their petrol would not be enough for the journey to Pretoria. We reached home late in the evening and found that my mother had already been buried. When they did not arrive with me early, knowing that at times I spent weekends in Johannesburg, people thought they had not found me at home. So I had not exchanged words with my father or my mother when they died. All I saw was my mother's grave, and even today I don't know what her coffin looked like. Later my aunt told me that before mother died she told my sisters to care for each other and gave them much advice, but when asked about me said, 'He knows all. He will manage.'

That time I had not got permission from my employers to be away. I wrote them a letter from Phokeng to tell them that I was there because of my mother's death and did not know when I would return. I was away for a month, arranging my affairs, collecting all my father's animals together and giving them to my married sisters to care for until I needed them. I returned to Pretoria to face the world alone. A month later I received a letter from Ntobana Kgamphe, that her child Peggy was sick and I should come at once to see the little girl. I wrote to her that I would come later but hoped that she would be well soon. Two weeks later I received a sad letter from Ntobana that Peggy had died, and accusing me of being a heartless man who didn't care when told that his child was sick. She accused me further that my refusal to come as soon as she requested convinced her that I did not love her and the baby, and that, as usual, I must have been kept away by the girl friends she knew I was unable to keep myself from. My heart was broken. I wrote back expressing my sorrow, but denying all the allegations in the letter.

Thereafter our friendship soured, our letters conveyed quarrels and accusations which led to its breakdown. That year I knew that my dedication would be to African politics. I had no real girl friend but began to form secret associations with girls, mostly my friends' girl friends. I don't know how I developed that habit and why the girl friends of my friends could not resist me. I had no girl friend of my own but I was happy and lacked nothing a member of the opposite sex could offer.

As I continued to attend radical political meetings in the open-air near Marabastad, I got inspired by the ICU (Industrial and Commercial Workers' Union) speaker, Ismael Moroe, when he used to point at the police who were always at such meetings taking notes, saying, 'Don't be afraid of them, they are workers like yourselves; they are working, that is why they are here with us today. Their bosses are spending afternoons with their families and they are here, listening to what we are saying so that they can go and tell Hertzog, Smuts and Pirow about us.' Moroe used to stress that we should free ourselves from fear of the police and prison, saying, 'The police are men like us and prison is a house like the house we sleep in every night.' He used to get arrested himself, charged with incitement and sometimes going to prison. 'You can't stand up for your rights if you are not free from fear,' he stressed strongly.

XXVI Experiment

Ismael Moroe's insistence that we should free ourselves from fear of police and prison inspired me so much that I made up my mind to experiment. I had no doubt that if I were to go into politics, to take my stand against the pass laws and other forms of colour discrimination in the country, I ought to free myself from fear of police and prison as Moroe advised. I had already felt the handcuffs on my hands in Johannesburg when I was arrested by Sporting (Mr. Du Preez) but I still wanted to see the inside of prison and the treatment of people there.

I was also eager to become a speaker myself rather than to be a listener all the time. To become a politician in South Africa as a non-European meant arrest and imprisonment. Criticising those who governed the country and made laws which oppressed the non-Europeans and the Africans in particular was and still is interpreted as inciting Africans to break the laws of the land and hate Europeans. It was and still is a risk. Fear of the police and prison has always been the main thing that prevents many Africans organising themselves.

In nineteen-thirty-eight I decided to take the bull by the horns and to defy curfew regulations. One evening I went to visit one of my friends in Arcadia, the residential area of the rich Europeans of the city. Africans were not allowed to be out in the public streets to enjoy fresh air or to visit their friends after ten o'clock at night without written permission from their employers stipulating how late they permitted them to be out.

That night, because I wanted to be arrested, I left my friend at eleven o'clock and cycled to Marabastad where I lived. My friend tried to stop me and offered me a place in his bed, but I made the excuse that I had left my room unlocked because I thought I would be back early. I had all my other documents in my possession, all in good order, the bicycle I used had Cuthbert's name written on it, but all those things were of no defence to me at that hour under curfew regulations. I went by Church Street, the main street of the city, knowing well that I would not escape the police there. I had not gone far, and I was crossing the river which divides Arcadia from the centre of the city when a policeman came out into the middle of the street and flashed his torch into my face, signalling me to stop. I stopped and he asked me in Afrikaans, '*Waar is jou nag pas?*' ('Where is your night pass?'). I said I had not got one. That was enough. That

216

also relieved him of patrolling the area further because he had to take me along to the police station. There he charged me for being in a public street without a night pass authorising me to be there at that hour. That night my bedroom was a police cell which I shared with five others.

The next day, after a breakfast of salty soft porridge, we washed the cell yard with a hosepipe. The police informed my employers that I had been arrested the night before and if they wanted to release me the fine would be ten shillings, otherwise I would have to spend five days in prison. An hour before the court was due to start, I was handcuffed to another man who was in the same cell as me. With the other hand I could manage to push my bicycle. We went to court. In the yard, waiting for the court to start, I heard my name being called by one of the police, and when I reached him he handed me ten shillings and said it came from my employers. I knew that I was deprived of going to prison, which I was eager to see and also to have the honour of saying, 'I am no longer afraid of it.' That was my first arrest in Pretoria and my first night in a police cell. I was glad that I had crossed the first barrier and halved my fear of police and prison, but I was not yet satisfied.

From that morning onwards I was frequently to be seen, hand-cuffed, being marched to court with others for having defied curfew regulations. I remember one Boxing Day I was arrested in Arcadia and spent the night in Arcadia police station. The next day in court I asked the native commissioner, whose court dealt with pass offences, why even on days like Boxing Day we were still required to carry night passes, yet it was the day after the celebration of Jesus Christ's birthday. 'Can't we be free even one night?' I asked. In reply he told me that he was not there to change the law but to enforce it. The law required me to carry a night pass in a public street at that time of the night, yet I was found by the police without one. He did not fine me but warned me that next time I wanted to be out so late I should see that I had a night pass regardless of what time of the year it was.

On one occasion, still determined to get arrested and desperately seeking to see the inside of prison, I went to visit my girl friend, Ntobana Kgamphe, where she worked as a domestic servant in an area called Waterkloof. I was not aware that Waterkloof at that time was not part of Pretoria municipality. It was a rural area where curfew regulations did not apply.

After spending part of the evening with Ntobana, I left her to return to my place in Marabastad which was very far away. It was a journey of ninety minutes. When I crossed into the municipal area, I was stopped by two policemen, one European and the other an African, and asked to produce a special pass authorising me to be in that area of Brooklyn at that time of the night. I confessed to them that I had no night pass. Thereupon they arrested me and took me to Brooklyn police station, where I was charged and spent the night in a police cell. As always I found other Africans who had been similarly arrested already in the cell.

The next morning a large police van came along from the city to collect us. From Brooklyn we went to Hatfield and collected others arrested there; from there we went to Sunnyside police station and from there to Arcadia police station, to collect from each place. By that time we were packed so tight inside the van that we could hardly move. I was the only one with a bicycle, and it was with us inside. That time no one informed my employers where I was and they wondered what had happened to me when I did not report for work as usual. I had already been arrested several times for defying curfew regulations and each time when my friends saw me amongst the arrested, knowing that my breakfast that day had been salty soft porridge, they used to buy me delicious fish and chips which I ate before the court began. That day when I came from Brooklyn one of my tribesmen, Ratshikane Molotsane, who worked at the native commissioner's offices, who had bought me several packets of fish and chips, remarked when he saw me come out of the police van, 'Hey, I think that each time you want me to buy you fish and chips you look for the police and ask them to arrest you.' He was saying it as a joke, because he at once went out to buy a packet.

He used the telephone in the office in which he worked to inform my employers that I was not sick but arrested for having no special pass. Again money was sent to release me. I missed going to prison again as on the previous occasions. Every week when money was paid for my release, which was always ten shillings, it was deducted from my pay. Cuthbert and Company at that time was one of the best paying firms. I was earning twenty-two shillings and sixpence.

I was so anxious to satisfy myself and my friends that I was free from fear that I took another step. I became eager to become a public speaker. One evening I visited George Daniels, of the Radicals group, to tell him that I would like to try public speaking myself. George was impressed. He said to me, 'I am glad that you want to work with us organising our people against these things which make us suffer so much. The field is big,' Daniels said, 'but there are few workers.' He warned me that I was committing myself to a dangerous task. The police would begin to take note of me, they would hate me as they hated him and others, and they would do everything they could to frighten me by arresting me for anything they thought would make me realise that in speaking against the government and the law I was knocking my head against a stone wall. I would get hurt.

I told him that I would be more happy to be hated by the police for working for my freedom and that of my people than to be liked by them for being a tame donkey. He laughed and said, 'Very well, boy; on Sunday I shall call on you to speak as one of our group, the Radicals.' He encouraged me by saying, 'You don't have to speak for a long time, two or three minutes will be enough.' During the week I began to call myself a fool, wondering why I had committed myself to becoming a public speaker when I knew nothing about public speaking. I began to be haunted by doubts and fears that I should not go to the meeting that Sunday and pretend to be sick. It was not until Sunday morning the following week that I pulled myself together and said to myself, 'I must go. How will I learn if I run away? I must go and make mistakes. They will teach me.'

That Sunday was, like most before it, bright and warm and the sky was deep blue. After lunch I left my room without telling anyone where I was going or why, and went to the open-air meeting. I got there to find a few people had already gathered, George Daniels had not arrived, but the police were already there. I was not there long before George arrived carrying a Sunday newspaper with him. He laughed when he saw me and said, 'Boy, you kept your promise.' He took one of his men aside to tell him that they had gained a new recruit. The meeting started. As usual, George Daniels and Ismael Moroe were the chief speakers, spoke for a long time condemning the Hertzog-Smuts government, oppression and the pass laws.

At the end, when many speakers had spoken and the meeting was about to be closed, George called on me to say a few words. I was nervous, but did say a few words as George asked me. I remember saying that if we were like Mr. Moroe and Mr. Daniels, if we did what they told us, we would free ourselves from all the things we all complain make us suffer. 'We complain,' I said, 'that the passes are no good, but we don't want to do anything about throwing them away.' I remember saying, 'They tell us that the passes are good, but why don't they want to carry them? If they are good, why do they arrest us when we say we don't want them? They don't want us to throw away the passes because they make money from us. We pay them money when arrested and they make us work for little money because we are afraid that if we refuse to work for little money they will arrest us for having no passes and send us to prison.' I was getting into form and remembering the lectures I attended at the Left Book Club.

I stopped and was surprised when the audience cheered the end of my speech. George Daniels invited me to his house after the meeting to tell me that I spoke well, and to warn me again that I had exposed myself to the police; from that day they would watch me. I told him that I did not mind; I thanked him for having been kind and let me speak. George said, 'Oh no, boy, don't thank me – thank yourself for having given yourself to the service of African freedom.' I had supper that evening with George's family.

Afterwards I went back to my own place, pleased that I had joined the ranks of the fighters for African emancipation from colour discrimination and the pass laws. During the week many people I did not know before began to greet me when we met and told me that they knew me from Sunday's open-air meeting outside Marabastad. News from European countries was disturbing; newspapers were printing stories that black clouds of war were gathering over Europe and the war was getting near. Newspapers were also reporting that there were signs that Hertzog and Smuts held different views about the coming war.

Before I could officially join the Radicals, not merely to be their casual speaker, the leader of the group, George Daniels, fell sick, and within three weeks he died. It was a sad day for us all because the group had lost a brave and inspiring man. Like most organisations, the group had depended so much on Daniels' leadership that none of the members who worked with him bothered to learn things as George did. A dilemma set in, everyone wondered who was capable of stepping into Daniels' shoes to lead the group as he had. Like children who had lost their parents, the Radical group disintegrated and as a result it died like its leader.

In Pretoria there was big movement going on, a new location was under construction eight miles from the centre of the city. Though we were at first opposed to its construction, the first houses built there turned out to be far better than our old homes at Marabastad. They were of good bricks, with good gardens, concrete baths built in, a good running water system, one tap in the yard and one in the bathroom, electric light, a coal stove, steel windows, and two doors, one in front, one at the back. All had cement floors, but no ceilings or doors in the rooms, with the walls of the rooms not up to the ceiling. The houses were not plastered or painted inside. There were houses of four types, with two rooms, three rooms, four rooms and a few with five rooms. Compared with Marabastad and Schonplaats they were really a great improvement for the Africans of Pretoria. The location was also an improvement on Bantule–Newclare, which was far better than Marabastad and Schonplaats. The location was named Atteridgeville after a liberal European woman who, for many years as a councillor in Pretoria City Council, had campaigned for better houses for the Africans. The Africans nicknamed the location Phelindaba, which means 'All arguments are over'.

I, together with others, opposed the building of Atteridgeville on the principle of opposing segregation and colour discrimination, because most of the city councillors agreed to build Atteridgeville not so much to house Africans in better houses but as a policy of making segregation work and to remove the Africans from European residential areas. Nevertheless, Atteridgeville provided many Africans with privacy which they never enjoyed in Marabastad and Schonplaats.

Many African families which had lived in rooms in Marabastad and Schonplaats now enjoyed living in houses on their own, free from the control of landlords. Their landlord became the City Council of Pretoria. But as laid down in the Natives Urban Areas Act of nineteen-twenty-three, Atteridgeville had to have an advisory board with administrative officers, a location superintendent and his deputy to control the inhabitants. The houses of the superintendent and his assistant were built just outside the location near the main road to enable them to see who entered the place. Pretoria City Council deserves credit here, because, though the Native Urban Areas Act firmly stipulates that African locations controlled by municipalities must be fenced, have only one entrance with sentries at the gate, and also that non-residents must obtain the superintendent's written permission to go in for any purpose, Pretoria municipal locations, unlike Johannesburg and the municipalities of other big cities in the country, never fenced their locations and waived the entrance permits. The Native Urban Areas Act lays down that all visitors must be reported to the superintendent and their visiting periods known. When their periods have expired they should move out. Those failing to comply must be arrested and be charged with an offence. I can remember no case in which Africans in Pretoria City Council's locations were arrested and charged.

Nevertheless, Africans in Atteridgeville, like Africans all over the country in urban areas, were not allowed to brew or drink beer. There were improvements in the raiding for beer on African homes in Atteridgeville. Instead of state police coming in to raid for beer, as was the case in all locations in the country, raids were conducted by municipal police, all Africans, under the supervision of the superintendent or his assistant. Those arrested were taken or kept at the municipal administrative offices, and collected later by state police from Pretoria West police station. Until nineteen-fifty-six, Atteridgeville African residents did not pay separate bills for water and electric light. All were included in monthly rents which were mostly under three pounds.

The Industrial and Commercial Workers' Union of Africa (ICU) also suffered the loss of their leader, Mr. Ismael Moroe. Moroe, who had been in the forefront of the fight against the pass laws and colour discrimination for many years, did what we called crossing the line into the enemy's sector. He was given a job by the City Council of Pretoria to become compound manager of their African workers' compound outside Pretoria in a quarry at the place called Bonna-Cord. In accepting a job from the City Council, he became one of those who were by no means opposed to the passes. One of Moroe's duties as a compound manager was to see that every African had a pass and that it was in order. We were betrayed by the man who inspired me and encouraged me to live above fear.

Those of us who tried but failed to make him change his mind heard him say, 'I have a wife and children to support,' as though he was a newly-married man. We began to hear words flowing from Moroe's lips that it was useless to carry on, the Africans loved the passes, that was why they refused to burn them wholesale in nineteen-thirty when they were urged to do so. He had tasted the honey of being in control of a large number of workers, with a regular monthly wage packet, and the praises of the officials of the council and the police that at last he had seen the light of truth and as a wise man had left a useless cause which could do his people no good. He was also impressed by talk that at that time he was really working for his people and leading them along the right path. Moroe had changed, he was no longer the man I knew when I first attended the open-air meeting he addressed. On more than one occasion, when some of us went to see him, hoping that we could still pull him back to us, he made it his task to avoid us, sometimes telling us that he was busy or, when we met him in the streets, saying he was in a great hurry. He decided his fate. Members of the ICU group, too, had made a great mistake not preparing someone to take over from Moroe in case he died or put on another coat. The group attempted to carry on, but before long the real ICU as it was known in Pretoria went out of existence, like the Radical group at the time of George Daniels' death. Moroe became a respectable man seen only among people who claimed that they were not interested in politics.

Events having taken that turn, open-air meetings were no longer taking place, the second world war was on and I was greatly worried by the fact that South African Communists, following the lead of the Soviet Union Communists who held that the war was not a just one but an imperialist one, were not participating in it. I was disappointed because to me it was a war which all anti-fascists ought to support in order to defeat fascism all over the world. I retreated back to my room to continue to read newspapers and books, trying to understand more of domestic politics and those of the world at large. At the end of each day after delivering the parcels, I went straight back to my room to cook for myself and read before going to bed.

In September nineteen-thirty-nine, a man I got to know well through the African National Congress branch in Pretoria, who himself was working for Pretoria City Council's non-European section as a clerk, a man who had become one of my friends, decided to get married. His name was Maila Lekgetho. He lived not very far from me in Marabastad; we saw each other nearly every day but when he issued invitations to his friends for his wedding he left me out. I was wounded by his exclusion of me and decided to stay away. On the day of the wedding, which was a Saturday, knowing that there was going to be a reception and dance afterwards in the Orient Hall, I still stood firm to boycott the whole affair. In the evening I was alone in my room reading when I heard a knock on my door. It was one of my best friends called Papi Mabuse. He said to me, 'You with your books, can't you free yourself from them and think of something else? Come on,' he said, 'let's go to Lekgetho's wedding.' I said, 'I am sorry, I am not invited. I don't want to be where I am not wanted.' He said, 'I am not invited myself but we are going there merely to dance afterwards.' I tried to talk him out of it but he talked me into it. Eventually we left together for Orient Hall. It was a big affair.

I think that it was an hour before the dance started. While we were sitting down, listening to speeches and toasts to Maila Lekgetho and his wife, a pretty girl approached us. She was one of the waitresses serving people with refreshments. Mabuse, who knew her and her family, greeted her and introduced us. He told me that her name was Nana Tlhogo 'head', and thereupon Nana Tlhogo asked what she could get for us to drink. I said I needed nothing, but Mabuse ordered two glasses of orange squash. Nana offered to get us something else if we wished, but I insisted on having nothing else.

Later the dance commenced and as we moved round Nana became my partner, and I asked her why she was waiting at the wedding. She told me that my friend Maila Lekgetho was her cousin and her family was in charge of the wedding. She pointed at two other young women in the crowd and told me that they were her sisters. To my surprise I had not seen any of them before or heard of the Tlhogo family in Marabastad. They were well known amongst the devout church-going people in the location. They were a very reserved family which kept itself to itself. Their father was dead, in fact I was told he died when Nana was only a year old. She was brought up by her mother, a devout Methodist, who could not go to church on Sunday and leave her children behind. The children also grew up to be devout Methodists.

When the dance came to an end I asked Nana her address and she readily gave it to me. I wrote it down on a piece of paper, slipped it into one of my pockets and forgot all about it. A month later, one Sunday afternoon, I was alone, bored and with nowhere to go, got tired of reading a Sunday newspaper and began to think of where to go to wait for Sunday to pass off. During a deep search in my mind I remembered Nana Tlhogo. I had forgotten her address but remembered that I had it on a piece of paper somewhere. I went through all the pieces of paper I had in my pockets and finally came across it. I dressed up and went to look for Nana merely to pass the time. I reached her home, found her two sisters there, and wondered which one of them was Nana. Fortunately, the one I was looking for saw me coming, recognised me and came out of the house to welcome me. I was a complete stranger to the family. I asked for Nana, and before I got an answer from the sisters, she said, 'I am Nana', and she invited me into the house and offered to make tea, and I encouraged her. I spent that afternoon at her home speaking largely about the wedding where we met.

XXVII Nana

After that three weeks elapsed before I saw Nana again. At our
second meeting she invited me to their Eisteddfod competition,
which took place in the John Dougall Hall, Marabastad. The
trainer and conductor of their choir was her sister's husband, Mr.
Lazarus Masuana, who was the headmaster of the Dutch Reformed
school in Marabastad. After their performance I accompanied her
to her home, and before we said good-bye to each other we arranged
our third meeting. We met again one Sunday at her home and
again our talk centred on their performance at the Eisteddfod.

I began to try to avoid meeting her because I knew that with me a
tribal man and she a town girl it would be difficult for us to marry.
We tribal people still thought that townspeople had lost discipline,
they were more influenced by money than by personal values. They
in turn had developed fears of tribal people that they never married
girls unless they were told to do so by their parents and that by and
large they were still polygamists and would not be satisfied with one
wife. There was a gulf between us. As I tried to stay away from her I
fell in love with her, and she kept coming into my memories while I
tried to forget her. Again fortunately for me, in the Bantu Men's
Social Club, of which I was the secretary, was a member who lived
with his parents right opposite Nana's home, and their families were
great friends. The member's name was Lentsoe Sesoko, and his
father was the priest of an African independent church called African
Catholics. Nana was also a great friend of Lentsoe's sister and they
were always seen together and sang in the same Eisteddfod choir.
One day I visited Lentsoe at his home and there I found Nana with
his sister. When I left I called on Nana to ask her if we could meet
on Sunday at her home, and she agreed.

I think that at that time she had also fallen in love with me. She
asked me to come earlier as she wanted me to have lunch with her
when she came back from church. As arranged, I went that Sunday,
and after lunch I asked her to take a walk with me for fresh air. We
went out together and during our walk I felt that I should ask her
to become my girl friend. She then told me that she was already a
girl friend of someone else, a teacher who taught somewhere in the
country, but they were not engaged.

A month afterwards she agreed to become my girl friend. From
that time I became a frequent visitor at her home. During nineteen-

forty we met nearly every week courting. My people in the country knew nothing about it until the beginning of nineteen-forty-one, when I broke the news to them. My parents were no longer alive, so I was in a stronger position to resist tribal ethics without risking accusations that I thought nothing of my parents' wishes that a tribal boy should marry a tribal girl so that she could be a trusted and loyal wife to him. When I told my sisters, aunts and relatives about it, it seemed as though I was speaking a language they did not understand. They all asked me why it was that I could not find a suitable girl in the tribe or in other tribes to choose to be my future wife. They were terrified because she was Marabastad-born. They would not mind so much if she had been born in Thaba Nchu, a Barolong tribe in the Orange Free State where her parents were born. To marry a girl born and brought up in Marabastad was as though I was telling them that I was going to throw myself into the sea to get drowned.

My love for Nana was complete and there was no longer any other girl for me in the world. I don't know what Nana's people's reactions were, but I could see that they too were suspicious of me, they knew nothing of my background. They heard from those who knew me that I was the type of a boy who used to attend open-air Radical and ICU meetings. I had little school education and they feared that their daughter was throwing her own life away by seeking to marry me. I heard such stories from people who claimed to be close to Nana's sisters and mother. None of them said such things to me, but later on I came to believe those stories. In Marabastad there were some boys who had chosen to live above fear of the police and prison, and Rabi Morudu was one of them. Some people called him a jail-bird. One day, when I was on my rounds delivering shoes in Arcadia, I passed Rabi in the street and entered the yard of a block of European flats. I left the bicycle with a load of parcels down below while I went up to deliver a parcel. By the time I returned the parcels had grown feet; they were not there, but I knew that Rabi was responsible. In the evening in Marabastad, Nana's cousin who knew well that I was Nana's boy friend, and who was at the same time Rabi's brother's family's great friend, was approached by Rabi selling best quality shoes cheap. But knowing Rabi, she declined to buy them. She heard of my story, and the next day she told me in Nana's presence that she had seen Rabi selling the shoes I had lost. She was a teacher educated by Nana's mother, and had come to live with the family in Pretoria at the age of five. When I said that I was going to tell the police she saw Rabi selling the shoes we were looking for, she said her loyalty was not with me but with Rabi's brother's family and she could not do anything to hurt them. When I insisted that I was going to mention her name to the police she said that she would call

226

me a liar, saying she knew nothing of my story, and ended up by saying, 'If you dare to mention my name to the police, I shall hate you and your offspring if I shall in future know them.'

Having heard that, I smiled at her and she said, 'You laugh; I am not laughing, I mean what I say.' I did what she asked, I did not go to the police with the story. The shoes were never found, but the bicycle was found a week afterwards – with no wheels, saddle or handles – in the bushes on an open plot of land near the hill on which the Union Buildings stand. That gave me the impressions that stories that Nana's family was not happy with me were true. I was in love with Nana, and I said to myself, 'I want her, not her people or their treatment.' I carried on going to Nana's home to see her. I said to myself, her cousin wanted me to break with her. If I did I would be carrying out her wishes, not my own.

My friendship with Nana grew and we planned to marry one day when we were ready. My letters to my sisters and relatives in Phokeng increased, and nearly every month I went to Phokeng to convince my relatives that I was not throwing myself into the sea to get drowned. One of the main reasons my people were not happy at my marrying a townsgirl was that they would lose me. She would keep me away from the tribe, and they could not see how I could prosper anywhere other than with them in the tribe. Even when I told them that I had grown beyond the tribe's boundaries, that I had broadened my mind and was looking on the whole world as my home, they only thought that I was mentally ill.

During nineteen-thirty-nine two men workers of Woolworths in Johannesburg asked to be transferred to the branch in their home town, Pretoria. They were my friend Papi Mabuse's brother, Simon Mabuse, and Frans Raboroko. African trade unions were virtually unknown in Pretoria. In the City of Gold the two men had belonged to an African trade union called the African Commercial and Distributive Workers' Union. They knew when they left Johannesburg that preparations were under way for a breakthrough on the trade union front which would affect the African workers for the first time. At that time African workers were paid anything the employers wished to pay them, they could be dismissed without notice if the employer was hostile, they could work any amount of hours a day or week with no overtime being paid, and annual holidays with pay were things which seemed not meant for them.

Since people are not the same and would never be the same, some European trade unionists in Johannesburg had made it their business to help Africans organise themselves into trade unions. Most of those Europeans had been Communists early in their lives, some were Socialists and others were still members of the Communist party of South Africa. I shall mention only a few of them: the late

W. H. Andrews, Solomon (Solly) Sachs, Maurice Kagan, his wife Kattie Kagan, Issy Wolfson, Louis Joffe, Anna Scheepers, Johanna Cornelius, Betty du Toit, and many others who will always live in the history of the South African labour movement.

The one I am particularly discussing here was a young man I knew as E. Gordin. I did not know what his politics were. When I met him he was the general secretary of several African trade unions which he organised with African under-secretaries in the basement at Explorations Buildings, Commissioner Street, Johannesburg. During the war Smuts's government interned him and removed him from African trade unions for good. He was a charming and firm young man when I saw him before his internment.

Early in January nineteen-forty Simon Mabuse and Frans Raboroko received notices of a big meeting in Johannesburg to take place in the middle of that month at Mai Mai Sports Ground on a Sunday. It was a trade union meeting called by the African Commercial and Distributive Workers' Union and other unions which were organised and conducted under the guardianship of Mr. Gordin at Explorations Buildings. The purpose of the meeting was to celebrate an event which was worth celebrating, the coming into force of industrial law in the commercial and distributive trades, which for the first time covered African workers in that field of South African industry. A minimum wage level was laid down for unskilled men in the industry, which of course meant African workers. That was made possible, as I have already said, by European trade unionists who, whenever they made wage demands for their European members to the government and the employers, argued the case of the African workers.

Mabuse and Raboroko told me of the meeting, and I told three men I knew would be interested, Johannes Makou, April Rabolao and Mogotoko Mfete. The six of us planned to attend the meeting and arranged to leave together that Sunday morning for Johannesburg. The meeting was a very big one; Wemmer Sports Ground, which held thousands of people, could not absorb all those who came to attend. Those of us who came to the meeting were urged to join the already formed unions, or form others where none existed. Mr. Gordin was the main speaker, supported by the African secretaries who worked with him. Wages laid down for unskilled workers, the Africans, were far below those of Europeans, but at last the African worker was taken away from the mercy of the employers. He knew what pay to expect when he performed certain types of job in the industry, that he was entitled to overtime payments, sick pay, injury benefits and an annual holiday with pay. It was a big landmark for the African workers in the country, thanks to the European trade unionist, Gordin, and the Africans who gave themselves to the cause.

At the end of the meeting Mabuse and Raboroko met some of the African secretaries who worked with Mr. Gordin and told them about us, and that led to our meeting Mr. Gordin and his men. After the introductions we joined the union and the link with Pretoria was established. Back at home we began to communicate with the Johannesburg office and told them that there were many people in Pretoria who were attracted by the idea of forming a branch of the organisation in our city. After one month, on a Wednesday afternoon in March, the six of us again left in a taxi belonging to Mr. Legotlo for Johannesburg. I had already been chosen as the secretary of the Pretoria section.

We arrived at headquarters and found everything ready for us, and leaflets were already printed for a meeting to be held in Pretoria on Sunday week to establish a branch. I was given books and membership cards to start enrolling those interested, and also told to prepare for the meeting. Before we went to Johannesburg we had already engaged the John Dougall Hall in Marabastad for the Sunday from eight o'clock in the morning until one o'clock. The leaflets we brought from Johannesburg were printed accordingly. Mr. E. Gordin was advertised as the main speaker, to be followed by others. When we left the head office we found two detectives waiting for us at the taxi with Mr. Legotlo. Mr. Gordin came out with us and explained to them that we were mere trade union fellows from Pretoria, whereupon the detectives explained that they were investigating a complaint by a robbed man and wanted to make sure that we were not involved in that crime. As a result of Mr. Gordin's explanation we were not asked to produce our passes. If we had been, I for one would have been in trouble because I had no pass authorising me to be in Johannesburg. However, we returned home happy, and I was to act as secretary until the appointment could be endorsed at the meeting the following weekend.

Our meeting was well advertised and was well attended. On the day of the meeting Mr. Gordin was not among the arrivals from Johannesburg. Those who came were Daniel Koza, Daniel Cosani, Nkageleng Nkadimeng, P. Phoffu, an old man who bore the Dutch name of van Dassie, and another African whom I did not get to know well because he died soon afterwards. We were told that Mr. Gordin could not come because of some unexpected events. Soon after our return he had been served with an order by the Smuts' government not to leave the Johannesburg area until further notice.

At the Pretoria meeting many workers joined and my appointment as secretary of the Pretoria section was confirmed. I was still working for Cuthbert and Company and my office was my room in Marabastad. From those who joined at work, I took their money and particulars and the next day brought them membership cards.

Every week I had to send the money to the head office with the list of names of members who had joined the union. The arrangement was also that when I got complaints I should forward them to the head office and from there they would be dealt with. Before long I found myself in an awkward mess, having sent complaints to the head office and, when the victims came to enquire, always telling them that I did not know what was happening, that the head office was still working on the complaints and as soon as I knew the results I would let them know. A man who has paid his money always wants to know his fate. Doubts began to set in. Some suspected that I did not send on their complaints. To free myself of suspicion I had to write letters in their presence and let them post them. Mr. Gordin was interned; I did not know what was happening at the headquarters and there was confusion. Complaints increased and stories began to circulate that my union was only interested in collecting money, not in the settlement of members' grievances. I carried on. Before Mr. Gordin was interned he formed a body at Explorations Building to run the unions jointly and called it the Joint Council of African Trade Unions. That body sent a man to Pretoria to organise garage and filling-station workers. He was doing it full time and an office was opened at 253 Vermeulen Street. I transferred my office there but was still not working full time. The man's name was Malesela Modiba, an ex-teacher. I arranged for him to enrol members for me during the day, and for me to collect the money in the evening and to take complaints. If I finished deliveries late and could not do it, I asked my union to pay Modiba so much for the work he agreed to do for us.

Instead of things improving they went from bad to worse. There were complaints from my members everywhere. Those who wanted to join were warned by others to be careful. Fortunately for me no one could accuse me of having taken his money and then neglecting his complaint. But my colleagues and I made a mistake in thinking that Pretoria complaints could be settled from Johannesburg, and that only people at headquarters could settle complaints when there was in Pretoria a department of labour with industrial inspectors where we could have sent our members with grievances to get them looked into.

I don't know why people always think that they can't do something but others can and never think that what others can do they too can do if they only try hard enough. At the beginning I believed that I was not fit to do certain things, and that attitude prevented me from trying to see whether I could or not. Only afterwards did I regret that I had not tried, when I found that time had passed and I had missed my chance to learn. This attitude damages many people's chances. It leads one to mark time instead of marching forward. At first I thought Africans, my people, were the only ones who were the victims of that widespread attitude, but when I came to live and work with other people who were not African I found that they were victims as well.

XXVIII Pretoria Non-European
Distributive Workers' Union

The dissatisfaction of my members, which I shared, began to reach the ears of the European trade unionists in Pretoria. They advised us that there was no reason why we should not have an independent union of our own which we ourselves could control to see that our complaints were attended to quickly and to know the results quickly. Some of them, like Maurice Kagan, Mr. Rutherford, and Mr. Plunkett of the Trades and Labour Council in Pretoria, offered their services. I heard of the move and thought that the Europeans were out to disrupt African unity. I tried to persuade some of my friends to keep away, but I had nothing to offer because my union existed only in name. A Pretoria union was justified.

I attended the first meeting when the Pretoria union was born but disapproved of everything, though my own union was discredited. Nevertheless, the union was formed and two years later I became secretary. Its formation led to the formation of many other African trade unions in Pretoria which I later became closely associated with and led. As a matter of fact the African Commercial and Distributive Workers' Union which I joined and brought from Johannesburg never properly functioned in Pretoria. But it is fair to say that it was the mother of all African trade unions in Pretoria. The first secretary of the independent Pretoria union was my tribesman and good friend, Moagi Mokoe, who at first wanted to recruit me when Messrs. Lee and Kahn tried to form a group of the Socialist party in Pretoria. He joined the Communist party before me and, when he was the secretary of the Pretoria union, fell into temptation and earned himself expulsion from the Communist party and from the union itself. It is said that he settled a case for a worker with an Indian employer. The employer paid him in full what was due to the worker, but when he gave the worker the money, he held back part of it for himself and concealed the truth from the man. The truth came out one day when the man met his former employer, who asked him whether he was satisfied with what he got. The man said it was too little to make him satisfied, thereupon the employer told him what he had paid the secretary of the union.

In nineteen-forty-one I was married in the Methodist Church in Marabastad. The service was conducted by a man who belonged to another tribe not far from my own who in his early days lived with relatives in my tribe – Reverend Sedumedi Molope. He joined the Methodist Church while at their Teachers' Training College near Pretoria, Kilnerton Institute, and later trained for the ministry. Our first child, a daughter, whom I named after my paternal aunt Keidumetse, was born in nineteen-forty-two when the second world war was on.

In June nineteen-forty-one, a few months after our marriage, I was visiting my wife's cousin and her husband in Atteridgeville. We were still living in Marabastad in the one room I occupied first with my friend Rampei Madiba. It was Sunday and a newspaper man brought my host a Sunday newspaper. In big letters on the front page appeared the news that Germany had without warning attacked the Soviet Union and the German army was advancing on a very wide front. Though I didn't say anything to those who were with me, I was delighted by the news. Something I had long longed for had occurred; the war against fascism. I knew at once that the way for me to join the Communist party was open. I needed no one to tell me that the character of the war had changed. I knew that all anti-fascist organisations and persons would join the ranks of those who hated fascism and everything it stood for. I never disassociated fascism in Italy and Germany from the fascism I lived under in South Africa at the hands of Smuts, Hertzog, Malan and Strydom.

The following Sunday, without telling my wife, I left Marabastad and went to the Left Club, in Church Street East, opposite Pretoria Technical College for Europeans only. On my arrival I found the place full of people. An aggregate was being held that day, and in the afternoon a meeting took place and speeches I had longed to hear were delivered. It was a meeting of representatives of the inhabitants of South Africa – Europeans, Africans, people of Indian origin, and coloured people. They were Communists and non-Communists, as well as sympathisers who held left-wing views. Amongst them were my old teachers, Samuel Woolf, his wife Ethel, George Findlay, his wife Joan, Franz Boshoff and his wife Helen. For the first time I got to know that the Communist party had a large following in Pretoria and had a district committee of its own.

The emphasis had changed. There was unanimous support for the war against fascism. As an anti-fascist I thought that it was time for me to get away from standing on the fence to join the anti-fascist front. At the end of the meeting I went into the office of the party and asked for a form to apply to join the party. A week later I received a letter from the party secretary in Pretoria, telling me that my application had been considered by the district committee and accepted, but I was on three months' probation. During this time I was placed in the Marabastad area group. I was expected to attend party classes, sell party literature, and to perform other tasks considered party work, as well as paying party dues which were calculated according to members' earnings.

In the Marabastad group I found not only Africans, but Europeans as well, who lived in other parts of the city. The Communist party at that time was highly disciplined. To obtain membership one had to prove one was willing to work and discipline oneself. It did not matter whether one was influential or well known in the party or outside it, if one breached party discipline or did something which would discredit the party, expulsion was the only consequence. It was highly democratic; before expulsion, the accused person was given a good chance to defend himself after being charged. If not satisfied with the verdict, he could appeal to the Aggregate District Conference; if unsuccessful, to the National Central Committee; after that, as a last resort, to the National Congress. I began to attend party lectures and classes and studied hard to enable myself to understand more about the party, the country's politics and the politics of other countries.

Anxious to get a party membership card, I worked hard so that at the end of my probationary period I could have in my possession the card of the political party which impressed me as being the only one in the country working for a happy society in which all the inhabitants would have the right to vote and stand for all law-making institutions regardless of colour, sex, creed, or former place of origin; a society in which all children would have free education and equal opportunities. Above all it was an anti-fascist party which was opposed to all the oppressive and discriminatory laws of Smuts, Hertzog, Pirow, Strydom, Malan, the Dutch Reformed Church and all those who admired them and shared their convictions.

European members of the party had critics on both sides of the colour line. The anti-non-European and anti-Communist Europeans accused them of betraying their own people. They called them *Kaffir Boeties* – Kaffir's Brothers – and trouble-makers. In addition they were accused as agents of Russia who were willing to sell South Africa to that country.

The non-Europeans accused them of hypocrisy, that they were out to use the non-Europeans for their own ends, that if they were really against colour discrimination they should invite the non-Europeans into their homes to have dinner with them. We Africans who joined the party were accused by fellow-Africans of being weak – Europeans' good boys and girls who were on their knees begging the Europeans to bring us freedom in our own country. Those of us who also belonged to the African National Congress were accused of being there as spies for Europeans. Those like me did not worry because we knew that we were searching for a true and democratic

South Africa. We knew, and told our critics, that the European members of the party promised us nothing but hard, testing work for the South Africa we were all seeking. Unaware, our critics did not realise that they were reinforcing the upholders of fascism, against us and democratic South Africa.

In the end I was officially accepted into the party, which I later grew to love. I was always proud to be accused of being Communist. The first membership card I regarded as a certificate for the fight for the end of fascism in our country and the world over.

In nineteen-forty-two when the district committee selection came up, I was elected as one of its members. From that year I was elected to the Pretoria district committee every year until the party was dissolved in nineteen-fifty, a few weeks before Malan's fascist government passed the Suppression of Communism Act which has been used against anyone in the country who protests against the fascist Nationalist party and its government – now led by Vorster who openly, during the second world war, proclaimed his loyalty to Adolf Hitler and Benito Mussolini. His loyalty to fascism then earned him internment by the Smuts' government for working against the war effort in the country.

From the time of my election to the district committee I was always among the Pretoria delegation to the party's national conferences, which took place in the Transvaal until early nineteen-fifty. At the time of the dissolution of the party I was the chairman of the district committee. I was well known to the police as a Communist and I filed affidavits with Malan's Department of Justice declaring my membership of the party and that my district and I agreed with the central committee to dissolve the party because of the Suppression of Communism Act. As I had expected, the political field was rough, full of thorns, difficulties and poverty. But at the same time my love for South Africa and her inhabitants filled my heart with love for peoples of all nations and lands.

The party and its members were blamed mostly for what others had done. At the beginning of nineteen-forty-two, with the help of members of the party, several African trade unions came into existence; one of them was the Pretoria Non-European Municipal Workers' Union. At that time another wage determination, number one hundred and five, came into operation. It stipulated wages and hours of work for unskilled workers which, as I have said, meant the African workers, and covered labourers employed by municipalities in big cities in the country including Pretoria. For the first time Pretoria municipal workers, who were the lowest paid, got their wages raised to five pounds a month. Before that they were paid two pounds a month, or a bit more depending on the wishes of the council's officials. The determination stipulated that they should be

235

paid weekly instead of monthly as had previously been the case; also that they should be given twelve working days a year holiday with pay. Sick pay was another of the benefits provided.

A date was arranged on which the weekly wages were to be paid, and the workers were looking forward to the change with a good deal of excitement. Most of them were housed in the municipal compound. A week before the change was due to start, the council began to postpone the day, saying that they were not ready with the books. The assistant manager of the City Council's Native Affairs Department, Mr. Hardy, called a meeting of all the workers in the compound to tell them that the changeover was postponed for a week. He did not explain to them the reasons. Filled with suspicion that it was an attempt to keep them on the old system, the workers demanded the reason, but Mr. Hardy refused, telling them not to worry, that everything was all right and they would be paid weekly as promised. When they insisted on an explanation, Mr. Hardy told them that he was not under an obligation to give them one – they had to trust that he was telling them the truth.

When he left the meeting, the workers demonstrated and a riot broke out. They destroyed window-panes in the compound, smashed furniture in the offices, pulled out the doors and caused considerable damage to the City Council's property. Near the compound, to the west, is a European residential area called Pretoria West. The police were called, but they could not cope with the situation. Nearby on the race-course was an army camp.

The army was called out to put down the demonstration, which they did with brute force. They opened fire on the demonstrators and many African workers lost their lives. They gave as a reason for opening fire and killing many workers that, by the time they reached the scene, the Africans were marching in a hostile mood towards the European residential area. That left them with no doubts that the workers' aim was to attack the residents, hurt children and perhaps rape women. They said that they tried to stop the demonstrators and warned them to get back, but the demonstrators kept marching towards them and the European area. They found themselves left with no alternative but to open fire.

Thereafter a judicial commission of enquiry was appointed by the Smuts government to find out why the situation had arisen. Most of the union secretaries were members of the party, but at that time I had not joined them. The Commission had three members: a judge of the Supreme Court, an ex-attorney-general of the Transvaal and another. It met in Pretoria City Hall. I was still working for Cuthbert and Company, and used to go there to listen after quickly delivering the parcels. All those who gave evidence for the City Council endeavoured hard to shift the blame to the party and its members; one of the latter, Mr. Michael Muller, was working with African trade union secretaries as an advisor, drawing no wages from the unions but being paid by the party. The City Council's witnesses, including Mr. Hardy, worked hard to impress the Commission that the demonstration was instigated by the party, on whose shoulders the whole blame should rest. They argued that for many years before the party helped to organise African trade unions, there was peace in Pretoria, there were never troubles, the workers trusted their supervisors and regarded them as fathers; they understood one another. Since this troublemaking party came along to tell their men that they were not treated fairly, the peace had been disturbed. They pointed to Michael Muller's activities in the unions, saying that the party planted him there to stir up trouble. But they could not get away with their unfounded allegations. Members of the party who were lawyers, like George Findlay and Franz Boshoff, took turns to cross-examine them. Another progressive and sympathetic lawyer, Vernon Berrange, used to come from Johannesburg to carry out lengthy cross-examinations. They made Hardy and those who sided with him admit that they were not against Africans having trade unions.

Under cross-examination, Hardy admitted that he was under an obligation to tell the workers the reason why they were not going to be paid on the day promised and that, had he explained, the workers would not have demonstrated and damage to the City Council's property would not have occurred. Every one of the council's witnesses admitted under cross-examination that workers lost their lives because Hardy refused to give them explanations when they asked him to do so; and further, that if the workers had not organised, wage determination number one hundred and five would not have come into being. Hardy also admitted that, though he claimed to look after the workers he supervised like a father, he would never have recommended to the council that they should be paid weekly at a basic wage of five pounds a month.

The police told the Commission that, because the situation was so ugly, they did not attempt to ask for reinforcements, but that they thought the people to deal with it were the army. The army in South Africa is for Europeans only; no non-European can join it and carry arms. The police admitted under cross-examination that if they had called for reinforcements they would have saved many lives, and, though they too wanted to blame the party and its members, that Hardy was wrong to withhold the reasons from the workers and that his refusal resulted in a demonstration which could have been avoided.

When the army's turn came to be examined, they said they found great confusion; there was a deafening noise, with the demonstrators moving up and down Proes Street – but not, they admitted, moving to the European residential area but merely marching up and down. What discredited the army most was their admission that when they got to the scene they did not try to fire into the air to frighten the workers but fired straight into them and caused a large loss of life. When the Commission reported, the blame went to the people who deserved it: Hardy, the police and the army. That was all we heard of the Commission. The workers had lost their lives, Jan Christian Smuts was the ruler of South Africa, the second world war was raging, the children of those who lost their lives became orphans with no support.

XXIX Party National School

In nineteen-forty-three the owner of the place in Church Street East, where the Left Club in Pretoria was held, gave notice that he wanted it for his own use. While the search for a new place was going on, the party had to have an office somewhere. A room was acquired in the Rand Provident Buildings, Pretorius Street, opposite the old City Hall, and from that one room the party operated. I was a member of the district committee and there we met on one evening a week.

In June that year the national executive committee decided to organise a National School and asked each district to select and send the candidate they wished to have trained on a large range of subjects which ought to be known by advanced party members. My district selected me, but I remember well saying when I was chosen that I did not know enough to be sent to such an advanced school. One member, who later become one of my best European friends in the party, barrister Franz Boshoff, said, 'We know that you don't know enough, that is why we selected you to go to that school.' His words silenced me.

Franz Boshoff had begun his legal career as public prosecutor in Pretoria magistrates courts. He later became a staunch Afrikaner member of the Communist party. He was not the only staunch Afrikaner Communist in Pretoria; there were others too, like Thuys van Huissen, Michael Muller and David Cousyn.

At the end of June I left Pretoria for Johannesburg where the school was held. It was a thirty-day course of intensive training from eight o'clock on Monday morning to five o'clock on Friday evening. Our classes took place at the Johannesburg Left Club in Commissioner Street, opposite Progress Buildings where the Johannesburg party offices were situated. All party districts in the country sent students there. Our keep was paid by our districts. Johannesburg district had more students because the school was in their district and so they had less to pay for their students. I made friends from many parts of the country.

There I met a Zulu boy, an ex-teacher from Pietermaritzburg in Natal, and we became very close friends. His name was Harry Kwala. Both of us lived at Orlando African location built by the City Council of the City of Gold for the Africans. Unlike Atteridge-ville in Pretoria, Orlando had electric lights in the streets but none in the houses. The toilets there, unlike the Atteridgeville ones, did not have running water. There were taps in the yards but not in the houses as at Atteridgeville. The houses were of best brick, but had no ceilings. Compared with the two old African locations in the city from which the inhabitants of Orlando were drawn, Prospect and Malay-camp, Orlando was a paradise. The residents there, as at Atteridgeville, had privacy and small gardens and lived without daily orders and interference from landlords.

Orlando, like all African locations in the country, was not free from the Native Urban Areas Act. People there were not permitted to brew or drink beer. Like all urban locations, Orlando had an advisory board, which was supposed to advise the City Council of the City of Gold of African needs. When I was there one of the leading members of the Johannesburg district committee of the party, Edwin Thabo Mofutsanyana, was a member of the advisory board. He was the editor of the party's newspaper *Inkululeko* – 'Freedom'. He had originally come to Johannesburg from a Sesotho-speaking tribe in the Orange Free State to work in the mines, but had joined the party, got himself educated inside the party and been to the Soviet Union for further education. He was a powerful orator and was one of my idols.

On Saturdays and Sundays, when we were not at school, Harry Kwala and I moved about together, studying or testing each other whether we understood what we had been taught at the party school. Kwala lived with a Moema family and was very happy there. Mr. Moema was not a party member but a very strong African Congressman and a member of the advisory board. I lived with a Molefe family that looked after me so well that later I regarded myself as a member of the family. Mr. Molefe was a member of the party, but his wife was a mere sympathiser. It was very interesting living where there was such a large concentration of Africans. Orlando is more than eight miles from the centre of the City of Gold and most people there are workers in the city.

Some of the best friends I met at school were Ben Mnizi and Abe Manala who, like me, became trade union secretaries.

At the school a long range of subjects were taught; political economy, socialism in general, trade unionism, the difference between the Communist party and the Labour party, social democracy and communism, the origin of man and society, civics, the meaning of democracy, dictatorship, capitalism and its functions, the workings of markets, monarchy, capitalist republicanism, proletarianism, the meaning of the proletariat, the state and people, the rights of people in society and the state, the state's functions towards the people, colonialism, direct and indirect rule, the pricing of manufactured articles, class conflicts and interests in society, just and unjust

240

wars, public speaking, administration, running of offices, drawing up of reports, taking of minutes, filing systems, the rights of people to self-government and self-determination, health, education, revolutions and people's republics. We were also taught the meanings of chauvinism, anarchism and anarchists, and discussed national liberatory movements.

Our teachers were learned men and women, lawyers, professors, trade unionists, lecturers, architects, doctors and politicians. They came in turns and each one of them left us with something to study, and wanted to know how far we had gone with it or how much we understood the subject. Time was short, only thirty days, but we were taught at great length. We were keen to learn because we understood that knowledge is power. I understood full well that I was sent from Pretoria to learn, so that on my return I could pass on what I had learned there to the people of Pretoria, the place where all fascist laws made in Cape Town by the Europeans-only parliament are put into operation and administered. I was aware of all that when I left for the party school and during my stay there.

I shall not mention the names of all my teachers at the party school, but that does not mean ingratitude to those I omit. By naming their colleagues, I mention them all. They were Issy Wolfson, A. Weinberg, R. Bernstein, H. Watts, Dr. Y. Dadoo, B. Cohen, A. Burski, E. Weinberg, Dr. M. Friedman, Mr. Festenstein and others. I owe to all of them and the party a debt I can never repay.

I was in Johannesburg for the whole of July. On the closing day, I don't know why, I was asked to address the students, and my theme was what I had gained from the school. I remember well telling my fellow-students that when I came to the school I thought I knew half of all we had been taught. But now, I said, the school has helped me to know that I knew only a quarter of it. There was laughter. 'Now,' I went on, 'I am convinced that I know half.' There were cheers and laughter again.

I reminded my fellow-students what one of our teachers had said, that we were there to learn, not only for ourselves but for others who would come to us for advice and help. 'I hope,' I said, 'that when we are back at our homes we shall remember those words of our teacher and adopt them as a guide in all our endeavours.' I reminded them further that what we were taught at the school was meant to guide us into activity. The path we had chosen was not a smooth one, I pressed on, it was full of frightening things and lined up by people who will do everything they can to discourage us. 'The first,' I said, 'are in our own families. They are our parents, brothers, sisters and relatives who will all complain that we are degrading their families in the eyes of the neighbours, that we are bringing hardship on ourselves and our families and threaten to disown us. They will do that because they will believe that what we have chosen to dedicate ourselves to is not for us and for them but for someone else. Some of us, like myself,' I said, 'who are already married, may find opposition from our own wives who will bring before us the children and themselves and say, perhaps with tears, that we are ruining their lives and future; "if you don't care about me, at least care about your own children". If,' I said, 'what we have learned here has not convinced us that we have chosen the right cause, that of working for a better future for all our people and children, we shall agree with them. I don't want to say here that I shall not fall by the way, but I can only say that I hope my conviction will at all times be with me.' When I sat down there were cheers. We sang the Internationale and ended our school.

The next day, August the first, nineteen-forty-three, I left Orlando on my way back home. My employers thought all the time that I was in Phokeng attending to family matters. I arrived in Pretoria on Saturday, and rested with my wife in the room we rented in Marabastad the whole of Sunday. Friends who knew I was back called in to see me and everything was nice, and I was preparing myself to go to Cuthbert's shoe shop to start work. The next day I joined the others at Cuthbert's but I think that news had leaked out. Before ten o'clock that morning I was at loggerheads with the manager, Mr. Haupt, who sacked me on the spot and ordered me to call in the afternoon to collect what was due to me.

I went away to tell one of my friends, Mr. Papi Mabuse, that I had lost my job and he should help me to find one. He invited me to go with him to the general post office to post parcels for his employer. To get there we could not avoid passing Cuthbert's shoe shop. I think that when the manager saw us he changed his mind. As we returned from the post office, he came out of the shop, called over and asked me whether I still wanted to work, and I said that I was ready to work if he needed me. Thereupon he said, 'Come on, go and do your work,' which meant go and take the parcels to deliver them. I went in, took the parcels, packed them on the bicycle I was using and went out. I think that I had been unemployed for two hours.

On Tuesday evening that week I was at the party's district committee meeting reporting about the school, how I enjoyed the classes and what I thought I had gained from the school. I remember that we had a visitor, Mr. Harry Bloom, a barrister, who was chairman of Durban district, and in Pretoria for some reason. At the end of my report, he asked me, 'How do you feel now?' I replied: 'I feel that I am a little Marxist.' There were cheers and laughter. The die for my political future was cast. My friend, Moagi Mokoe, who had been secretary of Pretoria Non-European Distributive Workers'

242

Union, had been expelled from the party two weeks before my return from Johannesburg and the union was also in the process of terminating his services. Two weeks after my return, the union asked me to leave my job to take the secretaryship of the union, and I agreed.

At the end of August that year I left Cuthbert and Company's employment to start at 99 Boom Street as secretary of the Distributive Workers' Union. Mr. Johannes Makou was the union's treasurer. There I joined the secretaries of other Pretoria unions which I saw being formed: the Pretoria Non-European Municipal Workers' Union, the Non-European Railways and Harbour Workers' Union, the Non-European Match and Glass Workers' Union, the Non-European Cement Workers' Union, the Non-European Building and Allied Workers' Union, the Non-European Dairy Workers' Union, the Non-European Iron and Steel Workers' Union, the Non-European Laundry Workers' Union, and the Non-European Meat Workers' Union. They all had secretaries and committees meeting regularly every week.

It may be asked by some who are not familiar with South African politics why they were called non-European unions. Apartheid is the barrier. White and black workers cannot belong to the same union; mixed unions are forbidden by the law called the Industrial Conciliation Act. Another question might be, why not call them African unions? It was felt that it was sectarian to call them African unions, and that it would have supported Hertzog and Smuts' concept of segregation; to justify their concept, they could have pointed out that the Africans wanted separatism and did not want non-Africans to join their unions, and so called their organisations African. Those who did not know of the Industrial Conciliation Act would have believed them. That Act also denied African unions government recognition: African workers are defined in it as not being employees because they carry passes – as though they asked for them and enjoyed them. Only Europeans and non-carriers of passes are recognised as employees, and their trade unions are recognised by the state and by employers as such. As a result African workers are only employed to do unskilled tasks and thereby earn far less than the majority of European, Indian and Coloured workers. All the unions which I joined, and later led at 99 Boom Street, were formed with the help of the Communist party and progressive Europeans who held left-wing views and sought to raise African living standards.

In the trade union offices at 99 Boom Street I worked with my colleagues as union secretaries. Their names were Tlhokoa Sekati, Municipal and Railway Workers; Maesela Kola, Cement and Meat Workers; Percy Phala, Dairy and Garage Workers; George Moloto, Match and Glass Workers; Jackson Nemkula, Building and Allied

Workers; and Malesela Kekana, Iron and Steel Workers. After my arrival there I suggested the formation of a Bakery and Market Commission Agents Workers' Union, and the union came into being. Each one of us organised and acted for two unions. We fulfilled the two functions of organiser and secretary. The Laundry, Dry Cleaners' and Dyers' Workers' Union was run from Johannesburg, but their secretary was free to use our offices any time he came to Pretoria to see their members. We paid rent jointly and the place was hired in the name of Michael Muller, who worked with us as an adviser. Without using Michael Muller's name, we would not have obtained the place, because it was in a declared European area. Only Europeans could hire places there.

Mike Muller was a very hard-working man, and devoted to the African cause. He was not a native of Pretoria, he came from the Free State. His parents were staunch supporters of the Nationalist Europeans-only party, led at that time by Dr. D. F. Malan. He was an Afrikaner who, I was told, had been sent to Pretoria University, the citadel of Apartheid. While there he became attracted to socialism and joined the Communist party. He did not finish his studies, but left to devote his time and energies to helping the Africans. He could not understand why the Europeans wanted Africans to work for them, and yet refused to accept them as equals. Though I became very close to Mike Muller, I never asked him how he came into the party. All I know of him was that he gave everything he could give in the form of service to the Africans. Because he identified himself so much with the African cause, he was hated by the police – Europeans – who accused him of inciting the Africans by treating them as his equals. The Africans of Pretoria, even those who were not Communists, liked him and respected him. He had earned their love because they saw him working with their people for their people. But friends at times become foes. By nineteen-forty-seven, Mike Muller and I were not on speaking terms; we quarrelled over a strike at the Central News Agency. I had negotiated it, but failed to get all the workers reinstated. He accused me of having sold out; I ought to have kept them on strike until all were reinstated. I disagreed with him.

In the same year I went to 99 Boom Street. We met other African trade unions in Johannesburg and together we decided to form a trade union council which would speak for organised African labour as well as to help organise the unorganised African workers in other trades and industries. When we met, the Johannesburg unions were represented by Messrs. Gana Makabeni, Daniel Gosani, Daniel Tloome and David Koza, and Pretoria was represented by myself, Mike Muller, Tlhokoa Sekati and Maesela Tlolane. We met first in Johannesburg, then twice in Pretoria, each time discussing the drawing up of the constitution and the name of the council. Finally we agreed to call it the Transvaal Council of Non-European Trade Unions. Gana Makabeni became its first chairman, Daniel Gosani the first secretary, and Daniel Tloome the treasurer, all of them from Johannesburg. We formed the council consisting of the following men: Makabeni, James Philips, Gosani, Koza, Mogoye, Phofu, Tloome, Mokgatle, Tlolane, Mfete and Setemela. That was the first committee of the council. Its seat was in Johannesburg and I used to travel with Tlolane and Mfete to attend its meetings.

Things being as they were and still are in South Africa, there was a much stronger council of trade unions in the country called the South African Trades and Labour Council, which consisted largely of well-organised European unions and non-European unions of non-pass bearers like Indians and coloureds. There were powerful and progressive European trade unions in the Trades and Labour Council which stood firmly for the Africans to belong to the council, but there were also other bodies, similarly powerful, which were prepared to see that Apartheid was strictly maintained in the Trades and Labour Council. The constitution of the council recognised no colour bar, but the unions against the Africans joining were the majority. The African unions were not strong enough financially, not recognised by the state, not well organised; all that helped their enemies in the Trades and Labour Council to defeat all the progressive motions tabled at conferences. It was hard for Africans to organise because unsympathetic employers were encouraged by non-state recognition to ignore them. Some would say to the secretaries, 'Go and get the government to recognise your union first and then come here and we will recognise you.'

A branch of the Transvaal Council of Non-European Trade Unions was formed in Pretoria, and I was elected secretary. All the secretaries at 99 Boom Street were elected members of the Pretoria Council. It was hard for us all; some of us were lucky to get our wages regularly every month. The motto was sacrifice. Without it there would never have been African trade unions in existence in South Africa. Passes which we were forced to carry became barriers to our trade unions' recognition. They chained us to the pole of low wages and unskilled jobs. Through them our trade unions were declared no unions by the state and employers. Nothing has changed; the situation is still the same under Vorster as it was under Smuts, Hertzog, Malan, Strydom and Verwoerd.

The last monthly contract pass I had was with Messrs. Cuthbert and Company Limited. In the unions I made up my mind to go about without a pass, knowing full well that I was courting arrest. I did on many occasions get arrested for having no monthly pass in my possession. I was still determined to go to prison to see what

245

happened there. At times I got convicted at the native commissioner's court, but friends always paid my fines and stopped me going to prison. At times, because I was well known in Pretoria, I was cautioned and told to register myself as self-employed, but I refused to do that. I always declared, 'I am anti-pass therefore I see no reason for having one.' I remember, one day, that I arrived at Pretoria central police station, arrested by pass raiders, who were nicknamed by the Africans as '*Vang die Ketaang*' (Hold the Chain'), a police flying squad, under a policeman called Jan van Rooyen, whose task was to sweep Pretoria streets clean of all unemployed Africans. When he saw me, he said to his policemen, 'Why waste time with him? – we know all about him. We can arrest him any time we like, but we don't go and waste time in court with him, and let many other kaffirs get away. When you see him, ignore him. The time to arrest him will come and he will be sorry for himself.' He then turned to me and said, 'You are a kaffir like all other kaffirs. The law says you must carry a pass, who do you think you are, better than other kaffirs? You can go, I shall send for you when I need you.' Between nineteen-forty-three and nineteen-fifty-four I was so frequently arrested with other Africans for pass offences and other acts of defiance that the black maria was nicknamed Mokgatle's taxi.

By nineteen-forty-three the Europeans-only Nationalist party led by Dr. D. F. Malan, and the Ossewabrandwag, the extreme wing of the Nationalist party in which Dr. Verwoerd and Johannes Vorster played leading roles, had become convinced that Hitler's victory, which they had wished for and thought imminent, would not be forthcoming. They could see, like all of us who were watching the way events and the war were turning, that Hitler's Germany and Mussolini's fascist Italy had lost the war. They then turned their attention to the home front. As is the fashion among South African European politicians who seek fame and success to become law-makers, they launched an onslaught on the African people. To see which way the political storm-centre is moving, one has only to watch or listen to the conferences of the European farmers, the motions submitted and discussed, and the resolutions which emerge from them. First the farmers sound the alarm, then the Dutch Reformed Church blows the bugle, and the political parties go into action.

The supporters of the Nationalist party in the Farmers' Union began to raise a cry that farmers were finding it impossible to obtain African labour because the natives were drifting from the farms to the towns and cities, and the government and municipalities were encouraging them by allowing them to get jobs and allowing those who could not find jobs to stay indefinitely. The government – it was the Smuts government at that time – was accused by the farmers of being weak and influenced by Liberals and Communists to allow natives to drift to urban areas unchecked. The next place to watch was the Dutch Reformed Church's conferences. While the farmers complained of shortage of African labour, the Dutch Reformed Church spokesmen raised the scare that European towns and cities were no longer safe for European women and children to walk about in because of the large numbers of natives who roamed about at will, not working, living largely by crime, attacking European property and individuals. The government and municipalities should join hands to keep natives out of European areas, the predikants demanded firmly.

The third place to look at then becomes the Nationalist party conferences. The resolutions of the farmers' conference and the Dutch Reformed Church would come up framed in different words but demanding the same strong action to be taken by the government against the Africans – who are made political vehicles to carry European politicians to power and success in the country. No European politician, provincial councillor, or town or city councillor will get elected to power in South Africa if he does not show that his stand against African advancement is stronger than those who compete with him.

Having been armed by the farmers' demands and the Dutch Reformed Church's frightening allegations against the Africans in urban areas, the Nationalist party found no difficulty sharpening its weapons to force the government to act against the Africans in the urban areas. When Parliament was in session, Malan, who was leading the Opposition against Smuts' war-time government, stood up, cheered by his supporters who knew what he was going to ask Smuts, and asked, 'What is the government doing for the farmers' legitimate grievances that they cannot obtain native labour because the government encourages them to leave the rural areas for urban areas?' Smuts, for his government, said, 'There is no truth in the allegations that the government's policy is to encourage or allow the natives to drift to the urban areas.' 'What is the government doing,' asked Malan, 'to stop this mass influx of natives into urban areas, not to work, but to live by criminal methods?' 'The government is watching the situation closely. At the right time the government would take action to remedy the situation,' Smuts answered. 'When is the right time? Is the government weak or afraid to act, is the influence of the Liberals in the government and the Communists outside this house so strong that the government finds itself incapable to act?' Malan asked again. 'I am afraid I have nothing more to add to what I have already told the house.' At that point I knew that we were about to be attacked on a united front by all Europeans who, regardless of their party affiliations, are totally against African advancement in the country. 'We have lost the war in Europe, we must win it at home', said the Nationalists and their allied bodies.

When nineteen-forty-four dawned, Smuts had already made up his mind to act, to show the Nationalists that he was no less against the presence of Africans in the urban areas than they were. In order to win the next general election, which was only three years away, he prepared the amendment to the Native Urban Areas Act of nineteen-twenty-three which was amended by Hertzog's government in nineteen-twenty-five. All amendments were meant to hit the Africans hard below the belt. The war against fascism was on. Smuts claimed to be against fascism, for human progress, and against oppression and race hatred, but he saw nothing wrong in himself and his supporters amending the Act in such a way that it would make it impossible for Africans to leave rural for urban areas without the permission of the native commissioner, a European in the rural districts, and written permission from the town or city council where the African wanted to go and seek work. Thirdly, an African asking the native commissioner for a permit to leave had to show that a job was already waiting for him, and give the name and address of the employer who needed his services. Fourthly, on arrival, carrying the commissioner's permission and a certificate of the employer's willingness to give him a job, he still had to ask the local authority for permission to work in its area. That amended Act gave the control of the pass system to the municipalities and empowered them to set up what are known today as labour bureaux, where Africans who are in search of jobs – with the permission of the local authority – must register and wait for anyone who may come along looking for a worker. The Act virtually took away the Africans' right to choose a job. It armed the municipalities with the right to allow or refuse an African entry into the urban area, and it authorised them to expel Africans at will from urban areas. Once an African's documents are stamped 'refused entry', he is at the mercy of the police. Jobs for Africans in this plight would be on the farms, in the mines if they handed themselves to the mines recruiting office, or in prisons where farmers would pay their fines and take them to their farms to work the number of days, weeks or months they were convicted for. Today in South Africa large prisons built by farmers with state aid are operating alongside large farms, and farmers in the country use convict labour. Many Africans go there but never return. They die there due to ill-treatment, beatings and other inhuman methods of torture. That is South Africa in nineteen-seventy.

The amended Act gave the municipalities one right the Europeans-only governments have denied the African people since nineteen-ten, the right to brew beer of their own. It empowered the local authorities to brew and to sell African beer to the Africans. In almost every city in the country there are places called native beer halls where Africans go for their beer, and which are patronised by those lucky enough to be allowed to work in the urban areas. The amended Act was passed by the Smuts government in nineteen-forty-five and came into operation in nineteen-forty-six. With it and its severity on the African's movements, Smuts was sure to win the general election of nineteen-forty-eight – but he had misjudged the Nationalists and their hatred for him for having supported the war against Hitler and fascism in Europe. I know all about this because politics was the game I was involved in. I saw the blueprints being drawn up, the finishing of the article and the operation of the machine.

In Pretoria I was deeply involved in fighting the operation of the bureaux, the expulsion of African workers who had worked in the city for many years, the denial of re-entry to Pretoria to those who had been away visiting their families in the tribes for more than three months. The Act, amongst other things, stipulated that those Africans who are granted permission to enter urban areas should be allowed to stay seventy-two hours and thereafter seek extensions from the local authorities. From nineteen-forty-six, monthly contract passes were issued by local authorities through their bureaux. That resulted in thousands of Africans being arrested by the police every day in Pretoria and in other major cities of the country. Can honest people really say that the country has never been under fascism? Or that only after the Nationalists took over, in nineteen-forty-eight, did the country start moving towards a police state? I have always said that it became a fascist and police state the day the Act of Union was approved in nineteen-o-eight and put into operation in nineteen-ten.

In nineteen-fifty-eight I received in London a telegram from South Africa telling me of my nephew's death. Later I got a letter from my sister, his mother, saying that he was arrested in Johannesburg for a pass offence and sold to a farm prison. There on the farm he saw an African being beaten to death. He ran away but that sight could not leave him.

Far away from the farm, a hundred or more miles away in our tribal village Phokeng, my sister's son was haunted by fear that the police were looking for him, would trace him and take him back to the prison farm. His mother and friends tried to console him saying that he should keep calm, it was not easy for the police to trace him, but one morning he was found hanging from a tree. He had ended his own life rather than see himself going back to the farm. His name was Sebepi Rakhudu. Fascism and the police state, which are the order of the day in my country, not only affected me personally but also caused death in my own family. And my family was just one of many thousands of such families which have been caused to lose dear ones. Perhaps we were lucky because my sister buried her own son. The family of the one my nephew saw being beaten to death did not bury their son. Many families do not know how their sons died and where they were buried. That was what happened in Germany under Hitler; that has been happening to the Africans in South Africa under Smuts, Hertzog, Malan, Strydom, Verwoerd and Vorster.

I am mindful that some people who read these accounts will try hard to persuade others to disbelieve them. But what I describe here is not what happened in the past but what happens today. South Africa is not a fiction, is not an abstract state which can only be told about in stories; it can be visited, my descriptions can be tested. The bureaux can be visited; police arrests are taking place every day, and they can be seen; farm prisons are filled with convict labour, and these can be visited and the convicts there can be spoken to. Europeans who emigrate to South Africa must know that they are invited to go there to help to make all those things work; to keep the Africans down, to deny them human rights and democracy. Musical artists who claim that they are not politicians and therefore go to South Africa to entertain Europeans only must search their consciences. They must choose between money-making and upholding human rights.

Economists who find pleasure in describing South Africa as a prosperous country with a sound economy perhaps do not know why there is such prosperity. Never before have so few enjoyed life and pleasure at the expense of so many.

XXX Native Representative Council

During my time as secretary and organiser of trade unions I found time to attend sessions of the Native Representative Council's meetings in Pretoria City Hall, listening to the debates and speeches of its members. The meetings were held every two years in the banqueting hall. The Nationalists, having succeeded in forcing Smuts to enact the new Native Urban Areas Act, started a new and more vicious attack on the African people and the Communists in the country. They accused Smuts and his government of having abandoned Apartheid, encouraging the natives to claim equality with Europeans. They cited Pretoria City Hall as the place where the natives were told that they were as good as Europeans by allowing them to sit on seats used by Europeans, from which they were encouraged to demand equality with God's chosen people. They alleged that speeches made by members of the Council were Communist speeches, inciting rebellion against European authority in the country – despite the fact that there was not a single member of the Council who was a Communist or a Communist sympathiser.

So they asked the Europeans-only voters to give them South Africa at the next general election to do what they said Smuts was afraid to do, to suppress the Communist party and abolish the Native Representative Council. They accused the Council further of being a group of African intellectuals who were ashamed of their own people, of men who, because they were educated, wanted to be white men in black skins. I have already explained that the functions of the Native Representative Council were purely advisory, and Smuts' government listened to them and ignored their recommendations.

The general election was drawing near and Smuts tried to show that he was also against the natives using the seats used by the Europeans in the City Hall and ordered that the next meeting of the Council must be held outside the City Hall. But before that happened, in nineteen-forty-six, the African mine workers, under the leadership of John Marks, a member of the Communist party, went on strike for higher wages after long and patient negotiations with the Chamber of Mines along the reef in the Johannesburg area.

At that time John Marks was the chairman of the Transvaal Council of Non-European Trade Unions, of which I was one of the founders and an executive member. The day before the strike I was summoned to be in Johannesburg to attend the executive committee meeting the next day to plan what was to be done to see the strike through. On the day of the strike, the Native Representative Council's meeting was taking place in Pretoria.

The next morning, I left Pretoria with my colleague Malesela Tlolane, who was secretary of the Office Workers' Union and a member of our Trade Unions Council, for the City of Gold. The strike was already on. When we left Pretoria railway station we rubbed shoulders with some members of the Native Representative Council arriving in Pretoria for their meeting. Everything was tense, and we were wondering what they were going to do or say at their meeting. On our arrival in Johannesburg we proceeded to Rosenberg Arcade, where we held our meetings, and there without wasting much time we went into session. All the newspapers were full of reports that the strike was a hundred per cent supported by the African workers employed in the mines all along the reef. We were faced with the problem of how to get to the workers, since most of them lived in mine compounds, the urgent need being to get them money to buy food during the strike period. The first thing we thought of was to make appeals to progressive European trade unions and other progressive bodies for financial and any other help they could offer us.

At about eleven o'clock that day, two European detectives from Marshall Square, the Scotland Yard of Johannesburg, arrived and found us in session. They called the chairman away from the meeting and talked to him outside, then went away. Mr. Marks told us that they asked him what we were doing, and he had said we were discussing the miners' strike. By lunch-time we were through with our plans; it only remained to roneo appeals to bodies we had agreed to contact. Afterwards we met again to start the ball rolling, but it was not long before three detectives arrived from Marshall Square and, in the middle of our meeting, our chairman was arrested.

With our leader, the leader of the striking men, arrested, we were overcome by confusion. We were beset by two problems at the same time. We then agreed to meet the next day to proceed with what we had agreed upon, and to see what could be done to release Marks, without whom our work to help the miners could not go ahead. The first thing to do was to get in touch with progressive lawyers in the city to get them to find out what bail was needed for Marks' release. Malesela Tlolane and I left that part of the work to our Johannesburg colleagues and made our way back to Pretoria. When we purchased afternoon newspapers we were delighted with the news that, despite police intimidation, the miners were holding out and that most mines were without African labour for the first time since they had started in Johannesburg.

The other bright and heartening news was from Pretoria. When the councillors of the Native Representative Council assembled in the banqueting hall of the City Hall under the chairmanship of Dr. Mears, who was the Secretary for Native Affairs, they unanimously refused to discuss the agenda laid before them, saying that it was the same as the one they had discussed at the first meeting of the Council several years before, that none of their recommendations had been met by the government, and that they therefore saw no point in discussing it. They passed resolutions demanding recognition of African trade unions, the abolition of passes, free equal education for African children, the franchise for the African people and the abolition of all colour discrimination in all sectors of South African life.

Dr. Mears promised to pass their demands to Smuts' government and that the government would give them their reply. That was the last meeting of the council in Pretoria City Hall. The Europeans-only general election was only a year away and Smuts had to prove to the Nationalists, to Malan, to his critics in the Farmers' Union and in the Dutch Reformed Church, that he was no less an upholder of white supremacy than they were. Two days later, the African miners were forced to return to work with brute force by the police. They were shot at and many lost their lives. Smuts was thereby repeating what he had done to the European miners in nineteen-twenty-two when he ordered the army to open fire on them at Fordsburg, Johannesburg, and, by killing many of them, forced them to return to work. That was Jan Christian Smuts, the idol of many people who never lived under his rule in South Africa.

To prove further to Malan and his followers that he was no less anti-Communist than they were, Smuts blamed the Communist party of South Africa for the African miners' strike and ordered the arrest of the whole central committee of the party. The headquarters of the party was in Cape Town, and most of the members were there; only a few were in Johannesburg. Those in Johannesburg were transported to Cape Town to join the others in preliminary proceedings. Among those taken from Johannesburg was a European, a patriot South African and a true friend of the Africans, who gave his time and energies to helping to organise the African Mine Workers' Union. He was not a member of the Communist party. His name was Louis Joffe. Without his consent he was taken to Cape Town to be tried with members of the party's central committee. Amongst these was William Henry Andrews, a veteran trade unionist, and one of the founders of the South African Trades and Labour Council, the South African Labour party and of the Communist party of South Africa. He was the national chairman of the party at the time and well advanced in age.

In Pretoria one day a detective's motor-cycle pulled up in front of our trade union's office, 99 Boom Street. A European detective came in and told me that they had come to take me to my room in Marabastad, which was to be searched. I left with them, and as was the habit in Marabastad when the sound of a detective's motor-cycle was heard, people came out of the houses to see what was happening. Usually a man brought to his house by detectives was someone accused of having stolen goods, and when people saw me with the detectives they had no doubt in their minds that I had stolen something and the police had brought me to search for it. My wife, too, was surprised to see me coming home during the day accompanied by detectives. Before they started their work they handed me a warrant signed by the chief magistrate to search my room for documents connected with the miners' strike. They searched every corner of my room, went through all my papers and books and everything they could lay their hands on. The people outside were waiting to see my fate. Eventually the detectives left without me and the people began to come in to ask what the reason was. Those who were my enemies were disappointed to learn that it was not connected with stealing but with the miners' strike in Johannesburg. My son Matshediso, who was two years old, helped the detectives by giving them some of my books to search.

The police carried some of my books and documents away with them, but after several weeks returned them. I was not arrested, but this was the introduction to what would follow later on. We lost our office the same year; the landlord refused to renew Michael Muller's lease, and that brought our occupation of 99 Boom Street to an end. It also brought disintegration into our unions. Without an office most of the secretaries were forced by starvation to leave the trade unions to look for jobs where they could earn a living. However, I carried on, arranging to meet the workers at appointed places to take up their grievances, to take them to municipal offices, or to challenge their expulsion from Pretoria, since they had worked in the city for many years. It was a hard job. Others were already living with their wives and children in Pretoria, having recently arrived, but were expelled simply because their old passes showed that they originally came from the tribes. Bureau officials argued that they still belonged to those tribes and must go back there. Most cases were heart-breaking because once a man had his pass stamped 'refused entry into the Urban Area' he was afraid to come to me, fearing that on the way he might meet the police and get arrested. Wives came to see me with tears in their eyes, saying, 'My husband is ordered to leave me and the children to return to where he originally came from.'

The first chief of bureaux in Pretoria was Mr. Kingsley. I was frequently to be seen with groups of African men with documents stamped 'refused entry' in his office, challenging his officials' orders. Above him was the manager of Pretoria City Council's Native Affairs Department, Mr. Brent. I was frequently in his office too, arguing against Mr. Kingsley's rulings. In some cases I won and in others I failed. I found myself fighting on two fronts, on the passes front and on the wages and other grievances front. Bureau officials hated me; the police also hated me intensely. My work in these fields can be seen in the records of the bureaux in Pretoria from nineteen-forty-six to nineteen-fifty-four.

In nineteen-forty-seven I went back to 253 Vermeulen Street, where I started in nineteen-forty. The place was occupied by an African tailor by the name of Joseph Motau, and I asked him to give me a space where I could run my trade union. He agreed and we shared the rent. The building belonged to the Muslim mosque.

At that time I was the only one of the Boom Street trade union secretaries left, and the workers were coming to me with their complicated cases and grievances. First I attempted to form a National Non-European Distributive Workers' Union with other interested trade unionists in the country. I met a trade unionist from Cape Town called Reginald September, and another from Durban called Mbonambi in the offices of the European Distributive Workers Union, and with the help of Mrs. Katie Kagan (who before her death was the secretary) and others we agreed to form our National Non-European Distributive Workers' Union. I was provisionally appointed president and Mbonambi treasurer. We agreed on a provisional constitution and agreed also to keep contact by correspondence, to arrange a national conference to establish the union officially. Correspondence was the only link between us, and our National Union never left the ground. I was in the north, September was in the south and Mbonambi was in the extreme east, all very far from one another. That was our first and last meeting.

Trade union work became so heavy for me at 253 Vermeulen Street that I felt the need for help. I approached some of my old colleagues but they felt that to start from the bottom again was rather difficult for them. So I carried on single-handed. Later, one of Mr. E. Gordin's under-secretaries in Johannesburg came along to join me, to organise the Dairy Workers' Union which was his union in the City of Gold. His name was Jacob Thipe, but he fell sick and died a few months later. I was again left alone in the field. That year temptation stared me in the face. I was well known to the Labour Department's industrial inspectors for the role I was playing in helping to settle African workers' grievances with them. I did not know that they admired me, because I always argued with them a lot, but one afternoon when I arrived there, one of them, a lady called Miss Drost, told me that the senior inspector, Mr. van Koppenaggen, wanted to see me. When I reached his office, Mr. van Koppenaggen told me that they had a job for me, to work with them as an interpreter and translator of African letters, and if I agreed to take the job the divisional inspector, Mr. Eve, was ready to recommend my appointment to the Minister of Labour and was sure that my appointment would be accepted. I turned down the offer and they all called me a short-sighted fool.

The trial of the central committee of the Communist party took place in the Supreme Court of Johannesburg. A judge from the Free State was brought in to try them with Mr. Justice Roper. On the day of trial I took my seat amongst the spectators to see men and women who were at the head of the party I had grown to like and admire convicted and sent to prison by Smuts' government. I did not want to read the news in the papers, but wanted to be there to see for myself how Smuts treated his opponents and how he wanted to silence opposition to colour discrimination and the doctrine of the master race.

I was expecting fireworks from Smuts' attorney-general, Mr. Lutge, and the assistant attorney-general, Dr. Percy Yutar, but instead fireworks came from the defence side. The central committee was represented by a barrister, Mr. Williamson, and the one man who was not a member of the Communist party, Louis Joffe, was represented by barrister Dr. Lowen, of whom I was told later that he came as a refugee to South Africa escaping from Hitler's terror. His English was fluent but dominated by a German accent. Before the accused persons were called upon to plead guilty or not, Dr. Lowen challenged the court's competence to deal with his client's case on a very strong legal point that Mr. Louis Joffe was taken to Cape Town to stand trial there against his will and without his consent being sought; that Dr. Percy Yutar, who prosecuted there on behalf of the attorney-general of the Transvaal, Mr. Lutge, had no right in law to do so, and that Mr Lutge had no right in law to send him to Cape Town. On those grounds Dr. Lowen challenged the court's authority over the case. Before my own eyes I saw the apple cart being upset for Smuts' attorney-general and his assistant, from which they never recovered. The judges asked Mr. Lutge and Dr. Yutar to help them with a legal answer to Dr. Lowen's submissions, but they had no answer. The whole case, which had taken months for Smuts' legal men to prepare, collapsed within ninety minutes. The court dissolved itself. But Smuts was determined to show that he was as anti-Communist as Malan if not more so. While the argument went on in court, Smuts' men, aware that their case was blown sky high, obtained another warrant to arrest all the discharged persons. Before they left the court as free men and women, they were arrested again. At the later trial they were discharged.

Nineteen-forty-seven was a year pregnant with political explosions in South Africa. The Europeans-only general election was only a few months away, and all European political parties were making their voices heard, each making appeals to show that it was more anti-African and anti-Communist than the other, without openly proclaiming itself as such. Jan Smuts and his United party were under fire from the Nationalists and the Afrikaner parties, accused of being weak, afraid of abolishing the Native Representative Council, encouraging the Africans to demand equal rights with the Europeans, and allowing Communism to spread in the country unchecked.

In reply, Smuts had to resort to actions rather than words. The Native Representative Councillors were summoned to Pretoria to get the government's reply to their demands at the time of the African miners' strike when they declined to discuss the agenda laid before them. Malan and his Nationalist party had won the first round: Pretoria City Hall and its seats were to be for Europeans only. There were no other halls in the city where they could meet, but luckily there was a religious hall in Sunnyside a mile or more from the City Hall, whose doors were opened for the Council to meet there. It was the Theosophical Hall. I knew that hall well, but did not know that members of that religious sect practised no colour bar.

Jan Hendrik Hofmeyr, who was Smuts' deputy prime minister, the man whom many African intellectuals respected because of his membership of the Council for Europeans and Africans, a body brought to South Africa from the United States of America early in the 'twenties by an African, Dr. Aggrey; Hofmeyr, whom the Nationalists and members of the Afrikaner party hated most, the man they kept under constant fire as a deadly liberal and *Kaffer Boetie*, was chosen by Smuts to deliver his government's reply to the demands.

I was in the Theosophical Hall when the councillors assembled, and I made a point of sitting very close to the platform on the row of seats behind the councillors so that I could hear every word uttered by Jan Hofmeyr. The South African sun was bright, the sky was clear and deep blue and it had not rained for several days. As is the habit of newspapers, we were already informed what the reply was going to be.

Ten minutes before the appointed time, half-past nine, the hall was already packed with people who had come to listen They were Europeans and Africans, and Apartheid was suspended in the hall, where it was never practised. Five minutes before the meeting was due to begin, the Dutch-Afrikaner intellectual Jan Hendrik Hofmeyr, accompanied by Dr. Mears, entered with their secretaries. We all rose to our feet in honour of personalities who were equipped to deliver the Smuts government's reply. A few minutes later the gathering opened and, as was the custom of the Africans, instead of singing *God Save the King* or *Die Stem van Suid Afrika*, the African National Anthem *Nkosi Sikelela Afrika* was sung. Afterwards Dr Mears, who chaired the meeting, read the notice calling the councillors together and the reasons why they were called, at the end of which he called on Mr. Hofmeyr to present the government's reply.

Mr. Hofmeyr began by telling the councillors that the government found it impossible to believe that they, a body of learned and responsible men, could ask the government for the impossible; things they knew the government could not agree to or grant. The councillors, he went on, knew that their demands were unattainable but insisted on putting them forward. Such demands, Mr. Hofmeyr proceeded, serve no purpose, do no good for themselves, the councillors or the people who look to them for leadership and guidance.

The government, he went on, was ready to give a sympathetic ear to reasonable demands, designed to produce results. In putting forward demands, such as the ones to which the government had delegated him to deliver their reply, they were not helping the government to help the African people but placing obstacles in its path. By creating this body, Mr. Hofmeyr told the gathering, the government had been and was still seeking help, not frustration. In his last words, Mr. Hofmeyr told the councillors that the government could not concede to their demands. They were unacceptable. The things they wanted removed were for the protection of the Africans.

In his closing remarks, Mr. Hofmeyr appealed to the councillors to show responsibility, to think of the people who elected them to the council, people who were in desperate need of help, to co-operate with the government to seek the best ways through which the African people could be helped. He appealed to them to rescind their resolution, which had done nothing but hinder progress, and discuss the agenda which had been placed before them in nineteen-forty-six. He expressed sorrow that the councillors, when they refused to proceed with the meeting of nineteen-forty-six, had not seen how much time would be wasted and how they had deprived their people of some things which might have resulted if they had exercised wisdom and proceeded with their meeting. He felt sure, he said, that after hearing the government's reply the councillors would lose no time to proceed with their agenda and debates.

When he sat down Professor Z. K. Matthews, who was the chairman and spokesman of the councillors' caucus, rose to present the vote of thanks on behalf of his colleagues. During his remarks he said that if the government had conceded to the demands of the African people, they would have helped them and the country. But, Professor Matthews went on, the government's rejection of those demands had helped the African to know and understand that they could go on talking but all would be in vain. The African people agreed to and accepted the council in the hope that through it their voice would be heard. Now, he proceeded, they were told that their voice was heard but nothing would be done. He ended by putting forward a plea that the councillors would like to discuss the government's reply in the presence of the deputy prime minister. To that request Dr. Mears said he was sorry the minister could not be detained any longer, he had an appointment at the Union Buildings and to avoid being late he was leaving at that very time. Mr. Hofmeyr gathered his papers and when he left the platform we rose again from our seats and sat down only when he had left the hall.

Afterwards Dr. Mears ruled that he would allow no discussion of the government's reply – it needed no discussion, things stood where they were. Dr. Mears also appealed to the councillors to forget the past and look to the future, and go with him into the business of the council. Professor Matthews then asked for time to allow his colleagues to discuss Dr. Mears's request, to give their considered reply in the afternoon. The meeting closed until after lunch.

In the afternoon, when the council's meeting was resumed, it became clear to everyone present that the cow had put its foot into the bucket of milk. Dr. Mears asked the councillors whether they were ready to start with the agenda before them, but Professor Matthews rose to say that they were unanimous that there was no point in proceeding with the agenda when they were denied discussion of the government's reply which they had been summoned to Pretoria from all over the country to hear. If, Professor Matthews went on, they were given the chance to discuss the reply they might in the course of time find it right to discuss the agenda as the chairman asked. In reply Dr. Mears said that as chairman he had made a ruling and that ruling stood. That signalled the death of the Native Representative Council which was born out of the Hertzog and Smuts law of nineteen-thirty-six, which abolished the African franchise in the Cape and Natal. Africans in the northern provinces, the Free State and the Transvaal, had never enjoyed the franchise.

Without wasting more time Dr. Mears closed the meeting after the African National Anthem *Nkosi Sikelela Afrika* had been sung. The next morning, newspapers reported the meeting in full but commented that the councillors were not wise in refusing to discuss the agenda because, if they had done so, the government might have reconsidered their stand and given a sympathetic ear to what they had asked. Their refusal, some newspapers said, had not improved things for the Africans but had hardened the government's stand, and the actions of the councillors had deprived their friends of arguments in favour of the Africans' case. Only the enemies of

African advancement had won and had cause to rejoice. We, who had been following the debates of the council from the day it first met, approved everything the councillors had done.

At that time, when the Native Representative Council got its reply from Jan Hofmeyr, the Nationalist party and the Afrikaner party, led by Niklaas Havenga, were busy demanding the abolition of the council and the taking away of African education from the missionaries. This, they said, was poisoning the minds of the Africans and creating the type of African who was in the council thinking that because he was educated he was no longer part and parcel of his people and wanted equality with Europeans. Up and down the country their spokesmen were telling the Europeans-only voters that as long as Smuts and liberals like Jan Hofmeyr were allowed to govern the country, the danger of the non-Europeans being granted equality with Europeans was real. Save South Africa and save the Europeans who were in the country to perform God's mission.

At the Theosophical Hall meeting I saw and met Albert Luthuli for the first time. No one knew at that time that one day he would be president-general. He did not speak and seemed shy, but he followed the line he and his colleagues drew in the caucus meeting. I don't know whether he was then a member of the African National Congress. Some of us who were watching closely the actions of members of the council could see that there were some, a few, who were willing to carry on with the meeting, but were afraid of being exposed to their people as men who were only interested in what they were getting from the government as councillors. African welfare cut no ice with them.

During the campaign for the Europeans-only general election, the spokesmen of both the Afrikaner and Nationalist parties brought a new slogan to the fore: *Kaffer op sy plek* ('kaffir in his place') and *Koolies nit die land uit* ('coolies out of the country'). By coolies was meant people of Indian origin. The Nationalists promised that if they got elected they would deport them back to India. Other slogans were *Stem Nasionale, teen Kommunisme en die swart gevaar* ('Vote Nationalist, against communism and the black danger'). Among their promises were that if they got elected as they asked, they would invent education to suit African children: education which would teach them that there is no such thing as equality between white and black.

I vividly recall reading a speech made by the Nationalists' leader in the Transvaal, Johannes Strydom, addressing the farmers he represented in the Europeans-only parliament, at Waterberg, where he was nicknamed *die Leeuw van die Nord* (lion of the north). He was reported to have said that Smuts was finished, he was old and was no longer interested in South Africa. His whole interest was with

England, and he was campaigning for Jan Hofmeyr. If he won the election he would retire and give the country to Hofmeyr and the liberals in the United Party. Strydom asked his listeners whether they knew that Hofmeyr wanted inter-marriage between white and black in South Africa. He was reported to have said that, if Hofmeyr became prime minister, within the first five years of his premiership he would pass a law permitting their pretty daughters to be married to kaffirs. The farmers roared with great disapproval, but when they had finished Strydom was reported to have said, 'Oh no, fellows, your disapproval here is not enough, it won't throw Smuts and Hofmeyr out of power. Amongst you in this place tonight there are Smuts' and Hofmeyr's supporters. Some of you are going to vote for Smuts on the election day, some of you are already urging others to vote for Hofmeyr on that day.' The farmers roared that they would do everything to see that everyone in Waterberg voted against Smuts that day.

The report said that he was satisfied with what they had promised him, but gave them a last word of advice. This was that on election day those who owned cars must carry those with no cars to the polling station to vote against Smuts. 'Those who can't get cars must walk, regardless of the distance. If there are sick ones who can't be picked up by car, carry them on your shoulders; if you have wheelbarrows, push them in the wheelbarrows to register their votes against Hofmeyr.' The farmers roared and cheered their Lion of the North. That was how Smuts' downfall was planned and that was how politics work in South Africa. I have already said that Smuts could only reply with actions not words. Already in his efforts to convince his critics that he was no less anti-non-European than they were, he had passed a law called the Residential and Representation of Indians Act. Its purpose was to drive the Indians out of European areas and create locations for them as was the case with Africans.

Jan Christian Smuts was the architect of the police fascist state which is the order of the day in South Africa today. He was famous and very much liked in Britain. He was hailed as a philosopher, soldier and statesman. When he died he was a field-marshal in the British army. Back in South Africa he was disliked by the majority, the Africans, and the majority of his tribe the Dutch-Afrikaners. Their reasons for disliking him were not the same. The Africans rightly regarded him as their oppressor. Those of his tribe who disliked him accused him of being more English than the English.

He started building the Apartheid state, the police state for Africans, at the end of the Anglo-Boer war in nineteen-hundred-and-two; he had been one of the Dutch leaders who negotiated peace with the British at Vereeniging. At those negotiations, and when he negotiated the establishment of the Union of South Africa, he saw to it that Africans were not informed or consulted, as if they did not exist. He took part in the drafting of the Act of Union, the constitution on which the Europeans-only state, parliament and government stand. On that rock Apartheid flourishes.

He was a schemer and a man who managed until his death to disguise the real nature of his Europeans-only state and present it to the world as democratic. That is why even today nations of the world recognise and defend the tribal state he built. He never failed to make his way into gatherings of the nations. Outside South Africa he wore a garment of democracy while deep in his heart was anti-democracy.

Early in the 'twenties he was one of the first to arrive at Geneva to help found the League of Nations. There he disguised his belief and his actions against the non-Europeans so that he won the hearts of all who listened to him and worked with him. That disguise won him the Territory of South West Africa, regardless of whether the inhabitants, the Africans, agreed to be taken over by him. He managed to convince the League of Nations that they were not worth consulting.

At the end of the second world war, in nineteen-forty-six, he crossed the Atlantic Ocean to the United States of America to help in the establishment of the United Nations' Organisation. As at the time of the League of Nations, he wore a garment of democracy and won. He took part in drafting the United Nations charter, talked loudly about human rights, liberty and fraternity, while he knew deep in his heart that he was only paying lip service to those declarations. It is said that he produced some of the words which appear in the preamble of the Charter of the United Nations; those words are 'We, the Peoples of the World'.

On his return from the founding of the United Nations' Organisation, Malan, in the Europeans-only Parliament in Cape Town, exposed him to the world, but no one took any notice. I remember reading in one of the newspapers that Malan, who was leading the opposition, rose, cheered loudly by the Nationalists, and said to Smuts, 'We don't know where we are with you; you go about the world in our country's name and make declarations which are contrary to our custom, tradition and belief. You have just returned from the founding of the United Nations' Organisation and you are reported in full as being the originator of the words which are printed in the preamble of the charter of that organisation. The words,' Malan said, 'are "We the Peoples of the World". Where do we stand in relation with the non-white races? Do you include them in those words?' 'I am surprised that the honourable member of this house desires to be believed that he did not know what I meant in those words. You know well', Smuts told Malan, 'that I did not include them in those words. They are not our equal and they will never be our equal.' All those present cheered and Malan sat down satisfied. That was Smuts telling the world that he was paying lip service to the world organisation. He died having lost no honour, no respect at the United Nations' Organisation.

In full view of a world audience at the United Nations' Organisation he refused to give the people of Indian origin in South Africa human rights when he was challenged, and a case was brought against him, by India's representative Mrs. V. Pandit, who later became the President of that Organisation.

Jan Smuts defied nations and got away with it. All nations which were granted trusteeship of territories taken from Germany at the end of the first world war by the League of Nations, nations which are more powerful than Smuts' tribal government, agreed to place those territories under the United Nations' Organisation's Trustee Committee when they were requested to do so, so that the people in them could be prepared for self-government; but Smuts refused to place South West Africa under the UN Trustee Committee. Nothing happened to the South African tribal government and Smuts, and now the territory is ruled by Vorster, as it was ruled by Smuts, with force. The nations do nothing about it. Smuts laid the foundations that Hertzog, Malan, Strydom, Verwoerd and Vorster have built on.

I remember I used to discuss with other Africans, who had made politics their devotion like me, the way Smuts used to break our hearts during the second world war. Large numbers of Italians were captured in East Africa, and as prisoners of war they used to walk the streets of Pretoria and other cities and towns of the country with more dignity, respect and pride than we non-Europeans. They entered hotels, restaurants, cafés, cinemas, and enjoyed outdoor life in the parks, all denied to us. Africans who served them were ordered to call them 'master'. Because of Smuts' doctrine of white superiority, the master-race concept, they lived in South Africa far better than we did. They wore their army uniforms and spoke no English or Afrikaans, but South Africa was a paradise for them. That was the Jan Smuts whom I knew and saw several times. The last time I saw him, he was deceased, passing through Church Street, carried on a gun carriage to be buried.

XXXI African General Workers' Union

Nineteen-forty-eight dawned and found me still working alone trying to keep the spirit of trade unionism alive in Pretoria. It was an uphill struggle which needed patience and a strong mind. The struggle for more wages was becoming secondary, because African workers were hit hard by being refused permission by the bureau officials to seek work of their liking. Africans who had worked in Pretoria for many years but had left their families out in rural areas in the tribes found that when they lost their jobs, instead of being given a chance to seek a new job, their documents were stamped 'refused entry', which meant that they should leave Pretoria never to return, without obtaining the prior consent of Pretoria City Council. My time was more taken up by pass complaints than by wage complaints.

In the middle of the same year I moved from 253 Vermeulen Street to 56 Potgieter Street, not very far from the main influx control office. I was still living in one room with my wife and son in Marabastad. While I was working at 56 Potgieter Street, a man who later became my colleague made a habit of visiting me each time he was in town from the African freehold location outside Pretoria called Lady-Selborne. His name was Stephen Sondag Tefu, and he was an African radical who in the late 'twenties and early 'thirties joined the Communist party in Johannesburg but got expelled. I never knew why. He was a very brave man but unpractical in every way. He was incapable of starting any movement but always the first to join them when they had been started.

Because of his bravery he had been inside prison many times. He was living above fear of the police and prison. One day when he called I invited him to join me, and told him that most unions in Pretoria had disintegrated, that the workers were going through difficult times, and the struggle was twofold – for more wages and for the right to be in Pretoria and work in the city. I told him that I wanted to form an African General Workers' Union, which would cater for all the workers regardless of their place of employment. I needed help, I told Stephen Tefu, so that we could organise the workers and try to help them with their 'refused entry' problems. He agreed to join me and after a week we distributed leaflets throughout the city, inviting the workers to a meeting to form an African General Workers' Union. The meeting was held on a Saturday after-

264

noon in an open plot outside Marabastad near where I first attended the radicals' meeting. The new union was born there.

I managed to rent 56 Potgieter Street because it was owned by an Indian landlord and next to it was a Chinese grocer's shop and therefore that part of the street could be hired out to non-Europeans. 56 Potgieter Street became the headquarters of the Pretoria Non-European Distributive Workers' Union and the African General Workers' Union. I acted as secretary for both organisations, and Tefu became the organiser and chairman. The Europeans' tribal general election campaign was on and Good Hope, the area where our office was situated, was a hotbed of Nationalists.

Twice a week we used to lead a group of workers to the influx control office to show Mr. Kingsley's men that they were wrong in stamping this or that man's documents 'refused entry' when he had worked in Pretoria for many years before the influx control system was introduced in its rigid form. Our successes meant more work. Influx control officials became careful because they knew that there were two men watching them. They used unconsciously to pass information about our office to workers who did not know that we existed. They used to say angrily, 'I am not allowing you to be in Pretoria, you don't belong here. I know you think that you can go from here to Mokgatle and Tefu's office and that they will help you. They are nothing, they are mere "won't-works" who want to impress on you that they have your interests at heart. Your going there won't help you.' When we succeeded they would turn round and say it is not because of Mokgatle and Tefu that we have changed our minds, we found afterwards that you deserved another chance.

Trade union work made me read about industrial law as well as the laws which caused African suffering. When I argued a case for a worker I used to put my own interpretations into it which used to weaken the influx control officers or employers, and as a result would get gains for the workers out of the employers and influx controllers. Workers used to think that I had changed, I was not the man they knew, and others thought that I was a lawyer – especially those I helped with documents stamped 'refused entry'. It was like having brought a dead person back to life. For an African worker who had seen his 'refused entry' documents destroyed and new ones issued, and that the work of an African like himself, it needed hard work to convince him that his helper was not a lawyer. Of course, there were also failures, which disappointed me a great deal.

Through the trade union work, I came to like law very much, and I began to enjoy reading law books and to admire lawyers and their profession. Through reading law books I discovered how people throw away their rights when they are told by an official that they are not entitled to certain things. People always think that the man at the counter or behind the desk has the final authority to decide issues. They never know that there is someone above who would overrule him. I found that even in courts of law, people always think that magistrates are final deciders in legal matters. They have no idea that there are three stages through which they have to go before they reach the dead end. I discovered and learned these things when I was doing trade union work. I learned that there is always a high level to which one can address oneself if one is not satisfied with the lower level decisions or conclusions.

Once I acquired that knowledge, there was not a single case of mine that did not end in the highest court, the supreme court. Each time a native commissioner or magistrate convicted me, he knew that before the end of fourteen days he would have my appeal in his possession, arguing my own case against his judgment and the conviction. Pretoria Supreme Court can furnish records of appeals drawn up by myself and cases where I appeared before the judges arguing my own case. I won and lost. While the Communist party was a political school for me, trade union work became my legal school.

In the trade unions, too, I learned that the courage of a leader strengthens his followers. One thing I never allowed to happen to me was to be intimidated by officials, whether in government or in municipal offices. In such offices Africans were expected by officials to speak standing on their feet. They were further expected to hold their hats in their hands. I knew that to create confidence in those I was engaged to help, I must first show them that I was not afraid of men behind counters or desks. Before I spoke in any office I put my hat on the counter or desk, sat down on a chair and then started to relate my mission. So that even when I did not succeed, the workers would say, 'He was not afraid of them, he did his best.' I also developed a habit, when I wrote a letter for anyone who wanted my help, of writing it, reading it to him and then asking him if he was satisfied with the contents. I then gave it to him to post. That created trust and confidence.

Every worker who came to the African General Workers' Union for help was enrolled first and given a membership card showing the amount he paid. Because most of the workers came to the union when they were already in difficulties, I drew up the constitution of the union in such a way that the joining fee was two shillings and sixpence and the subscription two shillings a month. But the other clause stipulated that if a member joined and wanted services at the same time, he should pay two years' subscription before his complaint was taken up.

From the subscriptions we paid rent for the office, bought stationery, paid the telephone account and drew wages. Our constitution stipulated that money received from subscriptions must be recorded in receipt books, the money must be banked and withdrawals made for administrative functions. First we banked the union's money with the Permanent Building Society in Pretorius Street, but we were expelled from there because one day when we were depositing money I had a quarrel with a male clerk who ordered me to take my hat off the counter. I had done that because the weather was so hot that I wanted to cool myself off while waiting to be served. I told the clerk that he was there to serve me not to order me about. As a European I think that he had not been spoken to in such terms by a native, as we were called at that time before Malan came up with his own term 'Bantu'. The clerk refused to serve me, but one of the young ladies who had listened to the whole argument served me, and thereafter we left.

A few days later we received a letter from the manager of the society telling us that we had behaved badly before customers in the society, that they had decided to close our account and we should come along to collect what belonged to us there. The Pretoria Non-European Distributive Workers' Union had an account at the Rand Provident Building Society in the same street, and we banked all our money there until we were attacked by Malan's government. It was a very hard struggle for survival.

During the same year, nineteen-forty-eight, I was allocated a house by the Pretoria City Council at Atteridgeville. That meant that I had to say good-bye to the one room in Marabastad I had occupied before I got married and for several years afterwards, the Madisha family whom I lived with in Third Avenue, friends I had made in Marabastad, and the old tin location itself which had produced Atteridgeville because it was said that it was too near European areas. I moved out of Marabastad with my wife and my son. My daughter was already living with my wife's mother at Atteridgeville. It was in May, the month of the Europeans-only tribal general election. I was sick when I was moved to Atteridgeville. I had contracted a very heavy cold, and was carried in the same way as the furniture.

The house I was given was at 37 Molope Street, named after the Methodist priest who married me in Marabastad. It was a three-roomed house standing on its own with a garden in front as well as at the back, like most of its kind throughout Atteridgeville. It had two taps in the yard, one inside the house and one at the back of the house. I have already described what Atteridgeville houses for Africans are like, but it was a great improvement on the room which was everything in Marabastad.

I left Marabastad on the eighth of May when the Europeans' election was only four days away. I had hoped that I would be well enough to see them vote against communism and black danger. To my disappointment on the twelfth of May when the votes were cast I was lying sick. Luckily I had bought a second-hand radio, and through it I was well in contact with the world beyond my sick bed. I did not see them vote but I heard how they voted. When the polling stations closed at midnight I knew that Smuts had already suffered a crushing defeat at Standerton in the eastern Transvaal, the seat he had held since entering the Europeans-only parliament in nineteen-ten. I knew from that day that Smuts' days of life were numbered, but he had left a monument which would need bitter struggle, sacrifices and the loss of many dear ones before it could be brought down. His monument is the division of the inhabitants of South Africa into white and non-white zones in a fascist police state which is fertile ground for hatred, suspicion and deep rooted self-deception.

The next day it was all over. Smuts had lost and Malan and Havenga had won. They had voted Nationalist against communism and the black danger: a danger which never existed but was invented by fascist European leaders, the preachers of the master-race doctrine. The fascists proclaimed it a new era, and indeed it was a new era. They proclaimed also that God to whom they prayed, God who sent them to South Africa to perform his will that a black man and a white man are not the same and must be kept apart, had heard them. They proclaimed further that the Europeans of South Africa gave them a mandate to outlaw communism, to invent a new type of education for African children, to take away from the missionaries the school buildings and the teaching of African children, to split Africans into ethnic groups, to abolish the Native Representative Council and, finally, to establish Bantustans. From that day the philosophy of Apartheid was proclaimed.

That was South Africa in nineteen-forty-eight. I was there, I was a physical part of it, I was affected by everything which happened there, I was the victim. The Europeans who hated democratic South Africa staged celebrations and victory demonstrations because at last they had found the answer to communism and to the ghost created in their minds by their leader, the black danger. When all that happened, Malan was in Cape Town. A few days before his arrival in Pretoria to form his government I attended a meeting uninvited and unwanted at five o'clock in Church Square, a meeting which was addressed by Smuts himself. I listened carefully to Smuts' voice and detected the voice of a dying man. I was not interested in his death because I knew that it could not bring the downfall of the monument of hate he had built in our country. I knew further that Malan was not taking over from him to ease things, to bring the day of democratic South Africa nearer, but to intensify brutality, hatred and the permanent division of the inhabitants of South Africa. I recognised that if world public opinion was going to give Malan and his doctrine the same reception and tolerance as it gave Smuts' government and leadership, the whole world would be poisoned by the theory of master race, Apartheid and fascist ideas that white is superior and non-white inferior. People from other countries would go there, get injected with that doctrine and those ideas, leave South Africa having become pregnant with them and go back to their countries to spread them and to inject their people with them. It is happening in many countries twenty years later.

As the general secretary of the Pretoria Non-European Distributive Workers' Union and the African General Workers' Union, and a member of the Communist party, in nineteen-forty-nine I was elected chairman of the district committee of the party. The Europeans-only Nationalist party and the Afrikaners' party were in power. They had formed a coalition government and were busy putting into effect their general election promises. The first thing on their list was to deal with the Native Representative Council which, according to their ideas, was a body of Communists demanding rights and equality with Europeans.

Dr. Mears was no longer secretary for native affairs. A man who was for many years chief inspector of African education in the Transvaal was now the secretary, Dr. W. W. Eiselen, who had never been a civil servant but an employee of the Transvaal provincial council. The minister for native affairs at that time was Dr. Jansen, who later became the governor-general. There were other men in the native affairs department who were entitled to succeed Dr. Mears, but Dr. Jansen brought Dr. Eiselen in from outside to take the post. That appointment produced quarrels amongst them that Dr. Jansen had not consulted their civil service commission, which was the body to make recommendations as to who was to be appointed when a head of department retired or resigned. To make them shut up Dr. Jansen explained that he appointed Dr. Eiselen because he believed in Apartheid, was for it and would carry it through. That was why Dr. Eiselen became the Nationalists' secretary for native affairs. It was he who changed its name to the department for Bantu affairs.

That year newspapers reported that members of the Native Representative Council were summoned to Pretoria to meet under the chairmanship of Dr. Eiselen. The venue was to be the Theosophical Hall in Sunnyside, where they had last met to be addressed by Jan Hofmeyr under the Smuts government. A few weeks later news reached us through the newspapers that members of the council had decided to come to Pretoria to ask Malan's government to tell them what they meant by Apartheid. I felt that the councillors were trying to play with words to avoid a showdown with Malan's government because Malan and all his followers had explained clearly more than once during their election campaigns that Apartheid meant kaffir in his place, permanent *baasskaap*, white supremacy, and the denial of rights and human dignity to non-whites in the country.

Having got the information about the councillors' intentions I planned a line of action. I decided that before the councillors arrived in Johannesburg and Pretoria for their meeting I would write them letters individually and send them by post to reach them a day or two before their meeting began. I knew the addresses of those who would board and lodge in Pretoria but not of those who would live in Johannesburg. I found no difficulty in that; I decided to use the address of the newspaper *Bantu World*, which was edited by one of their influencial colleagues, R. V. Selope-Thema. I was sure that each one of them would receive his letter before they all assembled before Eiselen. I informed my colleague Stephen Tefu of what I had in mind and he endorsed it. We then waited for the time to arrive.

We bought a ream of paper, a stencil and got ready to act. A week before the meeting I drafted the letter and got Tefu to approve the wording. Afterwards I sat behind a typewriter, cut the stencil and went to the office of the party to roneo them. Three days before the meeting took place the letters were going through the post office sorting department on their way to those they were aimed at. But I did not trust the editor of the *Bantu World*; I suspected that after receiving his, he would know what they were about and withhold the others. So I addressed the other letters to the Theosophical Hall in order that when the councillors arrived there on the day of the meeting they would find the letters waiting for them.

I sent out the letters under the auspices not of the party but of the African General Workers' Union, as its general secretary, on behalf of our members, ourselves and the African people throughout the country. The wording read as follows: 'We are surprised and alarmed to learn that you are coming to Pretoria to ask the Nationalist government to tell you what they mean by Apartheid. The Nationalists have explained in great detail what they mean by Apartheid and we can't understand how you can pretend to be ignorant of the meaning of Apartheid. You know well its meaning; what you desire is to make a deal with the Nationalists in order to shake off their accusations that you are Communists, agitators and a group of men who claim equality with Europeans. If you wish to surrender, do so openly, instead of hiding behind the shield of not knowing the meaning of Apartheid.'

I went on in the letters to say: 'We take this opportunity of explaining to you what Apartheid really means since you claim ignorance of its meaning. Apartheid means total segregation of the African people and all non-Europeans in the country, permanent denial of human rights, permanent *baasskaap*, master race, and inferiority for anything non-white. That', I said in the letter, 'is the meaning of Apartheid. You will not enter the Theosophical Hall not knowing the meaning of Apartheid as you claim, but in full possession of the meaning.'

I well remember writing: 'When you enter the Theosophical Hall, you will be like actors appearing on the stage, your audience being the African people behind your backs, and before you Dr. Eiselen the Apostle of Apartheid and others who share his views. Beyond the borders of the country the nations of the world will be watching. You bear big responsibilities to the African people, and all of us will be watching whether you are going to sell out or whether you are going to go down fighting for human rights, dignity, the end of Apartheid and votes for all the inhabitants of the country.'

Three days later all roads led to the Theosophical Hall. My colleague Tefu and myself joined the crowds. I was there before Eiselen arrived to judge the moods of the councillors. Only one knew me, R. V. Selope-Thema, the editor of *Bantu World*. He didn't say anything to me or indicate that he had received my letter, but I was satisfied that the councillors had got them. The meeting was attended by many Europeans who were sympathetic to the African cause, some were spokesmen for the Africans in the Europeans-only parliament created under the same act which created the Native Representative Council in nineteen-thirty-six.

Dr. Eiselen arrived to chair the meeting and everyone of us there knew that he was not going to stand any nonsense. The council must proceed with the agenda of nineteen-forty-six or face a death sentence. Those were Malan's orders; and Eiselen was there to see that the kaffir was in his place. The meeting began with *Nkosi Sikelela Afrika*. After reading the notice which convened the meeting, Dr. Eiselen repeated what Hofmeyr had said: that much time had been wasted and the councillors should proceed with the nineteen-forty-six agenda. Professor Z. K. Matthews, as spokesman for the caucus, moved the suspension of the agenda so that they could discuss government policy. The motion was seconded and carried. Dr. Eiselen then said that as chairman he overruled the motion.

Again I was sitting very close behind the councillors so that I could watch and hear everything being said. Faced with Dr. Eiselen's ruling, Professor Matthews moved another motion: for the adjournment of the meeting until the afternoon to consider the ruling and to give their considered reply. The motion was carried. We left the hall, but made sure that we were there again in the afternoon. When the meeting opened, Dr. Eiselen asked the councillors for their reply and the spokesman for the councillors delivered it. It was again a cloudless day; we were all in light shirts, and I can't remember when last we had rain.

Professor Matthews made it clear that they saw no point in proceeding with the agenda when they were denied the right to discuss the policy of the government in power in relation to the life of the African people. He went on to say that they were being accused of not co-operating with the government; they were further accused of frustrating the government; but they knew of no time when the government wanted to improve the economic, social and political positions of the African people. Then he dealt with co-operation and said: 'If we are expected to co-operate with the keeping down of our people, to that we are unwilling to co-operate. We are ready at any time,' said Professor Matthews, 'to assist the government to solve the problems which stand between us and the other inhabitants of the country. We have therefore resolved that we shall not proceed with the agenda unless we are first afforded the opportunity to discuss the Government's policy.' He sat down. Dr. Eiselen then asked whether that was the feeling of them all, to indicate by raising their right hands. All hands went into the air, and that signalled the death of the Native Representative Council, created by Hertzog and Smuts, strangled by Malan and Havenga.

When we had left the hall and were still standing in its garden, a European senator called Malcomess, who represented Cape Africans in the Europeans-only parliament, came over to Selope-Thema, from whom I was not very far, and said, 'Thema, why did you allow this to happen?' Before Thema could answer, Senator Malcomess said, 'I came all the way from the Cape to hear you speak on the pass laws and nothing happened.' I replied: 'He has been speaking on the pass laws all these years and nothing has happened.'

A tall, elderly European lady, whose face was new to me, opened her handbag, took out one of my letters and said angrily, 'You are happy about what has happened, you are the cause of it all. Your people will suffer as a result and they will never forgive you.' I did not reply to her protest. The Native Representative Council was dead and buried. She was right, I was happy about it all. She said that my people would suffer as though they were not already suffering. I was suffering with them.

We left the Theosophical Hall and lost touch with each other. Newspapers reported the proceedings in full, but commented that the councillors allowed themselves to be influenced by outside forces and gave the Nationalist government a chance to abolish them. If they desired to discuss the government's policy they ought to have proceeded with the agenda and then in course of time forced the government to reveal its policy. Those newspapers wrote as though the council had not been in existence for more than ten

272

years. It had recommended many things, among them the abolition of the pass laws and of colour discrimination, and the franchise for non-Europeans in the country, but they had been told that they were asking for impossibilities and unattainable changes.

I had always maintained that the Native Representative Council, like the urban native advisory boards, was brought into being for the sole purpose of giving the Africans a toy to play with, letting them think that one day the Europeans-only government would grant some of their recommendations. Like advisory boards, it was my contention that it was meant to divide the African people so that they could not think of organising themselves into one solid body with which they could struggle for the recovery of the human rights, dignity and true citizenship they lost in nineteen-ten when the Europeans in the country formed the Union without their consent and without consulting them. Some members of the council and advisory boards saw no need to belong to the African National Congress and condemned it as a useless body which would never achieve anything for the African people. They misled themselves by thinking that they were in better positions to talk to the authorities because, although their recommendations were rejected, they were at least listened to. Some of them seemed to think that because they were in those bodies and were called masters or councillors during their meetings by their European chairmen, not boys like the rest of us outside the meeting rooms, they were respected.

I carried on with my trade union work and the chairmanship of the district committee of the Communist party. The situation for us was worsening. Malan's government was on the march, putting into effect the promises they asked the Europeans-only voters to vote them into power for. They appointed a commission to investigate how African education could be taken away from the missionaries, what type of education would be suitable for African children, and what amount of hours the children should be allowed to go to school – meaning those who were lucky to get a place in schools run by the churches. The state never encouraged or built schools for African children, for whom there has never been free and compulsory education. If the churches had not taken the initiative there would never have been members of the advisory boards and Native Representative Council, men like Professor Z. K. Matthews and others. Free and compulsory education for African children was one of the recommendations put forward by the Representative Council and rejected by Hertzog's and Smuts' governments.

For many years, too, Nationalists like Dr. Albert Hertzog, son of the first Nationalist prime minister, accused progressive European trade unions of being run or dominated by Communists. They were supported by the Dutch Reformed Church, who claimed that gods

Afrikaner girls and boys in trade unions were being indoctrinated by Communists with ideas that there was no proof as to whether there was God or not. They demanded government action to remove those they accused of being Communists from the unions. It is true there were unions, like mine, headed by Communists, but the members knew of our political convictions and were satisfied with our services. The commission to investigate African education was headed by the man of Apartheid, Dr. W. W. Eiselen, and it came to be known as Eiselen Commission.

Another commission was appointed to investigate the activities of Communists in the trade unions and to recommend how they could be removed. The Trade Unions Commission was headed by Professor Botha, an economist, a man before whom I had appeared with other African trade unionists for many years in wages board investigations of African wages and conditions of employment. When I first appeared before him, he was vice-chairman of the wages board, and he later became the chairman. These commissions were only a foretaste of the bitter things to follow.

XXXII Suppression of Communism

While Dr. Eiselen's commission was going round the country mixing poison with which to kill African education – education which none of the Europeans-only governments since nineteen-ten had encouraged or provided – Dr. Botha's commission, appointed by the Nationalists to oust militant trade unionists from progressive European trade unions, and to kill African trade unions unrecognised by the state, was also going about the country mixing a poison to end African trade unions. When the time came each came out with its product. The Eiselen commission gave birth to what is known today as Bantu education. Under it the direction of Bantu education came under the control of the Bantu Affairs department, that meant under Dr. Eiselen himself. History, that is world history, and geography became forbidden subjects. All that was needed, they recommended, was for the Bantu children (as they preferred to call us) to be taught about their immediate environment and to be able to read messages so that when employed they could deliver those messages to the right places. That would remove from their minds that there is or can be equality with Europeans.

Later Dr. Botha's commission came out with its report and recommendations. It recommended that Africans in employment should appoint one amongst themselves and delegate him to deliver their grievances to the Department of Labour or to the industrial inspectors of labour in their areas. That meant that if an African was not employed by a firm he could not act as spokesman for the workers of the firm. That was sentencing African trade unions to death. They also recommended that African workers should not be allowed to strike, no matter how justifiable the grievances. As a result of their recommendations, the Nationalist government framed and produced an industrial law known today in South African industry as the Native Settlement of Disputes Act. These are not fictions, they are things which hang on the necks of the Africans today.

What methods were then applied to get rid of militant trade unionists? Dr. Botha's commission was empowered to summon all the unions for investigation by calling on them to submit their minutes, audited financial statements, bank accounts covering a period of ten years, and to appear before the commission for interrogation by the commissioners. It must be remembered that under the

275

Industrial Conciliation Act, African trade unions were not trade unions. So, when it came to the killing of trade unions, African unions were included in the list of those which were called upon to submit books and financial statements. Suddenly, because they had to be strangled, they merited recognition as trade unions, and the Botha Commission had to deal with them in the same way as recognised unions. I was waiting in Pretoria for my turn to come. Eventually it came and I received a letter from the commission instructing me to submit minutes of my union, the Pretoria Non-European Distributive Workers' Union, mentioning even the time before it came into existence. The penalty for refusing to comply was a fifty pounds fine, six months in prison or both. At first I decided to refuse to submit documents on the grounds that my union was not a trade union under the meaning of the Industrial Conciliation Act and therefore was not obliged to comply with the Botha commission's instructions. Later I changed my mind and decided to appear before the commission to speak my mind. I sent them three documents, a copy of the minutes, a membership book and a bank book. On the day of the proceedings, I left with my colleague Stephen Tefu for the Labour Department building where the commission was sitting. Ironically, we found the commission holding its interrogations in the same room where we used to argue cases for our members before Dr. Botha, then chairman of the wage board.

A group of African trade unionists from Johannesburg was being interrogated. When they had been dealt with, we were called in for our dose of the poison. Dr. Botha knew me well because at one time I had a fierce quarrel before him with coal merchants who challenged me on the grounds that I was not a spokesman for their workers. They demanded that before I could be allowed to speak, I should disclose how many members I had in their yards. To stop the row Dr. Botha ruled that, even if I had only one member, I had the right to be there to put the member's case. I don't know what methods were used on those who were interrogated before me, but when I took the stand an electric recording machine was connected to my jacket lapel with a receiver which looked like a telephone receiver so that every word I uttered was correctly recorded by the machine. First I was told that I was under oath and that the commission wanted more documents than the ones I had submitted. I told the commissioners that I had no further documents to submit because I burnt the rest as soon as I heard that the commission was appointed. The commissioners then asked me if I had something to hide by burning the documents.

In reply I told them that I had nothing to hide, but felt that it was wrong for me to submit the documents of an unrecognised trade union to a commission appointed by a government which refused to recognise it. I then got heated and said that in my opinion the commission had no legal right to demand documents from unrecognised African trade unions. I submitted the documents they were not satisfied with under protest and force because we live under the system of 'might is right'. Dr. Botha then intervened to tell me that I was before a legally appointed government commission, not at a political meeting. One of the members asked me whether I was aware that I was placing myself in an awkward position, the consequences of which I would regret; he said that my self-admission that I burnt the documents rather than submit them to the commission amounted to refusal to comply. I contested his argument, saying that I had complied, I had submitted documents and appeared before them against my conviction that I ought not have done so.

One of them asked me if I agreed with them that I refused to submit documents and refused to answer questions on them. I reminded him that they had my documents before them and that I had answered the questions they asked me. He then told me that, as far as the commission was concerned, I had refused to give them the information they sought, having destroyed vital documents which they wanted, and brought only what I thought was enough. These documents, he told me, conveyed no information; from them they could only arrive at the conclusion that I was unreliable, dishonest and untrustworthy.

Dr. Botha then told me that, wherever they had been, they had had co-operation from the unions, European as well as African. Why did I think that I was different from the others? I came in in a big way. I said: 'Doctor, history repeats itself. In Germany after Hitler took power he appointed a commission headed by an economist, Dr. Ley, to investigate trade unions. The results are well known: death to the trade union movement in that country. Here,' I went on, 'we are being investigated by an economist, Dr. Botha. The results will be the same, our death. Kill us without my co-operation,' I concluded. I was dismissed and given my three documents to take with me. I knew it was not the end but the beginning

Two weeks later a detective arrived at my office with a warrant for my arrest. I spent lunch that day in a police cell at Pretoria central police station, but late in the afternoon, when I was convinced that the cell was going to be my bedroom for the night, I heard cell keys rattling, the door was opened, and a European policeman said 'Come on.' I followed him, thinking that the black maria was waiting outside to take me and others to the central prison in Potgieter Street, but he led me to the counter, where I found an Asian friend of mine, Ramthula Keshavjee, waiting for me with a car to take me home. He had paid twenty-five pounds bail.

The next day I appeared in front of the regional court magistrate

charged with failing to give the industrial commission the information they needed in their investigations. The case was postponed for a
month. When the trial came I defended myself, arguing that I gave
them the information they needed. They asked for documents
and they got them; they asked me questions and I answered
them.

One new ground I brought out in court was that I resented the
composition of the commission because it consisted only of European
members. I submitted that, though the Commissions' Act empowered the governor-general to appoint the commission, it did not
empower him to appoint Europeans only. I asked for the Act from
the court's library to read the relevant section. After reading it I
challenged the prosecutor to show where it empowered the governor-
general to appoint Europeans only. The magistrate overruled me;
the Act empowered the governor-general to appoint that commission and that was enough. I was found guilty and convicted, but I
was surprised when a fine of only five pounds or three weeks in prison
was imposed. I appealed against the conviction. After several weeks
my appeal was heard in the supreme court before two judges, Mr.
Justice Murray and Mr. Justice Neser. There, too, I argued my own
case, my main ground being the composition of the commission. I
lost the appeal. Mr. Justice Murray said that the Act did not forbid
the governor-general to appoint a commission of Europeans only. I
did not go to prison; my friend allowed his five pounds to take my
place. That was one of the ways in which I resisted fascism in South
Africa.

While that was happening Charles Robert Swart, who was
Malan's minister of justice (I called him minister of injustice) was
also mixing a poison to kill all opposition in the country. Like
Hitler's minister of injustice whom Swart admired, he disguised its
motive and purpose and called it the Suppression of Communism
Act of nineteen-fifty. Its title misled many people, but we who drew
lessons from history saw its motive and purpose. We knew that
Hitler had used the same methods and misled many people in
Germany. We knew well that Swart's Suppression of Communism
Act was loaded with bullets to be fired not only on the Communist
party and the Communists, but on all democrats who criticised
fascism in the country. I remember well that when that measure was
debated in the Europeans-only parliament in Cape Town, the central
committee of the party sent us stickers to stick wherever we could in
Pretoria saying 'The Suppression of Communism Act threatens you,
oppose it'. That was a warning and a call to the people of South
Africa to step off the railway lines before the train came along and
ran them over. Did all see it that way? No, of course not, they
laughed and some said, 'Communists are in danger, they want us to

help them.' The Italians had said the same in nineteen-twenty-two, the Germans repeated it in nineteen-thirty-three and the South Africans had not learned the lesson in nineteen-fifty.

I remember talking to Nimrod Tantsi, an African parson, a staunch African National Congress man, an anti-Communist but nevertheless a great friend of mine, trying to convince him that Swart's Act was going to be used against anyone who opposed fascism, all democrats who desired a democratic South Africa; that if the people understood its real motive and purpose, they would rally against it before it was too late. My friend laughed and said with strong conviction, 'Mokgatle, it's not true, its title is plain; they know I am a churchman, I was never a Communist; how can they be so blind and use it against people like me?' That was the mood; but what we said came true. At the beginning of that year I attended the last party conference in Johannesburg. It was presided over by a new chairman, a Cape Town architect, Oscar Hurwitz. I was delighted later that I had spoken at the last conference of the party which gave me political education.

When Charles Robert Swart, who later became President of the Europeans-only Republic in South Africa, rushed his measure through their parliament in Cape Town, the central committee of the party decided that when the measure reached its last stage, the party must dissolve itself rather than wait for Swart, Malan and the rest to dissolve it. Some people will tell you that Smuts' party, the United party, was in opposition, or is still in opposition, first to Malan and in nineteen-seventy to Vorster. Let me take you back to nineteen-fifty. During the debate on the Suppression of Communism Act, the Nationalists said that those convicted under it should be imprisoned for ten years, but Smuts' party said: 'No, that's too mild, they should be sentenced to death.' That is not a fiction; records in Cape Town will confirm it.

The central committee of the party circulated a notice of its intentions to dissolve, asking us to inform all members and to obtain objections and consents. I rounded up most of the membership of my district, gave them the confidential news, and one evening we assembled in the party meeting room and approved the central committee's intentions. The next day I communicated my district committee's views to Cape Town. A week before Swart got his Injustice Act through their parliament the Communist dove had escaped his trap. From that month, June nineteen-fifty, I was without a political home.

Well, I was not the only unfortunate one. I was one of the many, whose convictions I shared, who had suffered the same fate in Italy, Germany and other lands. The next question for me was whether I was going to give in and say I was never a Communist or whether to say to Swart: 'You chose the Nationalist party and I chose the Communist party of South Africa.' I decided to continue to wear the coat I had chosen. To change meant to me the admission of the triumph of fascism in South Africa. All I had to do was to wait for events to take their course. I was not an elector, I did not elect Swart, Malan and their government to power, so why, I asked myself, should I acknowledge their legality? I spent the last half of that year quietly carrying on with my trade union work, but at the same time thinking hard. I knew that Swart's attack was imminent. During that time I received a letter from the liquidator of the Communist party appointed by Malan's government telling me he was compiling names of Communists in the country, and that he had evidence before him that I was a member of the party and wanted to know whether I had any objections to my name being placed on his list. I ignored him.

In the year the Communist party was outlawed, nineteen-fifty, I took a train one Sunday morning from Pretoria to Johannesburg with my colleague Stephen Tefu and others to attend a huge rally. At that time the African National Congress president was Dr. James Moroka, a Thaba Nchu surgeon in the Free State province, who had been a member of the Native Representative Council when it died at the hands of Dr. Eiselen. The purpose of the rally was to welcome him and his wife to the Transvaal and to express loyalty to his leadership. We arrived at the City of Gold's main railway station, called Park Station, to find great excitement and a very large crowd. People came from far and near and from many areas near Johannesburg. There was singing and waving of banners; all sections of the inhabitants of the country were represented. There were Europeans, Indians and Coloured people. I think that the president of Congress himself was surprised to find so many people waiting to welcome him. Congress supporters in Johannesburg had brought a horse-drawn landau to carry him through the streets of the city. From the station the crowd moved southwards along Eloff Street on the way to the City Hall, the use of which was denied to the non-Europeans of the city.

The Congress welcoming committee had decided, though they had not bothered to ask for the use of the City Hall because their request would have been rejected by the council, to take him there and see if they could find unlocked doors and hold the reception in the City Hall. If they failed to get in, they decided to hold the reception outside on the City Hall steps. But others with weak knees had decided to lead him to Gandhi Hall, where the reception could be held without trouble. When the procession passed the City Hall on the way to Gandhi Hall there were protests, but it was too late. However, we proceeded to Gandhi Hall, where the reception took place. It was an exciting occasion. The people were in a mood for action against Apartheid.

In Gandhi Hall moving speeches of welcome were made by leaders of Congress, many people pledging to do anything their president wished them to do, and expressing their feeling that the time for action had come; what they needed was an order for action against colour discrimination and the denial of human rights. In the end it was resolved that, to start with, on May the first that year, all Africans should launch a political strike by staying at home, so that the employers of African labour and Malan's government should see that the non-Europeans were no longer willing to be denied rights and be discriminated against. The rally was held in March.

All other non-Europeans, and the progressive Europeans who were there, pledged to support the declaration and on that day to stay at home in support of the Africans' political strike. The resolution was not only meant for those living and working in Johannesburg but for the whole country. We all said that at last something positive had been decided, and that it was the duty of us all to see that it was carried out. It was agreed at the rally that when we returned to our localities we should see that the message reached the people in our areas, and work hard so that on May the first the people stayed at home to bring the industries of the country to a standstill. There was great enthusiasm for the resolution, and before we left Gandhi Hall the president of Congress addressed the rally, reminding us that we had taken a decision, and that it was ourselves who were to carry it out and see that others carried it out with us. He went on to say that the resolution was a Congress resolution, and we were Congress. Without us, he said, there would have been no such resolution, and without our dedication, devotion and hard work, people would go to work on May the first. He suggested that from that day we should salute each other by saying May the first, to keep the day in the minds of the people throughout the country.

A committee was set up in Johannesburg to raise funds for printing leaflets and sending them to all parts of the country where committees were functioning, preparing the people for May the first. The order was that people must simply stay at home and avoid going into the streets, so that there could be no violence and trouble with the police. It was to be only a one day stay-at-home strike. In the afternoon we left Gandhi Hall in a large procession for Newtown Market, where we were addressed again by the president and by other Congress leaders still urging us to be firm. I left the City of Gold for Pretoria with those who came with me; all vowed to work hard amongst our people to see that May the first was observed. In Pretoria, like other centres, we formed a committee to campaign for May the first. The Johannesburg committee supplied us with all the leaflets we needed. We held meetings in all localities around our city and explained in great detail the resolution and why people should stay at home on that day. As we went round, police followed us to record our speeches. Before March was out some members began to have many excuses.

By the middle of April the work of holding meetings and distributing leaflets was entirely done by my colleague Stephen Tefu and myself. The police had found that the best way of frightening some of our members was by saying that the May the first agitation was not a Congress campaign but a campaign launched by the Communist party. They cited my colleague and myself as an example, that we were the people who were keen on it and wanted to see it through. We were indeed the only two in our area at that time who were distributing leaflets day and night, addressing meetings in the evenings and to be seen shouting at the top of our voices on Sundays at public meetings.

Wherever we went, people came in large numbers to listen and to pledge their support. Newspapers now began to take part in supporting the police allegations that the campaign was Communist-inspired; the Communists were using Congress and the leaders of Congress to further their own ends. The African people were harming their own cause by allowing themselves to be used by Communists in disguise. As April moved towards its end it was already clear that the Congress leadership was looking for a way out of the campaign; however, in many areas the people were already pregnant with the message of May the first. To force Congress out of it the police accused Dr. Moroka of being a Communist. The newspapers took up the story that, though he was not a member of the Communist party, he showed signs of being a Communist at heart. That forced the President to come out against the campaign that he himself had launched and urged the people throughout the country to support. A week before the end of April Dr. Moroka issued a statement in the press that he had never supported the May the first stay-at-home campaign. He said further that he approved the principle of staying at home, but Congress's day that year was June the twenty-sixth. Confusion was at once sown. Congressmen who had all along disapproved of the May the first campaign came out to say that the day mentioned by the president was the one to be observed. The police, Malan's government and the newspapers had won hands down. But we did not give in, we went on with the campaign telling the people that the president was frightened by accusations that he was being used by Communists, and May the first was the day on which they should stay at home. I remember well one Saturday afternoon at Atteridgeville where I had organised a rally, Nelson Mandela came along as the leader of some Congress youth league members to tell the people that the president had named June the twenty-sixth as the day and those who listened to other voices were disobeying him.

Johannesburg, being the centre of political activities, the place where, more than in any other city of South Africa, political demonstrations and conferences always take place, the message of stay at home on May the first was as strong as in Pretoria. People were talking about the day, meetings were held in nearly all localities explaining the importance of this political strike, and nearly everywhere the people were openly saying that they would stay at home on May the first. The message had gone into the people like fever. In it the people saw a chance of expressing their resentment to the powers that be, and also of showing the outside world that the time for them to take positive action had come.

Malan's government, the police and the employers saw at once that Dr. Moroka's dissociation of himself from the campaign, and the confusion they had hoped he would cause, had come too late. They began to take action on their own, sending police into big firms, and places where large numbers of African workers were employed, to intimidate them. In the presence of the police the workers were asked, 'Are you going to stay at home on May the first or are you coming to work?' Trapped in that fashion the workers said individually, 'I would like to come to work but I am afraid that if I come my people will kill me in the evening when I get back.' The police then said, 'Don't worry, all those who want to come to work will get police protection.' The police would be stationed in the locations the night before May the first. They would be at bus termini to see the workers into the buses, and at railway stations to see the workers into trains, and they would accompany them to the cities to work. The employers, on their side, asked the workers to come and sleep at their places of work, and for the first time the employers undertook to feed the workers on the night before May the first and the whole day of the political strike. With such strong pressure, the workers' arguments of being afraid of getting killed fell to the ground. For the first time in the history of South Africa, newspapers appeared written in African languages as well as in English, telling the workers that the government would give them protection, and the police would escort them to and from work on May the first. Leave was cancelled for the army and police so that they could be within reach when they were required. But for the first time in the history of Pretoria the Africans of the capital were determined to strike politically on that day. That was largely because of my work and of my colleague Stephen Tefu.

We who were determined to see the May the first political strike through, stood firm and went on urging the people to stay at home.

We knew from the very beginning that as soon as the Malan government saw that the people were on the move against the denial of human rights, colour discrimination and Apartheid generally, they would not hesitate to attack. The president of the African National Congress and those who retreated from the campaign were not sure whether the people would go to work or stay at home. We, on the other hand, knew that the odds were against us; Congress was no longer for stay-at-home strike action, and the government, the employers and the press were lined up against us. But we made it plain to our people that if the strike failed, it would not be our fault but theirs. We asked them to ask themselves why the newspapers were written in their languages for the first time, why Malan's government, their bitterest foe, was at that time promising them protection, why the employers had for the first time invited them to become their guests to sleep at their places of work and were willing to spend money on feeding them. The protection Malan's government sought to give them, we told the people, was against freedom.

As night follows day, May the first came. The day was a Monday. On Sunday afternoon the situation was tense; the police and the army began to move into Atteridgeville and establish their camps by the municipal offices near the bus terminus. Tanks and all the most frightening weapons that we had never seen before were on view. I was well known to the police but not to the soldiers. Each time I passed near the camps the police said to the soldiers, 'That's him, the trouble-maker; he needs shooting.' Lady-Selborne too, where my colleague Tefu lived, was turned into an army and police camp. I was told, and I read in the newspapers too, that the same display of 'might is right' was in view all over the Reef and Johannesburg locations.

On the Sunday evening the police, accompanied by the army, began to transport workers to their places of work to sleep there. I went to the bus terminus to see what was happening. There I found the workers being taken away from their families to sleep at work, escorted by the army and police motor-cycles. When the workers passed me into the buses their heads were hanging down.

The next day, Monday May the first, I got up early and went back to the bus terminus. I found a long queue of workers lined up by the police and the army getting into the buses. Their bus fares were also being paid by their employers. Those who usually travelled to work on bicycles were being conveyed on buses. I passed very close to the queue and again the police said, 'Here he is, the trouble-maker,' but I uttered no word. Light was beginning to break through; I stayed nearby until after sunrise, but when the time for the white-collar workers came, mostly government workers, they jeered at me and said, 'We are going to work, try and stop us. Now

284

you are afraid, you see the police and have nothing to say.' I still uttered no word, just looked at them, knowing they did not realise that they were hurting themselves and their own cause, as well as mine. After nine o'clock I took a taxi to Lady-Selborne to find the situation there similar to Atteridgeville. With others who stood firm with us we took the same taxi to other locations to see what was taking place there. The reports were the same; the police and the army were there. The political strike was broken up, but I claimed it as a victory for us. Because of our work, things which had never happened before happened. We forced Malan's government to come out to force the African workers to go with the army and police. The police state came out into the open. In the evening the workers were escorted back to their homes. In Pretoria we were lucky there was no loss of life. In Johannesburg, at locations like Alexandra, police opened fire on the people and there was loss of human life. Reports of similar occurrences came from other centres. That was how the May the first stay-at-home political strike ended in nineteen-fifty.

Later some workers at Atteridgeville came to me to apologise, but they told me that they were pleased that I did not say anything when I passed them in the queue. They said that if I had ordered them to return home, they would have fallen over each other running away and the police would have got a chance to shoot me. They congratulated me, saying that for the first time in their lives, and some were old men, they saw machine guns, tanks and fearful weapons brought to them.

Dr. James Moroka's backing out of the May the first stay-at-home political strike in an attempt to show the Malan government that, like them, he was against Communism did not help him and those who supported his actions. He forgot that, during his membership of the Native Representative Council, he had stood with others and demanded abolition of the pass laws, and the franchise for non-Europeans in the country, thus ending all forms of colour discrimination. He forgot that, in the opinion of Malan and those who shared his convictions, anyone who demanded equality with Europeans was a Communist.

He was arrested with others and charged with inciting Africans to break what Malan and his government called the law of the land, as though those who were charged were voters who took part in electing them to power to enact the so-called law of the land. They were charged in Johannesburg and, after a trial which took a few months, were convicted and given suspended sentences. They were under restraint for five years, during which time, if they were arrested for a similar offence, they would be sent to prison for nine months. That was as far as Dr. Moroka could go in the struggle for rights for the Africans, who had had high hopes that in him they had found a leader who would go the whole way with them, on their march to freedom, despite the hardships.

XXXIII Pretoria Market Meetings

Towards September that year, I received a letter from the liquidator of the Communist party, telling me that because I had not made representations to him he had put my name in the list of Communists he was compiling. I treasured the letter very much; I framed it and hung it in my house at Atteridgeville. I treasured it because the Communist party was outlawed, but its haters were recognising me as a Communist. I treasured it because to me it was admitted evidence by Malan's government that I was a fighter for freedom, one of those who stood for equality between all inhabitants of the country regardless of their colour, creed or sex.

Before that, after the collapse of the May stay-at-home political strike, I carried on with my trade union but was at all times mindful that Malan was getting ready to attack. I began to get into contact with the outside world. I wrote to the Trade Union Congress in London asking for financial aid and explaining at great length our plight in the African trade unions. I wrote also to the British Communist party asking for the same things and explaining the coming danger to us as I saw it. Across the Atlantic, I wrote to the American Federation of Labour (AFL) and the Congress of Industrial Organisations (CIO) appealing for financial help and at the same time explaining in detail the conditions under which African workers worked and organised. After several weeks we received financial help from the AFL; I can't remember the exact amount, but it was over eighty dollars, which helped to keep our office open for a few months. My letters asking for help also reached the Italian Confederation of Trade Unions, the French Trade Unions' Confederation, all the trade union confederations in Eastern Europe, the Indian trade unions and China's Trade Union Federation. Not only did I write to trade unions but to Communist parties in those countries as well. The only unions I avoided were Russian, to avoid accusations of receiving Moscow gold, and the Latin American countries, because I lacked the addresses of trade unions there. My appeals were twofold. First we needed money to continue the hard task of organising African workers in the period of Malan terror. Secondly, I knew that Malan's attack was imminent and that when it came I hoped we should not be strangers to the workers and progressive peoples of the world. At that time, during the last half of nineteen-fifty, Malan, with the Suppression of Communism Act, was threatening people with ten years' imprisonment, and it seemed that many leaders who were active before its birth had decided that the best thing to do was to be silent. Malan's government was moving up and down the country like a lion in a game reserve, forcing all the weaker animals to hide from its path. With the passing of their Suppression of Communism Act the Nationalists were satisfied that they had silenced the progressive voices of the oppressed non-Europeans of the country.

Pretoria, unlike Johannesburg, has always lacked determined politicians, and no conference worth mentioning ever started in Pretoria with a message to engulf the whole country. Johannesburg is the place where political activities start and then move on to other centres. When there is no smoke in Johannesburg, then it's right to assume that there is no fire throughout the country. My colleague Stephen Tefu and myself waited to see smoke from the City of Gold but the year ended as though there were no more issues to be fought. The Malan government had inspired so many people with fear that it seemed unchallengeable. My letters were continuing to cross oceans telling our friends abroad what was happening, though I knew that they were as well informed about events in my country as I was, if not more so. I noticed that as the year moved to a close my colleague and I were beginning to talk as though there was nothing we could do by ourselves. We had begun criticising leaders who had been highly respected, honoured and famous before Malan came with the Suppression of Communism Act. 'Where is so and so, what is he doing? He used to pretend to be brave in those days, why is he silent today?' we used to ask. We drew up a list of men we knew in the Communist party, Congress, the Indian Congress and other organisations, and say, 'Where are they, what are they doing?' Gradually it dawned on me that we were merely talking and doing nothing.

I made up my mind that the following year must be one of great change. I said nothing to my colleague Stephen Tefu, but kept my thoughts to myself, until in January, nineteen-fifty-one, one afternoon in our office at 56 Potgieter Street, I said to him: 'We have complained enough about other men doing nothing, but we can also be accused of doing nothing. They too may be wondering why we are silent and doing nothing. Perhaps,' I continued, 'if we start something here in Pretoria, we shall give them courage to join in, and political activities will be resumed against Malan's government and their vicious policies. After all, our silence does not protect us in any way. Both of us have been listed by the liquidator of the Communist party as Communists; we shall have much to gain if we oppose them openly.

'There is no Communist party in the country but we are Communists, there is a chance for us to expose the Malan government, to show our people that they can in fact be challenged.' I said further: 'It is time for both of us to force them to arrest us. When we are arrested we can speak from the court room against them, their policies, and then even ask the court to bring them along to answer our questions about their oppression of our people.' Tefu did not take long to agree with my suggestion. He then asked me, 'How are we going to do it, we haven't formed a political party?' I replied, 'We call meetings in the name of the African General Workers' Union but devote our entire speeches to politics.' 'Good idea,' Tefu remarked with enthusiasm. He asked where we would hold our first meeting. I answered by saying, 'If Malan hesitates to arrest us, Pretoria City Council will start the ball rolling for us. Our first meetings will take place in the centre of town at Pretoria Market every Friday at lunch-time from one to two o'clock.' Tefu's feelings were already fired. We then began to plan the meeting. We agreed to February the sixteenth as the starting date. We began to get leaflets ready to be distributed in the city at bus queues, inviting the workers and everyone interested to attend. We kept the secret to ourselves until we began to hand the leaflets out to the people.

On the sixteenth of February, nineteen-fifty-one, at the time mentioned in our leaflets, we began to speak at Pretoria Market. We opened meetings by first singing a song to attract people, and after five minutes we started speaking, one in English and one interpreting what was said into Sesotho, which is the dialect spoken in the Pretoria area. I was always the first speaker and Tefu interpreted. Each of us spoke for twenty-five minutes to allow the audience to ask questions and still to return to work in time. The first meeting was attended only by ourselves. People listened from afar, fearing that we would be arrested at once and they would become the victims as well. The market place is so well placed that at such an hour many people pass there, walking along Church Street. Our platform was at the corner of Church and Prinsloo Streets, and along Prinsloo Street too there always moved a large number of people. On the eastern side of Prinsloo Street was a concentration of Indian shops as well as some shops owned by Europeans. By not taking action against us, Pretoria City Council enabled the people to see that there was nothing they could do against us. And people could see too that Malan's government might be challenged.

We did not mince words in our speeches in denouncing Dr. Malan as a fascist, his ministers as a group of fascists – racists who had no legal right to govern the country because they were elected by the minority, for the minority. We stressed strongly that they were an illegal government which had no legal right to make laws for the country, that they had no right to enter into contracts or agreements with legally elected governments of the world in the name of South Africa and her inhabitants. During our speeches we said that since nineteen-ten South Africa had never had a national government, but tribal governments chosen by the European tribes in the country. We claimed that we had more right to speak for South Africa at home and abroad because we represented the majority, the non-Europeans, and those European inhabitants of the country who did not support colour discrimination and racial oppression.

Our week-by-week Pretoria Market speeches, which were fearless and powerful, established us firmly in the minds of Pretoria people. Every week meetings became bigger. Europeans, too, began to join our audience. Some brought sandwiches with them and sat in cars near the meetings so that they could hear every word spoken. As the audience grew we also grew fiercer in our speeches with which we desired to impregnate the people. From the very beginning the secret police joined us to record every word spoken. Some we knew and others we did not know, thinking that they were newspaper men.

I remember some speeches I delivered personally at those meetings. At that time Verwoerd was the so-called minister for Bantu affairs. In one speech I said that we had formed a democratic government in the country; I was the prime minister, Tefu was the minister of justice, and I went on to read fictitious names of ministers in our fictitious government. I said: 'Some of you here are laughing, some are beginning to say that Mokgatle is mad. But,' I said, 'I want you to tell me if there is any difference between me and Malan. We only differ in colour. He is older than I am and that is all.' I went on to say, 'Malan and myself are products of two persons, a man and woman. We were conceived in exactly the same way. My mother was pregnant with me for nine months and Malan's mother was pregnant with him for nine months. Malan and I could not walk until we were over six months old. Both of us could not make ourselves understood in speech until we were over two years old. Where then,' I asked, 'is the difference?' There was applause and laughter. 'Remember,' I requested our audience, 'Malan and his admirers claim that they are superior and that I am inferior.' There were again cheers and laughter. 'I can and I am,' I claimed, 'the best prime minister of South Africa. In the government Tefu and I have formed there is no colour discrimination. All the inhabitants of this country are equal, all are voters, regardless of the language they speak and the religion they have adopted and whether they are men or women.' There was laughter and cheering again. I said further, 'We have arrested Malan and his entire ministers and you will not see them in Pretoria until July, some not until the end of the year. We have imprisoned them in Cape Town.' (Malan and his ministers were attending their parliament in Cape Town at the time.)

I remember vividly two of the speeches I made among many at our Pretoria Market meetings, dealing with Malan and Eric Louw, who had been Hertzog's ambassador in France in the 'thirties, returning to South Africa at the time Hertzog and Smuts came together to form the United party. He returned specially to join Malan in his crusade for continuation of hostilities towards the non-European inhabitants of the country. Though Eric Louw spent some years in France, where non-Europeans were not discriminated against, a country where some members of Parliament were non-Europeans, who must no doubt have rubbed shoulders with Eric Louw at state functions and other important occasions, his hostility and his fascist frame of mind never left him. As a hypocrite and an opportunist he felt it right to mix with non-Europeans abroad on equal terms, to regard them as equal to himself, not inferior beings, but never to meet them on such terms as soon as he crossed into South Africa.

When they had been elected to power by the European tribal voters, Malan made him his minister for external affairs. While our market meetings were in progress he was invited to pay a state visit to the Belgian Congo. In South Africa Eric Louw, like all who shared his views and convictions, said that he was totally against Africans being trained as soldiers, being recruited into the army and being armed with European fire-arms. Africans, he used to tell his people, are incapable of learning the military art, they can never become real soldiers and therefore should never be called soldiers or given the knowledge to use European fire-arms. The Belgians held contrary views to those of Eric Louw. In the Congo, they recruited Africans into the army and trained them with European fire-arms – something Eric Louw said he disapproved of strongly and disliked intensely.

He went to the Belgian Congo aware that there Africans were in the army and were soldiers. He was aware that on arrival there he would be provided with a guard of honour consisting entirely of Africans. That was what happened when he put his foot in Leopoldville. The South African newspapers showed him, with pride, inspecting the African guard of honour. I took him up on that at our market meetings. That day there was a large number of Europeans in our audience. I held the newspaper picture up and said, 'Look at the cheat and hypocrite Eric Louw.'

I said, 'You Europeans have allowed yourselves to be misled by him. . . . This picture in the newspaper is an admission that he has been telling you deliberate lies. I know,' I said, 'that some of you will say that the Belgian Congo is not South Africa and that he is not there to tell the Belgians how to run their colony. That argument,' I said, 'is all nonsense. If you were honest to yourselves, you would agree with me that the Belgians have exposed him in front of your very eyes. The Belgians have revealed to you that he is nothing but a hypocrite.'

I said further, 'I am going to ask you a question which I hope you will answer with honesty. Supposing a friend of yours knows that you don't eat pork, you never touch it, that you are on record as having said that you will never allow it to be eaten in your home. Your friends invite you to dinner but prepare a pork dinner for you; would you accept the invitation or, if you did accept the invitation, would you eat pork just to please your friends under the pretext that you are not in their homes to tell them how to cook or what sort of meal to provide?' There was a loud cry of 'No!' but I can't guarantee whether the loud 'No' came from Europeans or the non-Europeans in the audience. But not a single European contradicted the loud 'No' reply I got.

I then turned to Malan himself. I said, 'In the same way he bluffs you that for him it is Afrikaners first and others later. You believe him,' I said, 'you swear that he is one hundred per cent for the Afrikaner folk. I say that he is lying to you, he is not for Afrikaners as he says. After the war they brought German orphans to South Africa to care for them. Malan adopted one of the little girls and named her Maritje.' I said, 'I am not against children who have no parents being adopted, whether they are white or black or from which country they are taken. What I want you to tell me, on behalf of your Malan, is why didn't he first adopt a little Afrikaner orphan girl, or adopt one after Maritje? He didn't do that,' I said, 'because he is not one hundred per cent for the Afrikaners but only wants to use them for his benefit. Like Eric Louw, he is a liar and hypocrite. I challenge him from this platform to adopt a poor Afrikaner orphan.'

Our Pretoria Market speeches were biting deep into Malan's government's flesh. They were getting regular reports from the police, who were recording our speeches every week. Our meetings were drawing large crowds, and people outside Pretoria who could come into town and return home the same day made Fridays their shopping days so that they could be at the meetings to hear the speeches which had never before been heard inside the city against the tribal government which had struck fear into the people's hearts. We held meetings regularly without a break.

In June nineteen-fifty-one, Malan's tribal government could not stand it any longer. One morning at about ten o'clock we saw three cars drawing up in front of our office, 56 Potgieter Street, and out of them came six detectives led by Detective Inspector van der Berg, armed with a warrant signed by the chief magistrate of Pretoria to search and to seize documents from our office. There were four Europeans and two Africans. We knew them well; some of them were regular visitors at our meetings. They, through Chief Detective Inspector van der Berg, gave me the warrant to read, and after doing so I gave it to my colleague Stephen Tefu to read, but before Tefu finished they were already busy going through every file, cupboard, drawer and book they could lay their hands on. While they were busy selecting what they were going to take away I telephoned a barrister friend of mine, George Findlay, to tell him what was going on in our office. He asked me if they had a warrant. When I confirmed it he advised me not to hinder them but to see that they gave me a receipt for everything they took with them.

After seizing the documents, they said that they were taking us to my house at Atteridgeville to search, and we left in three cars for my house. They needed no lead; they knew where I lived. I travelled in the middle car driven by Detective Sergeant Visser, sitting in the front seat. Tefu travelled in the one in front and Detective Chief Inspector van der Berg followed in the third car. My wife was surprised and so were the people of Atteridgeville. At my house, too, after the warrant had been read, a search commenced and many documents and books were seized. I was given a receipt for them all. From there we went to Lady-Selborne to search Tefu's home. The same procedure was adopted there, but Tefu kept no large documents or books. What they found and thought would help them they took.

In April of that year, before the South African gestapo raided our office and homes with warrants, we had planned to hold a May Day demonstration in the centre of Pretoria. Our aim was to march along Church Street carrying banners displaying slogans against the pass laws, denial of human rights and denunciations of the Europeans-only tribal government. Towards the end of April, as was our custom, we roneoed leaflets telling the workers that on May the first, for only one hour, we would assemble at the market and from there march along Church Street to the Square, where we would make political speeches. We knew that the first leaflet we distributed would fall into the hands of the police. We distributed the leaflets widely in the city, urging all workers and sympathetic people to attend regardless of their colour. We made it clear in our leaflets that we were not against Europeans as such but against their tribal government which was inciting them against the non-European citizens of the country. The day following the distribution of the leaflets the police arrived at our office to tell us that our planned demonstration was banned by the chief magistrate of Pretoria and that we should call it off. We told the police that, since we had already planned our march, there was no way of cancelling it! Only the workers could cancel it if they did not turn up on the day. Two days before the demonstration a local newspaper announced that we had planned an illegal march in the centre of the city and that the chief magistrate had banned it. It warned that if some people allowed themselves to be led into disobeying the order of the chief magistrate they might find themselves in trouble which they would regret when it was too late.

The next day we received a telephone call from the police to come up to the main police station. We went and there we were warned that if we demonstrated the police would break up the demonstration. We insisted that we were committed to it; it was going to take place. We had everything ready, banners written, slogans shining on them.

When we left the police station and were walking along Pretorius Street eastwards towards the market, we were met by Major van den Berg, chief of police in the Pretoria and district division. He stopped us and said that he had heard we were still intending to go on with our demonstration. We said that was correct, and he warned us that the police would break it up and we would be held responsible for whatever resulted from that. He left us and went his way and we went on with our mission.

On May the first that decision of ours still stood. At twelve o'clock sharp we were already at the market with all the banners, waiting for the workers to come along to start the march. The atmosphere was tense, the police were there in a full force to show strength. They were fully armed. Everyone could see them and their intentions were obvious. One o'clock struck. The presence of the police frightened the workers away. Very few gathered; we waited for more, but that was all we could get. At a quarter to two I announced that our demonstration had failed. It lacked support, therefore we were not going to demonstrate with so few people against such heavy odds. We dispersed and the police formed into lines and were marched back to the main police station.

I am sure that if the police had not gathered there to frighten the workers off I would have delivered a speech in Pretoria Church Square that day. I knew that the police would not have broken up our demonstration at that hour when Church Street was full of traffic and people were rushing for their lunch, Church Street being the main and fashionable shopping centre where many shop windows would have been broken and great damage done. We would have been arrested that day. We wanted it to happen so that we could bring the mayor of the city and his councillors to court, to ask them why we, as citizens, were not allowed to demonstrate in the city when Pretoria University students were free to do so when they demanded strict enforcement of Apartheid. One of the important files the police confiscated from our office in June that year was the one I called the international file, which contained copies of letters and replies from countries we had written to. When they found it, Chief Detective Inspector van der Berg, who was in charge of the raid, remarked, 'They are already in touch with the whole world.'

XXXIV Arrests

In June of that year we were still anxious to keep the spirit of the stay-at-home political strike alive. Some people in Johannesburg, like ourselves, who had been disappointed by Dr. Moroka's actions the year before, were still willing to go on with the African National Congress version of a stay-at-home on June the twenty-sixth. We pledged ourselves to organise the people of Pretoria to stay at home on that day. The organisation was poor at that time; our aim was only to make people understand that if there were improvements to be gained they would have to sacrifice themselves for them. Together with those in the City of Gold, we printed and roneoed a large number of leaflets, which we distributed widely in Pretoria. Some Indian friends joined us in an attempt to make the strike a success. They helped by conveying us in their cars to places we could not reach and also helped with the distribution of the leaflets. They were my friends Ramhtula Keshavjee, G. Sooboo and Sandie Nicker: all from well-known families in the Indian community of Pretoria.

On the twenty-fifth of June Ramhtula Keshavjee's car was loaded with a loudspeaker and a large quantity of leaflets and the three of them came along to me at Atteridgeville to help strengthen the morale of the people to stay at home the next day. To make the Indians and Africans feel that they are not the same, the laws of Apartheid forbid Indians to enter African locations without a permit from the superintendent. We had arranged with a staunch Congressman, Theodore Ngamana, to collect the car and leaflets from our friends outside the location so that he and I could distribute the leaflets and broadcast the last message through the loudspeaker in the evening. Theodore Ngamana drove the car while I broadcast the message. My voice was well known to the municipal police, Mr. Zimmerman the superintendent and the people of Atteridgeville. That evening we went all over the location distributing the leaflets while I broadcast the message urging the people to stay at home the next day. While we were doing that the Pretoria West police were called by Mr. Zimmerman to arrest our friends who were waiting outside the location for allowing us to use their car. While we were moving around in the car, which was still full of leaflets and some in our pockets, we were stopped by the superintendent with his municipal police and arrested. Without knowing how or why, we were joined by someone, Lucas Moleele, an African who was never in the campaign.

When we reached the municipal offices we found our Indian friends waiting there with the Pretoria West police. We were taken together in a black maria to Pretoria West police station, and there all of us were charged with inciting the people of Atteridgeville to break their contracts of employment by staying away from their work. I had heard before that Lucas Moleele was a police informer but had no evidence of it. While we were waiting in the station to be charged, I overheard one policeman saying to the other, 'Our man is also here,' and the other one said, 'Don't worry, we know all about it.' From that the allegations against Lucas Moleele were confirmed to me; that he was the police's man.

We all slept in the cells at Pretoria West police station. Lucas was drafted into the same cell as me. I knew then that I had to hold my tongue, but Lucas did not know what I had overheard about him. He tried to speak to impress me that he was more in favour of the stay-at-home strike than I was, but I told him that I was too tired, I needed to sleep. Early the next morning Lucas was called out. I only saw him again in court, where he told me that a charge against him was withdrawn against his will and he was angry about it.

When the court proceedings began I found that I was heavily indicted, and it was so arranged that if a conviction against me could be secured, then it would be easy to convict others. We had all pleaded not guilty. When that happened I looked round the courtroom to see whether there was anyone I knew who was brought in to testify that he or she did not go to work that day because I threatened them. There was no one. I decided to make that my defence.

Municipal police, all Africans, were the first to give evidence against me: that they saw me during the previous day distributing to the residents of Atteridgeville the leaflets displayed in court. Before that no one had talked about not going to work. When the superintendent's time came to give evidence he stressed firmly that he knew me well and that I was one of the influential people in Atteridgeville. My influence, he thought, could be harmful to people who were not mature enough to think for themselves. In the evening he said he listened to my broadcast for a long time before he called Pretoria West police to come along to help him. He feared that if nothing had been done to stop me, there might have been trouble in Atteridgeville the next day. Before he called the police he made an inspection of the whole location and found that every yard he visited was flooded with leaflets I had distributed, and everywhere in the streets my leaflets were lying about.

The case was before a man who later conducted the preliminary trial when I was arrested under the infamous Suppression of Communism Act with my colleague Stephen Tefu. While Mr. Zimmerman was giving evidence, the magistrate asked him whether I was a visitor at Atteridgeville or if I lived there. He replied that I was a registered tenant of Pretoria City Council in the location. I was surprised that at the end of his evidence the magistrate took up my defence before I could say it; that all that was brought before him were leaflets alleged to have been distributed by me. He went on to say that not a single person was produced in court as evidence that because of my influence he could not go to work that day. He followed that by saying that the municipal police gave evidence that they saw me distributing leaflets, but he could not understand why they did not take me with the leaflets to the superintendent or call the superintendent to see me distributing those leaflets. The superintendent himself, the magistrate went on, said I was a registered tenant of the council, that I lived in Atteridgeville, that every yard he saw was full of leaflets similar to the ones in court and the streets were also full of such leaflets. It was likely, he said, that as a resident I might have found them in my yard, or picked them up in the streets and put them in my pocket to read, and those may have been the reasons why they were found in my possession. He said that he found that the Crown case was not proved against me and the whole case fell to the ground.

While this was taking place I had no idea that the police and their superiors were busy framing against us an indictment under the Suppression of Communism Act. Our market meetings were going on week by week, and my attacks on Malan and his ministers were heard by those who attended our meetings and people who happened to pass the meeting place on Fridays at lunch-time. In Atteridgeville, the advisory board elections were getting near, and I had joined our men who were dissatisfied with the work of the current advisory board. I had contested other elections before, but failed to get elected. I was determined to get nearer to the city council's so-called Bantu affairs department, where I could ask for any councillor to be brought to our meetings and question him as to why they were so keen to reject the recommendations of the advisory board, after they had said they needed it in order to know the needs of the African inhabitants of Pretoria.

At that time my letters to overseas countries were going off week by week, and week by week we were receiving replies. A new international file was building up again. On the evening of the seventeenth of August nineteen-fifty-one, I held a meeting of the men with whom I had decided to contest the advisory board elections at Bantule Newclare, eight miles away from Atteridgeville. We were planning our action, and the way we were going to conduct our campaign against the board in power, which was well endowed with women: their best organisers were women. We did not finish our discussions until midnight. I travelled home in a taxi with other Atteridgeville men, not aware that the next night my bedroom would be a police cell. I arrived to find my wife worried, though she knew I was attending a meeting at Bantule. The next day I went to the office as usual, but Tefu failed to arrive at his customary time. At about half-past ten a worker entered the office to tell me that he saw Tefu being marched to the police station with men arrested for pass offences. I left at once to fetch Tefu. I found him before Jan van Rooyen, head of the pass squad, who warned us that unless we got ourselves new passes like everyone else we should always be arrested for not carrying them with us. He said that he was giving us a last chance to get ourselves fixed up at the influx control bureau. That was the turning-point.

Before this, in the period of our Pretoria market meetings, I drew up a petition and read it at one of the meetings. It said that we, the Africans in particular, did not recognise the government of the country elected by the minority; we considered their laws illegal; their parliament, from which the majority are barred, illegal; the act of Union constitution of South Africa, which ignores the majority and gives the minority the right and power to establish a European tribal government, illegal; and we demanded that a new convention be called, where all the inhabitants of the land would be represented, to draw up a new constitution which would be democratic and enable all adults to vote and to be voted for in general elections. In the petition I listed many points to show how undemocratic the Act of Union was and why a government elected under it should not be recognised. It was long and had many items and reasons.

My purpose in drawing it up was to indict the Malan government and others before it before the International Court of Justice at the Hague, Holland. As I read it, Tefu explained the contents to the audience. It was approved. At our office we roneoed many copies of it and sent one copy to a famous British barrister, D. N. Pritt, KC, asking him to be kind enough to act for us in presenting it before the International Court of Justice. Mr. Pritt was kind enough to write back acknowledging its arrival but advised that the International Court at the Hague would not deal with it because the court was set up to deal with disputes between governments. He advised us that the right place for the petition was the United Nations Organisation at Lake Success, New York. After the arrival of Mr Pritt's letter we wasted no time and forwarded the petition to Lake Success. That time Malan's government was at loggerheads with their judiciary, quarrelling about the removal of the Coloured people of the Cape from the voters' roll. Before we sent off our petition, newspapers published a picture of the men who drew up the South Africa Act,

298

and there was not a single non-European amongst them. We sent a few copies of the newspapers' pictures with the petition to strengthen our case that the dice had been loaded against us from the very beginning.

Several weeks later we received an acknowledgement of the arrival of the petition at the United Nations and the promise that it was receiving attention. We then felt it our duty to give it to the South African Press Association (SAPA) to publish, and it received publicity. When the gestapo raided our office, they took a copy of the petition, the letter from Mr. Pritt, and the correspondence from the United Nations Organisation in the first international file.

As we left Jan van Rooyen in the large police yard behind the main Pretoria police station, we saw one of the men, Detective Sergeant Visser, coming towards us. He stopped us and told us that he had been on his way to our office when he saw us talking in the police yard to the head of the pass raiders' squad. He opened the file he was carrying, gave us a warrant for our arrest to read, and then placed his hand on my shoulder, saying, 'I am arresting you under the Suppression of Communism Act.' He did the same thing to my colleague Tefu and invited us to follow him into the police station. As far as I know we were the first in the country to be arrested under that vicious Act. We were locked up in one cell and during our confinement we talked and discussed our future plans, but we were above all delighted that it had happened, that we were going to be used as guinea pigs and had a chance to show that the Suppression of Communism Act was not something which the people could not stand up against. Under it, if convicted, we faced ten years in prison.

We spent the whole day in that cell and it also became our bed-room. I don't know what Europeans' cells are like inside, but non-European cells are empty, bare, cement-floored, inhabited by lice and, at that time of the year when the weather was still cold, only three rough dark blankets were provided for each person. No furniture, no bed or mattress. The food, soft salty porridge, no bread, no tea or coffee. That was how we faced life in the cells at the hands of the police state in South Africa, the land of our birth, under the tribal government we did not choose, and the government we repeatedly said had no legal right to govern us or to arrest us. The next morning we were forced to clean our cell, and also to help wash the cell yard with water and a hosepipe.

Afterwards we were given prison breakfast, soft salty porridge of mealie meal. Later we were handcuffed, together with the rest who were arrested for pass and other offences, and marched to court, which is next to the police station. There we were told by the magistrate that we were arrested under the Suppression of Communism

Act; we were not going to be tried that day, the date for our preliminary examinations would be fixed later, but we were remanded in custody. We were told further that our bail was one hundred pounds each. Then we were removed from the dock to wait in the court cells for the black maria to take us at lunch-time with the convicted ones to central prison, Potgieter Street. We had our lunch that day in the main Pretoria prison and it was my first experience inside it, though I had always wanted to go there to see for myself what it was like. On arrival, after undergoing a thorough search and being given a prison card and number, we were ordered to strip naked and to go in groups under cold showers to wash our bodies; soda soap, no towels, to be dried by the sun. I protested and was taken to the chief's office and there he told me that I was in prison, I had lost my liberty, I was subject to prison regulations and was there to do as I was told.

After that we were taken to prison cells to wait for our date to be fixed. The order was that I should be separated from Tefu. In the prison cells, as in the police cells where we spent the first night, we had no furniture, no bed, no mattress, cement floors and three blankets. I cannot remember the measurements of the cells, but we slept twelve in each cell. We were locked up in the cells in the afternoons at half past four after the last meal of soft salty mealie meal porridge, with two buckets, one as our toilet and the other as our fountain for drinking water. I don't know what European prison cells were like, but prisoners who cleaned them told us that they had beds and furniture. In the mornings we had to carry our buckets out to empty them, clean our cells in turns and in turns wash the yard with hosepipe and water. We used the yard for sitting down. We were not allowed to talk until after lunch at twelve, when we were locked in again to enable the warders, Africans and Europeans, to have their lunch. That gave us a chance, Tefu and I, to share a cell in order to discuss our case and future plans.

Each week we were visited by a high prison officer who asked each one for complaints. Tefu and I complained to him that we were locked up with others who were not arrested for the same thing, that we were political prisoners; we should be given our own cell, given books to read and not forced to work in prison, since we had not been convicted. He said that he would look up the rules and when he came next time he would give us a reply. When he came the following week he told us that we were not political prisoners so we were subject to the same treatment as others, but he had ordered that we should be given books to read. When the books came they were books about dogs, ships, hunters and things we were not interested in, and I personally could not understand. When he came again we told him that we were given books we didn't want and asked if we could tell him the sort of books we would like to read. His reply was, 'You asked for books, you were given books. If you don't like them it's your problem.' We withdrew our request.

In prison, awaiting trial, we were forced to go under cold showers with soda soap and no towels twice a week. We were allowed visitors once a week and we could be brought something to eat from outside, but we had to show everything to the warder. We could write letters but they were to be closed and sent off by the chief officer. Twice a week, on Wednesdays and Sundays, our last meal of soft salty porridge was mixed with carrots and pieces of meat. One Saturday, when it was my turn to join others in washing the yard, I refused. The warder took me to the chief, who asked me the reason. I replied that I was not yet convicted. That earned me solitary confinement in a small cell upstairs with no food, only water, until the next day.

On two occasions when we were waiting for our day to be fixed we applied to be taken to the magistrate's court to plead for our bail to be reduced. Each time in court the magistrate told us that we knew the bail; if we paid it we could be let out. Towards the end of August we received papers from the public prosecutor's office that our examination would start on the third of September, nineteen-fifty-one. At last we knew that our test was on the way and we got ready for it. When that day came, we left with others in the black maria for the battle to begin. We found Detective Sergeant Visser with his men, African and Europeans, ready to read the notes they had prepared on speeches we had delivered at our market meetings.

We had decided not to seek legal defence, we wanted to conduct the case ourselves. There were lawyers in Pretoria and Johannesburg who would have come to our aid free of charge if we had asked, but we avoided that, knowing that they would conduct it on purely legal grounds. To us it was a political struggle which must be waged on political fields. When we saw Sergeant Visser with his men, each carrying a notebook, I said to Tefu, 'We must pull every one of them down with us.' The proceedings opened; they began to read their notes, which refreshed our minds; some of them made us wonder whether in fact we did deliver such brilliant speeches, and it strengthened our determination to fight and to be ready to receive the consequences.

After each man had read his notes we took him up on them and asked if there was anything untrue in what we said at our meeting; that we were not voters, that we were discriminated against, that we were forced to carry passes when others were free of them, that we were the majority in the country, that the Act of Union was drawn up to deny us true citizenship and treat us as though we were people from outside imposing ourselves on the Europeans uninvited, that our adults were called boys and girls regardless of whether they had grey hair and were over a hundred years old. Every one of them, Africans and Europeans, agreed that everything we said was so in South Africa.

Every day a new group was brought in to give evidence on their notes. We were surprised to see that some of the men we had thought were newspaper reporters when we saw them at our meetings, were expert shorthand writers from various government departments. We adopted the same system with them too. On the last day, which at the time we did not know was the last, the fifth of September, a man I once asked at a meeting to write down everything I said, thinking that he was from the newspapers, came to give evidence from his notes. Before he began he was asked by the prosecutor to explain his position to the court. He gave his name as Mr. Khoury, chief short-hand writer of the supreme court, Pretoria. He went on to say that most of the supreme court records were done by him, that his accuracy was never challenged and that he was a graduate of Pretoria University. When he read his notes, I found there were gaps which he read as dot, dot, dot. He had left some words out, for instance when I talked about Malan's mother and mine.

As an acclaimed expert, I knew that Mr. Khoury was brought in to level the whole circus. I said to Tefu, 'He is my target, I am going to make him angry first and then confuse him.' When he had finished, the first question I asked him was 'What are you?' Angrily he shouted at me, 'What do you mean, what am I?' The magistrate told him, 'You can't ask him a question, tell him what you are.' He said he had already told the court that he was a shorthand writer of the supreme court. He was heavily suntanned, he suspected that I thought he was a Coloured man. I then told him that I wanted to know whether he was a European. Again he replied angrily, 'Of course I am a European.' I asked him whether he was born in the country; he said he was. I asked him his age and he told me. I asked him whether he was a voter; he said he was. I asked him if he voted in the nine-teen-forty-eight election which brought Malan into power; he said he had. I asked him whether he voted when Pretoria city council was elected – he said he did – and whether he voted when the Transvaal provincial council was elected, and he said he did.

I then reminded him that in his notes he mentioned that I said we were not voters, that everybody elected by Europeans only was illegal and had no legal right over us. He agreed. I asked whether, in any of the elections he participated in, he voted with Africans or non-Europeans. He said he did not. I asked him whether at any time he saw them voting. He replied that he had never seen them voting. Lastly I asked him whether he knew that they were voters at all? He said he did not know. I then drove him into admissions that what I said in his notes was correct and true – he said it was. I said, 'So you agree that I did not invent anything but stated facts'. He kept quiet. The magistrate asked him to reply, and his reply was 'Yes.'

I reminded him again that under oath he had said that his records were never challenged, but before he replied I said, 'I am challenging them today.' I asked him about the gaps in his notes and he said they stood for words he thought silly and not worth recording. I asked him about my speech about my mother and Malan's, and asked him why he did not record the speech in full. He said he found it silly and irrelevant. I asked him to admit that because of the gaps his whole record was unreliable and not correct, to which he said it was for the court to say. I left him feeling happy that I had demolished him. In the end we were told that it was the last day of the examination.

Having not been able to pay a hundred pounds bail each, Pretoria central prison continued to be our home. We were taken back there to wait for our real trial. The cells there, with cold, cement floors, a small window at the back with iron bars, thick steel doors, no mattress, no bed and no furniture except the two buckets, continued to be our bedrooms. None of us had ever had a hundred pounds in his possession, or held that amount in our hands.

One day towards the middle of October I was called out to the offices and taken in a police van to the magistrate's court, where I was taken down into the cells but not given any reason why I was there. At about twelve o'clock I asked the keeper of the cells why I was brought there, and he answered that, like me, he did not know the reason; all he knew was that he had to unlock the cell, put me in and wait for the next order. As long as he got no further orders he would not ask why but only make sure that I was there. I had lunch and late in the afternoon he let me out. A policeman took me to the office, where I signed papers and was told that my bail had been paid. From there I had to walk back to prison to collect my possessions. I found that everything of mine was held ready, and after checking it and confirming that it was all there, I signed for it. I was led to the main gate and released. When I stepped on to the pavement I had a guilty feeling that I was deserting my colleague Stephen Tefu, but there was nothing I could do.

I hurried to catch an Atteridgeville bus. Many people looked at me as though I was a stranger, someone they had not seen for a long time. Not a single person spoke to me, but I noticed that those who did not see me were made aware of my presence by others. When I got home I found my wife waiting, and my two children cried with joy when they saw me. My bail had been paid by an Indian shopkeeper, Mr. Abdool Rahman, who had been patronised by my wife's family for many years. The next day I left for our office to see what correspondence had been coming in since August the eighteenth when we were arrested. I found a pile of letters, some from abroad. After reading them all I left for Lady-Selborne to see Tefu's mother, with whom he lived, and sister, to see whether, with their help, we could find bail for Tefu. I did not worry the old lady about the bail, but went to his sister, who with her husband had a stand and a house·

After I had convinced Tefu's sister that our trouble would not involve her and her husband in any way, she left with me for Mr. M. Shapiro's shop where her husband had worked for many years, to ask the husband to ask Mr. Shapiro to help with the bail money. The husband was a bit nervous at first, but I convinced him, too, that our trouble would not engulf them in any way. Mr. Shapiro knew Tefu and when approached did not take long to feel sympathy. He promised to pay the bail the next day. So I spent only one free day without Tefu, who was also released from prison on the second day. When he came out I was there to welcome him. On the way to the Lady-Selborne buses I told him everything I had done since he last saw me.

After seeing him to Lady-Selborne I went to Church Street to see some friends who did not know that we were out on bail. I met two African girls, and while they were admiring me and saying how glad they were to see me, not very far away I saw Detective Inspector van der Berg, the man who had been in charge of the raiding of our office and homes, standing looking at me as though he did not know that I was out on bail. When his eyes and mine clashed he quickly walked away.

We did not open our office until the following week, and suspended our market meetings until we knew our fate. Many people and workers had thought that we were finished, and were astonished to see us carrying on with our work in the office. Our determination to help the workers with pass difficulties and other matters connected with their grievances at work continued. Those who had told our members that we were finished were disappointed but could not help admiring our bravery. We avoided going to see the lawyers in Pretoria who we knew would be ready to take up our defence free of charge for the reasons already stated.

As time went on I said to Tefu, 'Tefu, we are going to be convicted and we know already that we shall be imprisoned for ten years. During our trial we must throw mud about, throw stones, which will remain in the minds of our people for a long time.'

I suggested that when the time came for us to defend ourselves, I should ask for Dr. Malan to be brought to court; I wanted to question him in my defence. After him I would ask for Verwoerd, then Eric Louw. 'You,' I said to Tefu, 'should ask for Charles Robert Swart, Ben Schoeman and Dr. Dönges.' Tefu agreed fully with my suggestions. I then said to him, 'Our requests will be rejected, but we will have scored a big triumph because the newspapers will report our requests and the court's rejection, and that will strengthen our people to resist further. Newspaper men,' I went on, 'may come along to interview us to find out why we wanted those men to be brought to court, and that will be our chance to tell the whole world about the police and fascist state we live under. Our request will be so dramatic that newspapers will find them impossible to suppress.

'The court's refusal to grant our requests will enable us also to say that we were denied justice and that our case was prejudiced and that we were not given a fair trial.' Tefu was greatly attracted to my suggestions. I said to him, 'In this we stand to lose nothing and to gain a great deal. If those men could be brought to court we should expose them before their admirers, we should show them that they are not untouchable as many of them think, that they are mere human beings like anyone else and not as clever as some of them think. We shall have proved that the court protected them from being exposed, and that when they are being challenged on their policies and convictions they would fall apart like a house of cards.'

I then said to Tefu, 'We have planned our secret weapon and we must keep it secret. We must not even tell our families about it; they will be frightened that, instead of us trying to get out of trouble, we are trying to do a foolish thing, driving ourselves deeper into trouble. They will try to bring in people they think can convince us that we are embarking on a foolish path and the whole secret will be known before we reach the court room. We don't know,' I said to my colleague, 'what the police and the attorney-general's office are planning against us. They must not know what we are planning for our defence. They may surprise us; we must surprise them too.' We agreed fully that our families and none of our friends should not know about our secret weapon.

As I foresaw, our market meetings and the biting speeches we made there gave our people confidence in themselves and removed many of the fears they had had for a long time. Our arrest and the stand we made in court inspired them enormously. At that time there had occurred within the African National Congress a movement of young people called the African National Congress youth league. The young people's wing of Congress was formed by students and others of that age who felt that the older leadership in Congress was not militant; Congress had in fact become a mere debating society with no programme of action. Nelson Mandela was one of those who took part in founding the youth league.

When I returned from prison I found that one of them at Atteridgeville had saved a copy of their roneoed newspaper called *The Lodestar* for me to see. There was an article in it which described how we conducted our case at the preliminary trial in the magistrates court

305

and how we held our chins up in face of great difficulties and odds. The article ended with these words: 'Never before in the records of people struggling for emancipation have so few served so many so well: Tefu and Mokgatle.' That was the first realisation for me that, though we had no way of knowing whether our actions inspired our people, at least they were appreciated. I treasured that copy, and kept it among my papers, which were later confiscated by the police in nineteen-fifty-six during the great raid on many leaders and people all over the country. The results of that raid are well known; from it resulted the famous Treason Trial which took four years without any of those who were accused being convicted. I was already in England at the time. The Europeans-only tribal government knew I was not in the country, their police knew I was beyond their reach, but my house at Atteridgeville was raided and my books and papers taken away. My wife and children were still in the country at the time. If I had been in the country I would have been amongst those who were tortured by the police during the Treason Trial.

In December nineteen-fifty-one, when the African National Congress held its annual conference in Bloemfontein, Dr. James Moroka was removed from the presidency and Chief Albert Luthuli was elected president-general. Because of the influence the youth league had in Congress, a resolution was passed launching the defiance campaign of nineteen-fifty-two.

The defiance campaign resolution was weakened because it was said that the campaign was against the unjust laws, as though there was a single just law in South Africa which applied to non-Europeans, particularly the African people. The pass law and night curfews were the first selected to be defied. People were also told to sit everywhere in parks on benches reserved for Europeans only, and to ignore (at public places like the railways and the post office) counters and entrances reserved for Europeans only. They were told to go in and demand service at those places or counters. The people were rightly told to court arrest, to go to prison, be convicted and fined. They were not to pay fines or seek aid from lawyers. The campaign was weakened further in that the people were told to volunteer, and Congress committees all over the country were to select volunteers and send them into places they thought ought to be defied. We supported the campaign but complained that if those methods were to be used the people would suffer and gain nothing in the end. We argued that when the people had been told fully what the campaign entailed and how much suffering they would have to go through, if they came forward to volunteer, selection of volunteers was not necessary; the people should be instructed to go into action, to defy in large numbers. We pointed out that the police in all the cities and towns would not be able to cope with all the people, the courts would not be in a position to deal with large numbers of arrested people, prisons could not accommodate them, many employers of African labour would be without workers, chaos would result and the whole machinery of Apartheid would break down in clear view of the world audience. Our advice and protests were ignored by Congress leaders.

The campaign was so popular and so widely supported that everywhere that Congressmen held meetings to recruit volunteers, hundreds and thousands of people of all ages gave themselves up to defy the government they had not elected and the cruel laws made against them and applied solely to them. Workers left their jobs, students interrupted their studies to make the campaign a success. But hundreds and thousands were *turned away* by Congressmen and few were sent to defy, enabling the police to cope with them and the courts to cut them down with ease, and new groups were not sent in until others were released from prison.

I remember talking to a group of Congress youth league men at Atteridgeville. They were holding their meeting next door to where I lived and it was very well attended. Nelson Mandela was national volunteer-in-chief, which meant that he had to go all over the country to see that committees were formed and that the people were defying everywhere. I was not a youth leaguer, but I asked for permission to come along to say a few words and it was kindly granted me. I said to them in Mandela's presence that if they were serious and wanted to break the Apartheid machine, the right way to break it was to throw into its spokes, its wheels and all its parts everything they could – sand, rags, stones – to jam it. By that, I told them, I meant that hundreds and thousands of volunteers should flood police stations, courts and prisons. I told them, further, that their methods were not aiding the people, but Malan's government. I said that their actions were like throwing things into a machine, then allowing the owners to dismantle it, clean it, sharpen it and put it together again before throwing in another thing. My advice was in vain.

Wherever I met Congress leaders I protested. One day I went with Tefu to see some volunteers being dealt with in Pretoria magistrates court. When they came into the court from the cells, a lawyer appeared and told the magistrate that he was appearing for all the accused. He was Mr. Sita, the son of Nana Sita, leader of the Indian Congress in Pretoria. I lost my temper and shouted in court, saying, 'They are volunteers, why bring in a lawyer to defend them?' The magistrate warned me that if I repeated my outburst I would be charged with contempt of court. Mr. Sita was sent by Congress in Pretoria to defend them. He told the magistrate that all his clients pleaded guilty. They were all convicted, fined and sent to prison. That was how the African National Congress conducted the defiance of the so-called unjust laws in nineteen-fifty-two. If Congress had really wanted to break the Apartheid machine, the chance was in their hands in that year. The people were ready but not mobilised. So an onslaught was never launched against the police and fascist state headed by Dr. Malan.

At the beginning of January nineteen-fifty-two, we received papers from the attorney-general's office at the palace of justice, Pretoria, informing us that our trial was scheduled to start on the twenty-second of February that year. At last we knew that it was coming and that we should get ourselves ready for our defence. Newspapers reported the date on which we were to be tried, and what remained was to wait to see what would happen that day. We expected nothing but conviction and ten years in prison.

In the face of all that, we continued with our trade union as well as communicating with the outside world. Some of my letters reached the American embassy in Pretoria requesting the ambassador to forward them to the United States government, pleading for mercy for Julius Rosenberg and his wife Ethel.

One afternoon early in February, while we were carrying on with our work in the office, a car with a Johannesburg registration number pulled up in front of our office. Out of it came a man who at the time of writing this book is serving a life sentence in prison, Abram Fischer, accompanied by a man who was the general secretary of the Communist party of South Africa, Moses Mauane Kotane. They had come to see us about our trial. They told us that they had discussed our trial with other people in Johannesburg and felt that we should be defended. They asked us if we accepted that offer, and we did. They then informed us that two progressive lawyers, Vernon Berrange and S. Slovo, were ready to take on the defence. We knew both of them very well and knew that if we were defended by them there would be fireworks at our trial. Mr. Fischer then gave us each a pound for fares to Johannesburg.

On the following day we were in the train on our way to Johannesburg to see Messrs. Berrange and Slovo to prepare our defence. This was the fifteenth of February, so that when the funeral of King George the Sixth was taking place at Windsor, we were deep in discussion with the men who had volunteered to defend us free of charge. We found that they had in their possession written records of speeches we made at Pretoria Market and went through them with us. In one of them I remember Mr. Berrange reading a passage to me in which I said that Malan's government was a Dutch government. He asked me whether I still stood by that. I did not give him a quick reply; I was still thinking what to say, but he laughed and said he didn't know why I was hesitating to reply, because it was nothing but the truth. All its members were from the Afrikaans-speaking section of the population of South Africa. As lawyers do, in the end they did not promise us anything out of the ordinary, but said that they would do what they could to see that we got a fair trial. They then told us that at the trial Mr. Berrange would be looking after me and Mr. Slovo would be looking after Tefu. The trial was only seven days away. We returned home to wait for the day.

On the twenty-first of February, the day before the trial, my aunt arrived in Pretoria in great distress, having travelled by train more than eighty miles from where I was born to see me. She told me that the purpose of her visit was to see me for the last time. I asked her, why for the last time? She said that people who were arriving from Johannesburg and Pretoria in my tribal birthplace were all saying that I was going to be sentenced to death and hanged. I laughed, and I don't know why but I said to her, 'I know you were born in a Christian family and that you read the Bible a lot. In the Bible,' I said, 'there are two stories which I think would put you at rest. They are the stories of Shadrach, Meshach and Abednego. They were thrown into the fire,' I said, 'but never burnt, because they stuck to their convictions. The other one,' I said, 'is that of Daniel, he was thrown into the lions' den, but the lions licked him instead of destroying him because he didn't deny his conviction. If,' I said, 'the two stories are true, my conviction and the truth I speak will stop them sentencing me to death. My lawyer,' I continued, 'will cover me with his legal gown and carry me out of that court without a scratch.' She laughed and said, 'I wonder why you didn't become a priest.'

The next day, the day of the trial, I left Atteridgeville with my wife and some sympathisers, and Tefu left Lady-Selborne with his sister and some sympathisers, for the palace of justice to be thrown into the lions' den. When we arrived our lawyers were already there, although they were from Johannesburg. Mr. Slovo was accompanied by his wife, Miss Ruth First, who was a newspaper reporter. The police were also already there waiting in the corridors with ther files, all of us waiting for the hour to strike. We still did not know what line of action our lawyers were going to take. We were scheduled to be tried by Mr. Justice Roper, the man who, with Mr. Justice van der Heever, was picked by Smuts' government to try the central committee of the Communist party in Johannesburg. I cannot remember who was to prosecute; I don't think it was Mr. Lutge himself, the attorney-general of the Transvaal division, but one of his aides.

When the trial opened I was called to lead Tefu into the dock.

When I was about to be asked whether I pleaded guilty or not, my lawyer, Vernon Berrange, rose to his feet to tell Mr. Justice Roper that his position was made difficult by the prosecution because they had not supplied him with what he asked. He said that he had written to the attorney-general's office asking to be supplied with the charge indicating what crime his client had committed, but he was still not supplied with the charge; therefore he found it difficult to join hands with the prosecution to proceed with the trial his client was brought to stand. The judge then asked the prosecutor whether Mr. Berrange was right and that he had not been supplied with what he asked for, namely the nature of the crime. The prosecutor admitted it but, like Mr. Lutge at the Communist trial, asked the court to proceed, promising that as he unfolded the case Mr. Berrange would soon know the crime.

Mr. Justice Roper found himself within the legal fence. He adjourned the trial for one hour to enable the attorney-general's office to supply Mr. Berrange with the information he had asked for. Mr. Berrange, like Dr. Lowen at the Communist trial, had thrown a spanner into Malan's legal machine. At the end of the adjournment, the judge asked the prosecutor whether Mr. Berrange had been told the charge, but got the answer that the charge had not been supplied; nonetheless it was requested that the trial should proceed. Thereupon Mr. Justice Roper dismissed the trial and directed that we must not be arrested. If that was to happen, an application was to be made to him and a complete new case started.

Our trial ended before it began. The police who came in full force to give accounts of what they heard and wrote at our market meetings returned to their stations and offices without having opened a single one of their files. Tefu and I were there, two advocates of peace, liberty, fraternity, harmony, and one South African nation, regardless of colour, language, sex or creed. We were put there to face a trial which seemed to many like a house which could not be penetrated, built by strong and clever men who claimed to be pure, chosen and superior. The indictment had seemed so powerful to many people that they saw no way for us to escape from it. But our lawyers came along to demonstrate in full view of everyone that the house which seemed so strong and solid was fragile, and the men who built it were not superior to or cleverer than anyone else. In less than two hours it lay collapsed and scattered about in pieces.

My prediction to my aunt had become true. Berrange wrapped me in his gown, Slovo wrapped Tefu in his gown and they went out of the palace of justice without us having been touched by Malan's men who had prepared their case from September nineteen-fifty-one to February nineteen-fifty-two. Many people who had come to see us for the last time could not believe their own ears when they heard that Malan's case had collapsed, and many who did not have the chance to be in the palace of justice with us could not believe their eyes when they saw us moving in the streets of Pretoria as free men.

Outside the palace of justice the man who was in charge of our case, Detective Sergeant Visser, came along, offered me his hand and said, 'Mokgatle, you have beaten me. This was my last case in the South African police force. As a matter of fact,' he continued, 'I am no longer in the police force, I have retired. I am now security chief at van der Byl Park steelworks in Vereeniging.' He told me that he had hoped he would start his retirement having put me away in prison for a long time. 'All I can say,' said Mr. Visser, 'is God bless the detective who will be assigned to look after you.' I listened to him all the time but uttered no word. He left and went his way and I went my way. Later Detective van der Merwe was assigned to look after me; he once complained, when he came to check up on me, that he could not go to play rugby in Australia because of me.

XXXV Banning Orders

When Malan and his tribal government heard that their case had collapsed like a house of cards they fumed with anger and launched another attack on us, again under the vicious Suppression of Communism Act. One afternoon in March that year the *Star*, one of the leading Johannesburg newspapers, came out with a report that a Cape Town African, Mr. Ngwevela, Stephen Tefu, N. H. Nyadioe-Mokgatle and Mr. Solly Sachs had been banned from attending gatherings and ordered to resign from their trade unions and other organisations for a period of two years. The *Star* went on to say that the bannings were made under the Suppression of Communism Act. This was the first time we knew that we had been banned and ordered to resign from our trade unions.

Two days later Detective Inspector van der Berg, with Detective van der Merwe and an African detective, Gabashane, arrived at our office to deliver the banning orders issued and signed by Malan's minister of justice, Charles Robert Swart. They were made and signed in Cape Town. As we received them we were made to sign for them.

The contents of the orders were that we were forbidden to attend public gatherings other than social and religious gatherings throughout the country for two years. Further, we were ordered to resign from the African General Workers' Union and the Pretoria Non-European Distributive Workers' Union and never to take part in their activities. We were further ordered to resign from the African National Congress and never to take part in its activities. That was how Malan, fearing the truth we were delivering at the Pretoria market meetings, muzzled us for two full years. I decided again that, since Malan's government did not make us trade unionists, they should not be allowed to drive us out so easily. I roneoed leaflets again, explaining to the workers in Pretoria that we had been banned from meetings for two years, that we had been ordered to resign from the two trade unions we were running, but announcing also that we had formed the Federated African Trade Unions of South Africa and the office was still at 56 Potgieter Street. We carried on.

I began to realise that more and more hardships were on the way. I began to write letters to all the organisations we had contacted before, telling them that our situation had worsened and asking for financial aid to enable us to leave the country to seek political asylum.

In October of that year I suggested to Tefu that, since the African National Congress defiance campaign was on, there was no reason why we should not defy Swart's banning orders. We decided to go back to Pretoria Market and hold a public meeting in defiance of Malan's orders. We roneoed leaflets again and distributed them widely in Pretoria, telling the workers and the people that we should be speaking from our platform at the market on Friday. That was the last Friday of the month.

At half-past twelve that day we were standing there waiting for the people to gather. By one o'clock the whole place was already covered with people who had come to hear us again. The police came in force, fully armed, but their presence did not frighten the people. At five minutes past one, when I began to speak, Tefu interpreting, the crowd was so large that I had to stand on a bench so that all could see me and hear what I had to say. Police officers in cars were also present at the meeting. I did not finish three minutes' speaking when a police officer, who told me that he was Major van der Herden, accompanied by other officers, called on me to stop, put his hand on my shoulder and said he was arresting us for defying the minister's banning orders. The crowd wanted to fight rather than let them take us away, but realising that the police were heavily armed and were going to shoot the people, I asked him to let me talk to the people to calm them down.

I appealed to the people not to fight, showed them that the police were heavily armed and would shoot them. 'Let them take us, they are taking us nowhere but to a house like the ones you are going to sleep in tonight. Prison is a house. There is no reason for you to die', I emphasised, 'because we are being taken to a house. Go home to plan how to get us released,' I ended. We were taken into police cars and driven off to the main police station to be charged. That night a police cell was our bedroom again. The following morning, Saturday, we appeared in court. Our case was remanded for a week and our bail was fixed at fifty pounds each. We had no money, so Pretoria central prison became our home again. We lived there for two weeks before our friend Ramhtula Keshavjee came along again to bail us out to wait for our trial.

During that time of waiting I went to see one of my trusted friends, George Findlay, QC, a well-known and highly respected barrister, for advice. He advised me that we ought to have legal defence because the character of our case had changed. I agreed wth him, but asked him to wait for our decision because I had not discussed the matter of defence with my colleague Stephen Tefu. When I told Tefu of my visit to Mr. Findlay and his advice, he agreed that we should be defended. We both went to see Mr. Findlay to tell him that we agreed that legal defence was necessary this time. He then told us to come and see him after three days, as he would try to get us an attorney who would take up our defence. When we saw him the second time he told us that Mr. George Aitcheson, of the firm of Aitcheson and Versfeld, had agreed to defend us free of charge. We were to go to his office to see him.

Mr. George Aitcheson was an experienced attorney, well advanced in age, and one of the citizens of Pretoria who had been working for many years for better relationships between Africans and Europeans. He was a member of the Pretoria Council of Europeans and Africans, a body which was mainly engaged in social work and in attempts to influence the city council to provide the non-Europeans of the city with better houses as well as sports facilities. He was one of those whom the Africans called sympathetic and progressive men.

In November of that year we were brought before the regional court, and Mr. Aitcheson was there with us. I cannot remember the actual words he spoke in our defence, but he put up a powerful fight. In the end we were convicted and given nine months' sentences, suspended for three years. That meant that if we defied Mr. C. R. Swart's orders before the end of the three-year period, we would be sent to prison for nine months. I appealed against the sentence and conviction, but Tefu saw no point in appealing. In December we lost our office at Potgieter Street, and we were without one until January nineteen-fifty-three, when we got another office in Vermeulen Street, next to a tea-room in a poor European area. Not very far from our office was a Chinese grocer's shop, which meant that in such an area non-Europeans could trade. When we left Potgieter Street I went to the post office to sign a form that all mail addressed to our old office should be forwarded to 253 Vermeulen Street, where we used to meet our members. In January, when we got an office, I went back to the post office to sign another form directing that all mail for the African General Workers' Union and the Pretoria Non-European Distributive Workers' Union be forwarded to our new address. But the police had been watching us all the time. We were acting openly for our members but using the letterheads of the Federated African Trade Unions of South Africa. We had also printed new membership cards which we issued to members. Because the banning orders did not forbid us to form or work for the new organisation, they did not know how to act to prove that we were still defying Malan's minister of justice's banning orders.

During January my appeal was heard in the supreme court, before the president of the Transvaal division, sitting with another judge, and I lost the appeal. I was back at the conviction and sentence passed by the regional magistrate.

After lunch on the ninth of February nineteen-fifty-four, Tefu and

I left the office to buy some papers in the city, not knowing that on that day our arrest was on the way. In Church Street, as we passed the general post office, detectives in two cars who had been sent out to collect us, saw us, but by the time they reached the post office building we were entering Church Square. They moved fast round the square, stopped at the eastern entrance, got out of their cars and came into the square to meet us. They were two Europeans and two Africans. I saw them first and made Tefu aware of them. They took us in their cars back to our office, where they showed us a warrant to search and to seize documents. Files, letters and copies of letters I had written for the African General Workers' Union and the Pretoria Non-European Distributive Union were found, as well as the new international file I had been building up. They took these as well as the typewriter we were using, and asked us to accompany them to Maritime House, the detective headquarters. There we were arrested for still defying the banning orders. The next day we appeared in court, and were given twenty-five pounds bail.

Pretoria central prison was our home for two weeks. In the middle of the second week we were taken to court, where we were remanded until the twenty-sixth of May. An order was made by the regional court magistrate that, if our bail was paid, we should report to the central police station every Saturday at eleven o'clock. On the Saturday morning of the second week I was called to the prison office, where I found my friend Ramhtula Keshavjee waiting to take me home by car. He had paid my bail. That weekend I did not spend in prison with Tefu. First Ramhtula took me to his parents' home, where I was given an Indian meal, then to Atteridgeville. No one knew I was coming home and my wife was surprised to see me arrive with Ramhtula.

Ramhtula was a fearless man; location regulations required him to enter with a permit, but he never asked for one whenever he came to Atteridgeville to see me. He was so light in complexion that he looked very much whiter than some of those who were beating their chests proclaiming that they were white. When he called for me at central prison the warders took him for a European, called him 'Sir', something a non-European never got in South Africa, and took him into the European waiting room to wait for me. Outside he said, 'They thought I was a European.' We just laughed it off.

On Monday Ramhtula raised twenty-five pounds from some Indian friends, and both of us went to bail Tefu in Ramhtula's name. I don't know what had happened to Tefu after I left him the previous week-end, but I noticed that he was not the man I knew. His enthusiasm had undergone a change. After seeing him off to Lady-Selborne I went to see George Findlay, and again he arranged

315

that Mr. George Aitcheson should defend us. Two days later, when I told Tefu about it, he remarked that he was capable of defending himself; he saw no point in defence being arranged for him without his consent. His remarks opened my eyes to the fact that Tefu was reaching breaking point. We went together to see Mr. Aitcheson and found him delighted to have a chance of defending us again, still free of charge. That was generous of the man. While we were waiting for our trial, Tefu kept complaining that he was not satisfied with Mr. Aitcheson's defence, he was not aggressive enough; our case, instead of being a political one, was being turned into a purely legal one. At times he threatened to ask Mr. Aitcheson to withdraw from defending him, until one day I angrily said, 'Why don't you? What are you waiting for?'

Our third arrest brought to the surface Tefu's reluctance to carry on with me. During the period of our reporting to the police on Saturdays at eleven o'clock, since we came from different areas, we had arranged to meet at a certain place and from there go together into the police station to show ourselves. Our agreement was that whoever got there first must wait for the other to arrive. One day I got there, found that my friend had not arrived, and as usual waited for him to come. I waited in vain, and at about quarter to twelve I went alone, thinking that something might have happened to him. It was after twelve when I entered the police station, and the sergeant to whom we always presented ourselves asked me where I had been; my mate reported earlier at the right time, did I think that I could report at my own time? I was surprised but made an excuse that I missed my usual bus, whereupon the sergeant warned me not to be late again and to remember that I was under a court order to report in time.

The following week, on Monday, when I asked Tefu what happened, why hadn't he come to our usual spot, he told me that he had not wanted to go there; after all I knew where the police station was, and the time. That cleared the clouds for me; I knew that my association with Tefu had reached a decisive stage and that we were travelling through a rocky land in our political journey. On the day of our trial in May, in the court corridor in front of many people, and in Mr. Aitcheson's presence, Tefu remarked that he was not interested in legal assistance. He preferred a political trial to the one forced upon him in which a lawyer would plead for mercy for him. I was disappointed, and Mr. Aitcheson, who was hurt by his remarks, said to him, 'Look here, Tefu, I am not forcing myself on you. If you don't want me to defend you, say so now, I shall withdraw. But if you want me to carry on, I shall conduct the case my way, not your way.' Faced with such a dilemma, Tefu did not ask Mr. Aitcheson to withdraw.

316

We went in, the case started, and Mr. Aitcheson defended us both his way. The police gave evidence about what they had found at our office, producing letters they had found to support their evidence that we were still carrying on working for the trade unions we were banned from. Mr. Aitcheson went for them one by one in cross-examination. The last witness I was surprised to see, was a man flown from Cape Town from the so-called department of justice to read copies of the banning orders served on us.

In his defence Mr. Aitcheson took the line that we were not carrying on with the work of the trade unions mentioned in the indictment and the orders read by the man from Cape Town. He said that the African General Workers' Union and the Pretoria Non-European Distributive Workers' Union, from which we were banned, were not the same as the unions we had organised and worked for at 56 Potgieter Street. We were at that time working for and organising the Federated African Trade Unions of South Africa, an entirely new body, in an entirely new office. He challenged the Crown to show that we were in fact banned from running such an organisation. He read a leaflet I had drafted after receiving the banning order, one of the many we distributed widely in Pretoria, telling the workers that we were banned from working for them by Malan's government and his minister of justice. He submitted that those leaflets amounted to our resignation from those trade unions. He went on to say that since we were also banned from gatherings, we could not call public meetings to dissolve those unions. The leaflets, Mr. Aitcheson pointed out, were the only possible way left to us to dissolve those unions. In conclusion he demanded our discharge saying that a *bona fide* case had not been proved against us.

In passing judgment, the regional magistrate rejected his contention and said that it was established beyond doubt that we were carrying on defying authority and challenging the banning orders. Things being as they were, he said that the Crown's case was proved, and he had to find us guilty. He convicted us and sentenced us to nine months in prison suspended for three years. With that our third trial in Pretoria ended. Mr. Aitcheson had done his best for us, giving us the use of his time and services, his office and stationery free of charge.

The end of our third trial also brought to an end my association with Stephen Sondag Tefu, my colleague since nineteen-forty-eight. While we were waiting for the trial, the police frightened our landlord, the tea-room owner next door, saying that he was endangering his own licence and position by allowing us to continue to use his premises for work we were banned from doing. He gave us thirty days' notice to leave, and we asked an African tailor at 253 Vermeulen Street to keep some office furniture in his place for us until the trial was over, and then, if we did not go to prison, we would look for a place and collect it. There were a small table, a small second-hand desk, two chairs, and two benches on which people sat when they came to see us. There was also a wooden cupboard for our stationery and files. The typewriter had been impounded at the detective headquarters.

That same month, May, our banning orders had come to an end. After the trial I stayed at Atteridgeville for two full days without going to the city. I was heavily engaged in thinking what we were going to do next. I knew well that we had no political future in the country, and I could see no alternative to leaving the country and seeking political asylum elsewhere. Malan's next attack was certainly imminent; the best thing was to leave the country while leaving was still possible. So I made up my mind to put the proposition to Tefu that it was best for us to leave before we were overtaken by the storm. I also made up my mind that if Tefu was not willing to leave with me, I was still going to leave. I planned my departure secretly. The Gold Coast in West Africa was the place to go – Ghana today. At that time it already enjoyed internal self-government. First I planned to go to Rhodesia, while there seek the way to Ethiopia, and while there plan the journey to Ghana. On Christmas Eve that year, when people would be busy with the festival, I would take a train from Johannesburg to Rhodesia unnoticed.

On the third day I went to the city. I was in possession of the receipt the police gave us when they took things from our office in February that year. When I got to Maritime House the police showed me Tefu's signature; the day after our trial he had been there to collect the things including the typewriter. From there I was going to court, I can't remember why, and when I was about to enter I saw Tefu.

We met and I told him that I had come from Maritime House and that they said that he had collected the things. He admitted having done so. I asked him whether he took them to where our other things were, but he surprised me by telling me that he hired a trolley and took everything to his home in Lady-Selborne. I asked him what was the meaning of that. He replied that he was finished with me and that he was going to run the office from there. I got angry and said, 'Look, if I want to be nasty, I can go in there,' pointing at the police station, 'to report that you have stolen those things. When I brought you into the unions you found me with those things, you don't know how they were bought and where.' I said, 'Never mind, I am finished with you,' and then walked away from him, filled with anger. Our parting came when we were standing between Pretoria main police station, where we used to be charged and put into the cells, and the magistrates courts where we used to be brought up for indictments and convictions. It was in the open in Pretorius Street. Tefu never knew of my plans to leave the country.

From my last meeting with Tefu I went to Mr. George Aitcheson's office to tell him what had happened between Tefu and myself. I thought he should know, if Tefu came there for help, that we had separated. Mr. Aitcheson laughed. He invited me to a small room where his firm stored some of the things they did not use or did not want, gave me an old typewriter and his old broken revolving chair and said, 'See if you can fix this chair; I think you can still use the machine.' He then gave me some advice, 'Stay out of trouble.' I thanked him for all he had done for us and for the things he was giving me. I took away the machine first and went back for the chair later. I was seriously thinking of appealing against the regional magistrate's judgment, but afterwards thought that it would look like abusing Mr. Aitcheson's kindness, taking advantage of the fact that he charged us nothing, and I dropped the idea. Life was becoming harder and more difficult every day, and my thoughts were engaged in leaving the country but not telling anyone – my wife, children or friends.

In June I wrote to someone in Rhodesia whom I did not know but had read about in the newspapers, asking him to receive me in his family as a visitor for a month. His name was Mr. Wellington Chirwa, and at that time he was a member of parliament there. I never got a reply – but of this, more a little later.

During the same month the second banning order came. I had no office in the city, I was not working; sand was running fast beneath my feet. The police knew me well, they knew the spots I always visited in Pretoria; they could not find me. They asked people if they had seen me during the day, and those who had seen me said so. The police knew that before they travelled to Atteridgeville, where I lived, they should try one last spot. At four o'clock one day I was sitting talking to an African tailor at 253 Vermeulen Street, getting ready to leave for home, and there stepped in three detectives, two Europeans and an African with a second more severe and more restrictive order than the first from Mr. Swart, Malan's minister of justice, whom I called minister of injustice. First they heard my voice from outside. When they got in one of them said, 'Oh yes, here he is.' They gave me the order to read; some people who were there thought it was a warrant for my arrest. After reading it, I said angrily waving it at them, 'Look, I cannot observe this. At five o'clock, you go and stand by the bus queues; I shall be among a large gathering taking the bus home. I must find you there to arrest me, that is the only way I can observe this order.' They made me sign for it; their leader said, 'You understand its contents, that is all we are interested in.' They left me with it.

That order obliged me to resign from the African National Congress, the Federated African Trade Unions, the African General Workers' Union, and the Pretoria Non-European Distributive Workers' Union, never to form or take part in forming any organisation, never to belong to any organisation, never to take part in the activities of any organisation, never to attend any gathering, political, social or religious, and never to leave the province of the Transvaal or enter the territory of South West Africa for a period of five years. Two days later Tefu came to see me to ask whether I had, as he had, received the second banning order. I told him that I had, but did not discuss it with him. He had forfeited my trust.

I always kept another typewriter that I had bought myself at home. I sat at it one day and wrote a long accusing letter direct to Mr. Swart, accusing him of being dishonest, and him and his government of cowardice. I said that in his second banning order he banished me from working, from political life, and from mixing with my own people, interning me in my own house, and making no provision for my welfare. How was I expected to live?

I asked, 'On the social side, does it mean that when my daughter gets engaged, or gets married, I must go away from her function; or if one of my family dies and people come along to help me bury him I must go away from them? Does it mean that for five years I should not stand in a bus queue with other people or travel in a bus or train with other people?' I then told him that since I got the order I had been in gatherings travelling in buses full of people and that I should continue to do so.

I said in my letter that he was interning me indirectly, but I demanded open internment. I said, 'Deport me to any place you like. I demand deportation. Deport me to a place where people will know where I am, where your government will feed me and my family, where my friends will visit me if they wish. If', I said, 'you and your government are brave enough and honest enough you will deport me in bright daylight so that everyone can see and know where I am.'

After two weeks I received a letter from C. R. Swart simply saying, 'Consult your own legal advisers on the matter.' That was my last communication with Mr. C. R. Swart, Malan's minister of justice, who later became their first president. I detested them, their government, the way they governed South Africa, and I still detest their tribal government under the fascist Vorster, together with those who share their views and convictions.

Having set my mind firmly on leaving the country at the end of the year, on June the third nineteen-fifty-four I presented myself at the native commissioner's office, Pretoria, for a reference book, which male Africans had been forced to carry since nineteen-fifty-two. My number was 1082386. The book is claimed to relieve the Africans of carrying many passes but makes provisions for recording everything required of Africans under the pass laws. Since its introduction I had refused to register myself for one, but at that time I felt that I needed some form of identification outside the country's borders. Until then I had refused to pay the poll tax which was required of me, on the grounds that I was not a citizen because I was denied the right to vote, to be voted for and not represented in the Europeans-only tribal parliament. I had last paid poll tax, which was a pound a year, in nineteen-thirty-nine. When I was married in nineteen-forty-one, I paid for three years and stopped paying again. When I got the reference book I paid one pound poll tax for nineteen-forty-three and never paid again.

I had no office at that time, Tefu had taken everything away from me. I was not working. Starvation was beginning to tell. I had some European friends who, whenever I called on them for help always came to my aid. Some of them are still in the country so I will not mention their names. All I can say to them is, 'You saved my life.' One of them even gave me a bicycle to move about on. I have already said that I wrote to Mr. Wellington Chirwa in Rhodesia and never got a reply from him; but when I met him in London in nineteen-fifty-five, he assured me that he did reply to my letter, telling me that he and his family would welcome me there as their guest for a month as I asked. I did not disbelieve Mr. Chirwa, because at that time many letters of mine were disappearing into police files. Some letters which escaped police interception contained passages enquiring why I had not replied to correspondence.

Before we were banned we received magazines and newspapers from many organisations overseas, and these too were banned. The British Communist party was kind enough to send us every week five copies of their paper the *Daily Worker*, which informed us what was taking place in Britain. The fascist axe fell on them too.

In reading the *Daily Worker* I saw a book advertised by the Central Bookshop in London, *Mother*, by Maxim Gorky. I sent the money required for ordering the book and later I got a letter from the Central Bookshop saying that the book had left London. Three weeks later, as it had become our habit to read the *Government Gazette* every Friday, I noticed that the book was banned in South Africa. I knew that it had arrived. The following week I got a letter from the customs and excise department that Gorky's *Mother* had arrived but had been confiscated as prohibited literature. A few days later I went to see the head of the customs and excise department at his office behind the magistrates' courts to protest that the book was mine; I had bought it for my own use only and they had no right to deny me having it. He told me that he was carrying out government instructions and I was not having the book. If I persisted I should apply to the supreme court contesting the government's right to deny me possession of the book. That was the end, I had lost the money and Maxim Gorky's *Mother*.

In the middle of June nineteen-fifty-four, while waiting for the Christmas festival to come to enable me to escape to Rhodesia, I decided to start something in the meantime. I founded Mokgatle's Agency. My purpose was to advise the workers in their troubles over their wages, conditions of employment, influx control difficulties and everything else that I could help them with. I went to see another African tailor, near Pretoria's main railway station, to ask him to give me a space in his back-room where I could meet people and work three times a week. He was glad to have me with him to help pay the rent. His shop was behind a row of Indian shops in Scheiding Street, directly opposite the railway goods sheds. His landlord was an Indian shopkeeper, whose sub-tenant I thus became. The first letter I wrote from there, to the influx control office protesting against the withholding of permission to seek work or to be in Pretoria from Africans who had been in the city working for many years, was enough to provoke the influx control department to send one of their inspectors to ask whether I had registered with them to open or run my agency there. I told him that I had registered with the city council a long time ago when he was perhaps sitting in his pram or at school. If he was interested he could get in touch with Atteridgeville municipal office. He left, angry, promising trouble.

I knew he was one of the Pretoria University boys who, when they were being polished up to become staunch Nationalists and for posts in the so-called Bantu affairs department, were sent by Dr. W. W. Eiselen, the chief Apartheider, to spend some months or a year in influx control administration. He had never before in his life been spoken to like that by someone he considered and was taught to believe inferior. From me he went to locate the real landlord of the place to threaten him that, unless he got rid of me, he would lose his licence and property for allowing a law-breaker to use his premises. It was not long after his departure that the landlord came up to ask his tenant, the tailor, how I came to be there. He was furious, saying that he did not want sub-tenants in the place, and if he had known he would not have given the tailor that place; he thought he wanted it only for himself. There was a row but I refrained from taking part in it.

In the end the landlord came to me and said he did not blame me, but his tenant asked me to leave and offered to carry my things in his small lorry free of charge to wherever I chose to go as long as I got away from the place. I calmly said to him, 'Very well, I shall look for a place and let you know.' I had one small kitchen table, one armchair, the typewriter Mr. Aitcheson gave me, one ream of paper and two files. The next day I went to Lady-Selborne, six miles from Atteridgeville, to look for a room in one of the houses. I went to see a friend of mine, my admirer Thipe Ditshego, who was a standholder and had a large house. He gave me a room to use and was pleased to have me near him to help him with some of his own problems. He was a medicine man, an old Congress man and one of the early fighters for African rights, now advanced in age. He was trying hard to organise African medicine men to struggle for recognition by the powers that be. He was full of wisdom, but he lacked the art of writing English letters. I went back to tell the Indian shopkeeper, and that same week on Saturday he transported me to Lady-Selborne, free of charge as he had promised.

Mr. Ditshego had his own typewriter and roneoing machine which became very handy for me. That Saturday afternoon I typed a stencil and roneoed the ream of paper I brought with me, informing all my friends and the organisations I had contacted overseas of my new address. The only man who knew of my intention to leave the country at the end of the year was Thipe Ditshego. He was dead against my leaving, arguing that my friends would say I ran away; but I admitted that I was running away. I told him that I could see dark clouds coming, a time when it would be difficult to escape, when all of us would be imprisoned, if we were lucky enough to escape being shot. He tried to pacify me, 'Lie low, do nothing, like everyone else, they will forget you.' He went on to tell me: 'After all, when there is more suffering, you will be part of us all, we shall share the bitterness with you.' I said to him, 'Don't shake off my admiration for your wisdom, you are the wisest African I know.' I pulled out one of the poems he wrote in Sesutho in which he said, 'We have been turned into slaves in our own homes, our homes are not respected, they are no protection for our wives and children, we work hard for next to nothing, our tears make them laugh, they entertain each other with our sufferings, our screams delight their children, we have become stories for pleasure by their firesides. Our fathers and mothers with us are called boys and girls. Will it ever end?' I said, 'There you speak for us all, but now you seem to suggest that one day they will change and become reasonable.' He got up from his chair and said to me, 'My reason for trying to stand in your way is that I know you will be a loss to us. I know,' he continued, 'what you say is true, but you have held the torch so long in the dark, that with your departure you will take the torch with you.' That was in July nineteen-fifty-four.

One day a young African came to see me; he was one of my

admirers and he had lost his job at Pretoria general hospital where he was a cleaner, because he was accused of being a labour ring-leader. He had spoken fearlessly for improvement in their wages and that earned him the sack. He was a clever young man with a fair knowledge of English, but like most African workers he was a migrant in Pretoria. When he went to the influx control for a permit to seek a new job he was refused and ordered to leave the urban area of Pretoria within seventy-two hours. He came to seek my help. I went to argue his case before Mr. Brent, head of the so-called Bantu affairs department of the city, and we succeeded.

After that I said to him, 'Look, this is temporary, it will happen again. Why not take on the Federated African Trade Unions of South Africa from which I am banned, and become secretary? I shall help you secretly with everything you find difficult.' I said further, 'Tomorrow, you go to influx control and register yourself as self-employed, working as secretary and organiser of the union.' He said, 'They won't agree, they will know that I got the idea from you.' To which I replied, 'They know already that you are one of those who are influenced by me, to them you stink like me. They can't refuse you registering as self-employed, paying two shillings every month. If they refuse we shall challenge them. I shall get Mr. Aitcheson into it; after that I shall get George Findlay, QC, to take it up to the supreme court.' That impressed him a good deal and he agreed. The next day he went and registered. According to him they mocked him by saying, 'You think where Mokgatle failed you will succeed. You will end the same way as him. He thought he was clever, now he knows he has been kicking a wall with spikes. He is finished, only fools like you will still listen to his nonsense.'

For the whole of July and August I trained the young man. His name was Samuel Maesela Maimela, the son of a lay preacher in the Methodist Church at Middelburg, Transvaal. I made him write all the letters first in draft form, which I would go through with him, correcting mistakes, and then allow him to type them. I did so because I knew that the police knew my methods of construction in writing, they would one day raid the office and, though the signa-tures were in Maimela's handwriting, they would question him to find out that I was using him only to sign the letters. I knew that when they questioned him on the contents they would find that he had the answer for every passage. That would be the way to beat them. I asked the old man Thipe Ditshego not to tell the young man that I was planning to escape from the country at the end of the year. That would frighten him off and make him feel that I was leaving him with a task too big to handle alone. Ditshego insisted that I should go to Swaziland or Basutoland, now Lesotho, where I could be reached when my advice was sought, but I said they would follow me. They would tell the governments there that I was a troublemaker and I would be thrown out. I was desperate, the year was not moving fast enough. Though I had received no reply from Chirwa, I was going.

XXXVI Departure

In the middle of August I received a letter from the Rumanian trade union council asking me why I had not replied to the letter which they said they had sent me in July asking me to come to Rumania to attend a world conference of chemical workers to be held there on the twenty-third of September, as a fraternal delegate, representing South African African workers. I had not received the letter, which probably found its way into the police files. They stressed that they were waiting for my reply. After reading the letter I showed it to Thipe Ditshego and he asked me what my reply was going to be. I said that I would acknowledge the arrival of the letter, point out that I had not received the first one and explain to them that being poor I could not manage the fare. If they could pay the fare and my keep, I would be with them when the conference opened. He looked at me in amazement. He said, 'You are too optimistic, how can you say a thing like that? You have no passport, they won't give you one even if you apply for it. Where do you think the first letter is? The police have it, they know all about it, they are watching.' I reminded him of my letter to C. R. Swart demanding deportation, and said, 'Let them stop me. I am going if my fare can be paid.' To cool him off I said, 'If I do go, after the conference I can come or go to any part of Africa.' We then called Maimela to tell him about the letter, but promised him that I should come back after the conference, or move on to another part of Africa. The young man said that my going to the conference would be a great help because people who did not know our situation would hear about it from someone who had suffered from it himself.

Like Ditshego, he expressed the feeling that they would not let me leave the country. I said, 'Let me write to see what will happen.' We all agreed. I took Ditshego's typewriter and the same day I replied along the lines I have already indicated. I was not sure myself that they would let me go. I posted the letter by airmail from Lady-Selborne sub-post office. All I could do now was wait. I carried on with my cover agency, helping Maimela and showing him how to do things the way I understood them. Each day I travelled fourteen miles each way to and from Lady-Selborne.

One day on a Wednesday, September the Sixteenth, I felt tired and lazy and decided to spend the day at home in Atteridgeville. By ten o'clock in the morning I suddenly got a feeling that there might be someone in Lady-Selborne who had come to see me from far away. It was not unusual for people to come in from distant farms to see me about their grievances on the farms, and many letters from me were in the files of native commissioners and district farmers' union offices protesting and asking them to investigate the grievances people had come to Pretoria to see me about. Workers who visited their families and relatives on the farms always gave those with grievances my name and address, telling them that I might help them or advise them what to do. I learned that even if you did not succeed, the mere fact that you made representations, and these were talked about by farmers they had thought were untouchable, was success in the eyes of those suffering people.

I set off and reached the city at half-past eleven, but decided to leave there for Lady-Selborne at two o'clock in the afternoon. I went into the place where I began my trade union work in nineteen-forty, the place I occupied at various times as my office, the place where my second banning order was handed to me, the place from which at one time I was thrown out under a court order for being in arrears with my rent: 253 Vermeulen Street. At that time it was occupied by two Africans, one a tailor, Motau, and the other a teacher of motor driving, Mahlangu. I sat there talking to Motau, waiting for two o'clock to strike. But people from afar had indeed been in Lady-Selborne looking for me. Maimela and Ditshego told them to go to Atteridgeville to find me, but first to try 253 Vermeulen Street. At half-past one a European and an African entered and said they were looking for someone called Mokgatle. Both were complete strangers to me. I said I was Mokgatle. From the uniform the African wore it was plain that they were not the police. They were from Johannesburg, representatives of Swissair airlines. The African was the chauffeur. They told me in the presence of my friends that they were to tell me that their office in Johannesburg had received instructions from Europe that my return air ticket from South Africa had been paid by the Rumanian trade union council, and that they should take me to Europe to attend a conference.

On the spot they asked me whether I knew of the conference and if I was ready to leave in a few days' time. I said 'Yes' to both questions. They then asked me whether I had a passport, to which I also replied that I had. They told me to get vaccinated and that the plane that would carry me to Europe left on Saturday, September the nineteenth, at ten o'clock from Jan Smuts airport. They would collect me, but wanted to know where they could find me. I said, 'Here at this very place.' 'Very well,' they said, 'we shall be here at eight o'clock in the morning on Saturday.' They left.

I begged my friends who had been listening not to spread the news because I was not sure that I would be going. Immediately after that I left in a hurry for Lady-Selborne, where I told Mr. Ditshego and Mr. Maimela who the two men were who had come looking for me early in the day and that it was all set, I was going. 'What about a passport?' they asked me. I said, 'I am going to make one out for myself.' They could not believe it, so I had to repeat that I was making one out myself. It became a joke. I took Ditshego's typewriter and began to type the following affidavit:

'I, Naboth Monyadioe Mokgatle, national registration no. 1082386, of 37 Molope Street, Atteridgeville–Pretoria, whose signature appears below, hereby declare and swear that I am a South African by birth and residence and I am a British subject, born at Phokeng–district–Rustenburg Transvaal province on the 1st April, 1911. I am 43 years of age.

'I am a trade unionist by profession and I am proceeding to Vienna–Austria for visiting purposes.

'I know and understand the contents of this affidavit.'

When I had completed it, I left hurriedly for the city to get it sworn by a commissioner for oaths, an Indian friend of mine, who was employed by the post office in the Non-European section. From there I went to show it to my friend Motau the tailor, who like others doubted whether I would be successful with it. I had it in my possession when I arrived home, but did not tell my wife that I was leaving the country on Saturday. All I told her was that I was going to Johannesburg that day to see some friends and that I would be back the same evening. It was not unusual for me to attend conferences in Johannesburg before I was banned.

The next day I went to Lady-Selborne to finalise things and to wait for Saturday to come. I told a few trusted friends about the journey and asked them to spread the news after they were sure I had left the country. One of them was Motau the tailor. Though he was a resident of Lady-Selborne, I asked him to travel to Atteridgeville on Sunday to tell the news to my wife and children if he did not find me at home. That he did, as I was told later by my wife. The other one was my fellow-tribesman and friend, Ratshikane Molotsane.

I asked Ratshikane to visit my wife late on the night of my departure. If he did not find me at home he was to ask to see me, and if my wife said that I had not returned from Johannesburg, then he would know that I had left the country and that he was to tell my wife I was not in Johannesburg but on the way to Europe. I was later told by my wife that he fulfilled his promise. I did not want my wife to know beforehand that I was leaving because she would have been afraid that I was deserting her and the children and that they would never see me or hear from me again. Althougn my wife was loyal to me, she never shared my convictions. She was always trying to pull me down, urging me to be like everyone else, and saying that I was making trouble for myself. On the nineteenth of September nineteen-fifty-four, I left my wife and children with a promise that I was going to Johannesburg. My son Matshediso, who was ten years old, was suspicious and wanted to know more than once why I was going to Johannesburg. Even when I had gone out of the house he came running after me to ask whether I would come back in the evening. I lifted him up and said, 'Yes I always come back.' This moved me and filled my heart with strong emotions.

The die was cast, there was no turning back. I carried no luggage, everything was on my person. In my pocket were three shillings and three pennies. At eight o'clock that morning I was waiting to be picked up. Half-past the hour the Swissair people arrived from Johannesburg, and with them I began my trip to Europe and finally to England. We arrived at Jan Smuts airport and for the first time they heard that I had no passport. The secret came out at the desk when I was asked to hand in my passport. I produced the affidavit I had drawn up myself and that was that.

I was the only black passenger at the airport and I was ready to fight. The man who was checking passengers' passports and other documents asked me to step out of the queue, so that he could deal with me later. I did so, and when he had dealt with all the others he turned to me and asked why I had no passport. I replied that I did not need one. He asked for my medical certificate and I said I possessed none. He then asked me which country I thought would let me in without a passport, visa or medical certificate; I replied that it was my affair. All the time he was speaking in Afrikaans. He then telephoned a certain department, I don't know which; all I could hear was him mentioning my name and saying that I was at the airport without a passport, only a piece of paper drawn up by myself, no visa to enter any country and saying that I was going to Vienna, Austria. He was asking for advice as to what he should do with me; then I heard him say, 'So I should let him go, I must not stop him.' When he had finished, he said to me, 'You will be sorry for this, you will suffer. No country will let you in. You are being foolish to think that you can just leave like this.' I said, 'I shall see when I get there.'

He gave my affidavit back and said 'Go and wait for your plane to take off,' pointing to the non-European waiting-room. I went to wait. Four or five minutes later a young man, a European, came along and asked, 'Are you Mokgatle?' I said 'Yes.' He said, 'We understand that you are leaving the country without a passport.' I did not reply, and he invited me to follow him upstairs. In the office into which he led me I found a tall, well-built man, a European, behind a large, well-polished desk. He introduced himself to me as Detective Inspector van Heerden of the South African police. I uttered no word. There was already someone else with him, so there were three of them while I was alone. He said, 'We have received a report that you are leaving the country but you have no passport.' I said, 'That is correct.' He said, 'I have instructions from the department of justice, Pretoria, to warn you that you can't leave the country with no passport. If you insist on leaving, you can do so at your own peril. When you want to come back, because no country will let you in without proper papers, you will not be allowed into the country. This is an official warning given in the presence of two witnesses?' He said, 'How do I know that you are Mokgatle?' I gave him my reference book. He said that is not good enough.

He said, 'Books like these are made by crooks like you all over Johannesburg; it doesn't make me believe that you are really Mokgatle.' I showed him the native commissioner's official stamp on it, but still he said he wanted further proof. I then took out the letter I had received from Mr. C. R. Swart advising me to consult my legal advisers in the matter I had written to him about regarding deportation, and said, 'This is from your chief, I hope it will satisfy you that I am the man.' He read it, took it with my other papers, gave them to one of the men who was with us as a witness and instructed him to copy them all in full for him. Ten minutes before my plane was due to take off he gave me the papers back and said I was to go back to the waiting-room again. When the plane was ready, all of us were called to go on board, and between the building and the plane I found him waiting for me with an automatic camera. As I moved towards him, his camera was taking snaps of me until I passed him to board the plane. As I passed him, he said, 'Good luck, Mokgatle.' I followed the other passengers into the plane, but I did not feel sure that I was leaving South Africa, my country, my home, the soil which gave birth to me and all my ancestors before me, the country in which I was deprived of dignity, human rights and all respect. Only when the plane had left the ground I looked down and asked myself, 'Am I really above South Africa? Am I really leaving torture and the pass laws which have been part of my life for the past forty-three years?'

Though I had read a lot about other countries, that my colour would mean nothing and they would treat me like everyone else, for me the whole world was South Africa under Malan, and before him under Smuts and Hertzog. To believe that I would find different or better treatment in other countries never settled down in my mind.

We flew non-stop from Johannesburg to Nairobi in Kenya,

leaving at ten in the morning and reaching Nairobi at half-past five in the evening. I was the only black passenger in the plane. Only the stewardesses spoke to me, but I was not worried. I suspected that since all the Europeans in the plane were flying from South Africa they resented my presence in the plane. I may have been wrong; perhaps they were not all South Africans, some may have been visitors to my country. It was at the height of the fighting in Kenya, the talk was about Mau Mau.

We spent an hour at Nairobi and from there we flew on to the Sudan. It was not until after nine o'clock in the evening that we landed at Khartoum. All of us left the plane for refreshments. It was very hot and I wondered how it would have been if we had arrived during the day. The Sudan at that time was enjoying internal self-government. While we were in the restaurant an African in light khaki uniform noticed that I was a stranger and came to sit next to me. He asked me where I was from. I told him I was a South African, whereupon he told me he was a police officer. Without asking about our situation in South Africa, he said, 'We know how you people live there, we are totally against the way you are treated. After our complete independence we will have to see that the pressure on you is ended.'

In reply I thanked him for his kind words and sympathy but said that the best way they could help us after their complete independence would be to build up a very strong Sudan. It would show the people who govern my country how wrong their accusations are that black people left on their own can't make any progress and can't govern themselves in a civilised fashion. 'When you have built schools and universities, offer our Africans scholarships to study in the Sudan. The education they will secure in the Sudan and the climate of being free from racial pressure in South Africa will give them encouragement and the determination to struggle for the democratisation of their own country.' I briefly pointed out to him that not all Europeans in South Africa are for keeping down Africans, but admitted that those who want to accept the Africans as equals are few. They too need encouragement and strengthening. The Africans, I pointed out, are not only oppressed physically, they are oppressed mentally too. They live in an atmosphere in which they are made to feel that they are clamouring for things they are not entitled to. It sounds odd, I said, but it is true. Most of them do in fact feel that it is pointless to struggle for the right to become prime minister in South Africa; that position is unattainable for them. I also said that most of the Africans, through lack of education, don't know what is happening outside their own country.

Before he had time to comment or ask me questions it was time for us to leave. I noticed that there was now another black passenger, a

Sudanese. He saw me and came along to share the seat I had occupied alone since we left South Africa. He told me his name was Mahdi Hussein Sherif, and he was an engineer in the government railways on a mission to West Germany to make purchases for the railways.

As we were travelling at night we were advised to sleep, because the journey to Europe would take the whole night. In the morning when I woke up we were about to cross the Mediterranean sea into Greece. We had breakfast. It was Sunday, the twentieth of September. The sky was clear, the sun was bright and the weather very warm. It was time for refreshments. When we got out of the plane and my feet touched the ground, silently I asked myself, 'Am I really standing on European soil, the Europe I have heard so much about?' The soil did not look different from the soil I was accustomed to in South Africa. But as if to prove to me that I was in Europe, something unique, something completely new happened to me. As Mahdi and I were walking to the restaurant, we were going the wrong way and a pretty young Greek woman came running to us and said with her Greek English accent, 'Excuse me, sirs, are you Swissair?' Mahdi replied 'Yes,' and she said, 'This way, please,' leading us to the right entrance. It was an historic day. In my entire life I had never been called 'Sir' by a European, let alone by a woman. Her words were a landmark. In the restaurant we were the only two black people, but no one cared. We were treated as human beings, nothing less. But the South African feeling was still part of me, the fear that there might be rows and objections against us.

At Ciampino airport in Rome, too, I was nervous about going into the restaurant. I did not want Mahdi to notice it. The place was full of people, all Europeans; and memories of South Africa were haunting me, that we might be attacked and thrown out, but nothing of the sort happened.

We reached Klotten airport, Zurich, at four o'clock in the afternoon, and there Mahdi Hussein Sherif said good-bye to me and took a plane for West Germany. I found myself alone at the airport, which was full of people, all Europeans. I could hear from the speech of some that they were Americans or Canadians. My plane for Vienna was not leaving until six o'clock in the evening, which meant that I had to wait there for two full hours. The waiting-room was full of people waiting to be called to planes for all parts of the world. In my memories I was still in South Africa, where the colour of my skin was a mark to Europeans that I was not a real human being but someone inferior, who if he wanted something to eat or a soft drink, must go into a restaurant or café, purchase what he needed and go out into the street to eat or drink it on the pavement; my country, where I was isolated into a lonely non-European

332

waiting-room at the airport because I ought not to mix with the real human beings, the Europeans.

At Klotten Airport I began to search for the non-European waiting-room. The day was warm, the sun was at times disappearing into the clouds. While casting my eyes all over the place wondering what to do I saw an Asian, sitting down, quietly reading a newspaper. He saved me. Seeing him there, I said to myself, 'Surely, if they don't throw him out of the place, they won't throw me out.' Because of him, I entered the waiting-room, to see what would happen. No one cared. I don't even know whether they noticed that I was there.

XXXVII Vienna

At six o'clock on Sunday the twentieth September, nineteen-fifty-four, I left Klotten airport. Unlike my fellow passengers on their way to Austria, I had no luggage, as everything I had was on my body. We were then conveyed by a British European Airways plane, and landed at Vienna airport after eight o'clock. There too I was an odd man out. When I reached my turn in the queue, the immigration officer who dealt with us found that I had no passport such as he would know, and no *visa* as was required from any foreigner who entered the country. To avoid detaining those with all the required documents, he asked me to step out of the queue so that he could deal with me later. He called a policeman who was on duty there to get a chair for me to sit down while waiting for my turn. That was an unusual thing happening to me, since in South Africa I could have been allowed to stand on my feet until my turn came to be dealt with. He vas very polite and, like the pretty young woman in Greece, he called me 'sir' when he addressed me. That was in Europe, where people in South Africa, who still claim to be Europeans, have created in our minds that Europeans think nothing of us and would never treat us as their equals. Within two days since my departure from my own country my whole life had changed and I had gained dignity and respect from those authorised to deal with people on behalf of their government.

The evening was warm and I sweated. While waiting I felt thirsty, so I interrupted him and asked for a drink of water. South African treatment of Africans still very fresh in my memories, I expected to be taken to a tap from which to drink with a communal tin mug. The officer again called on the policeman to get me water to drink. I was so surprised to see the policeman emerging with a tray, carrying a spotless glass of water; when I had finished he asked me whether I needed some more. Everything was done with extreme politeness.

When passengers with valid documents had been dealt with and left, I was called to the counter to explain why I had not the necessary papers. I produced the affidavit I was travelling with, my reference book which showed my photograph and explained that I was passing through Austria on the way to Rumania to attend a conference. I was stopping in Vienna at the invitation of the World Federation of Trade Unions, for only a day. The officer then asked me whether the WFTU people knew of my arrival, and I said they did, but that I was astonished that none of them was there to meet me. He asked me if I knew them, to which the answer was that I only knew them by the correspondence I had had with them for some years. He then asked me if I knew their address. I knew it by heart and recited it to him. Noticing that in my affidavit I had written that I was a British subject, he telephoned the British consulate in Vienna, told him that he had someone from South Africa claiming to be a British subject, but without a passport or *visa* to enter Austria, who was in need of help. He asked whether I should be sent to see him, but the consulate official said that they were not responsible for South African citizens, and that the South African consulate was the right place to contact.

After that he told me that it was his duty to detain me at the airport, but that he was going to be sympathetic and would allow me to go into the city to find my World Federation of Trade Unions people, but the next day at eight o'clock in the morning I should report to him at his office in the city. He gave me his address card; his name was Herbert Huber. He said a policeman would take me outside to the bus which would carry me to the terminus in the city, where there was a taxi rank. When I left the airport in the bus, it was already eleven o'clock at night.

When I arrived in a taxi at the offices of the World Federation of Trade Unions, I found the caretaker expecting me. After finding out that I was the right person, he asked the same taxi to take me to the Hotel Trieste where a place was booked for me, and to collect me again from the hotel the next morning and bring me to the office. During the night I wondered how the officials of that world-wide body could be so careless not to send someone to meet me at the airport, knowing well that I was arriving at night, a complete stranger to Vienna. Perhaps, I said to myself, I shall know the reason tomorrow at the office. I spent the night peacefully, after a delicious meal at the hotel.

The next morning, after breakfast, the taxi arrived to collect me. The lady who received me, together with others, said that they were pleased that I had arrived and welcomed me on behalf of the World Federation of Trade Unions. I expected an apology for having not been met at the airport, but no such apology was made. I showed them Herbert Huber's card and told them he expected me at his office, and could they telephone him that I would be arriving in a few minutes; they told me I had nothing to worry about, and they would see to everything. I then left the matter in their hands and stopped worrying about Inspector Huber.

I was sitting in a waiting room reading periodicals, and saw a tall well-built man going into the office of the lady who welcomed me.

They spoke in German, and I overheard them talking about me; my name and South Africa were repeatedly mentioned. Soon I had no doubt that this man was a detective. After he had left the lady came out to see me and, smiling, she told me that the man was sent to arrest me for not having reported to Inspector Huber's office, but she told him that they were to blame and would take me there the next morning. As far as I was concerned the matter was out of my hands. At their offices a delightful young Chinese showed great interest in me, and took me with him to lunch in the canteen. He asked me about life in South Africa. No one else seemed to notice me or bothered to ask me anything. The whole atmosphere was surprising to me – I though that friendship and solidarity were lacking.

In the afternoon I went round the city, admiring its beautiful buildings, clean streets and everything else my eyes could reach. I was not aware this was to be my last day in Vienna, and instead I was thinking I should spend the next day sightseeing before leaving for Rumania. But my stay in Vienna was brief. I remember saying to myself, here I am in one of Europe's capitals, going about without fear that round the next corner I may be stopped by a policeman and asked to produce my pass. It was in that great city of culture and music that for the first time I rode in a taxi used by Europeans. It was in that city that for the first time I shared a hotel with Europeans and slept under the same roof as them, though still imagining that my presence in the hotel would cause a revolt. The other residents saw me there, and no one objected.

The same morning, when I was waiting outside the Hotel Trieste for the taxi to collect me, I saw something which made me doubt my sight and wipe my eyes twice with a handkerchief to make sure that my sight was in order. There was a pretty young woman washing the windows of a shop! I had never seen anything like that in Pretoria and Johannesburg. In those cities of apartheid, European women were angels, and if they had washed shop windows, South Africa would have been destroyed by fire.

While I waited a chimney sweep came into the hotel carrying his tools and wearing an overall, his face covered in black by the ashes of other chimneys he had cleaned before coming to the Hotel Trieste. When he entered, there were several people in the foyer and when he saw me, he remarked: 'I am also black'. His remark caused laughter, he stood for few seconds, looking at me with happy expression splashed all over his face. 'I am also black', the chimney sweeper said again with pride. He was identifying himself with the colour that Smuts, Hertzog, Malan, Strydom, Verwoerd and Vorster would have felt highly insulted to be identified with.

The next day, officials of the World Federation of Trade Unions took me to an office, I don't know whether for immigration or for internal affairs. Two of them went with me by car. When we got there I was made to wait in a room while they went into another. Five minutes later I was called in. All my identification papers were copied by two girls, one of whom told me in perfect English that she had lived in London during the Second World War. I was in the office while my papers were being copied, but I was not asked a single question by a man who seemed to me the person in charge. Afterwards, I saw the two officers of the World Federation of Trade Unions paying a fine and being give a receipt for it. There was no sign of hostility towards me. Afterwards one of them told me that the fine equalled three pounds in English money, and that everything was all right. My papers were given back to me, and I was taken into another room. That was the last I saw of the two men who had brought me there. After half an hour, the English-speaking girl entered the room with another tall, well-built man who she said was a detective. I was arrested and taken downstairs, put into a black Maria and driven to the police station. As I had known such experiences before, I wasn't in the least worried. The only thing that did worry me was that the arrest would make me miss the conference in Rumania.

The conference was being held in Bucharest. At the police station, every method I knew was gone through; I was thoroughly searched, everything found in my pockets was taken out—tie, wrist-watch and braces were put into a bag, and I was given a receipt for them. I was then taken into another room, as I thought to be taken to the cells, but before that could happen I was given my things back and the two men from the World Federation of Trade Unions arrived. They took me back to their offices, where I was told that the Austrian government had decided not to imprison me but to deport me out of Austria. I was shocked when I was told that the organisation's secretariat has discussed my position at great length, with great care, and had come to the conclusion that for my own safety I should return home to South Africa. I asked how they could discuss my position without me and make a cut-and-dried decision. They told me that they had no time for that, the man who accompanied us from the police station was waiting to take me to the airport to put me into a plane back to Zurich, where I would take my plane back to South Africa. I became very angry and said to them that the deportation was all right, but to let me proceed to Bucharest to attend the conference I came to Europe to attend. They said there was no time for more arguments – the Secretariat had made its decision that I should be returned home. While we were still arguing the Chinese gentleman I had found there came in and said he had just come back from the Dutch airlines office, and

KLM had reserved a seat to take me to Bucharest, all they were waiting for was money to pay for the seat. But he was told that the Secretariat's decision could not be reversed, and that for my safety I was being returned home. I begged them again to let me go to the conference, after which I would return home. No, was the reply, there was no more time, the policeman who was taking me to the airport could not be kept waiting. I gave up, but said to myself, I am in Europe and I am not returning to South Africa. I shook the Chinese comrade by the hand and told him not to worry; he had done his best. The policeman was called in to take me away. I told them that I had no luggage and there was nothing to collect at the Hotel Trieste. I was now taken to Vienna airport, on my way back to Zurich. At the airport the policeman told me that I was entitled to a free meal as the guest of the Austrian government, I should choose what I liked.

My contact with the officials of the World Federation of Trade Unions was a very limited one; as I have already explained, I had a sad arrival with no one waiting to receive me in Austria. Even at their offices, the reception was a limited one. I saw only one lady official, but apart from her I met no one else. I mention no one's name because I met no one. They gave me the cold shoulder, but without a reason. They made no attempt to show me how the organisation to which workers organisations in many countries of the world were members worked. No attempt was made to show me round, and I never knew who was at the head of the organisation. I only heard of the Ghost Secretariat which decided my fate, aiming at sending me back to South Africa, where they knew through correspondence I had written to them for several years that I was persecuted because of my convictions. What blatantly exposed their hypocrisy was when they said they were sending me back to the police state in South Africa for my own safety.

I had never thought that I would find people like that inside the World Federation of Trade Unions. Their actions convinced me that they were not in the world workers' organisation to advance its cause but to disrupt it, to speak sweet misleading words, and to act against the workers' interests. They gave me a picture of the couldn't-care-less type of bureaucrats, who put themselves far above the people they pretended to serve.

XXXVIII Zurich

The policeman who escorted me to Vienna airport, carrying out my deportation order, was polite. In the airport restaurant he bought me a large and delicious meal, saying that I should not be afraid to ask for what I wanted, because the Austrian government was paying for the meal, not he himself. I asked him to do the choosing for me, assuring him that what he liked I would also like. While we were enjoying ourselves eating the delicious Austrian food, and waiting for the plane to take off to Zurich with me on board, I was scheming hard what to do when I arrived in Zurich. I had already decided that going back to South Africa was out of the question. Only fools could think that I would go back there.

I made up my mind that as soon as I reached Zurich, I would hand myself over to the Swiss police and asked them to convey to their government that I was in their country seeking political asylum. I also decided that, while my request was being considered by the Swiss government, I would ask to meet the press so that my request could be known in the country. My idea was that once my request was brought before the Swiss people, many would come forward to help me secure the political asylum I was seeking for. That was September the twenty-second, nineteen-fifty-four. The Bucharest conference was opening next day.

The time came for the plane to take off, and I shook hands with my escort at the door of the plane. We landed at Klotten airport, Zurich, at about six o'clock in the evening. From the plane I went straight to the inquiries office to find out when the next plane was leaving to South Africa. I was told that there was no plane till Thursday of that week. It was now Tuesday, so there was Wednesday before me. This came to me as a gift from nowhere. When I left the inquiries office, I met a man dressed in uniform, with the badge of British European Airways. I asked him to excuse me and told him of my desperate trouble, asking him to help me. He first checked when the next plane was leaving for South Africa and when he got the same information as I had he asked me whether I had any money – I had ten Swiss francs, given me by the WFTU office in Vienna – and he showed me the immigration office and said I should ask them for a twenty-four-hour transit visa. After I had done this, I went back to his office, and he told me his name was Murphy and that he was in charge of British European Airways planes at Zurich. He got me a hotel room, put me aboard a bus to the city, which stopped right in front of the BEA office, where a young lady was waiting to take me to my hotel. Needless to say there was no difficulty for her in recognising me. She invited me to go along with her, and side by side we walked to Hotel Trumpy where she left me in the hands of the management. After being booked in, I was taken to the dining room and left to choose what I desired to eat that evening. With only five Swiss france left (five had gone to pay for the visa) and three shillings and three pennies in South African money, I ate everything which attracted me on the menu. I sometimes wonder what would have happened if they had wanted me to pay my bills in advance. I was the only person of my colour in the dining room, but all the people there seemed to be pleased at being joined by someone who, though of a different colour, was like them in every other respect. Many of them can seldom have seen a black man, as I could see by the concealed way that they drew the attentions of others, who hadn't noticed me, to my presence amongst them. I went up to my room later to ask myself searching questions about what I was going to do the next day, which was the only day I was allowed to be in Switzerland. One thing I had already settled, that I was not going back to South Africa. The only alternative was to ask the Swiss government to grant me political asylum. I knew that Switzerland was a neutral country and that many people, including Lenin, had enjoyed asylum there. I could not decide at what time of day I was going to contact the police, but I fell asleep, still not having decided. I got up in the morning, like all residents, had a refreshing bath, and after the sound of the gong, went down to breakfast as though I had money to pay for it. After breakfast I went to ask in the office where I could get English-language newspapers, as I was keen to know what was going on in the world. She advised me to try at the railway station, which was not far away. On my way there I noticed that Swiss people were not accustomed to seeing black people in their country. Before I could greet them they greeted me first, and as I walked away from them they looked back to make sure that they really had seen a black man, as they would have a fascinating story to tell to others.

In front of the station, where I brought an English newspaper, is a busy square, with benches for people to sit down and pass the time. Having slept in a hotel with no objections, I convinced myself that no one would object to me sitting on one of those benches. But before I could do anything, my memories of South Africa came first. Would I be attacked or arrested for being in a particular place or doing a particular thing? I was haunted by my unbringing under the racist police state in my own country. I always remembered soon enough that I was not in South Africa but in Europe: people who passed me sitting there made sure that their eyes were not painting me black, but that I was really black. I remember an old lady coming up to me with excitement, asking: 'Are you happy in this country, do you like it?' – and, after I had replied yes, she stood by looking at me for a while and said: 'I am glad, good-bye,' and walked away. People who passed by in trams shouted out to attract my attention and waved, inviting others to see what they saw.

Not far from the station is a bridge over the river, where people had collected to enjoy the sight of passing boats and others were feeding beautiful snow-white swans with breadcrumbs. I was attracted by the number of people on the bridge, and went to join them. While enjoying the sight the thought came to me that I was in the home of the Red Cross. I said to myself, Red Cross people must settle my problem. I am a refugee, I convinced myself, my problem is a Red Cross problem. I felt strong and left the bridge at once. When I found the office and I knocked at the door, a middle-aged lady invited me inside and offered me a chair. First I asked her to write down my name, and then I told her of my political convictions, that I was a communist who had run away from political persecution in South Africa. In short, I claimed I was a political refugee in need of a help. I gave her my reasons for being in Europe and how I had come to be in Switzerland. After giving me much of her time, she asked me how I wanted them to help me. First, I said, I had to be out of Switzerland by the next day, and I had decided not to return to my own country. I didn't know where I would be going, and I was desperate and mixed up. I said I wanted her office to get me an extension to stay in Switzerland for a month while I sorted myself out, and as I was living in a hotel with no money, sleeping there and eating food which I would not be able to pay for, I suggested they adopted me and paid the bills. She replied that she was sorry her office could do nothing for me, they were concerned with orphans who had no parents and no homes. I didn't fall into that category.

I then asked her bluntly: 'What are you going to do for me?' 'Nothing, I am afraid,' she replied. I noticed that she was thinking about something, and I waited. Eventually she said: 'I shall send you to the World Red Cross office – they may do something for you.' At the World Red Cross office, I found an old man and old lady. Before them I laid my cards facing upwards as I had done at the Zurich Red Cross office. My requests were the same. They, too, after hearing me out, told me that according to their rules I was not a refugee, who was entitled to help from their organisation, which dealt only with displaced persons, who had suffered because of war. I landed on them the same question: 'What are you going to do for

341

me?' They said that they were extremely sorry, their hands were tied, there was no way they could help me under the circumstances.

The old lady then said they could send me to the Refugees' Committee and that I might get help there. At the Refugees' Committee office, a lady received me and introduced me to a Dr. Landau, who shook hands and invited me into his office. There, too, I left no stone unturned, and explained my political history in South Africa, my arrests and other persecutions, the purpose of my stay in Europe, and all the reasons why I was appealing to their organisation for help. I ended up by saying that for me to return to South Africa was as good as ending my own life there in Switzerland in order to get over all my problems.

While I outlined my position to Dr. Landau I noticed he was not only listening, but understood what I was telling him, and was sympathetic. When I had finished he told me that he was not the director of the Refugees' Committee, but the assistant director. He called in the lady who had received me, and asked her to give me some tea and biscuits. He then asked me to wait as he was going to consult the director about my appeal. He was away for ninety minutes, after which he emerged with an attractive middle-aged lady, whom he introduced as Miss Furrer, the director of the Committee. They left me, and I waited another hour. When they returned they said that they had got in touch with other directors of the Committee, and they had been authorised to help me. The three of us went into Miss Furrer's office and from there they telephoned the immigration office asking them to give me an extension to be in Switzerland for a month. The result was that they granted me three weeks grace. They asked the Refugees' Committee whether they were making themselves responsible for my actions and for whatever mischief I committed in Switzerland.

Miss Furrer told the immigration authorities that their Committee was prepared to take that risk, as they felt they could trust me. They were then told that the extension was granted on condition that for the next three weeks I should stay in Zurich and not leave the city area and also that I should not get in touch with the local communists. So at last my worries and problems were over, and they telephoned the Hotel Trumpy to book me in until October the third and to send all my bills to them.

Dr. Landau left me with Miss Furrer. She told me that Dr. Landau was himself a refugee who left Germany and came to Switzerland at the time of Hitler's persecutions; he was now a Swiss citizen, and had married and raised a family in Switzerland. I began to understand why Dr. Landau understood my plight and had been instrumental in getting me help. She told me with pride that Switzerland was a democratic country, but added that women still had no vote. I remarked that the Refugees' Committee should come to their aid. She laughed and agreed.

Then she told me of an English-speaking lady in Zurich, who had lived there since nineteen-nineteen, married to a Swiss professor. Her name, too, was Furrer, but no relative. She asked if I would like to meet her, and I said very much so. So she telephoned to Frau Furrer, and asked her if she would like to meet me, and her reply was to invite me to tea with her that afternoon. Miss Furrer gave me five francs and told me to go and have lunch in any restaurant, and when I ran short of pocket money, to go back and see them. I thanked her and Dr. Landau for everything, and asked her to convey my thanks to the other directors. I then left. In the afternoon I knocked at Frau Furrer's door, and she welcomed me with a very broad smile. We had tea together and I explained myself fully to her. Late in the afternoon we were joined by her husband Dr. Paul Furrer. I found them both very kind people, who offered me their home entirely all the time I was in Zurich. They said to me, 'This is your home, sleep at Hotel Trumpy, but you can have all your meals here if you like.' They were Christian Socialists and Dr. Furrer was the editor of the Christian Socialists' organ in Switzerland. I felt completely at home in their house and with them. They even told me not to wait for them to give me something to eat, but whenever I felt hungry, I should go into the pantry and get something. They also placed their typewriter and paper at my disposal, to write anything and to whom I wished.

The same evening they held a reception for me in their house to which they invited their friends. It was a most exciting event, something I had never known before in my entire life. Among the guests was a young lady teacher, who invited me to visit her school the next day. So the next morning I went there, and met the children. In the class-room was a large map hanging on the wall. After the children had sung a sweet-sounding song, she asked them, 'Where does he come from? Show me on the world map.' She made it easy for them by saying that she didn't want the country but the continent from which people like me came. As can be expected, some pointed at Asia, others to America, and it was not until one of them pointed to Africa that she said, 'That is right, he comes from Africa.' The children sang two sweet songs for me, which I enjoyed very much though I didn't follow the words, but the sounds were enough.

I didn't realise that other children in other classrooms were envious of those who had the opportunity of seeing me close to. They asked their teachers to let them meet me in the yard when I was leaving, so that they could shake hands with me. There was excitement in the school yard, and each one who touched me looked at his or her hand to see whether I transferred some of my colour to them. There was no rudeness in this – it only revealed how rare black people were in Switzerland. Some asked to touch my hair, which they enjoyed feeling.

I lived in the Hotel Trumpy, and had my breakfast there, but took my lunch and evening meals at Frau Furrer's house with her and her husband. It was from there that I wrote a letter to the World Federation of Trade Unions in Vienna telling them that I was not in South Africa but in Zurich, making plans to find a new home elsewhere. One day when I arrived at Frau Furrer's house I found the lady from Vienna, who was the only link between me and the World Federation, waiting for me. She said that she had been sent to see me and say that they were pleased I was safe and well. I said that I had nothing to say except to mention that I was as she saw me.

She had brought with her forty-six Swiss francs as a gift from the organisation, for me to buy whatever I was in need of. Though Dr. Landau and Miss Furrer had said that whenever I needed some money I should call on them, I never did, so the money I got from the WFTU helped me to buy two shirts, underwear and socks, and enabled me to get the clothes I had brought with me from South Africa washed. I never went to the Refugees' Committee for money because I felt that they were generous enough in taking over payment of my hotel bills and in making a standing offer of money whenever I needed some.

I found it very difficult to shake off my South African upbringing. One Sunday, Frau Furrer said to me. 'Tomorrow is my washing day, so go back to the hotel, fetch all that you want washed and bring it here so that I can do it with the rest of the family's washing.' That was a new revelation to me. On my way back to the hotel, I could not cease wondering whether she meant that I should wash them there myself or whether she, a European lady, was going to wash and iron them for me – which was exactly what she was going to do. That was something I never thought would happen to me in my entire lifetime. The relationships between Africans and Europeans in South Africa is so poisoned that even when I was in Switzerland I still thought that a fine person like Frau Furrer was thinking along the same lines as Europeans in my country.

While I was in Zurich a South African European lady on holiday in Europe, who had heard of me, traced me to Hotel Trumpy. I was at the Furrers's house, but she left a message that I should contact her where she was staying. One day I went to see her. She was very progressive and sympathetic, and I found that she knew people in Pretoria and Johannesburg whom I knew. After hearing my story, she asked what my future intentions were, and I told her that I was still undecided, but there was a grain in my mind that I should seek political asylum in Switzerland. Like Dr. Furrer and his wife, she said it would be unwise for me to do that because, first I would thus sever my connections with Africa and the African struggle for emancipation all over the continent and, secondly, in Switzerland I would have to begin from the bottom, learning to speak, write and read the language, which would take a long time at my age. As though she knew what the Furrers had been telling me, she added that I should think of going to the Centre of the World, London, strengthening her case by saying that there I would meet Africans from all parts of Africa, some who had been living there a long time, and others coming in and returning again, as well as people from every other part of the world.

She asked me whether I knew anyone in London – I said I had had correspondence with the British Communist Party and some of its members for some years, and that since my arrival in Zurich I had written telling them I was out of South Africa and trying to pave the way to go to London, but no replies had been forthcoming. With fresh memories of the World Federation, I doubted if they wanted to have anything to do with me. She then said she had friends in London and would write and ask them to receive me when I arrived there. She asked me further whether I knew the Reverend Michael Scott, whom I had met several times in South Africa, saying that he had an office in London called the Africa Bureau, helping Africans who came to have talks with the British government. She promised to write to them, too. She said again that in London I would find people ready to help me; and she, too, offered to help the best way she could. So together we planned the last stage of my journey.

My newly-found South African European friend then asked me whether I had money for my flight to London, to which I said no but that I thought the Refugees' Committee would be able to raise it. She replied that that was where she would come in – it would be paid by her. So she booked me to fly from Klotten Airport, Zurich, to London Airport on the third of October, nineteen-fifty-four. She is a South African, back in South Africa. For natural reasons, I cannot reveal her name.

Frau Millicent Furrer and her husband were delighted when I told them of my South Africa friend and her offer, and they were delighted, too, that I had been persuaded to go to England, as they had advised. I spent my last days in Zurich happy and with nothing to worry about for myself, but knowing what was happening in South Africa. I worried, too, over the people in Europe, who were giving me hospitality – how would I pay them back? I felt sorry that I was only taking, and that because I had lost South Africa, I would not be able to give in return.

345

I arrived in Zurich alone with no friends, no place to go to, no one to receive me, but I had confidence in mankind and knew that someone would listen to me and, hearing my words, would move others to join him. I had no friends when I arrived, but I had many to leave behind when I boarded the aircraft for London. My father once told me that when you want help from people, you must not be afraid to tell them you need it, or be ashamed to tell them your needs. That was a guide to me during bad days in Europe, days I shall always remember. Many exciting things happened to me in Zurich. The childen of the school I had visited, who had wondered whether the colour of my hand would come off, had themselves photographed, wrote their names on the picture and sent it to me as a souvenir before I left Zurich. I treasure it very much.

I moved about in Zurich unresented, I visited many places, rode in a mountain train, visited the swimming baths though I didn't swim, went in a speedboat on the lake, visited the house where Lenin lived and had tea or coffee in any place I fancied. In Europe I was treated for the first time as a man and a free individual.

XXXIX London

After lunch on the third of October, nineteen-fifty-four, I said goodbye to the Hotel Trumpy, the management and friends I had made there; and with my South African benefactor, the Furrers and a few others, left for Klotten Airport. The day was warm. Unlike when I left my own country, I was carrying a beautiful brown suitcase which I had brought in Zurich with the money I had been given by the World Federation of Trade Unions. The waves of my friends as we said good-bye still come back to me in memory, I can still see their snow-white handkerchiefs, as they stood on the balcony of the airport until I disappeared from their sight. It was a happy flight, and we reached London Airport in the evening after dark.

Like at Jan Smuts Airport and Vienna, I was the last to be dealt with. When my passport was called for, I presented the affidavit I drew up myself; then out came my pass reference book. When the immigration officer discovered that these were all the documents I had, he told me to sit down and wait; he would see me later. When my turn came to be examined, he asked politely to see my papers again. After reading them carefully, he asked me what else I could produce to satisfy them that I was from South Africa and a South African citizen. I produced two letters bearing my name and address on the envelopes, and the letter I had received from Charles Robert Swart, Malan's minister of justice. The man took them all away, then after half an hour he returned and gave them back to me – it was all right.

Without asking me further questions, the man kindly directed me to a bus outside. It was already dark, so I saw nothing on the way into London except street lights. I had no idea who was meeting me at the terminus but I was happy to find there a daughter of South Africa waiting to welcome me on behalf of the Africa Bureau – Mary Benson, who was secretary of the Bureau at that time. She had been born and grown up and been to school in Pretoria, near to a very hostile place of higher learning, Pretoria University. In Pretoria I hadn't known Mary Benson but I did know her parents, particularly her father. He was the general secretary of Pretoria General Hospital, and they were customers of Cuthbert and Company, the shoe people I worked for in my young days. I used to cycle to the hospital with the Bensons' shoes, and must have delivered Mary's as well. I was the only black man on the bus, so that when I alighted she waved and came forward to meet me, smiling, her face full of life.

From the terminus she took me by bus to Friends' International Centre in Tavistock Square, where they had already arranged for me to stay. After seeing that I was well received and giving me the address of the Africa Bureau and instructions how to get there, Mary left. The next morning when I woke up I found the room contained more beds occupied by other men, all Europeans. The South African climate still haunting my memories, I wondered why they didn't object and revolt when they found that I was sharing the room with them. They were happy and all wished me good morning

I found the Africa Bureau. The Reverend Michael Scott was in the United States at the time, attending a session of the United Nations, but I was introduced to Miss Jane Ursula Symonds, who was assistant to Mary Benson, Lord Hemingford, the chairman, and other supporters of the Bureau – Thomas Williams, a barrister; the former leader of the Liberal Party, Clement Davies; Commander Fox-Pitt, assistant secretary of the Anti-Slavery Society; Mr. Greenidge, secretary of that Society, and many people who were helping to make the Bureau's work in helping the peoples of Africa who were engaged in the struggle for self-government a success. I found that the Bureau knew well about Tefu's and my arrests, and the news had been published in their information magazine, *The Digest*.

That week I helped at the Bureau, still living at the Friends' International Centre. London seemed to me so confusing that I though I should never get used to it. For a long time I could not tell without a map which way was east, west, north or south.

The terror inflicted on the Africans in the fascist police state of South Africa builds into their nervous system a fear, which hardens like a block of ice left in cold storage for years. When it is brought into a warm place, it takes a very long time to melt. The terror is instilled through the mass arrests for passes, the permanent denial of human rights, cruel segregation, and constant police raids in the areas where Africans are forced to live, for beer as well as passes at any time of the day or night. I did not realise until I came to London that this life, as I had lived it in my own country had ruined my nervous system. For many months I couldn't get rid of that fear. Each time I saw a policeman in London, the first thing which entered my mind was that he might stop me and demand production of my documents questioning my right to be where he had found me.

It took me many months in London before I could go into a cinema, where I knew the people would be Europeans. I always had fears that the lady in the box office would refuse to sell me a ticket. And if she made a mistake and sold me one, I feared I would be thrown out of the cinema, by her people who would strongly object to my sharing the performance with them. For many months I struggled with my fears, suppressing them each time I wanted to go into a restaurant alone for a meal or for anything to refresh myself. I feared that I might be beaten up, the police called and then charged for causing disturbances in a place where I had no right to be. To form a bus queue and wait there with Europeans was for many months a torment for me.

When I was with the Africa Bureau, Mary Benson and Jane Symonds used to take me to lunch, and when I stepped into the street with them they would make me walk alongside them, in the middle while one of them walked on each side of me. As streets at that time of the day are always full of people also going to lunch, I used to feel very nervous, and in actual danger of being attacked by European men for walking with or between European women. At night, too, whenever I saw a policeman after ten o'clock, the first thing which struck my mind was the curfew, and I feared he would ask me to produce a night pass, to show that I had the authority to be there at that time of night.

My nervous system took a long time to get used to life as I found it in London. When people live in a concentration camp, where they are denied human rights and live in terror of mass ill-treatment, their nervous system is destroyed, and their power to think like other human beings is destroyed as well. Their will to demand and struggle for human rights is weakened because they have been brought to the level of doubting whether they were really entitled to human rights and humane treatment. Anyone who has doubts as to whether he may demand something he is entitled to has lost the will to struggle for it. This revelation came to me in London. Only then did I realise how the fascist police state erected in South Africa has damaged the Africans' will to stand up without fear for human rights, and for the right to share in the administration of their own country.

Many people in the world wonder why the Africans, being the majority, allow themselves to be downtrodden, oppressed and forced to carry that badge of slavery, the pass. I hope I have given the reason. An African, who was born and has lived in the police state, takes a long time to get convinced that he is as good as any human being regardless of colour or language. I have gone through that experience myself; I have seen myself carry the whole system of a police state system with me in my mind in European countries and in London. I was like a person who had been sick for a very long time, whose blood had been heavily poisoned by the sickness, and who could not get cured in his own country, so had gone to another country where doctors began to work on him. My sickness was a very old one and my cure was long.

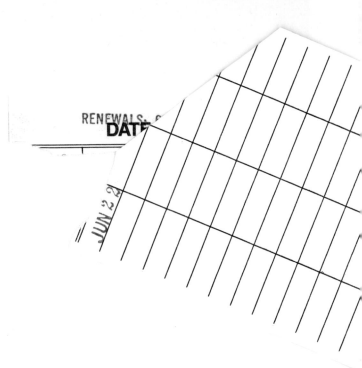